SPRING

AN ANNUAL OF
ARCHETYPAL PSYCHOLOGY
AND
JUNGIAN THOUGHT

1973

SPRING PUBLICATIONS
NEW YORK CITY, 16
Suite 306, 130 East 39th St.

CONTENTS

I. New Papers and Translations

Achelous and the Butterfly: Toward an Archetypal Psychology of Humor
David L. Miller 1

Mysticism and Humour
Henry Corbin 24
(translated by Cornelia Embirikos Schroeder)

Hephaistos: A Pattern of Introversion
Murray Stein 35

Jung and Marx
David Holt 52

On Reduction
Patricia Berry 67

Poetry and the Anima
Graham Hough 85

"Anima"
James Hillman 97

II. Excerpts from Works in Progress

The Incest Wound
Robert M. Stein 133

The Pit and The Brilliance: A Study of the 29th and
30th Hexagrams in the *I Ching*
Rudolf Ritsema 142

III. Jungiana

Three Early Papers:
    Sigmund Freud: On Dreams (1901)
    Marginal Note on F. Wittels: *Die sexuelle Not* (1910)
    A Comment on Tausk's Criticism of Nelken (1913)
C. G. Jung 171
(translated by R.F.C. Hull)

Prefatory Note to Jung's "Reply to Buber"
Edward C. Whitmont 188

Religion and Psychology: *A Reply to Martin Buber*
C. G. Jung 196
(translated by R.F.C. Hull)

Jung and Theology: A Bibliographical Essay
James W. Heisig 204

IV. Current and Controversial

Against Imagination: The *Via Negativa* of Simone Weil
Roger Woolger 256

Observations in Transit between Zürich and Milan
Luigi Zoja 274

Thoreau Goes West: Footnote to a Footnote
Philipp Wolff-Windegg 283

Letter
Edward F. Edinger 291

ACKNOWLEDGEMENTS

To Princeton University Press for quotations from the *Collected Works* of C. G. Jung (Bollingen Series XX) translated by R. F. C. Hull and edited by H. Read, M. Fordham, G. Adler and Wm. McGuire, and for quotations from the *I Ching or Book of Changes* (Bollingen Series XIX), the Richard Wilhelm translation rendered into English by Cary F. Baynes, third edition, 1967. (Both works are published in Great Britain by Routledge and Kegan Paul, London.)

Set, printed and manufactured in Switzerland for SPRING PUBLICATIONS Postfach 190, 8024 Zürich, by R. Sasek, Zeltweg 14, Zürich, and Buchdruckerei Schrumpf, 8123 Ebmatingen-Zürich.

ACHELOUS AND THE BUTTERFLY: TOWARD AN ARCHETYPAL PSYCHOLOGY OF HUMOR

DAVID L. MILLER
(Syracuse)

> To be yourself, just yourself, is a great thing. And how does one do it, how does one bring it about? Ah, that's the most difficult trick of all. It's difficult just because it involves no effort... nothing is unimportant. Nothing. Instead of laughter and applause you receive smiles. Contented little smiles — that's all. But it's everything — more than one could ask for.
> — Henry Miller, *The Smile at the Foot of the Ladder*

> This crown of laughter, the rose-wreath crown: to you, my brothers, I throw this crown. Laughter I have pronounced holy: you higher men, learn — to laugh.
> — Friedrich Nietzsche, *Thus Spake Zarathustra*

Lurking somewhere between the lines of Miller and Nietzsche is a modern truism which goes something like this: a sense of humor is vital to the authentic life of a self, a society, even to the vitality of the cosmos and the Gods. So indubitable is this sentiment in contemporary consciousness that questions are seldom raised about the matter of a functioning sense of humor. The truism lacks depth because we fail to imagine — to give image to — humor's figuration and meaning. Thus we ask: What collective fantasy informs man's happy hope about a sense of humor?

Dr. Miller lectures on Comparative Letters and Mythography in the Department of Religion at Syracuse University. He is the author of *Gods and Games*, and of a variety of articles in professional journals on the subjects of mythology, religion, and literature.

On the few occasions that this issue has been probed, the analysis has been prosecuted by those whose literalistic, positivistic, and behavioristic modes of thinking and speaking have functioned in fact to reduce the matter of humor's sense to a not-so-smiling and not-so-laughing conclusion, with the result that the sense-of-humor fantasy evaporates before our human understanding. What we are then left with is a residual and somewhat impotent senex seriousness that turns the truism into its moralistic opposite: namely, the conclusion that laughter is bad!

For example: Aristotle, in his intellectualistic way, cites two sorts of laughing and laughable men — the braggadocio and the boor. The one makes fun of everything, thereby laughing too much; the other takes everything seriously, thereby being himself laughable. Both types are to be avoided.[1] Saint Ambrose and Saint John Chrysostom are two of the theologians that the rationalistic and doctrinal Aquinas lists as taking quite seriously the Biblical injunction: "Woe to you who laugh".[2] In Freud's writings the philosophical and theological advice against laughter is qualified psychologically, and we are encouraged to think all jokes and witticisms phallically aggressive, hostile, and comparable to those other antisocial behaviors — the belch and the passing of air.[3] More recently there are those "sensitized" at Esalen Institute who, on discovering the function of their joke-telling and laughing *vis à vis* other persons, have given up the practice of joking altogether in the name of humanness.

This list of testimonies could be lengthened extensively, but the point that begins to take hold reminds one of the South American Indians who have a sacred taboo against laughter. About these tribesmen Lévi-Strauss tells us that eighteen of their twenty myths dealing with laughter connect it to death and destruction. The elders view laughter as effeminate and to be avoided.[4] One thinks also of the advice Lord Chesterfield gave his son. It is in the worst of taste, Chesterfield said, for a gentleman to laugh. Smile, perhaps; but laugh, never![5]

What is wrong here is the assumption that wit and laughter, jokes and smiles, are the only expression of a sense of humor, that humor is in their expressions. This assumption neglects the possibility that the smile of Miller's clown and the laughter of Nietzsche's Zarathustra may be metaphors of certain archetypal forms, imaginal patterns, rather than only overt behaviors. Our hunch here is that there is more to humor than its smile. To take humor at its face value also betrays a literal bias and moral-mindedness that can hardly be expected to give adequate account of the richness of humor's dimensions. Were we forever to leave humor in these hands, we would be neglecting to give humor a sense rooted in archetypal amplification. It would have no source and the sense of humor would have no sense. The present essay comprises some notes that hopefully may compensate this lacuna.

But there is a bit more in the present agenda. Nietzsche's epigrammatic aside, that laughter is "holy", linked to Miller's hope, that the smile is "everything", suggests a possibility that archetypal explorations in humor may disclose some coordinates of the matrix of religion and psychology. The pronouncements of Miller and Nietzsche subtly imply that humor may provide a clue to the "hidden harmony", as Heraclitus called it, of myth and psyche.

Earth and Water

An etymology will allow us a point of departure into the problematic of humor's sense. Though etymologies may be a sort of academic play with words, as Heidegger has observed, "it is not we who play with words, but the nature of language plays with us."[6] Hiding within words are eternal forms of human meaning, patterns and paradigms of psychic signification. The Gods and the Goddesses are there named. In searching a word's history (the story of its *mythos*), one enters, as if for the first time in full consciousness, the evolution of meaning. Etymologies are like therapy: they differentiate what is deeply and collectively unconscious. Potentially, therefore, an etymology can relieve the repressions of over-rationalized fantasies and provide new and compensatory resources in the dream-like depths of sense.

Unfortunately in the case of "humor" we are stuck with a seemingly uninteresting history. "Humor" does not belong to a large family of terms with many rich associations. "Humor" has as its immediate relatives only "humid", "humidity", "humidor" and "humoresque". Its lineage is from the Old French, and originally Latin, "*húmor*" or "*úmor*", which derived from "*húmére*" or "*úmére*", meaning to be "moist". Its ancient cousins are the Greek "*hugros*", the Old Norse "*vökr*", the Sanskrit "*uksati*", the Old Iranian "*fúal*", and the Indo-European root "*ug-*" or "*udh-*", all of which signify "moisture, sprinkling, and urine".[7]

The etymology is so disappointing that it may not be laid aside. Why, we may well wonder, when man wished to mean "humor" did he imagine "moisture"? What is it about wetness that suggests, not tears, but joy? Why did it once seem appropriate to picture in terms of fluid what we now think of abstractly as a sense of the comic. And where does one go for answers to these questions?

Ben Jonson provides a clue. Though the theory of the four humors was by no means novel with Jonson's writing, he handles this medieval medical hypothesis in a new way. Jonson links the old "humours" physiognomy to a theory of dramatic genres coined apparently by Roman schoolmen. The result is a new view of comedy.

In Jonson's "induction" to his play, *Every Man Out of his Humour* (1599), Asper explains that "humour" is an *"ens"*, an essence of man that flows from the idiosyncratic balance of his four fundamental fluids: namely, the blood, the phlegm, the choler, and the melancholer (melancholy). They are called "humours", Asper explains, because they have "moisture and fluxure", or, as he says later, "by reason that they flow continuously". But these "humours" may be viewed "by metaphor" to apply to "the general disposition":

> As when some one peculiar quality
> Doth so possess a man, that it doth draw
> All his affects, his spirits, and his powers,
> In their confluxions, all to run one way,
> This may be truly said to be a humour.[8]

The implication clearly is that one of the "humours" may take precedence in a particular person, acting as a sort of controlling metaphor or "objective correlative" for all the rest. Thus we may characterize a person as being sanguine, phlegmatic, choleric, or melancholic. It is not that the other fluids are missing; it is simply that they have been repressed, or better, pressed into the service of the one, all of them, therefore, running "one way".

A further step backwards, from the sixteenth- to the twelfth-century, will reveal the further peculiarity of colors being assigned to each of the humours: red for blood; yellow for choler or bile (compare our word "cholera"); dark blue or black for melan-choler; and green for phlegm. The medieval theorist located the source of the fluids in the *hypochondria* (literally, "under the musculature of the lower breast-plate", *i.e.*, in the center cavity of the body), and he called the name of the proper harmony of the fluids *"temperamentum"* or *"complexio"*. The opposite of having a tempered or temperate complex or complexion was, of course, a distemper or what we would now call disease.[9]

It is tempting to leap to the conclusion that the interplay of the humors corresponds to four modes of being human: irony and wit to the sanguine; dry humor to the phlegmatic; belly laughter to the choleric; and black or sick humor to the melancholic — the ideal humor of the humors being a precarious balance among the four. But this sort of conclusion would be superficial and simplistic. The matter of humor is deeper. Juggling words and concepts — matching modes of the comic with character types — will not do. In so doing a *problem* of words and ideas may have been solved on the surface; but the *mystery* of humor still evades our meditation, like the fluxure of moisture that continually flows in and out, waiting to be tapped as a resource of life.

The mystery of moisture as a source of life: it turns out that *this* is precisely the secret behind the secrets, like the humor of the humors, in several alchemical traditions. The spirit of life in everything was identified by certain alchemists to be a *humidum radicale*, a deep moisture, which was sometimes referred to as *aqua vitae*, the water of life. But by far the best water, the one whose energies held the power of transformation, was the *aqua vitae* which was also *aqua sicca*, or dry water; distilled seven times seven, it attained the quality of pure spirit. It was *aqua manus non madefaciens*, the water which did not make one's hands wet. This is the humor we are after: the deep humor of the spirit, whose mystery is unwittingly attested to in the alchemist's lore.[10] Indeed, it would be unadventuresome to stay with the tempting conclusion of the last paragraph when "the holy mystery of water" still flows before us. *"Felix sacramentum aquae nostrae"*, as the theologian Tertullian proclaimed it.[11]

*

Kerényi once wrote that "water is the most mythological of the elements".[12] Why? And in what sense? Of course there was the pre-Socratic philosopher Thales, in whose cosmological speculation water came to be identified as the first principle of everything. He also apparently said that "all things are full of gods".[13] Perhaps in light of his saying about water, the Gods to whom he refers are water Gods, *hudór theion*, which is the name of the alchemist's patron, Mercurius, "divine water" or *hydrargyrum* or *argentum vivum*, "quick silver".[14]

Aristotle links Thales not of course to alchemy, but to mythological stories, perhaps the sort Kerényi had in mind, about Okeanos- and Tethys, the waters above and the waters below, which, on converging, become the parents of creation, like the similar watery creation mythologems in Egypt and Polynesia.[15] In the Koran Moses is made to declare that he will not rest until he has discovered "the junction of the two oceans" *(majma' al-bahrain)*, as if the coming together of the waters above and the waters below has not only the function of original creation, but also that of re-creation, rejuvenation, and redemption in the ultimate day.[16]

What is most surprising in this mythologem is the frequency among diverse cultures of a theme reminiscent of what was later to become attached to the human body. When the waters above and the waters below come together at creation, the blissful Eden of the originative moment is characterized by the flowing of *four* rivers. The constitution of the body is a microcosmic recapitulation of the macrocosm. So in Genesis 2:10-14 we read about the four rivers of paradise flowing from the water of life that nourishes the tree at the center of the garden. But the testimonies are not limited to the Ancient Near East: in Hindu mythology the four rivers flow from Mount Meru; in Iranian tales they are located in the realm of the Blest and flow from the fountain of Arduisir; in Tibet, on the Hill of Hamavata, the four rivers flow from the root of the Zampu tree of life; in China the location is the Kwan-lum hills; in Slavic mythology the four rivers come from a magic stone, Alatuir, in the island paradise of Bonvan; in Scandanavian tales the four rivers come from the spring, Hvergelmir, in Asaheim, the home of the Gods. There are similar accounts to be found among the Sioux, Aztec, Mayan, and Polynesian peoples.

But note well what has become of the four rivers of paradise during the "fall" of the West! In Homeric epic we read of the four springs outside the cave of Circe. But by the time of Plato the rivers have had to go underground, as if another symbology attached to a very different sort of human meaning had taken ascendency. In the *Phaedo* Socrates tells a different story; it is his last tale. Contemplating the adventure and liveliness of his coming death, Socrates comforts his disciples by telling them that surely Aeschylus was wrong in describing the journey of the soul after death as following a single path. The topography allows for richer possibilities. The earth is a sphere suspended in ether. Inside the earth are hollows, and out of the hollows flow the underground rivers that will guide the soul on its way. Socrates names the rivers according to Orphic cosmogony: Acheron ("Mourning"), Kokytus ("Lamenting"), Lethe ("Forgetting"), and Pyrephlegethon ("Flame").[18] The rivers of paradise surely have shifted their shape!

The Greek description may be compared with the Jewish apocalyptic motif of the waters of life flowing from the cavity in the rock that lies under the throne of the Lord (see Ezekiel 47:1-12; Psalms 46:4; and compare Revelation 22:2). If the rivers of paradise went underground by the time of Plato, the tone remained, if not blissful, surely purgatorially neutral. However, by the time of the *Divine Comedy* the rivers flow out of the cavities of hell, and the whole scene is darkly negative in the extreme. Why? What has happened to transform the waters of life into the waters of death?

There is a clue in Western Christian iconography; paintings of paradise produce a curious datum. One might have thought that the four rivers of paradise would be a natural subject for representation. Indeed, until the thirteenth-century one does find, but only here and there, a manuscript page with the rivers pictured boldly.[19] But William Blake's sketch of the water of life (1805) is symbolic of the curiosity: he names the picture "Tree of Life". And so it is in the tradition. Characteristically, when paradise is imagined by Christian artists, it is the tree that appears, not the waters. The classic instance is the bay window at Chartres, and, as in this case, the tree in the garden combines with the tree of Jesse and the cross of Jesus.

Of course the waters do go with the tree. The latter needs the former for nourishment. But in the Western tree-tradition this is precisely what was forgotten. In *theological* and *philosophical* systems of thinking we do not have examples of the tree *as* lapis, or feminine numen, or serpent wisdom, but rather we have a simple one-sided "woodenness" that forgets its roots in the moist earth and whose rigidity is devoid of vital juices. The waters have gone underground, and we have lost touch with our sensing of the humors, because our traditional *axis mundi* turns out to be all bark.

Our tree-tradition has in the process grown quite proud of its ladder-like reaching toward heaven, forgetting thereby its source, which thereupon returned to the earth and became a shade in the dark depths of mourning. Masculinely aggressive and dogmatic theologies supported this movement so that the more contemplative mystical tradition, being fluid in its theological mode, haunted the orthodox lineage as a shadow and often became viewed as marginal at best and sometimes outright heresy. It is not surprising that such a tree and its concomitant theologizing has lost its liveliness in our own time. We may as well chop it up for firewood and pray for the wings of a Phoenix or the dance of a Shiva!

Barfield provides a tentative conclusion concerning the lost humors, the bodily fluids, when he says: "It seems for the moment as though some invisible sorcerer had been conjuring them all from inside ourselves — sucking them away from the planets, away from the outside world [here we have the mythological theme of the four rivers], away from our own flesh and blood [the humors of the body], down into the shadowy realm of thoughts and feelings. There they still repose."[20] When the mythological symbol-system dropped away in favor of a more sophisticated view of the cosmos, the rivers went underground into the human body. And when the ancient and medieval physiognomy was replaced by a more scientific view of anatomy, something else happened. It is this "something else" that does not allow us to stop here. Barfield's phrase, "the shadowy realm of thoughts and feelings", indicates where we have yet to explore. The rivers have gone underground into the unconscious.

*

Freud has already been mentioned on the *contra* side of wit and laughter. Therefore it is not surprising to find his hermeneutic identifying dreams of water as manifest contents signifying latent regressive tendencies toward an intra-uterine return. Though Freud may have moved us in the right direction in attempting to locate humor in the unconscious, he himself still belonged to the phallic-tree tradition, and therefore his aggressive view of humor, so like that of Hobbes, may be in need of some modification in the light of the mythological evidence we have adduced.[21]

Ferenczi helps in the modification. Taking into account the full mythological scope of water symbolism, Ferenczi re-envisioned Freud's hermeneutic. His focus was upon the mature sex act rather than upon infantile perversity. Coitus, he argued, is a recollection of the struggle of the primal creature among its ancestors who suffered the great catastrophe of the drying up of the sea. *Post coitus omne animal triste:* following copulation man suffers the drying up. The climax, therefore, is to enter the waters, swim freely there, finding that, in spite of the anticipation of castration or regressive fixation, one can emerge anew, only to re-enter and reach the goal once again.[22] The meaning is deep in the psyche and it is intimately connected with the fluids of one's body, as well as with the mythology of one's phylogenesis.

By returning the argument near to transformations like those of alchemy, Ferenczi moves us towards Jung's psychology. Jung often mentioned the "four rivers" when speaking of Gnostic and alchemical images of the self.[23] In the context of the physiognomy of the humors and the mythology of the four rivers, it would not seem overly bold to say that the humors are *the four functions:* thinking, feeling, sensation, and intuition. This nomenclature has the advantage of differentiating more precisely than did either Freud or Ferenczi the psychology of humor; but most importantly it places Jung's psychology of the four functions in a mythological, which is to say, an archetypal, framework.

Jung himself told us not to think of the functions as empirical descriptions. Rather, the function-theory is a *way* of seeing and of speaking about empirical realities. It is a *mythos*. And above all, Jung warned us, we should not use the functions as a way of "putting people into this box or that". He said: "It is no use at all putting people into drawers with different labels."[24] What is the "use", then, of the psychology of the functions? It is the same "use" that the physiognomy of humors (read the quotation from Ben Jonson again) and the mythology of the rivers have.

Jung's typology is a mythology, a fantasy. An archetypal psychology of the humor of the humors can help us to re-mythologize the very psychology that gives us clue to humor itself. When viewed in the context of a sensing of humor, our therapy may take on a moisture,[25] not being so analytic and "dry", but rather truly archetypal, possessed by a sense of humors, rather than being monolithic and overly-masculine in an unwitting and witless capitulation to a tree-tradition theology and an occidental rationalistic philosophy. Therapy then could be a making contact with earthy resources, where the water of life is still bubbling away at the crux of four rivers. The health of the humor is sensed in the harmony of the humors. It all happens at the emptied cavity in the center of the self, which is also, for purposes of psychic meaning, the center of the universe. It is out of the deep emptiness that vitality flows.[26] Albertus Magnus said: "In quiet and repose of the humors, the soul attains understanding and prudence."[27]

"In tranquil water how close the surface and the depths are",[28] Bachelard wrote. And Goethe, in one of his conversations with Eckermann, urged "aqueous affirmation", the drawing of the vapors into oneself, as opposed to "aqueous negation", the allowing of moisture to dry up in the air, earth, and fire of life. So it is that Jung wrote:

> The water of life is easily had: everybody possesses it, though without knowing its value. *'Spernitur a stultis'* — it is despised by the stupid, because they assume that every good thing is always outside and somewhere else, and that the source in their own soul is a 'nothing but'. . . . The treasure has sunk down again into the unconscious.[29]

And there it still reposes, said Barfield, meaning by the "it" the humor for which all men hope.

Fire and Air

It is indeed tempting to think that by identifying the psychology of a physiognomy of a mythology we have thereby completed an amplification of a sense of humor's collective fantasy. But to think this way is an academic seduction. There is still another side, a shadow of a shade, as it were, the fantasy of the fantasy itself. We are not finished — by no means. When earth and water go to sleep they dream of fire and air. The marvelous reveries on the elements by Bachelard make this point (see *L'Air et les songes; La Terre et les rêveries du repos; L'Eau et les rêves; La Psychanalyse du feu*). It is a mistake to go to sleep in the middle of one's own dream, the dream of the *felix sacramentum aquae nostrae*, the happy sense of humor's mystery. Yes, we would be remiss if we failed to point to the mistakes we have already made.

(1) A *methodological* problem has been plaguing our sentences. M.-L. von Franz has pointed to the *faux pas* of the intellectual who analyzes archetypal materials. By overlooking the emotional and feeling factors and by making archetypal images into patterns of thought, anything can become anything. Start with four rivers and the whole world can end up in a watery conflux! And all one has accom-

plished is betraying one's own psychology.[30] More directly to the case of our argument, Hillman has written that "attempts to equate the functions with these older principles do not quite work — feeling with water or with phlegm — since each age has its appropriate ciphers for expressing this archetypal metaphor and translations of it violate the context of the symbol."[31]

(2) There is a *mythico-religious* problem, also. Half the story has been omitted — in fact, the half that would have provided the feeling and intuitive contents (von Franz), and that would have re-placed the archetypal metaphor in its *symbolic* context (Hillman). Barfield, when speaking of "humor" divulges the other side of the story: "The medieval scientist believes with Hippocrates that the *arteries* (Greek 'aer', 'air') were ducts through which there flowed, not fluids but three different kinds of *ether* (Greek 'aither', 'the upper air') or *spirits* (Latin 'spiritus', 'breath', 'life'), viz. the *animal* (Latin 'anima', 'soul'), the *vital*, and the *natural*."[32] Apparently the breaths of life, the anima, are vaporized humors, whose transformation is important for a deeper humor.

(3) Jung, with the help of alchemical symbols, reminded us of the *psychological* dilemma that confronts us. The waters that are manifested as the four rivers of paradise whose axis is the tree with serpent atop and lapis at the base ("the paradise quaternio") tend not to stay put as an image of meaning. Rather, the waters become transformed through a dynamic alchemy into the image of the four elements centered by a lapis top and a rotundum base ("the lapis quaternio").[33] Just as an adequate picturing of the alchemical process does not allow the four waters to stagnate, so a proper archetypal psychology of humor is mistaken if it fails to follow the humors through their various transformations. A monomorphic archetype will never be able to account for the *dynamic* aspect of humor.

(4) There is, too, a serious *theological* problem in the humors business. Saint John of the Cross warned the novitiate on the mystical path never to confuse the authentic aridity that characterizes the true purgation of the soul with its masquerading look-alike, humor.[34] Heraclitus bears witness to the same phenomenon of spirituality when he notices that it is "death to become water", since "the dry soul (*psyché*) is wisest and best.[35] Saint Paul, too, noticed that entering the waters at baptism is a kind of dying.

All these problems — mythico-religious, theological, psychological, and methodological — could be transcended were not our argument and its image of humors-as-waters so ponderous. Were the matter lighter, had it more levity, in short, more humor, we would feel it to be dynamic, lively, human, and natural. The waters cannot flow — indeed, they get trapped in the earth and grow stagnant, if there is no air flowing through them to keep them bubbly. Or to put it differently: just as fish cannot live in waters that are devoid of airs, neither are the humors humor without some vaporization and recycling. We need air in the waters.

One way to get on with the story, so as to get the air into the water, is to tell how the air *(spiritus, psyché)* got left out of the water, producing the humorless onesidedness we have suffered in our theologies, philosophies, and perhaps in our psychologies too. The story will reveal that it was not a vaporization that caused our lack of spiritedness and vitality, but simply that the air drowned in the waters. It all has to do with imaginal attempts to express the self; and the story, like our very Western being, has its roots in Greece. It is the story of *psyché*, and it begins with Anaximenes.

In imagining the self in its spirited aspects, Anaximenes used both *psyché* and *pneuma,* and he meant by both the image of air-soul *(aér).* Yet the usage of *pneuma* did not catch on at first, and *psyché* was the dominant metaphor. The analogy between *psyché* and *pneuma* is in fact striking: *psyché* is to *psychó* as *pneuma* is to *pneó*.[36] This is simply to recognize the commonplace that both *psyché* and *pneuma* body forth the active, verbal image of breathing or blowing, as the wind.

In Homeric literature *psyché* was *eidolon,* a "phantom", as an image reflected in water. Also, the *Iliad* uses the image "smoke" to picture *psyché,* and the *Odyssey* uses "shadow", this latter corresponding to Pindar's picturing of *psyché* as a "second self" or alter-ego. Pindar also equated *psyché* and *kardian.* So it was believed that if a person could not see his *eidolon* in a mirror, it was a sign of impending death. This belief is similar to the custom among Florida Seminoles, who, when a woman was dying in childbirth, held the newly-born infant over the mother's face to receive the parting spirit, a sort of artificial resuscitation.[37]

At the beginning of the evolution of spirit's consciousness, Heraclitus gave us these enigmatic words:

You could not discover the limits of *psyché*, even if you traveled every road to do so; such is the depth *(bathos)* of its meaning *(logos)*.

(Psyché) is the vaporization out of which everything else is derived; moreover it is the least corporeal of things and is in ceaseless flux, for the moving world can only be known by what is in motion.

Psyché is vaporized from what is moist,
A dry *psyché* is wisest and best.[38]

Sometime later, in a time when mythological and poetic imagination had already become transformed into philosophical and rhetorical modes, the Greeks found *psyché* too fluid a term. Its usage died out and *pneuma* (a term Aristotle used to mean "flatulence"!) replaced *psyché* as the image of the spirited self. At this time *psyché's* usage is relegated to its secondary meanings, and the word and its cognates (e.g., *psychros*) come to mean "cold". Life goes out of *psyché* as one moves from myth to philosophy, from Dorian and Ionian settlement to City-State, from peace to war, from oral to written tradition, from the enervating warmth of a deep breath to the damp chill of death that is an-aesthetized Being without meaning.

Apuleius' fairy tale, "Amor and Psyche", discloses another reason for the death of *psyché*. Since Psyche is feminine, Eros can only have life through Psyche, and Psyche only in Eros. Psyche without Eros and Eros without Psyche is death. But the conjugation of the two results not only in life, but also in *new* life: "soon a daughter was born to them — in the language of mortals she is called Pleasure".[39] This tale, and presumably its potential Pleasure, goes underground when the moisture of Christendom's baptismal waters kills *psyché* by a usage of *pneuma*. Western Christian culture adopted *pneuma* as a neuter, never feminine, grace. But the "eternal feminine" cannot forever be forgotten.[40]

It is a long way — the transformations of the image of *psyché* — such is the depth of its *logos:* from the air/wind/breath of the Ionians, through the phantom/shadow/shade of the epics and the cult of the dead, the winged-daimon of the Orphics and Attic tragedy, to Socrates, about whose use of *psyché* Jaeger observes, "What shall it profit a man if he gain the whole world and lose his own *psyché?*"[41]

Pneuma could never do the imagination's realistic job, as *psyché* did. For *pneuma* leads too quickly to the non-imaginative and rationalistic *nous*. Spirit, in this fashion, like the German *Geist* and the

French *esprit*, "had come to mean rational, intellectual, ideological", and it therefore "belongs to the world of the decaying kind of man".[42] "The soul", writes Heidegger with a clue from the poet Trakl, "is the gift of the spirit — the spirit animates. But the soul in turn guards the spirit, so essentially that without the soul the spirit can presumably never be spirit."[43]

Unfortunately the Church Fathers, and thereafter the "wooden" Christian culture of the West, adopted *pneuma* as its image of the spirited self. Already in the New Testament *psyché* is used only fifty-seven times to *pneuma*'s two hundred and seventy-four occurrences. Over half the uses of *psyché* are in the Gospels and the Acts, and only four are in the Pauline Epistles. So much is this the pattern that Paul comes to call *psychikoi* bad and *pneumatikoi* good.[44] It is the same with the Fathers (with perhaps the exception of Clement of Alexandria, Origen, and Gregory of Nyssa, who hardly carried the day on the question of theological psychology). *Pneuma* is regarded as the opposite of *psyché,* in spite of the fact that in early Greek usage they meant *both* "soul" and "spirit".[45] The Christian culture learned much from the Greeks, but little of it had to do with the educated imagination. By the time the Christians got the myths, they were pure ideas, which the Christians made into categories of thinking and called theology. It was as if the Church, and then the civilization, systematically forgot what was an axiom to the early Greeks, that *pneuma* is the *psyché* of man.[46]

*

It would seem that the story of *psyché* leads to no humor at all — no way to get air into water, or some moisture into the airs. But right at the end there is a strangeness that changes the whole tale, if only we could feel its meaning. Plato had called *psyché* a "winged animal",[47] and he had said that *psyché*'s proper erotic, philosophic, prophetic, and poetic function is "to fly".[48] Aristotle, Theophrastus, and Plutarch, with neither etymological justification nor philosophical, biological, nor psychological precedent, use *psyché* to mean "moth" or "butterfly".[49] This is reminiscent of Eliphaz, when speaking to Job, making "moth" a surrogate term for God, though without having religious justification or precedent in Wisdom literature.[50] And it is like Jesus, in a culture-context in which moth is synonymous with destruction, likening the heart that treasures the Kingdom to a situation in which the moth does not corrupt.[51]

Jung had mentioned that "the Greek word *psyché* also means butterfly",[52] but he never said why, nor did he ever press the point. The Miller fantasies, particularly the "Song of the Moth" *(CW* 5) might have been a clue to help account for these odd uses of *psyché*, as might have been Freud's saying, had he taken his own image as something more than a mere figure of speech: "I believe I am in a cocoon, and heaven knows what sort of creature will emerge from it."[53]

Certainly the moth knows the secret of the transformation from moist humus to the airs whose true fascination is the element that itself transforms the moisture of earth into air: fire! But to say this is quite a different thing from seeing the "feeling and intuitive contents" of the fantasy in their full "symbolic context". For this human task only poets and mythographers suffice.

Serrano related the story of *Piktor's Metamorphosis,* a tale which the aged Herman Hesse had illustrated with watercolors and had given, as a token of friendship, to Serrano. The narrative recounts the process by which Piktor, whose name suggests both image-maker and victor, receives a new name and discovers "the truth of eternal metamorphosis, because he had been changed from a half to a whole". The central metaphor of this process of the psyche's alchemy is figured in a dream fantasy which is the answer to Piktor's question, "Where can one find happiness?" A bird with feathers like a peacock, reflecting all the colors of the spectrum, responds: "Happiness is everywhere — in the mountains and the valleys and in every flower." With this the bird stretched and shook its feathers. As it settled back it had become a flower, the feathers now leaves and petals, and the claws, roots. The flower then rustled its leaves and began to float upwards into the air, and Piktor noticed it was no flower at all, but a butterfly. It was a butterfly that now glided to earth, like a snowflake, and on the earth was transformed into "a crystal radiating a deep red light". But the earth seemed to absorb the light, for it was gradually disappearing into the ground. Piktor grasped at the jewel, held it tightly in his hand, "because it seemed a talisman for every adventure in the world". At that moment a serpent slid from a nearby tree and whispered to Piktor, "This jewel can transform you into anything you wish".[54]

John Keats ("Surely I dreamt today, or did I see / The wingéd Psyche with awakened eyes?"),[55] and Denise Levertov ("only those [butterflies] / that lie dead revealing / their rockgreen color and the bold / cut of the wings"),[56] among poets, are only two who join Hesse in his imagery of the butterfly-self. Among novelists, there is James Agee's remarkable ending to *A Death in the Family* ("Maybe 'miraculous' was the way the colors were streaks and spots in patterns on the wings..."),[57] not to mention the butterfly-passage in Thomas Mann's *Doctor Faustus* ("Genus Papilo and genus Morpho... regarded by the natives as evil spirits").[58] Portmann's 1954 Eranos lecture, "Metamorphosis in Animals," spells out in detail the mystical biology of butterflies, providing the background for understanding Mann's butterfly discussion in the Leverkühn family: "I must leave it to the reader's judgment whether that sort of thing is matter for laughter or tears."[59]

Little by little we come closer to the waters of transformation and to humor, but in so doing we should remember that the imagery of the poets and novelists is by no means new, nor even is it as recent as Aristotle, Theophrastus, and Plutarch. The reference by Mann to "the natives" is the clue to the final step in our trek.

Among the Aztecs, Xochipilli-Centeotl is a young God of life, morning, procreation, and vegetation, who, like Amor in Apuleius' tale, stands between night and day, and who, like Psyche among the Greeks, is mysteriously pictured as a butterfly.[60]

In northwest America the butterfly is shown on the lips of the Goddess as a breath-soul.[61]

In Samoa the butterfly was a family God.[62]

In Germany folklore makes the butterfly a source of babies.[63]

Among the Pimans, the Malagasians, and the Antimerinians the butterfly is the name of the soul who creates, and back to whom we descend at death, often in butterfly-form.[64]

Among the Finno-Ugric myths there are to be found butterflies which are *urts* or souls, and witches who act, in butterfly-form, as shaman-healers.[65]

Among the North Pacific coastal Indians the soul of the dead arises out of parted waters as a butterfly.[66]

The Japanese have a *kami-* or spirit-tale about "Mr. Butterfly and his Flowers" which parallels Hans Christian Andersen's tale, "The Butterfly".[67]

The African Swahili say that Kukuwazuka, the "fowl of the ghosts", is identical to Mantis, which is a butterfly, this being the totem object with taboo-function and mana-power.[68]

In Hawaii abandoned souls feed on butterflies.[69]

In England fairies sometimes take the form of butterflies.[70]

The Melanesians recount the story of a woman who, on hearing about a neighbor at the point of death, heard also a rustling sound and discovered a butterfly in her hut, caught it, took it next door, and opened her hands over the corpse's mouth — a fascinating form of not-so-artificial resuscitation.[71]

Why this uniform testimony? Certainly it is already clear in our deepest experience that butterfly-like fluttering is the crux of life and liveliness. It is a fluttering we feel deep down when we are extremely nervous, and so our language speaks of "butterflies in the tummy!" And our speech is right, of course. It would be true to our deepest selves, too, to name the fluttering feeling of a heart attack or a nervous breakdown by the name "moth". But happily the fluttering feeling is not always symptomatic of failing energies. The beating of butterfly's wings is metaphorically the proper name for the source of that gentle influx of spirit's energy that we occasionally feel when gently lifted sunward for a brief and quietly ecstatic moment of renewed vitality. Let us call it a sense of humor. But there is more.

Moths and butterflies are called *lepidoptera,* a name indicating that they have *scales* like fish but also *wings* like birds, as if *lepidoptera* transcend the earthly realm and are equally at home in the fertile dewy moisture and in drying airy skies. This imaginative clue from science tips us off to a double implication of the lepidopteran spirit of humor.

First, there is the important matter of the butterfly's many-colored wings, which (like the tail of the Peacock in the alchemical tradition, like the Coat of Many Colors for Joseph, and like the Rainbow for the Greek goddess Iris and for Noah) suggests spiritual maturity, a maturity of *psyché* that allows for the richness of many views, many voluntary associations, many colorations. Let us always remember that without those colors a butterfly cannot in fact fly; yet those colors are refractions of mere dust.

Second, there is the equally important matter of the moth and its flame. Goethe tells of this dimension of great Spirit in a poem titled *Selige Sehnsucht:*

> The stuff of life is what I praise,
> that longs to die in flames.
>
> In the assuagement of those nights of love which begot you,
> in which you have begotten,
> strange presentiments come upon you
> when the quiet candle gleams.
>
> You remain no longer
> held in the overshadowing darkness,
> and new desire sweeps you upward
> to more exalted mating.
>
> No distance makes you hesitate,
> you come flying and enchanted
> and at last, a moth eager for the light,
> you are burnt.

Then the poet concludes in his last stanza:

> Until you have grasped this:
> Die and be transformed! —
> you will be nothing
> But a sorry guest on the somber earth.[72]

Such is the dynamic of humor, the fire of Zarathustra that vaporizes moist tears into the quiet smiles of a master clown. When the poetess Sappho wrote, "my heart is a-flutter",[73] certainly the fluttering was the fluttering of butterflies' wings. When we are released from our ego-spun cocoons, the result is a gentle breath of air, as if the beating of the deep wings of *psyché* creates the wind that will support *her* very flight. There simply is no *pneuma*, no spirited self, without *psyché*, because, in the imagination's touch, there is neither breath nor wind, hence no humor, without the beating of wings which lift us sunward, out of the moisture, through the air, towards the fire, as butterflies are free.

"It is funny," wrote Christou (meaning that it is not funny at all), "how men are always seeking to bypass the soul *[psyché]* in their attempt to get a shortcut to spirit *[pneuma]*."[74] And now we may also say: it is funny (meaning what Christou meant by the word) how men are always seeking to bypass humor in their psychologies.

It is because of the cocoon. Bypassing and shortcutting are a syndrome of being all wrapped up, without humor. We may think there is a butterfly inside the wrapping, but it is only a worm. It is a butterfly when it emerges, which is why Goethe said, "Die and be transformed." To say that the butterfly is not inside the cocoon is to say also, as Christou does, that *psyché* is not in man. That is where we went wrong in our Western imagination, imagining *psyché* to be "inside", thereby subordinating *psyché* to ego, forgetting eros altogether. "The psyche is not in man, it is we who are inside the psyche."[75] Think of the butterfly and the moth — or rather, feel the fluttering — and the air and fire of the moisture will no longer be a problem, but an earthy mystery. There are many images of *psyché*, but the neglected image of *psyché* as butterfly is a clue to the humor archetype. It gives levity to moisture.

Naming the Gods

It may seem that there has been a considerable excursus from our original concern: namely, that of the collective fantasy regarding a sense of humor. But this is not at all the case.

Psyche *as butterfly* is the form of being at home in the interplay of the airs or ethers. This is so because she is the insect of shadows flitting light, and because some of her kind are keyed to the light of fire.

So, too, Achelous (for now we may say his name) as the river of rivers, eldest of the children of Tethys and Okeanos, is the form of being at home in the interplay of moistures (humors). This is so because he is the God and father of Castalia, who resists Apollo's ego and becomes the source of the Muses' creativity as a spring. Achelous himself resisted Heracles' heroic laboring and, though Achelous failed against Heracles, he is thereby in his failure eternally linked to the earth rather than to the vaulted sky. Achelous can have Castalia as an offspring because he is flowing always, archetypally in Psyche. He is the River within the Spring, who is within the Muses. Achelous is a deep resource. He is the underground of humors.

It is not easy to see the point about Achelous until one has encountered the butterfly. Achelous lives dynamically only in relation to the butterfly; they are together the Heraclitean fluxure that is composed of waters and airs. An archetypal psychology of humor should always focus on *both* the watery-chthonic *and* the airy-fire, so as to avoid *in its psychologizing* the either/or of a rigid senex and a fleeing puer (butterflies are too much at home in the shadows to fly too high).

In our civilization it is doubtless the case that Apollo will catch up with Castalia and ravage her, just as Heracles will impose his utilitarian will and power upon Achelous.[76] Similarly, the ego in such a civilization will think itself wind or flame *(pneuma)*, not noticing that the source of the air and the lover of the flame *(psyché)* is a deep resource considerably more shadowy than the wind that makes all things cold and more shadowy, too, than the flame whose end is apocalypse.

It would seem that a sensing of the humors in such a time might indeed be worthwhile, for ourselves and for our psychology. Achelous and the butterfly know how, for together they are the source of the interplay of a double archetype. They are the collective fantasy of an archetypal form. The poet Robert Duncan feels this as his moist tears turn toward "an orange butterfly with an eye / of turquoise staring / even as I stare, lost in setting four / factors of something I am making / into motion." And so he writes:

> the soul   .   recognizes wings
> as flight long known   the color
>   itself a universe   so near
> only my hands counting   and eyes
>   naming these things
> holds at bay   what is   from me.[77]

In recognizing the "wings as flight long known", the poet points toward the source of humors, a veritable Daphne, transformed and become Psyche, feeling herself Laurel, whose moisture desires Apollo's thinking to become erotic wind in her branches and water on her roots. The wind she wishes is, as Rilke said, not a rash breath, the song of the ever-too-young, but it is the breath round Nothing's tear, the emptied cavity at the center, whose presence is the very being of the interplay of waters and airs, and whose source, as it now appears to me, is Achelous' flow and the beating of butterflies' wings.

1 Aristotle, *The Ethics* (Baltimore: Penguin, 1955), iv. 7 (pp. 131ff).
2 Thomas Aquinas, *Summa Theologica* (New York: Benziger Brothers, 1947), Pt. II—11, Quest. 168, Arts. 2—4.
3 See Freud's book, *Jokes and their Relation to the Unconscious* (1905), and his article, "Humour" (1928). Also: Martin Grotjahn, *Beyond Laughter* (New York: McGraw-Hill, Blakiston, 1957).
4 Claude Lévi-Strauss, *The Raw and the Cooked* (New York: Harper and Row, 1969), pp. 122—133.
5 The letter is dated "London, March 27, o. s. [Old Style Julian Calendar], 1747. See: *Letters of Lord Chesterfield* (New York: Oxford University Press, World Classics, 1929).
6 Martin Heidegger, *What is Called Thinking?* (New York: Harper and Row, 1968), p. 118.
7 Eric Partridge, *Origins* (New York: Macmillan, 1959), p. 299.
8 Cited in: Paul Lauter, ed., *Theories of Comedy* (Garden City, N.Y.: Doubleday Anchor, 1964), p. 117.
9 Owen Barfield, *History in English Words* (London: Faber and Faber, 1926), pp. 136—138.
10 C. G. Jung, *Alchemical Studies*, CW 13, (Bollingen Series; Princeton: Princeton University Press, 1967), para. 255; *Psychology and Alchemy*, CW 12^2, para. 528.
11 *De baptismo*, I; cited in: Hugo Rahner, *Greek Myths and Christian Mystery* (New York: Harper and Row, 1963), p. 69.
12 Cited in: Gaston Bachelard, *The Poetics of Reverie* (New York: Orion Press, 1969), p. 177.
13 Philip Wheelwright, ed., *The Presocratics* (New York: Odyssey Press, 1966), p. 45.
14 See: Jung. CW 13, para. 255.
15 Aristotle, *The Metaphysics*, 938b 7; cf. Wheelwright, op. cit., p. 47.
16 See: *The Koran* (Baltimore: Penguin, 1961), p. 94; and cf. Theodore Gaster, *Myth, Legend, and Custom in the Old Testament* (New York: Harper and Row, 1969), pp. 26f.
17 Ibid. See, also, Jung, *Aion* CW 9, ii^2, paras. 288, 311, 336.
18 Plato, *Phaedo*, 107d—115a; cf. Giorgio de Santillana and Hertha von Dechend, *Hamlet's Mill* (Boston: Gambit, 1969), pp. 179—230. See, also: Walter Wili, "The Orphic Mysteries and the Greek Spirit," in Joseph Campbell, ed., *The Mysteries, Papers from the Eranos Yearbooks* (Bollingen Series; New York: Pantheon Books, 1955), pp. 64—92.
19 See the illustrations in Jung, *Aion*, CW 9, ii, pp. 130, 219. The classical instance of a description and explanation of quaternarian religious symbology is: Radulphus Glaber, *Historiarum libri quinque*, Lib. 1, Cap. 1, in: Migne, *Patrologia Latina*, CXLII, Col. 613, edited by Maurice Prou (Paris, 1886), pp. 2f. This text is explicated by: Joan Evans, *Cluniac Art of the Romanesque Period* (Cambridge: University Press, 1950), pp. 110—113 ("The Quaternities"), see also figs. 191a & 191b. At the top of several monastery columns the four rivers are sculpted into the corners of the pillar capitals.
20 Barfield, op. cit., p. 138.
21 For an analogous modification of Hobbes' view of humor, see the gloss by: Kenneth Burke, *The Philosophy of Literary Form* (New York: Vintage Books, 1957), pp. 318—320. And for an ingenious updating of traditional theories of laughter, in keeping with new researches in "double-bind" psychological theory, see: William Fry, *Sweet Madness* (Palo Alto: Pacific Books, 1963).
22 Sandor Ferenczi, *Thalassa: A Theory of Genitality* (New York: Psychoanalytic Quarterly Publ., 1938), p. 48.
23 See: *Aion*, CW, 9, ii^2, paras. 288, 311, 336, 353, 358, 373, 382.
24 C. G. Jung, *Analytical Psychology: Its Theory and Practice* (New York: Random House, 1968), p. 19. It should also be noted that Jung found there to

be clinical evidence for a strict correspondence in dream imagery between specific colors — red, blue, green, and yellow (like those of the humors!) — and the four functions of the psyche.

25 See: James Hillman, *The Myth of Analysis* (Evanston: Northwestern University Press, 1972), pp. 284f.   26 See: John 4:10—11.
27 Cited in: Gerald Vann, *The Water and the Fire* (New York: Sheed and Ward, 1961), p. 9.
28 Gaston Bachelard, op. cit., p. 197.
29 Jung, *Psycholgy and Alchemy*, CW, 12², para. 160.
30 Marie Louise von Franz, *An Introduction to the Interpretation of Fairytales* (New York: Spring Publications, 1970), pp. 8—10.
31 von Franz and Hillman, *Jung's Typology* (New York: Spring Publications, 1971), p. 76.
32 Barfield, op. cit., p. 137.   33 See: *Aion*, CW 9, ii, paras. 372—77.
34 John of the Cross, *Dark Night of the Soul* (Garden City: Doubleday, Image Books, 1959), p. 64.
35 Philip Wheelwright, *Heraclitus* (New York: Atheneum, 1964), p. 58.
36 Hjalmar Frisk, *Griechisches Etymologisches Wörterbuch*, Band III (Heidelberg: Carl Winter Universitätsverlag, 1970), p. 1142.
37 Cf. Erwin Rhode, *Psyche: The Cult of Souls* (New York: Harper Torchbooks, 1966), pp. 30—31, 46—47, 365, 442.   38 Wheelwright, *Heraclitus*.
39 Cf. Erich Neumann, *Amor and Psyche: The Psychic Development of the Feminine* (New York: Harper Torchbooks, 1962), p. 53.
40 Cf. H. J. Rose, *A Handbook of Greek Mythology* (New York: Dutton, 1959), pp. 286—287.
41 Werner Jaeger, *Paideia: Ideals of Greek Culture*, Volume II (New York: Oxford Press, 1943), pp. 40f.
42 Martin Heidegger, *On the Way to Language* (New York: Harper and Row, 1971), p. 179.   43 Ibid., p. 180.
44 I Corinthians 2:13—15, compare I Corinthians 15:44—46.
45 Cf. G. W. H. Lampe, ed., *Patristic Greek Lexicon*, Fasc. 4 (Oxford: Clarendon Press, 1965), pp. 1097—1098; 1546. Also: Rahner, Ernst, Smyth, eds., *Sacramentum Mundi: An Encyclopedia of Theology*, Volume 6 (New York: Herder and Herder, 1970), pp. 138—139; 143—145.
46 Cf. Gerhard Friedrich, ed., *Theological Dictionary of the New Testament*, Volume VI (Grand Rapids: Eerdmans, 1968), p. 357.
47 *Phaedrus*, 251a.   48 Ibid.
49 Aristotle, *Historia Animalium*, 551a 14; Theophrastus, *Historia Plantarum*, 2.4.4; Plutarch, *De causis plantarum*, 5.7.3.
50 Job 4:19.   51 Matthew 6:19—20.
52 Jung, *The Structure and Dynamics of the Psyche*, CW 8, para. 663.
53 Cited in: David Bakan, *Sigmund Freud and the Jewish Mystical Tradition* (New York: Schocken, 1965), p. 225.
54 Miguel Serrano, *C. G. Jung and Herman Hesse: A Record of Two Friendships* (New York: Schocken, 1966), pp. 16—17.
55 John Keats, "To Psyche", Richard Aldington, ed., *The Viking Book of Poetry of the English Speaking World* (New York: Viking, 1959), Vol. II, p. 773.
56 Denise Levertov, *With Eyes at the Back of our Heads* (New York: New Directions, 1959), p. 14.
57 James Agee, *A Death in the Family* (New York: McDowell Obolensky, 1956), p. 335.
58 Thomas Mann, *Doctor Faustus* (New York: Vintage Books, 1948), p. 14.
59 Ibid., p. 20; see: Adolf Portmann, "Metamorphosis in Animals", Joseph Campbell, ed., *Man and Transformation: Papers from the Eranos Yearbooks*, (Bollingen Series; New York: Pantheon, 1964), pp. 300—306.
60 Cf. Erich Neumann, *The Great Mother* (New York: Pantheon, 1963), p. 196.

ACHELOUS AND THE BUTTERFLY

61 Cf. James Hastings, ed., *Encyclopedia of Religion and Ethics,* Volume XI (New York: Scribner's, 1921), p. 729.   62   Ibid., Volume I, 1917, p. 506.
63 Ibid.   64   Ibid.
65 Cf. J. A. MacCullough, ed., *The Mythology of all the Races,* Volume IV (Boston: Marshall Jones, 1927), pp. 8—9, 13, 240f.
66 Cf. ibid., Volume X, p. 263.   67   Cf. ibid., Volume VIII, pp. 345f.
68 Cf. ibid., Volume VII, p. 288.
69 Cf. Stith Thompson, ed., *Motif-Index of Folk-Literature,* Volume II (Bloomington: Univ. Indiana Press, 1956), p. 506.
70 Cf. ibid., Volume III, p. 42.
71 Cf. James Frazer, *The New Golden Bough,* ed. by T. H. Gaster (New York: New American Library, Mentor, 1964), p. 199; Frazer here is taking his information from R. H. Codrington, *The Melanesians* (Oxford: Clarendon Press, 1891), pp. 207ff.
72 J. W. von Goethe, "Selige Sehnsucht", Leonard Forster, ed., *The Penguin Book of German Verse* (Baltimore: Penguin, 1957), p. 227.   73   Sappho, 2.6.
74 Evangelos Christou, *The Logos of the Soul* (Vienna/Zurich: Dunquin Series, Spring Publications, 1963), p. 102.   75   Ibid.
76 See also the downfall of Achelous before the Olympian power of Zeus, all understood as an archetype of human struggle: *The Iliad,* XXI, 195.
77 Robert Duncan, "Yes, I Care Deeply", Tony Stoneburner, ed., *Parable, Myth, and Language* (Cambridge, Mass.: Church Society for College Work, 1968), back cover.

MYSTICISM AND HUMOUR

HENRY CORBIN
(Paris/Teheran)

What is the connection between humour and mysticism? To begin with, I agree with the general opinion that there is no possible definition of humour. Even our British friends, despite their familiarity with the subject, have long ago given up trying to find a truly accurate definition. I shall therefore not make yet another vain attempt. But even though there is no satisfactory definition of humour, it may be possible to ascertain some of its effects. So I will suggest that humour implies the ability to establish a certain remoteness, a certain distance towards oneself and the world. That distance enables one to appear not to be taking quite seriously that which one's inner self takes, cannot but take, terribly seriously, yet without betraying the secret. Without that distance towards the object, one is in danger of becoming its captive and prey. Conversely, if the necessary distance is maintained, all the tension in features and gestures, the defensive and aggressive attitudes, may give way to a smile.

This brief indication may already suffice, or so I hope, to point out that the connection between mysticism and humour resides in the fact that humour may be the safe-guard of the mystic insofar as it protects him from the double hazard which I have described as "subjective peril" and "objective peril". And we may appeal to Sohrawardî himself to illustrate this statement.

This translation has been prepared from the second part of a lecture entitled "Mystique et Humour chez Sohrawardî, Shaykh al-Isráq" presented in Teheran, November 19, 1969, and which has been published in French in *Collected Papers on Islamic Philosophy and Mysticism*, (Institute of Islamic Studies, Teheran Branch, McGill University, Montreal), Teheran, 1971, pp. 16—38; this translation is of pp. 26—38. For further authoritative material on Sohrawardî, see the author's *En Islam iranien*, vol. II: "Sohrawardî et les Platoniciens de Perse", Paris: Gallimard, 1971.

Rather, I shall propose both the testimony of Avicenna (Ibn Sînâ) and of Sohrawardî since this first example comes from the "Recital of the Bird", written in Arabic by the philosopher Avicenna and translated into Persian by Sohrawardî. This "Recital of the Bird", as a mystical narrative, is one of Sohrawardî's small masterpieces. Its translation is in a book on Avicenna[1] in which I tried to show its place within the cycle of Avicennian stories — that is, situated in the context of what Avicenna's *Oriental Philosophy* would have been had its manuscript not been destroyed during the sack of Ispahan, and had Avicenna had the time to write it over again. Better still, this tale finds its place in the cycle that developed around the symbol of the Bird from Ghazâlî down to the great mystical epic of 'Attâr. Its origin is remote. The first reference that comes to mind is Plato's *Phaedrus* where the soul is imagined in the likeness of an Energy whose nature would be incarnated by winged horses driven by a charioteer who too is winged. Also, we find there the splendid image of the celestial procession of souls following the Gods, and of the fall of some of these souls. "The natural property of a wing", writes Plato, "is to raise that which is heavy and carry it aloft to the region where the gods dwell, and more than any other bodily part it shares in the divine nature."[2] So much for the symbol of the bird, other magnificent examples of which are to be found, for instance, in certain Manichean psalms.

Let us now turn to Avicenna's story, translated by Sohrawardî. Its prologue is full of pathos. "Is there none among my brothers who will lend me ear for a time, that I may confide some part of my sorrows to him?", asks the author . . . "Brothers of Truth! Strip yourselves of your skins as the snake casts his . . . Love death, that you may still live. Be ever in flight; choose no settled nest, for it is in the nest that all birds are captured . . ."[3] There are two splendid pages in this same style. Then the narrator tells his story: a party of hunters spread their nets and caught him together with the troop of birds to which he belonged. During his captivity, he forgot everything — his origin, his relation to another world and he eventually lost consciousness of the very shackles that bound him and of the narrowness of his cage. Then one day he noticed other birds who had managed to free themselves; he eventually joined them; they flew away together, cleared the highest peaks and travelled through the high valleys of Mount Qâf, the psycho-cosmic mountain, at the cost of exhausting efforts. They met their brothers near the City of the King, and in that very city the King whose beauty amazed them, received them; they made their way back escorted by the King's messenger who was bearing an order for those who had tied the bond and who alone could unbind it. I cannot insist on any detail, only on the sudden change in tone that occurs at the end of the story.

The reader was enraptured by his vision of "He who is all a Face that thou contemplatest: all a Hand that bestows",[4] when all of a sudden the narrator, anticipating the gentle irony that will greet his story, takes the place of the sceptics and writes the following lines:

> How many of my brothers will there not be who, my recital having struck upon their ears, will say to me: "I see that thou art somewhat out of thy wits, unless sheer madness hath fallen upon thee. Come now! It is not thou who didst take flight; it is thy reason that has taken flight. No hunter ever made thee his prey; it is thy reason and naught else that has been hunted down. How should a man fly? And how should a bird fall to speaking? ... 'Twere well to diet: drink a decoction of thyme dodder, take frequent hot baths, take inhalations of oil of water lily. Then go on a light diet, avoid sitting up late; and, above all, no overexertion of mind. For in the past we have always known thee as a reasonable man, of sound and penetrating judgment. God knows how greatly we are concerned over thy state. Seeing thee thus deranged, we feel utterly sick ourselves!"[5]

I believe that these lines in which Avicenna the physician's humour runs free have an exemplary quality; the mystic has spoken; he has tried to relate his adventure. But he knows beforehand how "rational" people will accept it; they will accept it in the same way many historians of philosophy received the teachings of the Neoplatonists — Proclus, Iamblichus, and their disciples. If he tries to confront them, meeting argument with argument, he will become infinitely vulnerable; he will convince none of the sceptics but he may increasingly convince himself of the excellence of his case. And then he will be lost, frustrated, ready for schizophrenia. On the other hand, if he is capable of taking that distance, of clearly and consciously formulating the objections that the sceptics and the agnostics will raise, then, what would have been negative, aggressive criticism is transformed into an achievement of humour that permits him to slip through their fingers. Humour is his double safe-guard, for while it protects him from ego-inflation and excessive exhilaration, it also obliterates the effects of what might have been an infringement of the discipline of the arcanum. Only he who is worthy and able will comprehend; the others will perceive nothing. But despite all and everything *his message will have been transmitted.* It is thus simultaneously that the mystic finds his protection against both the subjective peril and the objective peril that threaten him. This protection is offered by the language of *symbols.* And it may occur, as in the case of Avicenna and of Sohrawardî, that this language is inspired by a superior humour.

But then, what exactly is a symbol? In order to explain it strictly, it would be best to return to the meaning of the Greek word *symbolon.* In Greek, the verb *symballein* means to agglomerate, to join together. For instance, two men, quite by chance, happen to be fellow-guests. Before taking leave of each other, they break a ring or a potsherd in two; as each man takes one half, each of the two pieces becomes the *symbolon* of the other. Years may go by with all the changes they bring, but it will suffice that the owner of one *symbolon* joins it to the other in order to be recognized as the fellow-guest of old, or at least his deputy or friend. In the case of our mystical metaphysicians each *symbolon* belongs to its respective universe: the invisible world of *Malakût* on the one hand, the visible world of sensible perception on the other. The *symbolon* of one world joined to the *symbolon* of the other form a superior unity, an integral unity. Because the fact, in this context, that one *symbolon* conjoins the other proclaims that the visible world *symbolizes with* the invisible one — if we use the language that Leibnitz still knew how to speak. Here is the very source of Goethe's famous phrase at the end of Part Two of *Faust:* "All things ephemeral are but a symbol".[6] (We might even say: *nothing less than* a symbol.) The difference between "symbol" and what nowadays is commonly called "allegory" is simple to grasp. An allegory remains at the same level of evidence and of perception, whereas a symbol guarantees the correspondence between two universes belonging to different ontological levels: it is the means, and the only one, of penetrating into the invisible, into the world of mystery, into the esoteric dimension.

When I speak of the importance for a culture of having a philosophy that guarantees the function of symbols, it is the ontological, "objective" validity of the intermediary world, between the intelligible and the sensible, that I am referring to. The idea of this intermediary region implies the triple articulation of reality with the world of the Intelligible *(Jabarût)*, with the World of the Soul *(Malakût)* and with the Material World. The anthropological triad — mind, soul, body — corresponds to this triad. The day that philosophical anthropology is reduced to a dyad, be it soul and body or mind and body, that day signifies the end of the noetic, cognitive function of symbols. That triad, which has been suppressed in the West since the ninth century, has only survived in philosophical and theosophical schools mistakenly considered to be "marginal". Cartesianism recognizes nothing but thinking and extension. Sensible perceptions and abstract concepts of understanding alone remain. Then the vast world of Imagination, the world of the Soul proper, falls into disgrace; it is identified with the *imaginary*, with the unreal.

It is very striking to note how carefully Sohrawardî and the *Ishrâqîyûn* applied themselves to a metaphysics of Imagination. Because they realized its ambiguous role, they maintained it firmly centered between the intelligible and the sensible worlds. Its function in serving the intelligible, that is to say, the Intelligence — *nous* in Greek — is to present the *Veiled Idea* in the form of the Image, that is, of the symbol. The characters and events in a parable are all symbols, and that is why a parable is also the only story that is true. In return, when Imagination allows itself to be entirely caught by sensible perceptions, fluttering from one to the other, it is literally "off center" and loses itself in unreality. In the first case active Imagination is the organ of penetration into a real world which we must call by its proper name, to wit: the *imaginal;* in the second case, Imagination merely secretes the *imaginary*. For Sohrawardî, Imagination in the first case is the celestial tree at the top of Mount Sinai, from which the Sages pick the high knowledge that is the "bread of Angels". In the second case, it is the accursed tree mentioned in the Koran. There is a great deal of talk at present of a civilization of the "image"; in this respect, I believe that we have much to learn from our philosophers, the *Ishrâqîyûn* and other masters. It is certainly a most complex subject, which makes me fear to appear obscure where I would only be concise. For time obliges me to stick to essentials only. We have here reached the source of Sohrawardî's genius, the source of an inspiration that enabled him to move from one register to another as if playing upon a grand organ; that is to say, to present through the media of the symbols and parables of initiatory tales what he expounded elsewhere, in his major works, in a theoretical and systematic form.

I shall restrict my choice to three examples only, culled from a treatise of Sohrawardî's. Its form is not that of a continuous narrative, but rather that of a *rhapsody* linking together several symbolic stories. In it appear the Tortoise People, the Fairy People, and the Bat People. The subject is obviously not zoology — these are symbols of humans spiritually ignorant, the blind men of the soul. They are recognizable in their symbolic form because their hidden inner form, therefore their true form, *symbolizes with* these manifestations. And therein resides the whole difference from their daily life, which reveals only their apparent form. In displaying themselves in symbolic forms, they appear to us as they really are in the *imaginal* world, in which their ignorance or their blindness fixes them in a wholly *negative* relation with the *Malakût,* with the world of the Soul. It is their truth, or rather, their inner falseness which bursts forth when projected against the background of superior evidence, and here precisely a great mystic like Sohrawardî gives full vent to his humour.

A first example: what is at stake is *Nâ-Kojâ-Abâd*, "the country of nowhere", removed from the dimensions of sensible space. (I discussed this "place" in *Spring 1972,* pp. 1—19.) One could write a scholarly metaphysical dissertation on hyper-space. But the doctrine may also be experienced, no longer a theory, but instead a real *event* of the soul. We see the mystic at grips with the Tortoise People.

One day the Tortoise People were watching from the shore the wheeling round of a many-coloured bird at the surface of the sea: sometimes it dived underwater, sometimes it surfaced. One of the tortoises asked: "Is the nature of that bird aquatic or aerial?" Another replied: "If it were not aquatic, what would it be doing in the water?" But a third one said: "If it were aquatic, it could not live out of the water." Among the tortoises lived a wise judge whom they questioned. He answered: "Study that bird carefully. If it can live out of the water, that means that it does not need it. For proof, take the fish who cannot live out of the water." Just then a strong wind arose; the lovely coloured bird soared and vanished into the clouds. Did the tortoises understand? Far from it. They began to ask the Sage to explain himself. He answered them allusively by quoting a few of the great spiritual masters' sentences, culminating with the declaration of the mystic al-Hallâj concerning the Prophet: "He blinked His eye outside of the *where*", meaning that his inner vision removed him from the dimensions and orientations of sensible space. The tortoises became enraged: "How", they asked, "could a being who is localized in space go out of *place*? How could he remove himself from the directions and coordinates of space?" (We may recall the end of the "Recital of the Bird".) The Sage replied: "But that is precisely why I told you all I have been saying." Whereupon the indignant tortoises threw dirt and rocks at him: "Be gone! We remove you from office; we no longer acknowledge you as our judge."

Here is a second example. The issue this time is the connection between night and day. What appears as daylight to the blind men of the soul is nothing but darkness for him who possesses spiritual vision; and conversely, what is full daylight for him seems like dangerous and threatening obscurity to those who do not have spiritual vision.

Thus a hoopoe (wise Solomon's bird) in the course of one of its journeys stopped off with the Fairy People. And, as everyone knows, the hoopoe is endowed with remarkably sharp vision whereas fairies are totally myopic. The hoopoe spent the night chatting with the fairies, and at dawn he wanted to set off again, but the fairies violently opposed this plan: "You poor wretch! What kind of new-fangled idea is this? Since when does one travel by day?" The hoopoe replied that the time had come to leave precisely because it was light. The fairies answered: "But you're quite mad! How can one see anything during the day since the day is dark while the sun is passing through the regions of gloom?" "But it is exactly the opposite", said the hoopoe. The discussion turned vicious and the fairies demanded an explanation, provoking the hoopoe to a formulation in which we hear the profession of faith of a great mystic: "Whosoever sees during the day can only testify as to what he sees. Here am I, myself, I see! I am in the world of presence, in the world of direct vision. The veil has been lifted. I perceive the radiant surfaces like so many revelations; doubt does not encroach upon me." Whereupon the fairies, exasperated by the behaviour of this bird who claimed he could see in broad daylight, fell upon his eyes with their nails and teeth, screeching at him derisively: "Hey, you who-see-clearly-during-the-day!"

The hoopoe finally understood that there was no way out — what he knew to be the broad daylight of supra-sensible universes was nothing but darkness, bewildering those who see no further than their carnal eyes can perceive. He realized that the fairies would kill him since they were attacking his eyes, in other words, his inner vision, and that a mystic could not survive in this world without the power of his inner vision. The hoopoe knew that he must revert to the discipline of the arcanum, following the wise rule: "Address people only according to what they are able to understand." So, in order to free himself from his enemies, he told them: "Of course I am like you. Just as everyone else, I see nothing during the day. How could I see in broad daylight?" Whereupon the fairies were soothed and stopped torturing him. The hoopoe pretended blindness until he managed to escape, although this caused his soul to suffer a thousand torments. For it is hard not to be able to communicate to others the wonders one beholds. But the author reminds us of a divine law that admits no breach: "To reveal the divine secret to the unworthy is a crime of impiety *(kofr)*." The necessity for esotericism is founded on that very law.

The theme of the last example accentuates the story we have just read. This time Sohrawardî's parable introduces an innocent chameleon and the Bat People. How their quarrel began is left to our speculation. But the bats' hatred for the chameleon grew such that they plotted to imprison him under cover of darkness and to seek revenge by putting him to death in one way or another. They set off on their expedition and managed to drag their unfortunate enemy into their house of woe. They kept him imprisoned all night and consulted him in the morning. "How shall we punish this chameleon? What will be its death?" The worst torture for a bat would be to have to endure the sight of the sun, so they decided to punish the chameleon in this way. But what their bat minds could not even begin to apprehend was that this was exactly the kind of death the poor chameleon had hoped that God would send him. And here the author interrupts the bats' discussion with two of the mystic al-Hallâj's most famous distichs: "Do kill me, O my friends. In killing me you shall make me live, since for me dying is to live and living is to die." At sunrise the bats threw the chameleon out of their house of woe so that he should be chastised by the radiance of the sun. What they could not know was that the very thing that seemed like a torture to them was precisely the chameleon's resurrection.

Here are three mystical parables, at once very similar and very different. They draw upon the wealth of humour specific to Sohrawardî, a humour that conceals in its depths a profound sadness. It is the sadness of "he-who-has-understood" in the face of his impotence to overcome most men's incapacity to comprehend, because this incapacity is the "secret of destiny" and no human being can resolve that particular secret. I had been careful to warn you that there is no possible definition of humour. In trying to analyze Sohrawardî's humour too minutely, we would be sure of losing its presence.

But, what we can do before ending is to follow our sheik along the path of symbols. He was able to create marvellous ones, because he was endowed with the interior vision of the figures with which they symbolized. Perhaps a man must reach the summit of spiritual maturity — which bears no relation with his actual age — in order to create his own symbols. This summit is the self-knowledge which, as we noted, pervades Sheik al-Ishrâq's spirituality from beginning to end. The attainment of this self-knowledge blossoms in a visionary experience whose memory recurs throughout his tales. And this visionary experience gives shape to the most beautiful symbol of the Self that the philosopher goes in *quest* of, the Self of his transcending Ego, the celestial Ego that symbolizes with his terrestrial Ego. That symbol is the Figure of light, dazzlingly beautiful, with whose vision several of Sohrawardî's mystical tales open or close. It is the Figure of the Angel who, in Avicennian philosophy is the Angel of Humanity, Tenth in the Hierarchy of Intelligences, and whom theologians call the Holy Spirit. The remarkable thing is that this same Figure in the Western world also polarized the interior vision of those known as *"fedele d'amore"*, chiefly Dante's companions who had read Avicenna and Averroes; they named that Figure of the Angel *Madonna Intelligenza*.

Sohrawardî always calls the Figure of the Angel encountered in initiatory recitals a sheik. "Why a sheik?" asks Mosannifak, one of the commentators of these mystical recitals. The term has no bearing on years or old age, since the youthful features of the apparition are almost always underlined. The commentator goes on to explain that *sheik* means *morshed*, spiritual guide, and that the *Ishrâqîyûn* (the philosophers and spiritual masters belonging to Sheik al-Ishrâq's school) have no *morshed* other than this Angel of knowledge. That is precisely where they differ, he says, from the Sûfis who proclaim the need for a sheik or a human master. In any case, for the *Ishrâqîyûn* this master could never be more than a temporarily necessary intermediary because their sheik, their *morshed* or spiritual guide, is the Angel himself, the Angel of their vision and their nostalgia. Thus, we may say that this experience of the Angel for the *Ishrâqîyûn* is very close to the experience of the personal interior guide, the invisible master called *sheik al-ghayb, ostâd e ghaybî* in the school of Najmuddîn Kubrâ. And this is also why this Figure of light, who rules the mystic's inner horizon, is the *symbolon* par excellence, the Figure with whom one's most intimate personal being symbolizes; it is the Self reached through self-knowledge by the subject who is its mere earthly counterpart. Here we touch on a fundamental inner experience that could be illustrated with a great number of texts; the entire Valentinian gnosis could be cited in confirmation.

By the same token, one may catch a glimpse of Sohrawardî's "actuality". I apologize for using the word "actuality" in this context, as it is really too full of unpleasant associations. I would prefer "presence, urgency" ... In saying this, I am thinking of a man who died recently[7], a playwright and a novelist, who at first sight might seem as far removed from Sohrawardî as possible, but a particular page of his suggests the comparison with which I would like to end this talk. I am thinking of Audiberti, whom most of you probably know, and whose extremely diverse works are admired by an equally diverse public. But any reader of a book such as *Les tombeaux ferment mal*[8] will agree that he was a mystic and something of a visionary. Yet, I am referring to an episode from another book, a book called *Dimanche m'attend*.[9] This episode is set in one of Paris' many churches, the Eglise Saint-Sulpice. The architecture of this monument may not be altogether admirable, but it contains two treasures: its great organs and, in the first lateral chapel to the right of the entrance, Eugène Delacroix's huge painting of Jacob's struggle with the Angel. That is doubtless what suggested the comparison to my unconscious, although Sohrawardî's experience of the Angel is a struggle *for* the Angel rather than *with* the Angel. Nevertheless, without having read Sohrawardî, whenever Audiberti happened to be in the neighbourhood of the church, he was wont to go meditate before Delacroix's picture for a few minutes, and his meditation readily turned into a visualizing experience. This is how he ends the account of one of his visits:

Jacob and the Angel, after bending sarcastically over my confusion, regain their attitude . . . I begin to feel the cold, the church grows empty. Outside, rain glazes the square. Between the stopped cars (stopped but not arrested) walks a young girl in boots, wearing a toque and a grey coat whose sleeves are replaced by wing-shaped cloth. Her eyes are very slanting and her hair blonde. I gaze at her in wonder. But, come to think of it . . . believe me if you will, I rushed into the church.
"The Angel was still there . . ."

Well then! Here again is an example of the *sui generis* humour that belongs to a somewhat visionary mystic. How could he tell us what he *saw*, not merely what he *thought he saw*, without admitting that he went back into the church to check if Delacroix's Angel was still there?

Here all philosophical reflexion must stop, for it would destroy precisely what gives value to this humour. There is only one last thing we must do before parting, and that is to recall this verse of Rimbaud: "J'ai vu parfois ce que l'homme a cru voir".[10]

Translated from French by Cornelia Embiricos Schroeder.

1. H. Corbin, *Avicenna and the Visionary Recital*, trans. Willard R. Trask, (Bollingen Series, LXVI) New York and London, 1960. (Orig.: *Avicenne et le récit visionnaire*, Département d'Iranologie de l'Institut Franco-Iranien, Teheran, and Librairie d'Amérique et d'Orient Adrien Maisonneuve, Paris, 1954).
2. Plato, *Phaedrus* 246e (Version used by the translator of this article: *The Collected Dialogues*, edited by Edith Hamilton and Huntington Cairns, Bollingen Series LXXI, New York, 1961, p. 493; *Phaedrus* trans. by R. Hackforth).
3. Corbin, *Avicenna*, pp. 186—87.
4. Ibid., p. 192.
5. Ibid., p. 192.
6. Goethe, *Faust*, Part II, Act V: ("Alles Vergängliche/Ist nur ein Gleichnis"). My translation of the author's: "Tout l'éphémère n'est qu'un symbole".
7. Jacques Audiberti died in 1965.
8. J. Audiberti, *Les tombeaux ferment mal*, Paris: Gallimard.
9. J. Audiberti, *Dimanche m'attend*, Paris: Gallimard, 1965.
10. "I have sometime seen what man believed he saw" would be the literal rendering of Rimbaud's line.

HEPHAISTOS: A PATTERN OF INTROVERSION

MURRAY STEIN
(Houston)

The murals on the walls of the Detroit Museum of Art, commissioned by Ford and executed by artist Diego Rivera, depict scenes in the life of the industrial worker: heavily muscled men wielding wrenches and hammers, massed together around glowing furnaces and along endless assembly lines, some of them wearing gas-masks, others struggling mightily with glowing ingots of red-hot steel. Neatly dressed managers of the industry stand off to one side plotting how further to direct this mighty force of labor to their best advantage. In some of the upper panels, heavy-breasted primitive-looking women are bearing children, the next generation of exploitable workers. The whole of this impressive painting is suffused in a noxious, greenish light that gives the scenes a distinctly underworld tone. Ford, it is rumored, was not pleased when he saw what his money had paid for.

The Marxist image of the proletarian worker-masses may be largely a Hephaistian fantasy: the rejected of the earth, by whose labor and sweat civilization has grown; class-conscious and seething with pyromaniacal resentments and grudges; endlessly creative and the source of most of the world's supply of genius; restless, volcanically explosive and ready to take up arms against tyrannical masters, yet not lovers of war and strife but rather peacemakers and natural humanitarians; simple as fire itself and equally energetic. As the proletarian worker is seen by the Marxist to be the work-horse of industrial society, so is Hephaistos the only Olympian God who works. The workers of the world unite under the banner of Hephaistos. Bearing something of the mark of an inferior child who has to take up a trade, Hephaistos stands on the fringes of the power circles that govern the Olympian world, a servant-artisan figure who builds the palaces of the Gods "with skilful hands"[1] and sometimes plays the court buffoon to the great amusement of his fellow Olympians.[2]

Hephaistos is a quintessential fringe-person on Olympus. Included at the edge, he looks uneasily in, into the wheels-within-wheels that make up the Olympian social structure. But nervously and uneasily, too, he watches the power conflicts, remembering how Zeus "seized me by the foot and hurled me from the threshold of Heaven. I flew all day, and as the sun sank I fell half-dead on Lemnos".[3] Trying somehow to stay in touch with the center, maybe to be ready for the worst or to know what's coming next, he knows all the while that it's impossible really to belong there — there, where they tolerate the fringe-people as long as the work gets done, but where they can never act and feel quite easy and neighborly with them. Hephaistos-consciousness drifts a bit toward the Frankenstein phenomenon: his brother is the monster Typhon, but that goes beyond the fringe of Olympian society.

The feet of Hephaistos tell volumes: they are turned back to front, and when he walks he goes with a rolling gait that strikes the other Gods as somehow hilarious and breaks them up with mirth — "a fit of helpless laughter seized the happy gods as they watched him bustling up and down the hall."[4] On this particular occasion his buffoonery has the effect of keeping the Gods from each other's throats.

In one story the feet of Hephaistos are misformed at birth, and Hera, his mother, goes into shock (she had bred and borne him by herself to show Zeus what she could do without his help!), grabbing him up and flinging him with disgust from the portals of heaven. This boy-child was supposed to be something she could hit Zeus over the head with, to show off with, to prove that she was as good as he (he had given birth, through his head, to the mighty and highly respected Athene); instead, to her acute disappointment, this misformed cripple shows up her inferiority and embarrasses her, and this (of course) is intolerable. The crippled child threatens to put her on the fringe, too.

The other version tells that Hephaistos' feet were crippled when he hit the ground on the island of Lemnos, having been hurled from Olympus by Zeus who had a fit because the boy was sticking up for his mother, Hera, in one of the many quarrels between the royal pair. As a rule, Hephaistos remains close to women; he's not much in the company of men, except for the blacksmiths. Zeus sometimes passes for his father, but most stories tell that he had no father, only a mother. And since it is generally the father who shows the boy the ropes of society and leads him out into a "position", etc., it begins to make sense why he is so much on the edge of things in the patriarchal, masculine world of the Olympians.

Rejected by his "father" in a rather no-nonsense, brutal way, Hephaistos lands on Lemnos, where he makes friends with the Sintians. Lemnos becomes his home-away-from-home. In fact, this island may be his original home. There was on Lemnos a tradition of Hephaistos-worship on the part of the native inhabitants, those "foreign-tongued people the Sintians".[5] This island-home of Hephaistos throws much light on his background.

The islands of Rhodes, Samothrace, Delos, Lemnos were much associated with a race of creatures variously called Daktyloi, Telchines, Kouretes, Korybantes, or Kabeiroi; on Lemnos they were called Hephaistoi, in the plural.[6] These names refer to dwarf-like servants of the Great Mother Goddess.[7] Invariably they occupy themselves with metallurgy at subterranean forges, deep in the body of the Mother herself, for the islands were in earliest times identical with the Great Goddess.[8] As the Idaean Daktyloi ("Daktyloi" meaning "fingers", thus as the "fingers" of the Great Goddess), these smith-dwarfs learned their metallurgic arts originally from the Great Mother herself.[9]

The dwarfish smiths are not only the servants of the Great Mother, they are also her sons and lovers, her son-husbands: "It will be remembered how she, the Great Mother, always had with her Daktyloi, Kouretes, Korybantes or Kabeiroi, whom she had bred from within herself and with whom she also bred further . . ."[10] The name of this Mother-Wife was (sometimes) Kabeiro; she was the mother of the Kabeiroi, and her name was variously transmuted into Rhea, Demeter, Hekate or Aphrodite.[11] When Hephaistos mated with Kabeiro, she bore the boy Kakmilos, who again, in turn, mated with her and bred the three Kabeiroi and three Cabirian Nymphs.[12] Hera, the Olympian mother of Hephaistos, preserves associations from earlier, pre-Olympian times with beings of a Dactylic nature.[13] The importance of this incestuous pattern in the Hephaistian configuration is central.

Invariably the mythical smiths were set apart by some physical defect or oddity.[14] Often, also, these dwarfish, crippled or otherwise mutilated, craftsmen were, according to Eliade, associated with "strangers" and "mountain folk",[15] that is, with primitive populations[16] of "unfamiliar character who were surrounded by mystery".[17] Undoubtedly this cripple-motif, as well as the mysteriousness of these populations, hangs together with their incestuous bond to the Great Mother. Here we can perhaps see what lies behind the outcast character of Hephaistos: he is a fringe person and slightly monstrous because of his connections with the historically and psychologically regressive servant-son-lovers of the Great Mother.

This Daktylic background places Hephaistos, also, in proximity to the magical arts of the underworld. The left-handed Daktyloi, that is, those who originated from the fingers of the Goddess's left hand, were magicians.[18] And the cousins of the Kabeiroi of Lemnos, the Rhodian Telchines, were famed as evil magicians.[19]

Hephaistos cannot be separated from his fires. In fact, his name is said to mean "fire";[20] sometimes, too, he is called *"ephoros tou puros"* ("ruler of the fire"),[21] or again his "breath" is fire, and his "glance" is a "blaze".[22] But the fire of Hephaistos is fundamentally not a daytime, Olympian fire but a subterranean fire,[23] and here he connects with the Roman God Vulcan, who ruled over and in the volcanic Mount Etna on Sicily. The Hephaistian fire *per se* sprang from a hole in the earth on Lemnos, "on the small mountain of Mosycholos, where his companions were certain Kabeiroi called the Karkinoi, 'the Crabs'"[24] alluding perhaps to their strong fingers and masterful hands.

Another association connects Hephaistos to a pre-Olympian background: in one story, Hera brings the baby Hephaistos to the island of Naxos and hands him over to Kedalion, who is supposed to act as his tutor. The name Kedalion "was as much as to say 'the phallic one'".[25] Kedalion belongs to the ancient order of the Cyclops, who, besides the Titans and Giants, were the original children of Gaia and Ouranos.[26] The race of Cyclops is intimately related to the Great Goddess of pre-historic Greek religion, both as her sons and lovers.[27]

His association to the Daktyloi and to the Great Mother goes a ways in explaining the surprising connection between Hephaistos and women's mysteries. In one set of stories, Hephaistos is the son of Prometheus, and the two of them are visited by Demeter who brings them her mysteries, "just as she brought these ... to the King of Eleusis".[28] His relation to the feminine mysteries of childbirth and fertility has its reason in the Daktylic background. The Idaean Daktyloi, those "Idaean Fingers" to whom all the dwarfish smiths are related, came into being in the midst of the childbirth event: Rhea, worshipped in Asia Minor as *Meter oreia*, "Mountain-Mother", had fled to Ida to await the birth of Zeus, and there, when the time came due and labor pains set in, "she supported herself with both hands on the soil. The mountain at once brought forth as many spirits, or gods, as the goddess had fingers."[29] These spirits are the Daktyloi and procede to busy themselves in her service.

These numerous connections between Hephaistos and the Daktylic-Great Mother-pre-Olympian background would place the subterranean fire of the smith-God in touch with the dark, internal energies of the Mother's creativity; the Hephaistian fire would take its light and energy from the central fires which are at the heart of nature's creativity. Hephaistos is, then, a split-off animus of the Great Mother who "mimics" the creative processes in the depths of the Mother and brings to birth through this transforming mimicry his works of art.

Indirectly, Hephaistos has quite a lot to do with the origins of mankind. Out of his relations with the Great Mother Goddess "Lemnos" unravel the first sisters for the primordial brothers, and these form three pairs, the first human couples. Until this possibility of brother-sister incest arises, the sons remain incestuously attached to the Mother in a kind of pre-individual, anonymous, not-yet-human cluster.[30] In another mythic tale, Hephaistos is again responsible for bringing the first woman into being: he formed Pandora. Hephaistos fashioned this first human image of woman at the behest of an angry Zeus, who was contriving to punish mankind for possessing fire.[31] Heretofore the human race had been purely masculine, and to create confusion among them Zeus asked Hephaistos to form the image of a beautiful maiden. The story is well-known of how Pandora opened the box and released misery, disease, suffering, etc., into the world, snapping shut the lid just before the last content, "hope", could escape. What interests us here about Pandora is not, however, her character or what she may indicate about Greek prejudices on the subject of women. What catches our attention is Pandora's artificiality.

The name Pandora, as Kerényi explains, means "the rich in gifts", "the all-giving", and this is, significantly, a name for the earth itself.[32] "In an old portayal of her", Kerényi remarks, "the name written beside her is actually Anesidor, 'the sender-forth of gifts', which is one of the names of the earth-goddess."[33] Pandora is, therefore, a representation of the all-giving Mother herself, which has been scaled down to human size through the arts of Hephaistos.[34] But despite her life-likeness, and even her links to the Great Mother, Pandora is nevertheless "made"; she is an artificial product of skill and craft, but an *artifact* which resonates to the ground of nature in such a profound way that there is a kind of confusion between nature and culture, nature and art. Through Hephaistos, the Great Mother develops a "primordial imitativeness" which is the source of cultural and artistic creative energy. The forge of Hephaistos is therefore the birthplace of spirit. This "new" creativity, which nevertheless roots in and mimics the creative processes of nature, is what the Hephaistian fire symbolizes.

Some Renaissance fantasy supports this view. Because the Sintians were unknown to Renaissance scholars, they read *Sintiis* variously as *absintiis* ("wormwood"), *nimphis* ("nymphs") or *simiis* ("apes"). To justify the last reading, Boccaccio argued that Greek imagination gave Hephaistos to the apes because apes imitate man as man imitates nature. Man, he argues, imitates nature by practising the arts and crafts. Hephaistos is the God of *techne,* which means according to Aristotle "acting as nature acts".[35] Thus Hephaistos learns on Lemnos to "ape" nature and her creative processes.

Boccaccio goes on to imagine how Hephaistos (whom he naturally calls by the Latin name Vulcan), as "fire", forms the foundation of civilization, that is, how the keeping alive of fire "led to the formation of the first social units, to the invention of speech, and to the erection of buildings".[36] Boccaccio's fantasy follows closely the model given in the Homeric hymn to Hephaistos:

> ... he taught men
> work ...
> work that was
> noble
> for men to do
> on the earth
> men who
> formerly
> lived in
> caves
> in mountains
> like animals
> now on the
> other hand
> thanks to
>
> Hephaistos
> whose skill is
> so famous
> they know
> how to
> work
> life is
> easy
> the whole
> year
> long
> and they live it
> quietly
> in their
> houses now ...[37]

This hymn praises Hephaistos both as God of work and as God of the civilizing process, leading man from the caves and forests through imaginative, imitative work into his houses and palaces.

The greatness of Hephaistian art lies in its naturalness; his works are praised generally for being so astonishingly life-like. Examples of this abound. Homer heaps praise without end on the famous shield which Hephaistos forges for Achilles, precisely for the vividness with which the several scenes on it imitate real life. The shield is literally jumping with life — maidens and young men dancing, ploughmen driving their teams to and fro, reapers taking the harvest, sun, moon and stars shining brightly, and around the whole of it flows the cosmic river, "the mighty Stream of Ocean".[38] Indeed, the shield of Achilles contains the entire cosmos; all of nature is vividly recreated in this archetypal work of art. In miniature we find the same phenomenon in the wreath that Hephaistos weaves for Pandora — "In this wreath many beasts of the earth and sea were wonderfully portrayed, almost as if they were alive...".[39] Perhaps the most ingenious examples of Hephaistian artfulness are furnished by the female(-like) servants in his house: "Golden maidservants... They looked like real girls and could not only speak and use their limbs but were endowed with intelligence and trained in handwork by the immortal gods."[40]

The wife of Hephaistos, both in the *Iliad* and in Hesiod, is Aglaia, the youngest of the Graces. Her name means "the glorious", and Kerényi asks if she might not be a *living* work of art, for "grace" *(charis)* means also the "delightfulness of art".[41]

Through Hephaistos, the great forms of nature image themselves forth in art. His cousins the Telchines were the first creatures to build images of the Gods.[42] The springs of creativity, which are rooted in the depths of the Great Mother, take a turn in Hephaistos from concrete child-bearing and body-centered sexuality toward the realization of the cosmos as imagination and symbol.

The Hephaistian configuration remains deeply situated in the feminine mysteries of childbirth and fertility and has little to do with the labors and efforts of masculine heroism. The forges and fires of Hephaistos are in the earth, in the womb of nature. The furnace itself is an "artificial uterus", as Eliade has pointed out;[43] the smith stands in the service of the metallurgic processes that occur in the furnace just as the Idaean Daktyloi served the Great Mother in her labor. Whereas the heroes of solar masculinity perform great tasks to free themselves from bondage to the maternal background, Hephaistos remains always in the service of the feminine. And the Hephaistian passion for creative work is deeply of the Mother.

This intimacy between Hephaistos and the feminine world finds mythic expression through an incident of his boyhood. When Hera flings him in disgust from the gates of heaven, the crippled child falls into the sea and is rescued from drowning by the sea-nymphs Thetis and Eurynome, who take him home with them and nurture him for nine years. The Greek word for where they take him is *"mukos"*, which means "the innermost place", "the secret place", but also "the women's apartments in the house". During this sojourn in the women's quarters, the young Hephaistos puts his talented hands to work for the first time and fashions for his surrogate mothers many beautiful articles of jewelry. These nine years in *mukos* represent, of course, a second incubation period for Hephaistos, and it is during this period that he learns of his ability to create. Years later, when Thetis comes to the master-craftsman and begs him to fashion a shield for her son Achilles, Hephaistos forges the work that demonstrates the vast scope of his resonance to the primordial creative processes within the Great Mother herself.

Shifting for a moment from the archetypal background of the Hephaistian configuration to more personal psychological considerations, it is not hard to see that a man whose ego-consciousness is strongly influenced by the Hephaistian pattern will experience certain characteristic problems and proclivities. He will presumably find himself rather an outcast from a conventional world that requires ready adaptation to patriarchal and masculine dominants; he will be moody and given to swinging between inflation and depression; he will appear both to himself and to others, especially to the analyst, rather unheroic and uninterested in overcoming his close attachment to the world of women and mothers; indeed, he will cling to feminine circles and company, fascinated by the mysteries of creativity and often lost in a world of inner images and fantasy, bound hand, foot, and soul to the excitement and anguish of tending the "underground forges". He will seem to be quite anima-possessed, smoldering and crippled.[44]

Emma Jung, writing of the image-producing effect of the anima, describes a state of masculine ego-consciousness which is close to Hephaistian consciousness in a man:

> The transmission of the unconscious contents in the sense of making them visible is the special role of the anima. It helps the man to perceive these otherwise obscure things. A necessary condition for this is a sort of *dimming of consciousness;* that is, the establishment of *a more feminine consciousness,* less sharp and clear than man's but one which is thus able to perceive in a wider field things that are still shadowy.[45]

The analytic "treatment" of such a case of Hephaistian determination will be considered in connection with his association to Dionysos; for now it is sufficient to point out that the creativity of Hephaistos depends absolutely on his intimacy with the feminine world, for it is only as he is able to resonate to the deep maternal creative movements within the Mother that he can realize his creativity.

To the feminine ego the Hephaistian constellation may appear perhaps even more problematical and threatening. Hephaistos connects to her deepest feminine-maternal impulses, yet wants something other than simple maternity. The Hephaistian animus represents a subtle undermining threat to simple, natural feminine creativity, in that he tends toward creating the symbol that mirrors the creative process of nature but produces an artificial product which at once represents and substitutes for "the real thing". Hence the monstrousness of Hephaistian creativity for the feminine psyche: Hephaistos goes *contra naturam* (his feet are turned the wrong way round!) in a way that profoundly threatens to undermine or rechannel the essence of purely natural feminine creativity. Hephaistos may be, therefore, a monstrous offence to feminine naturalism, a sick-making disharmony in the tones that vibrate between feminine ego-consciousness and the Great Mother.

*

Returning to the Hephaistian configuration itself, we find in the contrast between the brothers Ares and Hephaistos several important points of differentiation that go far toward further clarifying the Hephaistian pattern. We come here upon a highly complex set of stories and motifs. The mythic links between Ares and Hephaistos pass through three nodes: their birth to Hera, both without paternity;

the love triangle among Hephaistos, Aphrodite, and Ares; the rite of passage episode when Ares tries by force, unsuccessfully, to bring Hephaistos back up to Olympus.

Like Hephaistos, Ares is born to an angry, jealous Hera. Zeus has offended her deeply, this time not so much by his promiscuity as by the affront of performing within himself the maternal task of bearing a child, Athene, and thereby demonstrating the superfluousness of womankind. This hermaphroditic act on the part of Zeus stimulates Hera to action: she does likewise. Her first effort results in the birth of Hephaistos; later attempts bring forth the monster Typhon and Ares, God of furious warfare and battle-rage. Hephaistos proves unsatisfactory in this competition because he measures up so unfavorably to Athene: "Without me he has born Athene", laments Hera, "who is glorious amongst all the immortals, whilst my own son, whom I bore, Hephaistos, is the least of all of us."[46] Dwarfish, lame, grotesquely comical, Hephaistos just will not do at all. But Hera's judgment of his inadequacy relates also to his deeper meaning: this animus of introverted *contra naturam* creativity, bound to the maternal depths and committed to a symbolic imitation of feminine creativity, simply does not begin to answer the extraverted challenge of Athene with her ear-splitting battle cry in a way that would satisfy the jealous rage of Hera. And yet, in a subtle way unseen by Hera, Hephaistos is a precise response to Athene, from hermaphroditic femininity to hermaphroditic masculinity. If, as W. F. Otto says, "Athene is a woman, but as if she were a man",[47] Hephaistos is a man, but a bit as if he were a woman.

Because she sees in Hephaistos a failure, Hera tries again and produces, finally, Ares. Whether or not Ares satisfies her is not said, but he certainly does reflect his mother's ferocious, battle-crazy animus. Ares, in contrast to the dwarfishness of Hephaistos, is gigantic;[48] the epithet *"artipos Ares"* ("swiftfooted Ares")[49] calls attention to his further physical superiority over Hephaistos, who bears the epithet *"apedanos"* ("the weakly").[50] In temperament, too, the brothers are very unlike, Ares thriving on strife and drinking deeply of the bloody waters of mortal combat, Hephaistos rather the peace-maker who tends to shy away from conflict.

But Ares is more than the split-off battle-thirsty animus of Hera, though he is surely that. He is also the fructifier, the masculine impregnator.[51] It is this underlined masculinity of his that distinguishes him sharply from Hephaistos, whose masculinity, in the sense of an aggressive, outwardly-fructifying flow of libido, is clouded by his intimate associations with the world of women. The crippled feet give an obvious clue of problematical sexuality in the Hephaistian configuration, feet having definitely a phallic significance.

The famous episode of the triangular relation among Hephaistos, his wife Aphrodite, and Ares her lover leads toward similar conclusions. Hephaistos, it is told, won the hand of Aphrodite as a reward for freeing Hera from the chains with which he had bound her. What sort of marriage this was remains in the dark, but it seems quite clear that Hephaistos spent much of his time on Lemnos with his smithy-friends, leaving the voluptuous Aphrodite home alone to mind the house. Her affair with Ares, begun during these interludes and carried on while Hephaistos was introverting at his underground forge, is marked by high erotic intensity: it is as though in the coming together of Ares and Aphrodite two sexual opposites meet which were simply not present in the Hephaistos-Aphrodite combination.

Not that Hephaistos is at all effeminate and soft. The many drawings and paintings of him show generally a robust specimen of the masculine sex with heavily muscled arms and thick neck. And he is, after all, God of smiths and craftsmen ("hardhats"!), probably the least effeminate elements in the population. When Hephaistos' temper flares, the volcanoes rumble in the distance. With the strength of his arm, he turns his furnace on Ares and sends him flying back to Olympus when the war-God comes to force him home, and his mighty deed in the Trojan War, scalding the river Xanthus with his dazzling flames, defeats any notion that Hephaistos is second-best in battle. But the masculine, fructifying libido in the Hephastian configuration, unlike that in the Ares constellation where it shoots actively and aggressively outward, instead moves in a kind of incestuous motion back toward the Mother, toward the subterranean forges on Lemnos.

Ares plays a secondary role in a story that tells of Hephaistos' return to Olympus and of a curious connection between the young smith and Dionysos. Angry at Hera for rejecting him, Hephaistos seeks revenge by constructing a throne for her that will bind her fast and levitate when she sits down on it. After the trap has sprung successfully, and Hera has suffered a while the mortification and discomfort of hanging suspended in mid-air on this trick-chair, the Gods send brother Ares down to bring Hephaistos back to Olympus by force. But Hephaistos drives Ares off with several blasts from his fiery furnace. Next the Gods send down Dionysos, and this God uses a cunning ruse instead of trying force: Hephaistos has never seen or tasted wine before, and Dionysos tempts him to try a bit. The smith drinks deeply, again and again, and soon suffers himself to be led away. Dionysos returns to Olympus, leading Hephaistos, who is drunkenly draped over a donkey, behind him. But Hephaistos is not so witless that he fails to bargain for the freedom of his mother: loosened chains in return for the hand of Aphrodite.

This mythic link between Dionysos and Hephaistos comes at an exceedingly important moment in the "development" of Hephaistos: the crippled child has been cast out of heaven, has sulked and sought revenge, has learned of his creative gifts, but has not yet found his maturity. His return to Olympus represents a rite of passage to maturity, to taking up a position within the Olympian hierarchy. The agent provocateur of this passage is his binding of Hera; the bonds he has applied to his mother provoke the crisis and force the issue. But his maturity depends on loosening the bonds with which he has tied her.

This act of "loosening" is effected through Dionysos and his intoxicating wine. As Hillman has pointed out, "Dionysos was called *Lysios*, the loosener".[52] Obviously he is the right God to send on this mission, for loosening is precisely what is called for, not only the loosening of Hera from her chains, but the prior loosening of Hephaistos from his *idée fixe* which is bent on revenge against his mother. The hardening of Hephaistos in this attitude of irreconcilable bitterness against his mother would spell absolute disaster for both, for it would leave the mother suspended and suffering in mid-air and the son cut off from the creative energies that flow into him through his contact with the Mother. Caught in his own trap, Hephaistos would wither in the self-destructive heat of resentment. A sort of anarchistic self-directed pyromania takes over in such cases, an attitude utterly devoid of creativity, rejoicing only in conflagration, even courting visions of pseudo-martyr death in the flames of its own kindling. The fire in the earth becomes an erupting volcano, and Hephaistos takes on the most terrifying aspects of his brothers Ares and Typhon. Only in Hephaistos, this anarchistic violence would be directed not outward, as with Ares, but inward against himself, against his own body and soul.

Dionysos comes, then, to save Hephaistos from himself, from suicide. The two Gods have several things in common. Dionysos was also born hermaphroditically, from the thigh of Zeus; one story tells that Hephaistos was born from the thigh of Hera.[53] Moreover, both Gods have deep linkages into the world of women. Even more than Hephaistos, Dionysos is "a man, but as if he were a woman". But whereas Hephaistos tends to tie down and fixate (a kind of compulsion to "show them"), Dionysos is the God of dismemberment, dissolution, and loosening. It is unclear where Hephaistos is when Dionysos comes to him, but one must suppose that he is still in the watery home of the sea-nymphs where he fell when Hera threw him from her. So Dionysos comes with his wine, with his spirit of drunkenness and eros, to free the fire of Hephaistos from its fixated imprisonment in water. By separating with his spirits the fire from the water, Dionysos frees Hephaistos from his submergence in the bitterly resentful negative anima; he frees the fire to follow its natural tendency upward, and by loosening his fixation frees him to touch yet more profoundly the creative energies in the core of the primordial Great Mother.

Loosening means separating without cutting off, rather healing and freeing to take a new look, to sink more deeply, to rise higher, to become flexible and plastic. For Hephaistos the solution to the mother "hangup" is not a heroic, aggressive battle against the maternal monster, but a kind of unfocused Dionysian intoxication which dissolves his claims upon her. Hephaistos rides back to Olympus, drunken, on a donkey, that phallic animal, and at the moment of entry into the Olympian gates his claim "transfers" from mother Hera to erotic Aphrodite. From this latter union, by some accounts, the God Eros was born.

The loves of Hephaistos, which begin with Aphrodite, tend to conclude in disappointment. Behind these disasters in love lies the incestuous, Mother-directed motion of his libido. Already somewhat apparent in his triangular relationship with Aphrodite and Ares, this pattern is dramatically stated in the story of his love affair with Athene.

The mythic ties between Hephaistos and Athene show, both in their quantity and profundity, a deep-going association between these two figures. More than Aphrodite, Athene is the "soul-mate" of Hephaistos. Yet a kind of cloudy mysteriousness shrouds their relationship; no single tradition was ever clearly established on this subject, and so what confronts us is a blurred image based on rumors and conflicting reports.[54] Despite this welter of tales, a few points seem fairly clear and the general outlines of a myth emerge.

Hephaistos was undoubtedly present at Athene's birth: many drawings and paintings attest to his presence there.[55] With his hammer he performed a mid-wife role, releasing the Goddess from the head of Zeus with a mighty, rending blow. It is highly significant that the contra-sexually colored Hephaistos should be the instrument of Athene's birth, for she is to masculine Zeus as Hephaistos is to feminine Hera: the product of a hermaphroditic birth-process decisively marked by the contrasexual parent. The birth of Athene heralds a significant development on Olympus, for she represents that inner space and capacity for reflection within the masculine world which is capable of containing affect and the chaos of conflicting, ambivalent feelings.[56] That she is a *contra naturam* content is clear, first because Athene springs (fully armed) from the *head* of her *male* parent, secondly because Hephaistos is her mid-wife and the essence of Hephaistos is a spiritual imitating of the procreative processes within the Great Mother. The Hephaistian configuration would seem to have a liberating effect on the Athene-pregnant head of Zeus: that is, the Mother-tuned, introverting Hephaistian attitude works on the dominant masculine attitude to release, loosen, free the Athene anima.

Immediately Athene springs forth with her "far-echoing battle-cry",[57] Hephaistos falls into desperate love with her. In other versions he first loves her when she comes to his shop for a spear, but always it is love-at-first-sight on his part and a distinct coolness towards him on her side. In some versions he marries her, in others not, in any case the outcome is the same: Hephaistos seeks impetuously and passionately to make love to Athene; at the moment of climax she pushes him aside, and his semen falls to the earth where it impregnates Gaia; the child of this misadventure is named Erichthonios. The marriage of Athene and Hephaistos and the fruit of their union were celebrated annually by the Athenians in a fertility festival named the Chalkeia.[58]

This story of Hephaistos' semen missing its intended mark and fertilizing instead the Great Mother tells of the introverted, incestuous course of his libido, and the offspring, Erichthonios, symbolizes the outcome of this movement. Erichthonios is closely associated both in art and story with snakes: in some accounts he is himself a serpent below the waist or has serpentine feet;[59] in other stories he is guarded by snakes which curl around him in "a covered, round basket, probably such as those which are used in the Mysteries";[60] in some versions he is even altogether a serpent.[61] "*Chthonios*", the stem of his name, means "sprung from the earth", and an epithet often applied to him is "*gaygenays*", meaning "born of Ge", of the earth. The claim of the Athenians to being *autochthonous,* i.e., indigenous to their soil, rested on their connection to Erichthonios as founder of the royal house of Athens; for after his birth Athene takes him up and cares for him, and when he comes of age she places him on the throne of Athens where he founds the royal line that culminates several generations later in the famous hero Theseus.

Hephaistos, then, not only mimics and transforms the creative energies in the dark, maternal, earth-bound background of the psyche, producing his art and culture-building artifacts, but he also impregnates the Mother with the incestuous, introverted turnings of his libido. And this impregnation of the psyche's fecund, inchoate background gives birth to an image of "natural man", unsplit between instinct and spirit, Luna and Sol, animal and angel, of man whose familiar is the snake. Perhaps it is to an intimation of this image of original man — at home with the earth, integrated, intact, intuitive, at one with himself, undivided by religion, unspoilt by civilization, creative, wise as the serpent, simple as his father "fire" and strong as his protectress Athene — that the Marxists have sung their paeans of praise. This Hephaistian turning of the libido back into the psychic depths fathers the birth of the ancestor-spirit fantasy (that "two million-year-old man")[62] and activates the symbol, the numinous images of the Gods.

1 Homer, *The Iliad*, Bk. I, 605. All quotations from the *Iliad* are taken from the translation by E. V.Rieu, Harmondsworth: Penguin Books, 1966.
2 Ibid., Bk. I, 590—600. 3 Ibid., Bk. I, 585—87. 4 Ibid., Bk. I, 600.
5 C. Kerényi, *The Gods of the Greeks*, London: Thames and Hudson, 1951, p. 72.
6 Ibid., p. 86. 7 Ibid. 8 Ibid., p. 189.

9   Cf. Rene Malamud, "The Amazon Problem", *Spring 1971*, p. 15. Also, cf. Kerényi, op. cit., p. 84.   10   Kerényi, op. cit., p. 211.   11   Ibid., p. 87.
12   Ibid.   13   Ibid., p. 158.   14   Malamud, op. cit., p. 15.
15   M. Eliade, *The Forge and the Crucible*, London, 1962, p. 105.
16   Kerényi, op. cit., p. 86.   17   Malamud, op. cit., p. 15.
18   Kerényi, op. cit., p. 84.   19   Ibid., p. 88.
20   Ibid., p. 156. Cf. also W. H. Roscher, *Ausführliches Lexikon der griechischen und römischen Mythologie*, Leipzig, 1916—24, vol. I, 2, p. 2037.
21   Ibid., p. 2038.   22   Ibid., pp. 2037—38.
23   Kerényi, op. cit., p. 156.   24   Ibid.   25   Ibid.
26   Their names meant "thunder" and "lightening". Ibid., p. 18.
27   Cf. for interesting amplification and interpretation of the Cyclops, Philip Zabriskie, *Odysseus and the Great Goddess,* unpublished Diploma Thesis, C. G. Jung Institute, Zürich, 1972, pp. 16—27.
28   Kerényi, op. cit., p. 212.   29   Ibid., p. 84.   30   Ibid., p. 211.
31   In some stories, Prometheus stole the fire, which he gave to man, from the Hephaistian forge on Lemnos (cf. Kerényi, p. 216). On the connections between Hephaistos and Prometheus, cf. Kerényi, pp. 212—13 and Roscher, pp. 2050—51. Like Prometheus, Hephaistos is a "*phosphoros*" ("lightbringer"), but the heroic and "tricky" features which are so prominent in Prometheus are clearly lacking in Hephaistos, who is as "simple as fire itself" (Kerényi, p. 212).
32   Kerényi, op. cit., p. 219.   33   Ibid.
34   In the story of Deukalion and Pyrrha, too, the identification between Pandora and Mother Earth is made: Deukalion, the son of Pandora, is told to throw the "bones of the mother" over his shoulder in order to create a new race of men; he obeys this command by throwing "stones" over his shoulder (cf. Kerényi, p. 229).
35   Erwin Panofsky, *Studies in Iconology,* New York: Harper Torchbooks, 1962, p. 38.   36   Ibid.
37   *The Homeric Hymns,* translated by Charles Boer, Chicago: Swallow Press, 1970, pp. 86—7.   38   *Iliad*, Bk. XVIII, 610.   39   Kerényi, op. cit., p. 217.
40   *Iliad*, Bk. XVIII, 417—20.   41   Kerényi, op. cit., p. 72.
42   Ibid., p. 88.   43   Eliade, op. cit., p. 52.
44   P. E. Slater, in his book *The Glory of Hera,* Boston: Beacon Press, 1968, includes under the general heading "Mythical Defenses Against the Maternal Threat", a chapter entitled "Self-Emasculation: Hephaistos". Slater discovers in the Hephaistian configuration a defense mechanism: the son, rejected by a jealous, authoritarian father (Zeus) and a narcissistic mother (Hera), "emasculates" himself by elaborating the style of fool and jester, thereby taking himself out of competition with his father, saying "You have nothing to fear from me, nor is there anything about me which should arouse your envy or resentment" (p. 193). The industry of Hephaistos belongs also in Slater's view to the defense, here against his mother: since he cannot present *himself* as an adequate object for "maternal display, he can create objects which will function as substitutes in this regard" (p. 199). This, it seems to me, is the view of Hephaistos obtained by looking at him through the eyes of Zeus, through the paradigmatic grid of a heroic, "mature" ego. This view certainly has its validity, but it is one-sided and ultimately betrays the potentialities inherent even in the "weakness" and "inadequacy" of the child of Hephaistos. What Slater fails to see, only because his method cannot cope with the inherent depth and subtlety of myth, is the pattern of meaning and movement within the Hephaistian configuration itself, and this reflects a fundamental failure of imagination. Instead of looking at and "explaining" myths through the concepts of an ego-building psychology (a psychology governed, it seems to me, by Zeus and Apollo), we are trying to let myth instruct our psychology, to broaden and deepen its visions, and to move us out of our narrow one-sided pre-conceptions of "what it means to be a man".

45 Emma Jung, *Animus and Anima,* New York and Zurich: Spring Publ. 1957/72, p. 25.   46 *Homeri Hymnus in Apollinem,* 309; quoted by Kerényi, op. cit., p. 151.   47 Quoted by Malamud, op. cit., p. 7.   48 Kerényi, op. cit., p. 150; cf. also *Iliad,* Bk. XXI, 400.   49 Roscher, op. cit., p. 2039, quoting *hy. in Ap. Pyth.,* 138.   50 Ibid.   51 Malamud, op. cit., p. 6.
52 J. Hillman, "Dionysus in Jung's Writings", *Spring 1972,* p. 203.
53 Kerényi, op. cit., p. 155.   54 Cf. Kerényi, op. cit., pp. 123—26.
55 Cf., for example, Kerényi, ibid., p. 119, and Roscher, op. cit., p. 2062.
56 Cf. Malamud, op. cit., p. 7.   57 Kerényi, op. cit., p. 120.   58 Roscher, op. cit., p. 2070.   59 Ibid., p. 2063; also Kerényi, op. cit., pp. 125—26.
60 Kerényi, op. cit., p. 125.   61 Ibid.
62 C. G. Jung, "Fragments from a Talk with Students", *Spring 1970,* pp. 177—81.

JUNG AND MARX

DAVID HOLT
(Oxford and London)

I

Students of the history of ideas usually present alchemy either as a woefully unscientific precursor to modern chemistry, or as a more or less bogus attempt to find sudden wealth through the artificial production of gold, or as an esoteric religious tradition that reached its culmination in Goethe's *Faust*. Jung recognises all three of these interpretations as partially valid. Yet for him alchemy came to mean something very much greater than any combination of these three traditions.

He has described in his autobiography how his interest in alchemy grew out of his own life.

> I had very soon seen that analytical psychology coincided in a most curious way with alchemy. The experiences of the alchemists were, in a sense, my experiences, and their world was my world. This was, of course, a momentous discovery: I had stumbled upon the historical counterpart of my psychology of the unconscious. The possibility of a comparison with alchemy, and the uninterrupted intellectual chain back to Gnosticism, gave substance to my psychology. *(MDR, p. 205.)*

This paper was read to the Guild of Pastoral Psychology in London March 2, 1972. It is the author's wish that it be printed in the discursive language in which it was delivered, as an exercise in persuasion that owes as much to feeling as to thinking. References to *Memories, Dreams, Reflections (MDR)* are to the Vintage Books edition, New York, 1963; references to the *Collected Works of C. G. Jung (CW)* are to the Routledge and Kegan Paul edition published in London. The author, a diplomate of the C. G. Jung-Institute Zurich, practises and teaches in London and Oxford.

> Since my aim was to demonstrate the full extent to which my psychology corresponded to alchemy — or vice versa — I wanted to discover, side by side with the religious questions, what special problems of psychotherapy were treated in the work of the alchemists. The main problem of medical psychotherapy is the *transference*... I was able to demonstrate that alchemy, too, had something that corresponded to the transference, namely the concept of the *coniunctio*... (*MDR*, p. 212–213.)
>
> This investigation was rounded out by the *Mysterium Coniunctionis*, in which I once again took up the problem of the transference, but primarily followed my original intention of representing the whole range of alchemy as a kind of psychology of alchemy, or as an alchemical basis for depth psychology. In *Mysterium Coniunctionis* my psychology was at last given its place in reality and established upon its historical foundations. (*MDR*, p. 221.)

Now what Jung is saying here is very odd indeed. It is so extraordinary that we may easily slide over it without feeling the sense of shock which we should. But if I am to persuade you that it makes sense to consider Jung and Marx together, we must pause to register shock, to emphasize just what an extraordinary claim Jung is here making. He is grounding depth psychology in alchemy. He is asserting a coincidence between depth psychology and alchemy.

How can we 'place' this idea within the wider history of ideas to which we are heirs? This is the question to which I am addressing myself in placing Marx and Jung alongside each other. I am not trying to interpret either one in terms of the other. I am not trying to reconcile the work of Marx with that of Jung, in the way that has been tried with Marx and Freud. Such an attempt I would regard as perverse. What I am trying to do is to open up a field of ideas wide enough, and contradictory enough, to give perspective to Jung's assertion of a coincidence between depth psychology and alchemy, so that this idea may have the 'space' it needs in which to move and grow if it is to do its proper work in helping to analyse the human problems of our technological civilization.

Let me start with Marx.

II

Up to about 1400 the economic life of Europe was essentially agricultural, concerned with problems of brute survival. There were exceptions which in retrospect can seem very significant. But taken as a whole, economic activity constituted a closed circle between man and nature. Between 1400 and 1700 this closed circle broke open and began spiralling, both 'out' and 'in', to include within the economic process a wider and ever increasing number of commodities and desires. From 1700 onwards this spiral became more like an explosion, until today we have a situation in which on the one hand the whole system can be kept going only by the creation of new needs out of luxuries that were themselves unheard of a generation earlier, while on the other hand it is becoming more and more widely accepted that this stimulation of new needs is destroying an essential balance within the natural environment. One can say, therefore, that within the closed system that prevailed — with significant exceptions — up to about 1400, money was essentially the medium of exchange, something to facilitate the barter of the market place. It served to lubricate a process of exchange whose driving energy was the natural cycle of agricultural seasons, supplemented by the skills and muscular energy of man. Since 1700, although it retains its old function of lubricating the economic system, money has *also* become the fuel which fires the engine which drives the whole system along. It is this change in the nature of money that Karl Marx described as the emergence of capitalism.

Marx is the prophet of this split in our experience of money. He lived and wrote at a time when the first industrial revolution had already transformed conditions of life in Britain, France, Germany and the Netherlands, and was reaching out to alter the face of our planet more radically — in relation to the passage of time — than in any previous revolution in the history of man. Marx insisted that something unprecedented was happening, and that the split in our experience of money, of which the power of capital was the outward and visible manifestation, was only one aspect of a much more pervasive and radical alteration in the whole balance between man and nature.

This unprecedented shift of balance between man and nature is today widely discussed in terms of ecology, in terms of the relationship between man and his environment. It is therefore perhaps easier for us today to understand Marx if we listen to what he has to say with the contemporary arguments of ecologists in mind.

Marx was deeply impressed by the way in which the split between money as means of exchange, and money as self-generating capital, seemed at the same time both to make possible and also to justify the technological exploitation of the planet on which the industrial societies of Western Europe had embarked. He argued that the result of this interpenetration of the monetary and technological revolutions was altering the very quality of human life. All previous history had been that of men living in a world that was *given*. But now men were learning what it was to live in a world that was to an ever increasing degree made *by* man, rather than given *to* man, in a world whose conditions were determined not by the gifts of nature, but by the manufactures of man. Marx's political economics studied the effects of this revolution on the social relations between human beings, but he emphasised again and again that to understand what was happening to personal relations within this new technological and capitalist society, man must be aware of what is happening to the much more fundamental relation between the creativity lodged in human labour and the material world of which man is part.

It is here that Marx touches the central nerve of meaning with which I am concerned in placing his work beside Jung's psychology of alchemy. So we must pause to consolidate our hold on his argument. We can perhaps best clarify how Marx understood this revolution in the relation between creativity and matter by looking briefly at his celebrated antithesis of capital and labour, and at the complementary idea of the positive abolition of private property.

III

Money has its origin in the market place where we go to exchange what we have, but don't need, for what we need, but don't have. Money is the medium which facilitates this exchange, but in so doing it converts the immaterial process of exchange into a thing, which can itself be exchanged for other things. It is as if when things are exchanged in the market place a new power is born, a power that breaks the circle of man's intercourse with nature. This power has no existence in nature, yet manages to establish itself in its own right as existing over against both man and nature.

Marx believed that with the coming of the industrial revolution, and of the concurrent financial revolution that made money out of credit, this break in the circle of man's intercourse with nature became absolute, so that the circle fell apart into a polarisation. On the one hand, we see the emergence of capital as an apparently autonomous power, able to breed out of itself with no sense of obligation to the material exchanges in which it had its origin. On the other hand, we see the emergence of wage labour, which is bought and sold in the market place like any other thing, and thus valued never for itself but always for something other than itself.

But Marx did not stop at this economic analysis. He gave it another dimension altogether, and it is in this dimension that his work continues to exercise its authority over the minds of men. He argued that with this polarisation between capital and labour a truth becomes conscious that has never been conscious before. He argues that in the consciousness of wage labour as it confronts the power of capital, nature becomes aware for the first time of what it feels like for matter, which in itself is virgin, to be used for a purpose outside itself.

So Marx saw the polarisation between capital and labour as the outward and visible sign of a far more momentous splitting, a splitting that we must think of as taking place within the transformative process between creativity and matter. It is in terms of this deeper and more pervasive splitting that we have to understand his insistence on the need to overcome private property.

Our civilization will fall apart, he prophesied, unless the polarisation between capital and labour can be transcended in some synthesis which takes up into itself the powers inherent in both. For such a transcendence the redistribution of property along the lines of reformist liberal or socialist policies is not enough. For the Marxist, the redistribution of property evades the issue. What is needed is an altogether different kind of 'going beyond' all private property. The value-creating power trapped within property has to return, consciously, deliberately, knowing what it is doing, to the material world in which it has its origin. Only then will human labour discover in itself an energy that is fulfilled not only in the productive-consumptive cycle, but also in the creation of the world within which we produce and consume. When that happens human nature, which is also the humanity of nature, will be realised.

It is an extraordinary vision. It has been compared with some justification to the Christian teaching of the resurrection of the body.

But it is so extraordinary that those who are not familiar with it may not appreciate at first just what is being said. So I shall summarize it again, using words and metaphors which good Marxists might avoid, but which may convey more to you than Marx's own vocabulary.

In buying and selling we exploit a moment of latent self-betrayal within nature. Money lends itself to this exploitation because it is, as it were, secreted like a potent juice by the act in which I, either as buyer or seller, take this thing not as something existing in its own right, but as something equivalent to something else. Every thing can be treated either as a *thisness* or as a *likeness,* because every thing can be true to itself or betray itself. Money materializes the act in which things betray themselves.

To use money as capital is to live off this act. This is what our industrial, technological civilization does. It lives off an act in which nature betrays itself. But because we ourselves are part of nature, this means that our civilization lives off an act in which we connive at the betrayal of our own nature. The more conscious we become of this self-betrayal, the more intolerable it becomes, so that we are driven in desperation to seek ways by which we can transcend the vicious circle in which we are destroying the sources of our own being.

It is, of course, unfair to Marx's voluminous, detailed and scholarly work to condense it into a few sentences. But I do not think my synopsis distorts the essential appeal, for those who call themselves Marxists, of Marx's theory of alienation. For that appeal lies in the simplicity, directness, and above all the humanity, of this central idea of a self-betrayal which is common to both man and nature, a shared loss of integrity in which nature waits on man to take the initiative in work that atones for a violation of which we are not fully conscious.

It is this central idea of a self-betrayal common to both man and nature which I want to compare with Jung's psychology of alchemy. And perhaps it will help you to follow the difficult transition from Marx to Jung if I say now in one sentence what I think I am doing in placing the work of these two men next to each other. I am contrasting the vision of a *world* divided against itself with the vision of *creation* divided against itself.

IV

Jung's interest in alchemy derived from personal experience, and in his researches into this obscure literature he was concerned to bring out the psychological significance of alchemy for himself and for some of his patients. But in order to do so he had to place alchemy in its proper perspective within the history of religious and scientific thought. This perspective turns out to be one that is familiar to us from studies of the Jewish and Christian origins of Marx's thought.

To study alchemy is to study the intercourse between man and matter at a level that was relatively accessible up to about the eighteenth century, before, that is to say, the technological revolution whose first fruits were witnessed by Marx. It is an intercourse of a kind that was grossly material compared to the Christian consciousness of its day, but which at the same time presupposes that matter is ensouled. Although the alchemists were embedded in a materialism deeply repugnant to the spiritual traditions of orthodox Christianity and Judaism, their materialism was never of that kind which exalts the *life* of the intellect over against the *deadness* of matter. For them matter was alive, and the intercourse of man with matter was not that of the objective scientist who puts nature to the torture, but of the worker who mixes his labour with the stuff in which his own existence is enmeshed. It is this quality in the work of the alchemists which reminds us so intimately of the writings of Marx.

But of course for the modern materialist, whether he be Marxist or not, the shocking thing about alchemy is that it is sacramental. Matter is not dead, but alive. The alchemist sensed himself to be involved in the materials on which he worked in a way which would prevent the modern chemist ever even beginning to set up an experiment, still less to accept employment by Beecham or Merck or Ciba. What possible relevance can such a materialism have for us who live in a complex technological civilization that would collapse overnight if we were really to believe that minerals had souls?

It has, I think, this relevance. If we believe, with Marx, that the civilization in which we live, on which we depend for our living, is built on the exploitation of a latent act of self-betrayal within nature, then the question arises: how are we, as members of that same nature, to react? As members of the natural order, we are involved on both sides of that betrayal. We are both the betrayed and the betraying, the exploited and the exploiting. What can we do to bring together these two sides of our being?

It is here that the introverted alchemical tradition can complement the extraverted bias of Marxism. But it can do so only if we are willing to take seriously something which is scandalous and repugnant to Marxist and non-Marxist alike.

This something is at the heart of what I am trying to say to you this evening. It is a something whose scandalous nature becomes more repugnant to our common sense the further we penetrate into it. We can distinguish four levels. At the first, we are asked by the materialism of alchemy to accept that matter is not dead but alive, which is offensive enough to many enlightened twentieth-century intellects. Then we are asked to credit that the aliveness of matter is to be thought of in terms of the intercourse between male and female. At a yet deeper level, alchemy confronts us with something even more improbable: the life of matter is not only compounded of a dialectic that is sexual in nature, but this dialectic wants to convert an intercourse which begins as an unintentional *incest* into the celebration of a deliberate *marriage*. And finally, the ultimate absurdity, we are asked to believe that in making this conversion, matter has need of a personal, human intervention.

How can we understand such absurdity? What conceivable relevance can ideas such as these have for those transformations of matter with which we are familiar in the modern laboratory, factory or supermarket?

There is, I believe, only one word able to integrate the absurdities of alchemy into our modern experience of matter. It is the word holy. In Jung's alchemical volumes we have a materialism that is baptised in the holy, a materialism sustained by an energy which is holy, a materialism that is alive only to those who come in reverence of the holy. Without this category of the holy, we cannot understand Jung's psychology of alchemy. Within it, the study of these strange and difficult writings enables us to assist consciously in that work of resurrection on which all matter is engaged.

So I want now to spend the rest of my time this evening in trying to convey to you something of how this category of the holy on the one hand helps us to understand alchemy, and on the other hand is itself materialised by that understanding. I shall hang what I have to say on two concepts, one taken from Jung, the other from the alchemists themselves. The first is Jung's concept of 'projection', the second is the alchemists' experience of being involved in a *double* work of redemption.

V

A central theme running through all these volumes is that when the alchemists described certain transformations as happening within the crucibles and retorts of their laboratories, they were *projecting the contents of their psyches into matter*. It seems to me that this is an extraordinarily difficult idea, and also an idea that is crucial to our understanding of Jung. The great danger, as I see it, is that we approach this idea of projecting psyche into matter in terms of an I-it dualism taken for granted by the culture in which we live. To do this is to lose the whole historical dimension of Jung's psychology. In writing about alchemy Jung is describing conditions prior to the subject-object dualism that first established its grip on western consciousness in the seventeenth century, and which is presupposed by the technological civilization in which we have to find employment. To question our projections is to question the distinction between mind and matter which has dominated and controlled the scientific revolution of the last three hundred years.

This can perhaps be illustrated by reference to what both Freud and Marx called *fetishism:* that process by which a thing comes to stand for something quite other than itself. Psychoanalysis has been fascinated by the way in which some part of the body — a finger, a heel, a breast — can come to mean some other part of the body, or indeed come, as it were, to contain within itself the whole body. For Marx a central characteristic of capitalist society was what he called the fetishism of commodities, that process by which a thing can be used for a purpose other than its inherent nature. Those thinkers who have tried to arrange a marriage between Freud and Marx have found in this concept of fetishism one of their more persuasive witnesses.

In writing about alchemy Jung is describing a world that glories in an indiscriminate fetishism. Transference of meaning is everywhere. The prima materia of the alchemists "has the quality of ubiquity. It can be found always and everywhere, which is to say that projection can take place always and everywhere". (CW 12^2, para. 433.) For, being unknown, the prima materia, like the unconscious, "is bound to coincide with itself everywhere" (ibid.). But, by analysing this universal fetishism in terms of the *religious* dynamism which sustained the alchemist in his intercourse with matter, Jung grounds his psychology of alchemy in an act which makes of fetishism not an evasion or betrayal of reality, as with Marx and Freud, but the enjoyment of reality as *created*.

This religious experience of creation is, I believe, crucial to our understanding of Jung's work on alchemy. So crucial is it that I must here pause for emphasis. We are at the fulcrum of my argument. If it slips, I am crushed by the weight of that which I am trying to move, and I will fail absolutely to persuade you of my meaning.

So as I continue please bear in mind that I am not using this word creation in the aesthetic sense which is today so common. I am invoking an experience of making which precedes the distinction between artificer and artefact. Theologians speak of it as a creation out of nothing, and are quick to warn that their words conceal as much as they reveal. Perhaps the closest I can come to it is in a metaphor of Gabriel Marcel's: "absolute improvisation".[1] The enjoyment of reality as created is possible only from within an act of absolute improvisation.

Jung's psychology of alchemy is, I believe, written from inside this act. As we read through these labyrinthine pages of esoteric lore, these dredgings in the mysticism of forgotten Gnostics, these anthologies of Jewish and Christian heresies, all further confused by the dreams of unidentified modern men and women, it is this act of absolute improvisation that we must constantly remember. In these volumes Jung is reminding us of an energy that sustains what IS between a beginning and an end of its own making; he is reminding us of a method by which men have worked to save that energy from wasting itself in a making that is in vain.

To follow the drama of this work through these pages we need to watch out for the word 'projection'. For this is the word which locates Jung's psychology of alchemy inside that act of absolute improvisation in which psyche and matter coincide. Every time we meet the word projection we must ask ourselves in what sense it is being used. Are we to think in terms of an I projecting onto a not-I, or are we to think in terms of a more 'original' act of projection, of making, which projects *both* I and not-I before there is any distinction between I and not-I?

1   *Being and Having*, Collins Fontana ed., London, 1965, pp. 21—22.

Let me give you an example of how this applies to the reading of these alchemical volumes. Here is a passage from *Mysterium Coniunctionis* in which Jung is describing the significance of Moon and Sun in alchemy:

> Properly understood, projection is not a voluntary happening; it is something that approaches the conscious mind from 'outside', a kind of sheen on the object, while all the time the subject remains unaware that he himself is the source of light which causes the cat's eye of the projection to shine ... For just as we perceive nothing of the real sun but light and heat, and, apart from that, can know its physical constitution only by inference, so our consciousness issues from a dark body, the ego, which is the indispensable condition for all consciousness, the latter being nothing but the association of an object or a content with the ego. The ego, ostensibly the thing we know most about, is in fact a highly complex affair full of unfathomable obscurities. Indeed, one could even define it as a *relatively constant personification of the unconscious itself,* or as the Schopenhauerian mirror in which the unconscious becomes aware of its own face. All the worlds that have ever existed before man were physically *there.* But they were a nameless happening, not a definite actuality, for there did not yet exist that minimal concentration of the psychic factor, which was also present, to speak the word that outweighed the whole of Creation: That is the world, and this is I! That was the first morning of the world, the first sunrise after the primal darkness, when that inchoately conscious complex, the ego, the son of the darkness, knowingly sundered subject and object, and thus precipitated the world and itself into definite existence, giving itself a voice and a name. (CW 14^2, para. 129.)

It seems to me that to understand this passage, we have to distinguish two axes on which the word projection is being used. On one axis, we are being asked to remember an act of creation sustained by a Creator who is beyond all human distinction between subject and object. On another axis, we are being asked to recognize the moment in which subject and object confront each other. The problem of how these two kinds of projection interact, to give on the one hand psyche and on the other hand matter, is the problem at the heart of Jung's psychology of alchemy.

What I want to emphasize here is that this problem confuses two kinds of experience which many of us have been taught to keep separate: the religious, and the scientific. Projections that have to do with the relation between creator and creature involve us in energies for which the only proper name is holy; while projections that have to do with the relation between subject and object are the proving ground of all science and technology. It is this deliberate confusion of the religious with the scientific which makes Jung's psychology of alchemy so difficult to 'place' in public discussion.

It is as if this psychology of alchemy were saying: to be man, to be this unique conjunction of psyche and matter, is to be engaged in two kinds of work. One has to do with worship, the other with proving. We worship a power that is wholly other than ourselves, the agent that has projected us and our world into being; and, at the same time, we put this power to the proof in our own projections onto matter. Man is the conjunction of these two movements of projection, the moment in which psyche and matter reflect on each other, and in so doing enable the holy to prove itself.

I know this can sound very obscure. For those who reject the idea of the holy as having place in a scientific world, obscurities like these confirm that they need waste no more time on Jung. But for those who are impressed by the ease with which science can enslave as well as liberate, I believe Jung is here saying something of immediate interest. He is reminding us that when we invoke the power to put nature to the torture, the power to test our own projections by experimenting with the transformations of matter, we are invoking the same power which distinguishes Creator from creature, and that whether this power enslaves or liberates depends on our attitude to the holy.

Let me now try to get a little closer to this central mystery of alchemy by considering the second theme to which I referred earlier: how the alchemists experienced themselves as engaged in two contrary yet interdependent works of redemption.

VI

This theme of man's involvement in a double work of redemption runs all through Jung's psychological explorations of religion. It has perhaps reached its widest public through *Answer to Job*, but it is also of quite special importance in the books on alchemy.

Writing of Paracelsus, Jung says:
Whereas in Christ God himself became man, the *filius philosophorum* was extracted from matter by human art and, by means of the opus,

> made into a new light bringer. In the former case the miracle of man's salvation is accomplished by God; in the latter, the salvation or transfiguration of the universe is brought about by the mind of man — *'Deo concedente'*, as the authors never fail to add. In the one case man confesses 'I under God', in the other he asserts 'God under me'. Man takes the place of the Creator. Medieval alchemy prepared the way for the greatest intervention in the divine world order that man has ever attempted: alchemy was the dawn of the scientific age, when the daemon of the scientific spirit compelled the forces of nature to serve man to an extent that had never been known before ... Here we find the true roots, the preparatory processes deep in the psyche, which unleashed the forces at work in the world today. Science and technology have indeed conquered the world, but whether the psyche has gained anything is another matter. *(CW* 13, para. 163.)

On the one hand, the miracle of man's salvation is accomplished by God. On the other, the transfiguration of the universe is brought about by the mind of man. How can we understand our human position between two such works of redemption?

My own feeling, as I try to relate these ideas to my experience, is that we have here an absurdity so great, so absolute, as to have only one resting place: the 'place of separation' between Christian and non-Christian. If Jung's psychology of alchemy is to assist future generations in the fullness of their time, I believe it is of the utmost importance that in studying these volumes we attend carefully to all that that 'place of separation' means to us. For this work unites Christian and non-Christian in a common dilemma. The processes described are incomprehensible without the Christian teaching as to the presence of Christ in the bread and wine of the Mass. Yet they also require us to believe in a work which betrays this central communion of the church.

For instance, comparing the alchemical transformation of matter with the Christian Mass, Jung writes:

> By pronouncing the consecrating words that bring about the transformation, the priest redeems the bread and wine from their elemental imperfection as created things. This idea is quite unchristian — it is alchemical. Whereas Catholicism emphasises the effectual presence of Christ, alchemy is interested in the fate and manifest redemption of the substances, for in them the divine soul lies captive and awaits the redemption that is granted to it at the moment of release. The captive soul

> then appears in the form of the 'Son of God'. For the alchemist, the one primarily in need of redemption is not man, but the deity who is lost and sleeping in matter ... Since it is not man but matter that must be redeemed, the spirit that manifests itself in the transformation is not the Son of Man but ... the *filius macrocosmi*. Therefore, what comes out of the transformation is not Christ, but an ineffable material being named the 'stone' ... *(CW* 12², para. 420).

Now this is very strange doctrine. It is no wonder that many poeple prefer to shrug it off as another example of the irrelevance of both Jung and Christianity for our modern world. But I think that for serious students of the history of ideas Jung has raised a question which cannot be so easily ignored. For in contrasting the alchemical and the Christian works of redemption in the way he does, and in deriving the modern scientific spirit from medieval alchemy, Jung is asking whether the failure of Christianity to contain within itself the scientific revolution of the last three hundred years may be due to a denial, common to both Christian and non-Christian, of the alchemical work which man must do if the world is to be saved.

Once we allow ourselves to entertain this question, a new doubt disturbs our enjoyment of the fruits of science and technology. We begin to look around us for evidence of such an 'undone work', and as we do so the doubt grows as to whether some of the problems of our *human* world may perhaps derive from an unfilled need within the *non-human* world. As this doubt spreads and deepens, people will, I believe, turn to the study of Jung's alchemical writings with the seriousness they deserve.

For in his alchemical works Jung has given us an analysis of how man, who is matter through and through, can prove himself more than matter in recognising that matter needs redemption. To those who reject the category of the holy, this need will present itself, as it did to Marx, as the consequence of some act of self-betrayal, of alienation, at the very source and fount of Being. To others, who are aware of the holy as that which psyche and matter have in common, this need presents itself as the mute entreaty of all those beings which can say nothing to resist projection: the entreaty that we assist the Creator in remembering His obligation to that which is always Virgin, and convert our conquest of nature into work which lets the world be.

VII

I said at the start that in presenting Jung's psychology of alchemy alongside Marx I hoped to raise a question which might remain with you: how can we understand a coincidence between the transformations of the psyche and of matter? Let me now summarise.

We make our living by exploiting the sources of our living. We are more and more aware that in so doing we trap ourselves in a vicious circle that we must learn somehow to transcend. Our public life is loud with plans for various kinds of social engineering which will enable us to recycle the powers of production and consumption and so prolong the exploitation which we enjoy. But such recycling, valuable and necessary though it may be, cannot spring the trap in which we are caught. For that trap is set outside the cycle of production and consumption. It is set when we pretend to ourselves that we can spend the Creator's power in our conquest of matter, while ignoring his intention to save matter.

In many and various ways, we and our children and our children's children, will have to learn to put that pretence at the centre of our shared world. Much will depend on how we come to interpret the legacy of Marx, on the one hand with his messianic vision of the atonement which man must make to his own nature, and on the other hand with his fateful rejection of the holy. Are we called to make good a *world* divided against itself, a world in which the holy is merely another trick to alienate man from himself? Or are we called to save a *creation,* a creation in which only the holy enables us to sustain our limited human position between two works of redemption? Here, in our uncertainty between a materialism which rejects the holy, and a materialism baptised in the holy, Jung's psychology of alchemy will, I believe, gradually unfold meanings of which we are at present only dreaming.

ON REDUCTION

PATRICIA BERRY
(Zürich)

'It was a great mistake on Freud's part to turn his back on philosophy."[1] So charges Jung, and in so doing sets for himself "the bittersweet drink of philosophical criticism"[2] as perpetual test, indispensable for the making of psychology. By remaining critical, Jung never stopped making psychology, but we have — in so far as we content ourselves with the piling up of amplification, the fitting of more and more cases into our selfsame puzzle, the reiterations turned clockwork, without at the same time or occasionally or at least making room for the bitter-sweetness of criticism. It is curious that Jung uses the word *philosophy* for this activity. Could he not as easily have said psychology (that is to say, a psychologizing of one's psychology), a self-reflection, or awareness? — words we are all familiar with and find fitting to our field. Most probably he did not use them for that very reason. He needed a word outside and beneath our conceptual ken. Jung continues:

> ... philosophical criticism has helped me to see that every psychology — my own included — has the character of a subjective confession ... I know well enough that every word I utter carries with it something of myself — of my special and unique self with its particular history and its own particular world. Even when I deal with empirical data I am necessarily speaking about myself.[3]
> It is perhaps here, where the question arises of recognizing that every psychology which is the work of one man is subjectively coloured, that the line between Freud and myself is most sharply drawn.
> A further difference seems to me to consist in this, that I try to free myself from all unconscious and therefore uncriticized assumptions about the world in general. I say 'I try', for who can be sure that he has freed himself from all of his unconscious assumptions?[4]

From the above we can now gather that what Jung means by "philosophy" in this patricular context is not necessarily its rational or logical

67

characteristics, but rather a basic questioning and, most importantly, a questioning not circuitously consumed by the very constructs it proposes to examine. And it is this psychologizing of one's psychology (for I think we can now call it that) which he declares to be *the* major difference between himself and Freud! It is with this critical spirit of Jung that we turn to the idea of reduction.

*

The term is one we use loosely to refer to "what Freud did", that distinctly factual, simplistic, causal tracing backwards that traps the personality in infantile events and prevents movement forward and into spirit. Reduction tends to stand for a familiar conglomeration of causal with factual with concrete (material), a lessening of number (from many considerations to fewer), a movement in time (back) and direction (lower) and away from spirit (evidently its opposite).

The reductive process sounds distinctly sinister, without hope, and rather un-Jungian. And yet Jung himself assumes its need.[5] What is this apparent contradiction? To take the contradiction at face value would be to become what we consider Freudian in regard to the "Freudian aspects" of a case (and in the very worst sense, since by employing the Freudian method piecemeal as Jungians, we lack the blessings of that orthodoxy), and then to become Jungian when we wish to deal with spirit, making of Jungian psychology a meager discipline, valuable only after the Freudian reduction is over, when meaning is important and inflation no consideration. But inflation is always a consideration, as is meaning. Spirit means nothing when disconnected from its home in psyche, and psyche nothing when severed from its roots in materia. If we are not to be Freudians in regard to all the areas that Jung says need reductive approach, what we need is a Jungian model of reduction. But in order to approach that we must first do some disentangling.

Reduction vs. Concretism

One aspect of the conglomerate we consider reduction has to do with the concrete. Reduction may move us toward the perceptible, "things", lumps of life seen as external facts and events. If we secretly feel that the answer to our and our patients' troubles lies in the discovery of a hidden fact about which our lives revolve, then the goal of our reduction is the concrete. But if, on the other hand, our hunch is that the trouble is of a different order, and not necessarily buried in a fact, then we are on another track, and oddly enough the same track Freud was on when he discovered seductions as psychic rather than actual events. Freud was humiliated when it became evident that the seductions reported to him by his patients, and which he had made much of, certainly could not have been the decisive cause of their neuroses, and may never have even happened. After the first wave of his defeat had subsided, however, he was able to confide:

> Tell it not in Gath, publish it not in the streets of Askalon, in the land of the Philistines, but between you and me I have the feeling of a victory rather than of a defeat.[6]

Not only was Freud's realization a significant victory for the future of psychology, but the metaphor into which he put this realization is more than notable. Whereas the Philistines would rejoice at his defeat, they would revenge at his victory, so best they not be told. For victory it was, over the Philistines. By allusion Freud seemed to have recognized that concrete event could be as much an enemy to psychological insight as was the common sense of the Philistine antipathetic to the emergence of spirit. Psychology and fact, and thereby spirit and Philistine, had at this moment of Freud's realization become separate. But we may draw something even more significant from Freud's discovery: the Philistine as a psychological entity, an archetypal mode of perception, what philosophers have referred to as the "common sense man", or the "plain man". This archetypal mode would justify things in terms of their being "only natural", nothing-but, bread-and-butter, down-to-earth, factual, practical. The perceptible, the material, would be for this viewpoint the "real facts" of life.

Both before and in many ways after this psychological realization of 1897, Freud proceeded Philistine intact, unaware of its workings. It was only natural that he take at face value his patients' reports. In this case, it wasn't until events no longer made sense to the Philistine himself — the facts just didn't make sense — that Freud was forced to admit a defeat that seemed at the time his own defeat (his hopes of success and wealth were "dashed to the ground"[7]) and to move on towards his real success: the founding of depth psychology.

What Freud alluded to as Philistine consciousness has generally been treated developmentally. Mankind in the course of time has developed from this primitive concrete thinking toward more independent, abstract thinking. But if, as we have suggested, the Philistine is also an archetype, then we must expect its continual reappearance. Freud did not get rid of it. For Jung, Freud even became it.

Jung's objections to Freud's mechanistic reductivism attest to Jung's own struggle with the Philistine, albeit now through the work of Freud. The struggle was fitting because the common sense to which the Philistine reduces all events is necessarily an enemy to emerging psychological spirit — Freud's, Jung's, whomever's. But certainly we cannot dispense with the concrete mode. It is after all a necessary function upon which we depend for basic orientation, and likewise for all situations in which action is more important than mind, doing more important than reflecting, object more important than image, practice more important than theory, the perceptible more important than the thinkable. But if this concretistic mode is archetypal, so too are the battles in which it is involved. Do we learn by doing, or is our doing a consequence of having first conceived? Do we theorize from the observable or observe on the basis of our theory? Which comes first is a question of philosophic and archetypal preference. Which archetypal mode is really most basic, most "real"? And of course we each end up with our particular mixtures, such as Jung's empiricism-cum-Platonism or Freud's materialism-cum-mythologism. Somehow psychology realizes that logical consistency would make for fallacious theory. So our problem is not consistency, but rather a psychological awareness of which mode we are using where. In the case of the concrete, this awareness is extremely difficult, because at the moment of realizing that we are using it, that we are now concrete, we are already partly out, partly metaphorical, relativizing our standpoint. The telltale mark of concrete procedures is one's total ignorance of having used them: one merely *is*, things merely *are*. To be concretistic one must be identical with the procedure one is using, the viewpoint one is in. Furthermore, like any archetypal problem or perspective, when the concrete mode becomes entangled with other equally valid procedures, it works to their detriment. But the concretistic mode is especially damaging to psychology, especially dangerous to spirit, because it is by nature anti-psychic, and anti-spirit. For Freud it was a sturdy

Goliath wanting no non-sense. But in whatever form it appears, the point is that it be located and grappled with, ceaselessly it would seem if one's business is depth psychology.

Jung too evokes the Philistine when referring to "Jesus' challenge to Nicodemus":

> Do not think carnally, or you will be flesh, but think symbolically, and then you will be spirit ... for Nicodemus would remain stuck in banalities if he did not succeed in raising himself above his concretism. Had he been a mere Philistine, he would certainly have taken offence at the irrationality and unreality of this advice and understood it literally, only to reject it in the end as impossible and incomprehensible ... The empirical truth never frees a man from his bondage to the senses ... The symbolical truth ... canalizes it into a spiritual form *(CW 5,* para. 335).

For spirit, in particular, the danger of the concretistic is its inertia, its only-too-natural gravitational pull downward into matter. It is understandable that much of religious tradition came to view matter as black and formless, the opposite of light (Delilah is popularly taken to be a Philistine), the flesh as sinful, the bull requiring defeat, Egypt requiring exodus, and so on. The Philistine played a major role indeed in the history of the Church — so major that in the continuous attempts to expurgate him, much of the concrete was thrown into his company as well. The animal, the body, the dark, the sensual, the feminine, lost psychic significance. No distinction had been made between the merely concrete and the concretistic attitude, better called literalism.

Literalism

Because our aim is psyche — and psyche has as much to do with matter as with spirit — we can have no quarrel with the concrete as such. Body, objects, the sensible-perceptible, facts, images, are all the prima materia upon which, and even within which, the psyche operates. But rather we quarrel with the literalism that would take these objects only at face value, robbing them of metaphorical value, i.e., soul significance.

When in his own land, the land of the concrete, nature, things as they are, the Philistine has an archetypal survival value. But when he is confronted with the Hebrews (read religious or psychological spirit), whose opus is against that nature, the Philistine becomes then the enemy. He applies his concrete attitudes where they do not belong: this makes for literalism.

An unfortunate result is that this literalism then blocks the way to the concrete. When approaching the concrete we meet instead the literal. Body, for example, then becomes only body, and we miss its metaphorical nature. The true sin of the flesh lies in its literal nothing-but interpretation, not in the flesh itself. Thus by shunning the sin, as the spiritual instinct necessarily does, we tend to miss the body as well. So our continuous need to redeem body from the literalism with which it is perceived, to free matter from a false spirit, which becomes reversed into freeing spirit from matter. Because the Philistine keeps literalizing matter, we are driven to fight him there, in matter, to redeem matter, whereas the sin is the literalism in which he has encased it. Thus it is even difficult to discover the appropriate matter with which to begin, difficult to return to nature, body, or anything concrete, without returning to the literalistic attitude as well.

An image at the end of Plato's *Symposium* might make this point clearer. We know that Socrates is a lover, a drinker, and a soldier. He can enjoy and endure the concrete. Moreover, in the passage we have in mind, Alcibiades compares Socrates to the wooden statue of a Silenus, that most concrete satyr. Yet, when the little doors to this figure are opened, the images of the Gods are revealed within.[8] The literalistic attitude would see the satyr and stop there, missing the Gods within. But once we have seen through the literal representation, the concrete body is itself a metaphor.

Curiously enough, when the concrete is denied, as in the case of the spiritual denial of body, images, or the senses, a concretism (or literalism) appears in its place within the spirit itself. Not only do the body, the images, or the senses, which are innocent enough and useful enough as modes of the concrete, become loaded with the literalistic weight of anti-spirit and anti-psyche, but also the concrete mode is displaced upward, creating literalisms of the spirit. This is the Philistines' revenge. The concrete that was defeated comes back to carry the day as literalisms. These appear as reified thinking, hypostasized ideas and metaphysical substances, and religions' investment in the letter of its dogma.

Hence Jung's lifelong battle to separate his ideas from Plato's hypostasized forms as well as from the substantials of the metaphysicians. Jung's aim was to keep the psyche both free from the left, Freud's literalizations of sexuality, and from the right, the hypostasizations of the metaphysicians. His course was to be that most subtle way of the metaphor, as yet uncharted by psychology.

In the spirit of this "as if" Jung insisted that his archetypes be viewed as psychic "possibilities", an insistence significant in light of Freud's reified archaic "memories". But Jung's deliteralization that is most often referred to appears in his treatment of the Oedipal question. For Jung, sexuality, apart from its concrete natural function, was psychologically meaningful in its symbolic aspect. Metaphorically incest had to do with "union with one's own being . . . simply the union of like with like, which is the next stage in the development of the primitive idea of self-fertilization".[9] This did not mean, of course, that he was advocating incest, but rather that he was distinguishing its metaphorical from its literal interpretation. On the question of the incest taboo, Jung responded with an anthropological argument, a concrete-literal answer, thereby putting the Philistine in his archetypal and appropriate place, the realm of practical considerations.[10]

What Freud implied by Philistinism, Jung elaborated in terms of primitive thinking. "Primitive thinking and feeling are entirely concretistic; they are always related to sensation. The thought of the primitive has no detached independence but clings to material phenomena."[11] In primitive functioning symbols are not distinct from object awareness. Symbols are literalized. What for the 'primitive' *is* becomes for us in our sophisticated awareness *as if*. The 'primitive' appears in the natural. So when we sense our "natural" viewpoint emerging, our "it's-only-natural" explanations, we must look as well to the primitive underlying *is,* the hidden literalism to which it is bound.

The innocent babe in the woods, the nymphic maidens, the nature spirits — trolls, elves, dwarfs, dactyls — bring us not only sparks of natural consciousness, but also hidden literal qualities. They carry not only the release of a complex, but somewhere else its fixation. The magic of the wood spirit has to do with the magic in primitive thinking, that literalistic attitude which binds psyche to physical signs, events. When I dream of the tricky little dwarf, I find in waking life new perceptions, quick insights, intuitive sparks. The world takes on a sense of magic and fairytale adventure. I jump from task to task as if enchanted, and the smallest events assume psychic significance; I see synchronicities and meanings everywhere. But psyche and concrete nature have merged into a narcissistic state, so that not only am I the world but the world is I, and psyche itself takes on a form as literal as the concrete objects to which it is attached. The bird that passed by, the letter in my mail box, the pot that boiled over, are no longer only concrete facts, but now have become pregnant with pseudo-psyche. Psyche has become magically bound to the literal events in which it has been discovered. It is as though the possibilities given by the nature spirits with one hand, the possibilities of psyche, are taken back with the other, the demand to be taken literally. The very moment we discover psyche, where before there were only concrete events, we again lose psyche to those same events, now taken literally.

The voice in us that says, "but that *is* the way it is!" Jung would place with the primitive, first level of the psyche, thereby emphasizing its initial self-protective purpose. Because of this voice we would know when to run, whom to avoid, that there *is* an out-there to be reckoned with. The difficulty, however, is like that with the Philistine, the image we have used where Jung uses primitive. What then takes more subtle, more metaphorical, handling is taken up likewise by this literal voice. In its most pathological form, we hear real voices, see real visions, take our fantasies and projections as "true". As an example of this, Jung mentions the primitive who dreamt that he was burned alive and who, in order apotropaically to avert this misfortune, put his feet in the fire and was badly burned.[12] This inability to take the dream other than literally, and likewise other than concretely to act out an attempt at its aversion, shows stunningly how literalism can make for a circularity, landing one in exactly the situation one had sought, by means of literalism, to avoid. This happens each time we take the danger in a dream as a literal warning, and act to avert it. As with the primitive, such literalism leads to a chain of undoing. By avoiding the person who constellates the worst in me, what he represents becomes all the more literally constellated in my psyche. I reinforce the literal quality of this psychic constellation (and any constellation has its Philistine face), making greater the possibility of my literally acting it out and then undoing it with an opposite and even more literal factor, in order to keep the initial threat in abeyance. Then this undoing has to be undone too. So I proceed through a chain of literalisms mis-using dreams as guides for my actions.

Since, as we have said, any psychic constellation has its literal aspect and can be taken literally, the problem in therapy becomes one of recognition and discrimination of the literal archetype. But the task is not easy, primarily because the plain man literalist also has his say about what psychology is and what it means to be psychological. Nevertheless, let us consider an example: the choice problem, the problem which "calls for a decision". Since the call for a decision already casts the situation into literal terms — should I or shouldn't I — the natural course would be to meet the problem within the area it has set for itself. Then we would discuss it with our analysts or, even better, with ourselves, swapping literalisms between parts of the psyche, giving to ourselves opinions drawn on past experience and practical counselling — all of which would meet the Philistine's view of what is psychological. Especially, this self-counselling would have reference to the facts: finances, schedules, advantages and disadvantages — my dinner last night, my mother's visit, my economic situation.

Another alternative would be to refuse the decision altogether, to hold that psyche has nothing to do whatsoever with the literal decisions of life. This is perhaps what psychoanalysis implies by its rule that no major alterations in the life situation be undertaken during the course of the analysis. A marriage, a divorce, a change in jobs would be at that time merely an acting out.

Whereas the first of these ways of meeting the problem of decision identifies life as psyche so that working on life and solving its problems holds the illusion of working on psyche, the second position places life as opposed to psyche, maintaining that they have nothing directly to do with each other. Both of these positions make life literal, and both deny the metaphorical, thereby disregarding Jung's statement that "every interpretation necessarily remains an 'as-if'".

There is yet a third alternative. This would be to refuse the practical discussion of the problem until we have had the right dream, and then to connect the dream with the problem. Here we feel we are being truly psychological, connecting psyche and life. But let us see by an example how this might work:

Say I am an American in Europe trying, once again, to decide whether or not to go back to America. Should I have had a "positive dream" of an American Indian, that would portend going. But just here the literalist has his victory, for he has made of the dream an oracle. Like a primitive he has magically confused metaphor with literal. And, more importantly, he has insisted that the dream, by either its confirmation or its denial, must correspond with a literal reality. The dream must serve the problem; the metaphorical must provide answer to the literal. The psyche has been forced into serving the concerns of the Philistine. This occurs even when we least notice it. When, for example, I say I cannot continue with this plan, work, relationship, because my dreams won't let me, I feel I am sacrificing the outer for the sake of the inner. I feel that the outer is serving the inner. But still I am reading the inner as a confirmation, warning, or denial of the outer. And the real loss is not the plan, work, relationship — but the psyche.

The literalist has taken not only my quandary — should I or shouldn't I — at face value, but also has robbed my psyche of its dignity. He has not respected psyche as a function every bit as valid in its own right as is the ego and its decisions. To give the psyche its due would be to recognize the literalism (decision problem) as the reflection of a fantasy, a way in which the fantasy is expressing itself. Because the fantasy has been taken up by the literalist, I now want to know what to *do*, practically speaking. I think that is my problem, as the literalist always thinks *his* concerns are the problem. Decision-making itself benefits the literalist, confirms him and makes him stronger. Neglected are the psychological values in the metaphors "America", "home", "going back" (both in the sense of regression and in the sense of return), as well perhaps as the counterpole of "exile", "alien", "foreign", "outside the fold" (and all the pathology inherent in these), to say nothing of "crossing the great water"!

The point would be to find the metaphorical background, the context from which the literalism emerged, actually to see the literalism psychologically — and by so de-literalizing, to return it to psyche. Like Perseus, we must see this Gorgon through a mirror, through the reflection of metaphor, else we become the Gorgon ourselves, meeting literal with literal and thereby neglecting the reflective indirection of the psychological.

ON REDUCTION

After this analytic hour with myself, the literalist feels, of course, vaguely dissatisfied. He had expected to come out with a clear list of reasons for-and-against, or to have turned the Indian of the dream into a magical "coincidence", which would thereby have solved the problem. Yet in some way too this plain man has been relieved, his ferric nature softened and made more yielding; the weight of ego identification with which he has been burdened has been shifted to wider and more fertile, metaphorically more substantial ground.

Part of the great difficulty we have with the literalist is that he operates relatively, and therefore cannot be easily pinned down. He does not always say the same thing or have the same viewpoint. He appears anyway less in literal definitions than in a literalistic attitude which can shift from one aspect of the psyche to another. We see this in our interpretations of the dream ego.

Given a certain sophistication, probably the most concrete mode a dream interpreter could fall into would be to take the dream ego as identical to the most literal aspect of the waking ego: dream ego = I. (I should not go off this weekend because I have just dreamed I was in a car accident.) A second level of interpretation would be to distinguish the waking "I" from the dream ego. (In this dream my ego is doing such and such — not I, but my ego.) In this case, the "I" which works on the dream is at least given a point of reflection over and above that of the dream ego. A further level of deliteralization then would take this particular dream reflection as an attitude, one of the many guises, of the ego. (My ego is here behaving in its role of spoiled child, kind parent, successful general, or whatever.) Yet further would be to see that that particular guise is the result of the interplay of the dream scene, dependent upon it, and that the reality of the dream is only in terms of its participants. When my ego is doing this and this, so the dream setting is particularly such and the participants constellated in a certain manner. The point here is to realize the context within the dream itself, the particularity spun out of the relationship of all the parts. To draw any behavioural precepts or "shoulds" out of the dream constellation would be again to take it literally, and out of its own metaphorical context, neglecting the real and psychological task: to lay out and analyze the constellation, to sharpen and fill out the metaphor that the psyche has presented, and to resist the cheapening predictions, the temptations of the Philistine, his practical advice.

PATRICIA BERRY

Towards a Psychological Reduction

We may return once again to the question of reduction. If the process of reduction must be identical with the literalism we have been discussing, as Jung supposed when speaking of Freud's reduction, then certainly, since our business is psychology and soul-making, such reduction would lead us very far astray. Yet again we must ask ourselves why Jung — who never ceased to stress the "as if", who championed metaphor against so many Philistines, who never spoke in terms of nothing-but, by which he defined reduction — nevertheless did speak of the need for a reductive process. My suspicion is that Jung intuited something very much deeper about the essential nature of this process than was apparent in its practice. Jung was not contradicting himself when he both stressed its need and yet denied its methods. Was he perhaps sensing another kind of reduction, a reduction devoid of the literal and in keeping with his own psychology?

His later alchemical work certainly returns Jung to reduction. There we delve into what had been the seeds of his earlier intuition. By that time Jung no longer mentioned the term reduction, with its Freudian associations, as a tool of analysis. Perhaps Jung's own sort of reduction had already made its way into his thought, via the more highly differentiated concepts within alchemy. One must note the reductive significance of processes such as: mortificatio, putrefactio, separatio, calcinatio, coagulatio. Such reductions have little to do with literalism, though their basic metaphors involve concrete substances. In one notable passage, Jung even uses the term reduction as synonymous with the psychological idea of synthesis. "The aim of the tetrasomia is the reduction (or synthesis) of a quaternio of opposites to unity."[13]

As reduction in the Freudian sense would connote a return to beginnings, a causal tracing back in time to childhood, the primal scene, the Oedipal complex, the basic traumas and libidinal fixations, so alchemy would move toward beginnings — the radix elements or the prima materia, in any of its many forms. A basic difference, however, does appear in the use of cause. Freud's use of cause is more literal, more in the sense of efficient, more mechanical. Psychoanalysis leads one back in time, through actual life history and toward causes buried in the earliest years. Reduction is taken literally as re-duction, leading back or leading again, in the sense that going through the same events again may free one from them. Alchemical reduction moves rather toward the prima materia at the core of the complex, which need not be seen as prior in time but as prior in ontology, status, or value. This unformed is never fully formed and always present. It is as it is always. As a core it is the basic matter of what's the matter, and it is always described by the alchemists in metaphorical terms, terms of outlandish perplexity so that one could not possibly confuse them with actual incidents of an actual life.

Because the entire alchemical process is based on the metaphors of the prima materia, the process too is metaphorical, even if here our literal man jumps again into the works to take "the process" literally. This time he attempts to make process a linear event in which each successive stage transforms the preceding and thereby most probably loses it. Because of the literalist's penchant for "process", complex gives us perhaps a better image, for its definition insists upon a nucleus, an archetypally (as-if, metaphorically) based but pathological core to which increasing numbers of associations adhere. Nothing is overcome or left behind, because the movement is not literally linear. Instead projections are taken back, dissociations rejoined, all of which leaves one feeling much sicker than before. Whether one *is* sicker or not is another matter — a matter of great interest to the plain man in us all. We want to see progress and so strive to set up some criteria which answers this need. We pay actual money and sit actual hours with our analysts, and in keeping with this constellation expect actual cure or actual betterment. Yet this literalism too is sooner or later broken and replaced more metaphorically, for we *feel* sicker, our sense of sickness having become perhaps more subtly attuned. The health/sickness dichotomy has merged into a more highly differentiated sense of daily-life pathology. By deliteralizing diagnostic prototypes, we see their "as if" relevance in our own lives — our "as if" schizoid or paranoid mechanisms, our areas of psychopathy or hysterical responses. This is not, by any means, to devalue the real sicknesses as described by psychiatry, but rather to see them as prototypes, reals from which to make metaphor. If I have not acquired this sense of sickness, then either my analysis has not intended to touch the pathology (or archetypes) at all, or it has refused to proceed in that direction because of its literal ideas of reduction, as something only negative, only destructive, only Freudian.

Reduction gives the sense of pathology, and at the same time, because it is deliteralized, makes pathology meaningful. Pathology becomes the touchstone of the psychological. The difference between me and my mental hospital prototype becomes qualitative rather than quantitative: she more literal in her psychic connection, I more metaphorical. But the root of the matter (our psychic matter) is similar. Should I, in the course of my analysis, remain still separate from my sickness, encapsuled and protected, then the benefits of my analysis, the changes in my awareness, the conscious insights, should all be called into question and examined to see if they too are not just additional, albeit more complicated, more subtle (and therefore more insidious) defenses, my very individuation a defensive system. But certainly if my pathology seems to have disappeared, my analysis has failed. And the failure is due to a faulty view of reduction.

Reduction keeps us in touch with prime psychic matter. Because as Jungians we make much of building (synthetic approach), finality, process as progression, and the teleological implications of completion, wholeness, becoming conscious, transcendent function — we are ever in danger of losing a sense of the depths. If we give reduction away to the Freudians, we lose one of the ways of maintaining this depth. Without our own kind of reduction, even the opposites, which were meant by Jung as a means of deepening, a way of realizing the ambiguity and complexity of psychic life, become instead an ego defense, a way of balancing, and thus a way of keeping out of the depths.

The whole point of reduction is precisely that it goes too far, off the end of the balance, to the roots. Its aim is the radical moisture, the *radix ipsius*,[14] the "secret hidden in the roots",[15] the prime matter to which there is no opposite, no other principle, but contains in its radicality its own internal opposition. To go down and back merely because it leads up and forward, to confront the negative with the positive (or vice versa), or to apply a bit of reduction as a therapeutic technique in order to "integrate some shadow", is perhaps an artificiality, probably a simplicity, but assuredly a literalism. When the opposites are taken in this manner the aspiring mathematician, wildly spinning formulas in his attic, is told to come down to earth and take up gardening, or to live among the peasants in the mountains and chop his own firewood. Had Einstein "balanced" his life by chopping firewood, the world most probably would have had no Einstein. He probably would have cut off his foot, thereby leaving the theory of relativity spinning footless in the heavens. But his theories had a foot, and they were grounded; within his eccentricity the opposites were at work, and to the benefit of the world.[16] According to Jung, once a person

> ... has seen the Faustian problem, the escape into the 'simple life' is closed for ever. There is of course nothing to stop him from taking a two-room cottage in the country, or from pottering about in a garden and eating raw turnips. But his soul laughs at the deception. Only what is really oneself has the power to heal.[17]

What is really oneself can only emerge out of one's nature, but not out of a nature that has been recommended.

For when the balancing of the opposites is taken up by the literalist it becomes a prescription *a priori*, rather than a description *a posteriori*, thereby cutting off the possibility of an individual, or unique, development before it begins. When Jung said that *les extrêmes se touchent*, he did not mean it as a literal device to be put into practical application, touching each thing with a bit of its opposite, especially since the opposite for each psychic content cannot be known in advance. It is the unconsciousness buried in the reduced state itself. Compensation and balancing by opposites — because it is in the hands of the literalist who has his ready-made high for every low (and low for every high), and his literal inner for every outer, etc. *ad inf.* — are to be eschewed until we are quite sure the Philistine and the daughters of the Philistine and their daughters' daughters have all been through a psychological analysis. Of all the haunts of the plain man (and he has many, as we have seen, such as process, primitivity, practicality, naturalness, life, magical synchronicity) none is more ruinous to the spirit of Jung's open-endedness than the neat little scales of compensation. The literalist wields the opposites in such a way as to make everyone more or less similar and like himself, a literalist and mediocre. The median and the statistical average are this same sort of balance in another form. This is not the uniqueness of self which Jung's work evokes.

Psychology has traditionally focussed its study upon the extremes, the aberrant, the pathological. Reduction would mean a return to these. Psychology's tradition is in the area of reduction, the area of the radical and the extreme: the extremity of our misfortune, the trapped aspect of fate, the un-understandable. Jung speaks of the hopelessness, the resignation in the reduced. And indeed what one seems to find, or at least expects to find, through the process of reduction is expressed as negative: putrefaction, mortifaction, nigredo. Even the fire of reduction is negative "because it burns all things and reduces them to powder: quicksilver is vinegar",[18] the tincture a "fiery and gaseous poison".[19]

Here Mercurius himself has turned sour and there is no compensatory sweetness.

Reduction's extreme is a concentrate of shadow, that which would undermine our ego's positions, no matter how "balanced", "right" or reasonably attuned. Reduction, by blacking in ego's shadows, would tone grey ego's rightness. The alchemical idea of the gold in the dung would reverse rather to show the dung in the gold. Wherever there is gold — each goal attained, each piece of conscious realization — would be also where to look for the dung. The best smells worst. But to be never far from the dung heap is also psychic body. Whereas all gold looks alike, psychic body makes for discrimination. Each complex has its own smell to the nose of instinct, and thus gold-making would require the help of reductive discrimination.

The negative tone of reduction still needs to be explained. Of course it belongs to the shadow or personal unconscious, to which Jung said it applied. However, its unpleasantness, difficulty, and extremity refer to the senex. And so our theme is oppressed by the lead of Saturn. Owing to this archetype, reduction is inevitably seen leadenly, opaquely, as concrete and as literal. Saturn forces reduction into the literalism of dirt, history, negativity, resignation, hopeless causality, depression. Even the primitivity of reductive thinking belongs to Saturn, who ruled at the beginning of time. Just as reduction prevents forward movement, Saturn swallowed his own children. But if we stop there, we have again reduced reduction to a nothing-but. For Saturn as well frees from the very literalisms he fosters. Saturn sees through to the ultimate realities, is the principle of abstraction. Perhaps this is what the journey through the planetary houses signifies, both beginning and ending with Saturn,[20] or the image of the white dove contained in the lead.[21]

A psychological reduction, and by this we imply one freed of all the literalisms to which reduction has been reduced — concretism, historicism, causalism, simplistic Freudianism, etc. — would be one of the operations of psychological work. It would go toward the extreme radix. It would be the way of arriving at the irreducible, the essential oil, the quintessence of one's nature, the indelible character traits that are concealed in the dross of one's case history.

Through these character traits one is involved with the daimones of one's fate and with the prima materia in the daily entanglement with literal problems, which, because they are prima materia, give the psyche the chance to move them from the literal to the metaphorical, thereby giving ground and body, relief to the literal itself. Reduction denies the free and easy flow of life. It makes for difficulties, constructs obstacles; it dams up and dampens down. Jung had in mind reduction as literal, and thus its goal as natural. But viewed as metaphorical reduction, the end becomes contra-naturam as well. Viewed metaphorically naturam and contra-naturam are one. Only the literal is solely naturam; and once world, nature, body, matter, are seen as image, sensed as metaphor, they are in psyche, transformed. Reduction by going into the concrete and the natural is the via regia of the opus contra naturam.

1 CW 4, para. 774.   2 Ibid.   3 Ibid.   4 Op. cit., paras. 775—6.
5 Cf. reduction: as caustic tool, CW 7, paras, 65—6; for resolving transference, CW 16, para. 286, CW 7, para. 96; for severe neuroses, CW 16, para. 24; when meaning is conscious and difficulty unconscious, CW 7, para 68; to phylogenetic basis and elementary processes, CW 6, para. 852, CW 16, para. 282; to reality CW 6, para. 427, CW 7, para. 88, CW 8, para 46; to the primitive or natural, CW 8, paras 93—5, 109, CW 4 para. 679; to 'simple' instincts, CW 16, para. 40; for youth, CW 7, para 88; as shadow realization, CW 16, para. 146; as dream, CW 8, paras. 496—8; as dream antecedents, CW 8, para. 452; as the 'objective' level of dream, CW 7, para. 128. Cf. also causal.

6 E. Jones, *Sigmund Freud, Life and Work*, (London: Hogarth Press, 1953), vol. 1, p. 294. See also II Samuel, 1 (19ff):
"Thy glory, O Israel, is slain upon
   thy high places!
  How are the mighty fallen!
Tell it not in Gath,
  publish it not in the streets of
   Ash'kelon;
lest the daughters of the Philistines
   rejoice,
  lest the daughters of the
   uncircumcised exult."

7 Jones, op. cit. p. 293
8 *Symposium*, 215bff.
9 *CW* 16, para. 419.
10 *CW* 5, para. 217.
11 *CW* 6, para. 697.
12 *CW* 8, para. 94.
13 *CW* 13, para. 358.
14 *CW* 12, para. 430.
15 *CW* 13, paras. 242f.
16 That Einstein was in some ways a 'simple man' is beside the point in this context, for whatever simplicity he had — he wore no socks we know — his extremity remained intact. For us, that is the decisive factor.
17 *CW* 7, para. 258.
18 *CW* 13, para. 103n.
19 Op. cit., para. 358n.
20 *CW* 14, paras. 298—311.
21 *CW* 12, para. 443.

POETRY AND THE ANIMA

GRAHAM HOUGH
(Cambridge)

In these lectures I shall be talking about some of the ways in which the anima archetype manifests itself in English poetry. I am using the word 'poetry' as shorthand for imaginative literature in general, like the German *Dichtung;* and it will include some fictions that are not in verse — partly because 'imaginative literature' is an awkward mouthful, and partly for another reason. To speak of poetry and to include in it some things that are written in what we would normally call prose directs our attention to the imaginative, the fictional element in literature, that which springs from our inner needs and compulsions, not that which springs from the mimetic impulse, the impulse to imitate or represent the goings-on in the outer world. In poetry it is often easy to isolate this imaginative element; in other kinds of fiction, in the novel especially, it is less easy. But in our present context if I speak of novels I shall be concerned not with how they represent the life of London in 1840 or Dublin in 1904, but with how they reveal underlying psychological patterns that have nothing to do with these particular times or places. And I must begin with a few theoretical considerations about the archetypal element in literature, some of which will be thoroughly familiar, and some of which will diverge a little from the usual habits of analytical psychologists.

We know very well, or should know by now, that the archetypes are not images; they are not pictures, or characters in a story. They have no predetermined content; they are pure potentiality. An archetype is not a pattern; it is the psychic predisposition to form a pattern of a certain type, an unconscious predisposition, therefore not open to examination. We cannot inspect the archetypes. All that we can inspect is their manifestations — in behaviour, in dreams, in myths, in literature. Jung himself is perfectly explicit about this:

> Again and again I encounter the mistaken notion that an archetype is determined in regard to its content, in other words that it is a kind of

unconscious idea (if such an expression be admissible). It is necessary to point out once more that archetypes are not determined as regards their content, but only as regards their form and then only to a very limited degree. A primordial image is determined as to its content only when it has become conscious and is therefore filled out with the material of conscious experience. *(CW* 9, i², para. 155.)

Yet in spite of this and many similar warnings we are all apt in practice to neglect this distinction and slip back into the mode of expression that Jung condemns. The reason is obvious: the unconscious really is unconscious; the only things we can see, the only things we can talk about are its manifestations that have already been formed and filled out by consciousness. Since these formed manifestations are the nearest thing to the archetypes that can ever be visible to us, we tend naturally to talk about them as if they were the archetypes themselves. This is perhaps unavoidable, and harmless enough — as long as we realise that behind these inspectable forms there lies the real mystery which in itself we shall never be able to inspect. I use the word mystery not as an incantation, but quite strictly to mean a factor that can be approached from many sides, can be guessed at distantly and partially, but in itself must always remain beyond human understanding. And now, having put myself doctrinally in the right, I shall in all probability go on to talk of characters in fiction, moods and images in legend and poetry, as though they were themselves the archetypes of which they are only the outward and visible expression.

It soon becomes obvious that these apprehensible manifestations of the archetypes in dreams, myths, and literature have been subject to very varying degrees of conscious development. In some the work of consciousness has been prolonged and intricate, in some it has been very slight. In the myths of primitive peoples it is slight; in the myths of the Greeks (a people who attained an extremely high degree of consciousness at an early stage of social and economic development) it is very considerable. Geoffrey Kirk has gone so far as to say that the Greeks have hardly left us a true mythology. What has reached us from them has already undergone a far-reaching process of literary and cultural manipulation.

Now if this is true of Greek myths it must be even more emphatically true of archetypal patterns as they appear in literature. By literature I mean written literature; and written literature is the product of a high state of culture. Above all, it is an individual product, composed by an individual poet, subject to his conscious will and to all the accidents of his individual psychology. What we see is a work of conscious art; beyond that, much can be explained as the work of the personal unconscious, the result of singular experiences and a unique destiny. In work of this kind the ultimate mystery, the unknowable archetype that we suppose to underly all human productions, seems very far away. It has been natural on this account for psychological research to turn away from sophisticated literature, the literature of high culture, and to go back to folk-tale or legend, above all to the myths of primitive peoples, which it feels to be nearer the source, less deformed by conscious elaboration. No doubt the tastes and interests of individual investigators has had something to do with this too. Jung himself engaged in anthropological research and made original investigations of his own in America and Africa. The feeling has therefore grown up that the Eskimos, the Pueblo Indians or the tribes around Mount Elgon can give us a direct insight into the archetypal background of our lives, while Dante or Shakespeare or Goethe or Keats can only supply secondary and decorative illustrations. Now I am going to be bold and say that I believe this to be a fallacy; and I want to spend a little time on saying why.

In the first place I should like, with all proper deference, to express a mild scepticism about anthropologists' reports on the myths of primitive peoples. From what I know of these matters I suspect that the sheer linguistic difficulties, the difficulties of verbal communication, are greater than is often believed, or than is allowed to appear in the final scientific report. And, since the whole frame of mind of the sophisticated European observer is so utterly alien to that of the primitive whom he is investigating, I think it must be seriously doubted how authentic or complete his understanding can ever be. I would not presume to cast doubt on the validity of the anthropologists' results within his own discipline. But students of the psyche need a subtler, perhaps a humbler, approach than students of institutions. So I suspect that our current accounts of primitive myth have in fact been subjected to a good deal of conscious modification, not by its creators but by its reporters, the anthropologists.

When we dream, as long as we are still dreaming, what we receive is a message from the unconscious, without conscious control. If we leave it at that, the message remains buried in the unconscious and the dream is forgotten, as happens with most of our dreams. We have been trained, or some of us have, to recall our dreams. We have pencil and paper by our bedsides, and the moment we wake up we write them down. But let us not be under any illusion. What we write down is not the message from the unconscious in its pristine, primitive state. Because we are now awake and writing, it has been filtered through consciousness; it has been put into words; it has been given a form different from its original one. The selection of what is important and what insignificant in the shadowy confused recollection of the dream has been made by the conscious intellect and the conscious will. Whatever the dream itself was, the record of a dream is always a collaboration between the unconscious and the conscious mind. So it is with the myths of primitive peoples. They have been received by a sophisticated observer; they have been put into the grammar and vocabulary of an alien tongue. The result is not the primitive essence, it is a joint effort, with the anthropologist playing the part of the waking mind in the case of the recorded dream.

Recent dream research has been somewhat disturbed by these considerations; but I think unnecessarily. We cannot discuss the unmanifested, but we can at least make informed surmises about it from the manifestations that we can see. I would even question the assumption that the presence of the archetype has been weakened or corrupted by conscious work upon it. Moreover, I do not accept a too common asumption that in primitive myth we are nearer to the archetype than in more developed forms of human expression. Primitive myth as we receive it has already been worked on by consciousness; sophisticated literature has been worked on more elaborately, and in a different way. But behind them both lies the archetype, unmodified, untouchable, forever inaccessible to consciousness. Literary works have of course been conditioned, culturally and individually; they have been overlaid with all manner of formal and linguistic elaborations; but these do not and cannot touch the hidden archetypal roots. Because of its simplicity of form, because the language in which it is expressed is a matter of indifference, primitive myth makes it much easier for us to sense the archetypal presence, but it does not follow from this that myth is a richer object for study than developed literature. Myth is often imperfectly recorded; it is fragmentary and incomplete; it often exists in varying and rival versions. In short, there is a great deal of sheer *muddle* in the study of myth, besides its legitimate mystery. A character in one of E. M. Forster's novels said, "I like mysteries, but I dislike muddles"; and the student of myth often comes to feel the same. In studying literature from the psychological point of view this element of muddle largely disappears. We have a definitive text; we know who is responsible for it; we can for the most part be sure that unintended hiccups and accidental gaps in communication have not interfered. It can even be maintained that conscious artistic elaboration does not deform or falsify the archetypal presence, but allows it to persist with considerable purity. This last point is a psychological fact that is more evident to students of literature than to students of psychology, so I should like to develop it a little.

If you try to write as directly and spontaneously as possible, without any restraints on form or choice of language, you might think that the unconscious would be able to express itself with the minimum of interference. But, except in the case of trance or some semi-dissociated condition (so-called 'automatic writing'), this is exactly what does *not* happen. Writing is an act that requires a high degree of conscious control; while it is being performed the conscious mind is ever awake, and if it has nothing else to think about beyond what is to be said, it is continually tugging, nagging and interfering. Many people find this difficulty in the practice of active imagination, and that is why they cannot make a success of it.

But suppose you give the conscious mind some moderately absorbing formal task to fulfil. Suppose for example that you are writing in verse that has to maintain a regular iambic rhythm, and whose lines have to rhyme alternately. This is sufficient to keep the conscious mind active and occupied; while behind its back, as it were, the unconscious is left free to make its suggestions. A particular verse rhythm suggests a mood that has not previously entered into consciousness at all; the need for a rhyme suggests an unexpected, apparently quite irrational word, and the word releases a whole train of thought that formed no part of the original consciously conceived plan. We are apt to think of the unconscious level as something that can be released simply by passivity and relaxation. But our conscious defences are so strong that often enough it does not work in this way. The unconscious has to be coaxed or tricked into revealing itself; and artistic form is one of the means by which this is done. So it is a mistake to think that the formal elaboration of a work of literary art suppresses or smothers the unconscious; on the contrary, it is one of the very means by which the unconscious contents are enabled to appear.

For all these reasons, therefore, I believe that literature, the consciously elaborated, artistically intricate literature of the highest civilisations, has far more to offer for psychological investigation than is commonly supposed, and perhaps more than the primitive material that is more often used as a source of psychological examples.

*

Archetypes are invisible, and that is one source of difficulty. They are also, it appears, innumerable. There is no directory of archetypes, and we cannot say that there are twelve of them, or forty, or a hundred. We cannot do this because they are not strictly separable or countable; they are forms of psychic activity that shade into one another, and doubtless there are many such forms that have not yet been isolated or recognised. But there are some of them that are so frequent and distinct, and realise themselves in so many areas of experience, that we are thoroughly familiar with them. Some of these, like the shadow, the anima and the animus, the mother, the old wise man, we recognise almost as characters, as personalities. There are others that realise themselves not as characters, but as patterns of action, trains of events — the life-plan of the hero, the quest, the rebirth archetype, for example. And all these relatively clear-cut and well-known forms of psychic activity are also forms of the artistic imagination. Anyone who is well-read in poetry and imaginative literature would recognise them as familiar elements of his experience even if he knew nothing of psychological theory.

If there is any one of these archetypal forms that is especially closely connected with poetry it is the anima. In several periods of our culture the poet is supposed to be always in love — that is to say in a state of permanent anima projection. Often the object of his love is a lady who is extremely remote, whom he does not really know, perhaps a *princesse lointaine* whom he has never even seen. And that makes it fairly clear that the real inspirer of his work is the anima herself rather than the real human being to whom his experience is so slightly attached. Literary criticism generally assumes that the biographical object of a poet's passion is not a matter of any great interest. This link between anima projection and imaginative writing is very much taken for granted; it has passed even into popular speech. The word 'romance', which originally meant a particular literary form, in newspaper language means a love-affair. We take all this so much for granted that it is apt to vulgarise our conception of the role that the anima plays in the genesis of poetry.

There is a more fundamental sense in which the anima is the inspirer of literary art. Traditionally the poet is inspired by the Muse, a semi-divine female figure who is clearly an embodiment of the anima principle. Sometimes there are said to be nine Muses; and this marks a tendency that is frequent in poetry towards the multiplication of anima images. Homer begins the *Iliad* by calling upon the Muse, the Goddess, to sing of the wrath of Achilles. At the beginning of the *Odyssey* he asks for her help in telling of the wanderings and trials of Odysseus. Milton begins *Paradise Lost* with a long intricate sentence —

> Of Man's first disobedience, and the fruit
> Of that forbidden tree, whose mortal taste
> Brought death into the world, and all our woe,
> With loss of Eden, till one greater Man
> Restore us, and regain the blissful seat,
> Sing, heav'nly Muse.

So the Muse, the Goddess, the feminine inspiring principle, is called upon to sing through the lips of the poet about warfare and heroic struggle, about perilous sea-journeys, about the whole destiny of mankind in this world and the next. In these majestic and central poetic examples the part played by the anima has nothing to do with eros, nothing to do with sexual love, no connection with what are known to the magazine-story public as 'true romances'.

Side by side with the idea that poetry is a learned art, a particular kind of skill, it is a very old tradition in our culture that poetry is essentially an irrational activity, not to be created or explained by conscious will or intelligence. Shakespeare's phrase "the poet's eye in a fine frenzy rolling" goes back ultimately, like all such expressions, to Plato's dialogue *Ion* (543 a—b), where we first encounter this long-continued conception of the poet and poetry.

> And as the Corybantian revellers are not in their right mind when they dance, so the lyric poets are not in their right mind when they are com-

posing their beautiful strains: but when falling under the power of music and metre they are inspired and possessed who draw milk and honey from the rivers when they are under the influence of Dionysus but not when they are in their right mind. And the soul of the lyric poet does the same, as they themselves say, for they tell us that they bring songs from honeyed fountains, culling them from out of the gardens and dells of the Muses; they like the bees winging their way from flower to flower. And this is true. For the poet is a light and a winged and a holy thing, and there is no invention in him until he is inspired and out of his senses, and the mind is no longer in him: when he has not attained to this state, he is powerless and is unable to utter his oracles.

Behind all the moral and social pressures, behind all the technical rules — the three unities, recipes for composing an epic poem, etc. — there lies this much older idea that poetry is not the product of consciousness, that it is only when the mind is flooded by the contents of the unconscious that poetry can come into being. So we see why the Muse, the Goddess, the anima figure, is invoked by the poet; she is the guide to the realm of the unconscious from which ultimately poetry must spring. The realm she introduces us to is a dubious one and her gifts are uncertain. The passage from Plato is indulgently ironical; the poet is a light, a winged, and a holy being, but he is also out of his mind. To Plato as a moralist and a rationalist poetry is deeply suspect, the nurse of falsehood and illusion; but since he is incurably a poet himself his objections can never be whole-hearted. He fears poetry because it is not subject to rational control, but he also loves it, and his repeated concern with it is an admission of its power. This is a typical anima situation — a psychic content that is deeply fascinating and attractive is also feared because it upsets the conscious rationally adopted stance. The shadow is feared and rejected; the wisdom archetype (the sage, the wise old man) is regarded with awe, but welcomed. It is peculiarly the property of the anima, to whom poetry belongs, to arouse these contradictory emotions — fascination and suspicion, love and a kind of fear. This then is the way the anima is most fundamentally involved in poetry — as its inspiring Goddess, its patron Saint.

*

In this sense the anima stands outside the poetry, at its threshold, as it were. Once the Muse has been invoked she is forgotten; she speaks through the poet's imaginative activity and is absorbed in it. But naturally that is not the whole story. Since the anima is one of the archetypes that manifests itself as a character it can very easily reappear within the poetry itself — simply as one of the characters within the poetic fiction. And here we are faced with an *embarras de richesse:* such anima characters are only too numerous and only too easy to recognise. Are all the heroines of romantic and idealised fiction anima figures? Yes. Are they equally anima figures regardless of the quality of the fictions in which they appear? I am afraid, yes. The unconscious is no respecter of the standards of literary culture. From Dante's Beatrice and Petrarch's Laura to the vulgarest heroines of soap-operas and girlie magazines, all are recognisable as anima images.

From the point of view of literature this is extremely uninteresting, and literary persons are often disconcerted by the tendency in analytical psychology to find illustrations of the archetypal world in works of little literary merit. Jung for instance cites Rider Haggard's *She,* Pierre Benoit's *L'Atlantide,* and a book by William Sloane, *To Walk the Night,* as examples of the collective anima in prose fiction. None of these is exactly a literary masterpiece. There is a reason for this. Books written as thrillers, ghost stories or popular supernatural entertainments correspond to collective demands. They do not represent any intense self-scrutiny on the part of their authors; they are a mere acting-out of unconscious pressures and do not involve the element of spiritual conflict that an authentic attempt at confrontation between conscious and unconscious requires. They therefore give us, often very clearly and simply, a generalised diagrammatic picture of unconscious contents, often valuable for purposes of psychological illustration — as lecture-room diagrams, shall we say. There are times when we want lecture-room diagrams in psychological study; there are also times when we want something more — not schematic knowledge, but insight.

Some insight can be derived from introspection, observation of our own behaviour, thoughts and dreams; some of it can be derived from our experience with others — our lived relationships with other people. But this can never be enough. Insight derived from these sources is always limited by our own historical and social situation, the obvious limits of our personal experience and range of human contacts. So we find Jung himself, with his intense and wide-ranging inner life, his enormous range of clinical experience, still continually extending his insight by his researches into mythology and alchemy. It is in this way that literature can serve psychology — and not the kind of crude and inferior literature that provides convenient text-book examples, but literature which is the evidence of a real psychic development, which is itself a part of the individuation process.

Rider Haggard's *She* is an example of the kind of good-bad literature that used to be commoner a generation or so ago than it is today. The Sherlock Holmes stories and the tales of John Buchan are of the same kind. I used to read them as a boy, and now wandering hopelessly round the house in search of something that isn't real literature, I sometimes read them again. Because they were written in response to not very subtle collective pressures they give a real and easy satisfaction. Because they belong to a phase of society that was still relatively sure of itself and relatively uncorrupt they are not disgusting or degrading as many of the corresponding things at the present time undoubtedly are. But it is not in works of this kind that we shall find the insight we are looking for. Psychologically speaking they are case-histories, specimens, but no more.

She, we may perhaps dimly remember, is the tale of an archaeological expedition to Africa which sets out to discover a lost kingdom. Its ruler is a mysterious female figure whose name is Ayesha (itself of psychological significance, for the homonymous continent of Asia is always for Westerners the realm of the supernatural, of unknown psychic forms); but she is generally known simply as She-who-must-be-obeyed. She is in appearance young and beautiful, but she is also thousands of years old. She is infinitely seductive, but she is also cruel and repellent. She promises infinite riches and possibilities, but she is also terrifying, leading the normal decent masculine explorer to death and extinction. She is both an inspirer and a destroyer. In short, she is a very crude and simplified diagram of the collective anima, and one can easily see why she served Jung for purposes of rapid illustration. But such a picture cannot lead us any further or bring us any new insight.

What are the right relations, the productive and progressive relations, to unconscious contents for the man who sees his life as a process of spiritual development. Not simply to stare at them in fascination. The right relation is a process of continual differentiation, of clarification and absorption. The tangled, self-contradictory yet always living mass of thought and feeling must first be realised for what it is — something outside the conscious personality, something even alien to it, yet profoundly attached to it; something belonging to us yet not belonging to us. Unless it is faced and experienced, life will always be partial and incomplete. But there is more to be done. At least for certain types of mind, the tangled mass must be disentangled, its complexities separated into their different strands. And one by one the different strands can be handled, can become familiar, can be woven into the fabric of our total experience. This process that Jung calls the integration of the personality is the process that is actually recorded in much great literature. Not only recorded, for in many poets the writing of the work *is* the actual process of integration. It is not that something happens and is then put on record as a work of art. The creation of the work of art is actually the happening.

This is not true of all poetry or imaginative literature. It is perfectly possible for poetry to rest on the level of normal social consciousness, or on the level of acquired technical skill. Robert Graves, the most anima-possessed of all modern English poets, actually makes this distinction. He distinguishes between Muse poetry — poetry inspired by the anima, or as he calls her, the White Goddess — and what he calls Apollonian poetry, the poetry of literary tradition and conscious art. It is with Muse poetry and Muse-inspired fiction that we are concerned; and it is very unevenly distributed through the history of our culture. In the courtly love poetry of the Middle Ages and its descendants in the Renaissance — the poetry that idealises women and the love and service of women — the anima moods and images are particularly obvious; but even here there are many imitations — poems not springing from any genuine experience of the anima, but simply literary copies of earlier and more authentic experiences. Romance literature is particularly rich for our purposes. By Romance literature I mean fiction that sits very loosely to common experience, that does not attempt to reproduce the actual conditions of ordinary life but deals in marvels, magicians and enchanters, supernatural helpers, talking animals, cloaks of invisibility and impossible journeys. In fictions of this type it is particularly easy for the inner demands of the psyche to find expression. When we come to realistic fiction, largely a modern phenomenon, the situation is different. Realistic literature sets out to represent an actual society at a particular period of history. It is obliged to observe the way things actually occur; it is crowded with accurately observed detail, and the interior drama of the psyche is obscured and overlaid by the demands of day-to-day representation. Yet even here we find again and again that the deeper rhythms of such fiction are conditioned, not by historical accuracy or the need for faithful representation, but by unnoticed yet imperious pressures from the deeper psychic levels. And at the extreme limit of realism, in that kind of literature that seems to bury us under a shower of observed detail, in which the inner life seems utterly lost beneath a mass of trivial and defeating circumstances, we find when we least expect it that the autonomous power of the psyche begins to reveal itself again, and the shadowy outlines of myth, of unconscious archetypal forms, make a surprising reappearance. It is no accident that each of Joyce's major fictions, *Ulysses* and *Finnegans Wake,* fictions in which we have been almost swamped in our accumulation of empirical fact, should end with the meditation of a woman — a woman who is also all women, the eternal image of the soul.

This paper served as an introduction to a series of four lectures, "Anima Images and Moods in English Poetry", held at the C. G. Jung-Institute Zürich, Autumn 1972. Professor Hough (of Darwin College, Cambridge) is a poet, and has written widely in the field of literary criticism and language. He also lectures at the Eranos Conferences.

"ANIMA"

JAMES HILLMAN
(Zürich)

> "...if a man does not know what a thing *is*, it is at least an increase of knowledge if he knows what it is *not*." C. G. Jung (last phrase of *Aion*).

This excursion is intended to supplement the main literature on the anima.[1] Since that literature provides a goodly phenomenology of the *experience* of anima, I shall look here more closely at the rather neglected phenomenology of the *notion* of anima. Experience and notion affect each other reciprocally. Not only do we derive our notions out of our experiences in accordance with the fantasy of empiricism, but also our notions condition the nature of our experiences. In particular there seems to me to be a sentimentalism suffusing "anima" which I suspect is embedded in the notion itself, thereby colouring pale and pink our experiences and the assessments of those experiences. So, examining our experiences cannot rectify this sentimentalism, since they have already been prejudged by the rose-tinted glasses given us, I suspect, by the notion. We do better looking into the notion, if that is where the sentimentalism lies. Of course, "anima" marks out a difficult region of the psyche, hardly lending itself to any sort of examination. But the difficulty we have with anima arises as much from our indistinct concepts of her as from her indistinct nature. Jung often explained the therapeutic value of concepts as ways of taking hold, of grasping and comprehending, so that precise conceptual thinking and feeling, especially in regard to such a vague and subtle *fascinosum* as the anima, serves psychological consciousness.

A review of the literature shows that since Jung's original work on the anima notion, there have been no further contributions, neither critical, nor conceptual, nor even the addition of observational data. Rather, there is contentment to reiterate Jung with less freshness and to confirm him by multiplying examples. The notion remains untouched; its uncertainties unexplored.

It may be argued that the very uncertainty is appropriate to anima, because conceptual clarification is to use intellect where it does not belong. Our concepts reflect her best when they are vague. To me, this all-too-familiar argument means having embraced the anima foolishly and having been dragged by her into the woods. As we are supposed not to let her rule in the realm of personal relationship where, as Eve, she would make us all too fleshly and literal, so too we may not let her dominate the realm of ideation where, as Sophia, she would make us confused and formless *(CW 13,* 452f). We can as well be victims of anima projection with sentimental ideas that cloud and turn our heads as with persons. The *sacrificium intellectus* in analytical psychology today sometimes becomes perverted from its authentic meaning — dedicating intellect to the Gods — to abandoning the burden of it for tendermindedness and fuzz. Neither Freud nor Jung had to cut off his head in order to serve psyche. If Sophia is one face of anima, then a subtleness in the application of mind is surely no affront to her and may instead be one of her claims upon the psychologist, and an exercise in which she delights.

Precision in regard to anima seems particularly relevant for two further reasons: first, because our society, and psychology as part of it, is in high tension concerning feeling, femininity, eros, soul, fantasy — all areas which analytical psychology has involved with anima; and second, because Jung has said that for the individual the *Auseinandersetzung* "with the anima is the 'master-piece'" of psychological work *(CW 9,i,* 61). Again, clarification of what the notion carries may afford some insight into the social and the individual confusions, including mine, as I write, and yours, as you read.

"Anima" receives several definitions in Jung. These can be taken as levels of distinction which we may separate before attempting to understand their inter-relation. By levels I do not want to imply a hierarchy of stages or grades of value, but merely facets superimposed upon one another. These several definitions need not be treated historically, for we are not engaged in a study of the development of the anima concept in Jung's mind. Rather, I would regard the notions phenomenologically, using the *Collected Works (CW),* and occasionally *Man and his Symbols (MS), Analytical Psychology (AP),* and Jung's *Letters (B, i, ii),*[2] as a single corpus without special attention to the chronological order of the anima notions or their contexts.

"ANIMA"

1. Anima and Contrasexuality

Jung and the literature of analytical psychology mainly employ "anima" to refer to the contrasexual, less conscious aspect of the psyche of men *(CW 7, 296—301; CW 5, 678; CW 11, 48, 129)*. "The anima can be defined as the image or archetype or deposit of all the experiences of man with woman" *(CW 13, 58)*. This basic definition, which places anima in the psyche of men only, is reinforced with a biological speculation: "The anima is presumably a psychic representation of the minority of female genes in a man's body" *(CW 11, 48; CW 8, 782; CW 9, i, 58, 512; B, ii, p105; MS, p31)*. Anima thus becomes the carrier and even the image of "wholeness" *(CW 14, 500; CW 10, 715; CW 16, 471)* since she completes the hermaphrodite both psychologically and as representative of man's biological contrasexuality.

If anima represents man's female lacuna, then a therapy governed by the idea of individuation towards wholeness focuses mainly upon her development. Anima development has thus become a major therapeutic tenet in the minds of many analytical psychologists, and the "development of the feminine", a major plank in the platform of analytical psychology. But as long as "anima" remains a portmanteau idea packed thick with other notions — feeling, eros, human relationships, introversion, fantasy, concrete life, and others we shall be uncovering as we proceed — the development of anima, like anima herself, continues to mean many things to many men. In the guise of "anima development" there takes place a rich trade in smuggled hypotheses, pretty pieties about eros, and eschatological indulgences about saving one's soul through relationship, becoming more feminine, and the sacrifice of intellect.

The first notion of anima as the contrasexual side of man is conceived within a fantasy of opposites.[3] Men and women are opposites, conscious and unconscious are opposites, conscious masculinity and unconscious femininity are opposites. These oppositions are qualified further by others: a youthful consciousness has an elderly anima figure; an adult pairs with a *soror* image near his own age; senile consciousness finds correspondence in a girl child *(CW 9, i, 357; CW 16, 521, B, i, p 244)*. Then, too, a social factor enters into the contrasexual definition. In several passages *(CW 7, 303—04, 521; CW 6, 803—11)* "anima" refers to the contrasocial, inferior personality. There is an

99

opposition between the external role one plays in social life and the interior, less conscious life of the soul. This less conscious aspect which is turned inward and experienced as one's personal interiority is the anima as "soul-image" *(CW 6, 803ff)*. The more a man identifies with his biological and social role as man (persona), the more will the anima dominate inwardly *(CW 7, 317—22)*. As the persona presides over adaptation to collective consciousness, so the anima rules the inner world of the collective unconscious. As male psychology, according to Jung *(CW 8, 782f; CW 9, i, 147)*, shifts after mid-life towards its female opposite, so there is a physiological and social softening and weakening towards "the feminine", all of which are occasioned by the anima.

No doubt experience does confirm this first notion of the anima which holds her to be the inferior distaff side of men. Indeed she is first encountered through the dream figures, emotions, symptomatic complaints, obsessive fantasies and projections of Western men. Anima is "the glamorous, possessive, moody, and sentimental seductress in a man" *(CW 9, ii, 422)*. "She intensifies, exaggerates, falsifies, and mythologizes all emotional relations . . ." *(CW 9, i, 144)*.

However, the syndrome of inferior feminine traits in the personal sphere, like other syndromes (conversion hysteria or raving mania, for examples), is relative to the dominants of the culture and the *Zeitgeist*. Syndromes current when Freud began psychoanalysis are less current today; the anima as a syndrome of excessive or inferior feminine traits is less evident as the culture moves towards incorporation of "typically anima" attitudes into its collective values. We should therefore not identify a *description* of the anima in a rigidly patriarchal, puritanically defensive, extravertedly willful and unsoulful period of history with her *definition*. Even if the anima exaggerates and mythologizes, her influence upon emotional relationships today when interiority of soul and contrasexuality are *de rigeur* will appear differently and be governed by other myths. The task now is to discover what descriptions suit her in this time and how is she mythologizing today.

Besides, quite independent of historical periods and their notions of effeminacy, there might be a sophisticated anima consciousness (in the troubadour, stage-actor, courtier, diplomat, painter, florist, decorator, or psychologist — although all these with a grain of salt) which refers less to unconscious femininity than to actual ego identity. A man may be mainly governed by anima without being unconscious, i.e., without showing undifferentiated or compulsive contrasexual traits *(CW 14, 225)*. A man may indeed be quite a child of the anima in overt social behaviour, living adaptedly in a collective consciousness that has again made room for what hitherto in this century would have been considered preposterously inferior anima subjectivity and feminine sensitivity. In face of these phenomena, analytical psychology is yet able to maintain its theory again by referring to the fantasy of opposites. This time "anima" is paired with the masculine shadow *(CW 10, p377n)*. When a man's ego shows a preponderance of classical anima traits, then the unconscious is represented by the chthonic male shadow; when the ego in a man is feminine, then his unconscious contrasexuality must be masculine. (Cf. *CW 9, i*, 146, 356; *CW 10*, 220 on male homosexuality as anima identification.)

Today the notions of "masculine" and "feminine" are in dispute. This dispute has helped differentiate sexual roles from social ones, and even to differentiate kinds of sexual identity, i. e., whether based on primary or secondary, manifest or genetic, physical or psychic sexual characteristics. It has become difficult to speak of the anima as inferior femininity since we are no longer certain just what we mean with "femininity", let alone "inferior" femininity. Moreover, archetypal psychology has placed the very notion of the ego in doubt.[4] Ego-identity is not just one thing, but in a polytheistic psychology "ego" reflects any of several archetypes and enacts various mythologems. It may as well be influenced by a Goddess as by a God or Hero, and it may as well display feminine styles in behaviour without this indicating either ego-weakness or incipient ego-loss. A man's ego may perform all the required functions of an ego without its being modelled upon Hercules or Christ. Neither captain, father, nor builder of cities, instead moving through the world as a child of Luna or of Venus, yet with all ego-functions of orientation, memory, association, and proprioception intact. We shall return to the ego/anima relation in section five below.

Because the fantasy of opposites keeps the anima in a social tandem with either the persona or the shadow and in a sexual tandem with masculinity, we neglect her phenomenology *per se* and so find it difficult to understand her except in distinction to these other notions (masculinity, shadow, animus, persona). We are always regarding anima phenomenology from within a harness, or from the opposite arm of a balance. Our notions are drawn in compensation to something else to which she is always yoked. And, as the differences between social and sexual masculinity remain muddled, and our ideas of ego have hardened into dogmatic clichés, the anima's definition tends to be derivative of — and not demarcated enough from — her cultural and historical occasions. Yet, the phenomenology of anima in the psyche existed before and continues to exist independently of the psychological framework into which she has been put. An archetypal psychology would attempt to see through the descriptions given of her by the various complexes in order to get at a more fundamental notion.

2. Anima and Eros

This implies that in trying to lay bare a definite idea of anima, we shall beware of whatever descriptive traits she currently bears. The first ones to be questioned are the erotic traits (*CW 13*, 60; *CW 14*, 322, 330, 333; *CW 9, ii*, 29; *CW 10*, 255–59; *CW 17*, 338; *AP*, p99). Erotic contents and feelings have become attached by the anima archetype, but do they belong necessarily to it?

Linguistically and phenomenologically *anima* and *psyché*[5] have more to do with air, the living air of the head as a holy seat of generative power (later, our *anima rationalis* or intellectual soul), with breath as Jung points out *(CW 8*, 664; *CW 9, i*, 55; *CW 14*, 748), with dew and heavy cool vapour, and even with earth and death (P'o soul, *anima telluris)*, than with fire and desire.[6] This vaporous soul substance, like the mists that hang over marshes, the water-fowl, the hollow reeds and the breezes stirring the reeds, has been brought into conjunction with the anima by Bachofen ("hetaerism"), by Roscher's *Lexikon* ("nymphs"), by Emma Jung ("Naturwesen").[7] Elsewhere[8] I have set out some of the traditionally contrasting phenomenologies of anima and eros so that there is no need to resume them but briefly here. The first is moist, vegetative, receptive, indirect, ambiguous; its consciousness is reflective and in flux. The second is fiery, phallic, spirited, directed, sporadic and unattached, vertical as an arrow, torch, or ladder. Anima refers to the archaic, historical, and traditional past.[9] Eros is forever young, has no history and even wipes out history, or creates its own, its "love-story". And where anima withdraws towards meditative isolation — the retreat of the soul — eros seeks unions.

Even where Jung speaks of "four stages of eroticism" (*CW 16*, 361) and correlates the four stages of erotic phenomenology with four grades of the anima (Eve, Helen, Mary, Sophia), the feminine images are not the eros itself but the objects of its longing *(pothos)*. A drive has a corresponding projection, a goal it seeks, a grail to hold its blood. These containers may be represented by the anima images which Jung describes, and a quality of eros may be correlated with each of these figures, but the figures are not the eros. They are not the lovers, but the beloveds; they are reflections of love. They are the means by which eros can see itself. When our desire is mirrored by a cheering coed or a nursing nun, through the specificity of the soul-image we are able to know more precisely about the quality of our desire. But the desire is not the cheerleader, not the nurse. The images are soul-portraits by means of which eros is drawn into the psychic field and can be witnessed as a psychic event.

Bachelard[10] associates anima with reverie (in contradistinction to animus and the activity of dreaming); Corbin[11] with imagination; Ficino[12] with fantasy (*idolum*) and fate; Onians[13] with life and death; Porphyry[14] with a damp spirit and "aerial opacity" (cf. *CW 12*, p278n, anima as "smoke"). These traditional phenomenologies of the notion of soul, including the lunar descriptions of anima in Jung (*CW 14*, 154—233), do not have markedly erotic traits. These notions do not identify anima with eros or attribute the eros principle to soul. Moreover, where anima has classically referred to an internally located function in deepest association with human life and its fate, eros is a daimon, external, that visits itself upon life and fate. We fall in and out of love or are carried and redeemed, or cursed, through its working, but that which love works upon is not love but soul. Soul is the arrow's target, the fire's combustible material, the labyrinth through which it dances. It is especially this structural notion that I would emphasize: anima as an *archetypal structure of consciousness*. As such it provides a specifically structured mode of being in the world, a way of behaving, perceiving, feeling, that give events the significance — not of love — but of soul. Now, what more can we say about this structure? What are its differentiating features, if they are not erotic?

Anima is inward (hence "closed" and called "virginal" in religious and poetic metaphors of the soul), devoted, yet labile, generous and generative, yet reserved (shy, shameful, retreating, pure, veiled —

these latter qualities presented by the virgin nymphs and Goddesses such as Maria or Artemis). To this interiority belongs a movement of deepening downward[15] (caves, deeps, graves) which in the phenomenology of Kore-Persephone connects her with the realm of the underworld. "*Anima* was not the usual name for the life-soul till after death."[16] She carries our death; our death is lodged in the soul. Again, these notions are far from any thought of the anima as the eros principle, especially where eros has come to mean — and not only through Freud — the libido, the life-impulse opposed to death.

This consciousness is mood-determined, a notion that has been represented in mythological phenomenology by images of natural atmospheres (clouds, waves, still waters). Anima-consciousness favours a protective mimicry, an *attachment* to something or someone else to which it is echo. Here we see the wood nymphs that belong to trees, the souls which hover over waters, speak from dells and caves, or sing from sea-rocks and whirlpools — and, most vividly, the succubus. That we conceive anima in tandems is already given by her phenomenology. So, we think of her in notions of attachment with body or with spirit, or in the mother-daughter mystery, in the masculine-feminine pairings, or in compensation with the persona, in collusion with the shadow, or as guide to the self.

In these pairs, like in the mythological imagery, anima is the reflective partner; she it is who provides the moment of reflection in the midst of what is naturally given. She is the psychic factor in nature, an idea formulated in the last century as "animism". We feel this moment of reflection in the contrary emotions that anima phenomena constellate: the fascination plus danger, the awe plus desire, the submission to her as fate plus suspicion, the intense awareness that this way lies both my life and my death. Without these soul-stirring emotions, there would be no significance in the natural places and human affairs to which she is attached. But, life, fate, and death cannot become 'conscious', so that with her is constellated a consciousness of our fundamental unconsciousness. In other words, consciousness of this archetypal structure is never far from unconsciousness. Its primary attachment is to the state of nature, to all things that simply are — life, fate, death — and which can only be reflected but never separated from their impenetrable opacity. Anima stays close to this field of the natural unconscious mind.

A consciousness that does not soar but stays attached, that hovers and flutters over the field of natural events, is imaged also by the butterfly. The fascination of moth for flame has long stood for the soul's fluttering attachment to eros, and the butterfly sucking its sustenance from the flowers of feeling again has represented the psyche-eros relation. The butterfly points again to air as the psyche's element. To be in the air, put on airs, be breezy, windy, breathless, or show shifts of atmospheric pressure all belong to anima. Low-flying in dreams, especially over furniture or persons in rooms (closed, interior, within), can be distinguished from puer-soaring, and is not necessarily a dangerous sign of "having no earth", of inflation, of being out of the body. I take this flying as part of anima phenomenology and air as a legitimate element for certain conditions of the soul. Low-flying in childhood dreams I take as an announcement of anima consciousness. (On anima and air, see *CW 13*, 201; 261—63.)

Like the butterfly, anima-consciousness moves through phases, bearing a process, a history. It is egg, worm, cocoon, bright wing — and not only successively but all at once. Our strongly evolutional approach to events and images makes us always see development first, forgetting that in the realm of the imaginal all processes that belong to an image are inherent to it at all times. There is not merely a *coincidentia oppositorum* but a coincidence of processes. All phases at once: no first and last, better and worse, progression and regression. Instead, soul history as a series of images, superimposed. The tale of their interaction the Mother would turn into growth, the Child into futurity, and the Hero into an evolutionary epic of achievement. Because our consciousness is in thrall to these archetypal structures, we are unable to envision a phenomenology of phases except as development, as if the butterfly were a moral pilgrim. But the choice of an image from nature does not imply the naturalistic fallacy in regard to its interpretation. *Psyché* as butterfly does not demand that we view the soul developmentally.

Despite these distinctions between eros and psyche and a characterization of psyche apart from eros, there remain of course the ladies of pleasure who pay their sensuous call in our dreams. They seem erotic in themselves, thus giving phenomenological ground to the notion of anima as eros.

Here I believe we do well to remember that all that is female is not necessarily anima, and that all that is anima is not necessarily Venusian. Venus phenomenology in dream and fantasy becomes ennobled by the word 'soul', which both overloads the aphrodisiac facet of the psyche and also undervalues Venus in her own right. The whore in a dream is a whore, who can take on deeper psychological significance (cf. the "great whore" *[meretrix]* in alchemy, *CW 14,* 414ff) as an archetypal image in her own right, and need not be the anima, my mistress soul, psychopomp to the self, that is, unless she be *numinous (CW 9, i, 59)* and carry all the fascinating bipolar perplexities by which the anima archetype is recognized *(CW 9, i,* 356) — old and young, frail and physical, culture and nature, innocent and vile, intimate and occult. We do injustice to the complexity of anima by calling every woman street-walking through our dreams an 'anima image'; and we neglect Aphrodite as an authentic structure of consciousness when we psychologize her into an 'anima figure'.

To take seriously Aphrodite's archetypal realm and its patterns of behaviour means to take them *as such* without conflating, and inflating, them with the import of soul. The seductive Venusian figures draw me into the realm of Venus as Ulysses went to Calypso and to Circe, or as Michael Maier journeys into the planetary houses *(CW 14,* 297f). But neither in the Odyssey nor in Maier's alchemy does Venus stand for soul. Ulysses has as guide Athene, and Maier's psychopompos is a sibyl — soul as psychological understanding rather than as eros. There is evidently more to soul than Venus, and more to Venus than soul.

On the one hand, giving soul to each chick and duck and silly goose that enters fantasy loads these images and the human relationships in which they appear with disproportionate significance. When analysts put soul values onto simply Venusian affairs they serve her as couplers, even while burdening the pleasures of life with 'anima development'.

On the other hand, Venus is one of the way-stations and she must get her due. Modern man has an accumulated debt to Aphrodite on which she is today exacting payments at a furious rate. It is as if she were actually demanding our souls for all the centuries that they were denied to her by Judeo-Christian repression. But we pay her back best in the true coin of Aphrodite. To pay her in the guise of soul-indulgences cheats the real cost. It is more comforting to visit her planetary house in the name of anima development than it is to suffer the venereal evils, entanglements, perversions, revenges, furies, and soporific pleasures for her sake alone.

The contemporary analytical confusion of soul with eros has its source, I believe, in the archetypal perspective of Aphrodite. She would insist that we look at phenomena through the eyes of Eros, her son. By maintaining this perspective she would be perpetually reclaiming this son to serve a Venusian and venereal view of soul and of femininity. She above all has an interest in keeping Eros on the feminine side of the coniunctio. By keeping Eros on her side, his eroticism will be stimulated in an aphrodisiac fashion, giving that cast to eros in our consciousness today in which it is so highly sexualized. (Socratic Eros — from where Jung says he took the expression *[B, ii,* p 81f] — is definitely masculine. This Eros had Hermes in his genealogy and so it has further aims than the Eros of Aphrodite which was for Socrates only one phase of erotic activity.)

But Aphrodite still awaits recognition for the influence she has upon analytical psychology's notion of anima. The realm of anima often seems nothing other than Aphrodite's realm, erotic relationships, or as they are transmuted into Helen's, who was imagined in antiquity as Aphrodite's incarnation. There we supposedly find anima and there we develop it. (So much does Helen-Aphrodite colour our notion that when Jung writes of the four stages of eroticism *[CW 16,* 361], it is to Helen in particular that he gives the qualification "anima figure".)

The paradigm of this erotic exercise is transference which in both Freud and Jung receives primarily an Aphroditic cast. This was so from the beginning in Paris at Charcot's clinic. Jung soon recognized the influence of Paris and Vienna upon the formulation of psychic events, and, in separating out the school of Zürich (a city where Venus is less at home), he first focused upon the libido concept, renaming it psychic energy. By de-libidinizing the very basis of psychoanalytic theory, the archetypal premise of the unconscious was shifted from Aphrodite to Hermes-Mercurius, and the soul's fluxions were removed from the sexual eroticism and personal concretism of Aphrodite.

But still she influences our notions. How we welcome her colour green *(CW 5,* 678; *CW 14,* 393) in fantasy and dreams, indicating to what extent Venus has coloured our view of psychic events. They are seen through the green lenses of her world, growth, nature, life, and love, so that individuation tends to mean increasing beauty and harmony of soul. Little wonder that contemporary psychotherapeutic work — encounter, sensitivity, gestalt, Reichean — has led finally into overt demonstrations of Aphrodite: non-verbal, nakedness, feel-and-touch, body awareness, orgasm.

We may know a good deal about the manifestations of Aphrodite in myth and in our personal lives. But we know far too little about how she governs the premises and conclusions of our thinking. These we naively think are based on empirical facts. But the very idea of concrete sensate facts suits her style of consciousness. The erotic 'facts' on which we build our ideas are her creations. Empirical evidence is never simply objective givens, lying around like moonrocks, waiting to be picked up. Empirical evidence of any psychological premise forms part of the same archetypal perspective: we find what we are looking for; we see what is allowed to fit in by the perceptual defenses in the archetypal structure of our consciousness. So we see the soul filled with sexual wishes when our premises and observations are Aphroditic. The Aphroditic cast of the anima in Jung's essay on transference *(CW 16,* 419 to end) is an excellent case to point.

Aphrodite may have given the correct perspective to transference and may have been the gateway to the repressed (in our culture between 1870 and 1960), but it is not the anima's only, or even main, perspective. Athene, Artemis, Hera, and Persephone produce ideas of soul that would show another twist. To place anima events upon the altar of Aphrodite puts Psyche back in her service, back to the beginning of Apuleius' tale, the rest of which and the very point of which displays a movement away from Aphrodite, both of Eros and of Psyche.

If anima is defined as the eros factor, then we are always bound to assume that sexual excitation is a soul message and cannot be denied — who would deny the call of his soul? And we are bound to assume that active human relationships and uplifting enthusiasms are anima-inspired, whereas in truth they are less promoted by the reflective moisture of the soul than by eros captivating the soul. For here we must concede that though anima is not eros, her first inclination is towards love. So she seduces, to be turned on, set afire, illumined. So she makes advances, in order to move pure reflection into connection. So she commands an incredible range of voluptuous imagery in order to draw eros down upon her for what Plato called "generation", or soul-making. Nevertheless, though love be essential to soul, as theology insists and psychotherapy confirms, and though soul be that by which we receive love, soul is not love.

By drawing them apart in contrasts of moisture and fire, serpent and hare, waterfowl and dove, reflection and desire, fantasy and impulse, nature and spirit, mind and activity, depths and ascent, I am following the alchemists' dictum that only what has been properly separated can be adequately joined.

3. Anima and Feeling[17]

Besides eros, feeling too has been generally attributed to anima, as if she were the archetype of the feeling function. This confusion has several roots. The first and simplest lies in the idea of inferiority. When the feeling function in men is inferior (as is generally claimed by analytical psychology), it merges with men's contrasexual anima inferiority *(CW 12,* 150; *CW 9, ii,* 58; *AP,* p99). Then we believe we discriminate the anima *by* discriminating feeling, whereas the task more likely is one of discriminating anima *from* feeling, from the human relatedness and personal evaluations that feeling has come to mean and which confine anima into the personal feeling world of Helen *(CW 10,* 75f; *CW 16,* 361; *B, i,* p333f).

Another source of the confusion between anima and feeling lies in an idea, only occasionally occuring in Jung *(CW 6,* 640; *CW 10,* 79; *B, i,* p77), but bruited widely by later analytical psychologists, that feeling is a feminine prerogative. (Women are more at home in the feeling world; men learn about feeling from women; the development of the feminine goes by way of the feeling function.) Since anima is by definition feminine, then feeling refers to anima. Next in these steps of spurious reasoning erected on questionable premises is the equation: anima development = feeling development. Behind this equation still lurks the idea of eros, that is supposed to be the force within both the anima and the feeling function.

Just as anima is not eros or its psychic representative, so too the relation between the God-daimon Eros and eros as an archetypal principle, on the one hand, and feeling as a psychological function, on the other hand, has never been established — neither empirically, nor logically, nor phenomenologically. The feeling function works mainly through the realm of feeling of which at least 1500 different ones have been named by psychology. Only some of this feeling has to do with eros. To give to eros either feeling or the anima puts too many events all upon one altar, claiming all for love. Not only is this biasedly Christian — in the sense of limited to only the one perspective of love — but authentic aspects of anima become judged only from the standpoint of love. Hatred, spite, suspicion, jealousy, rejection, enmity, deception, betrayal, cruelty, misanthropy, ridicule play their part in anima experiences. These emotions are appropriate to many of the cold-blooded witchy creatures whom we find in legend and poetry — and our dreams and lives — even where such "negative" emotions are far from the eros and the feeling function that would conform with the mediocre niceness of Christian humanism.

Yet another source lies in the idea of relationship. Jung (as we shall explore in section seven below) often calls the anima the function of relationship. He also sometimes *(CW 9, ii, 33; cf. CW 9, i, 487, p270n; MS, p31; CW 13, 60)* does consider anima to be that factor which can give "relationship and relatedness to a man's consciousness". Although Jung himself only rarely describes feeling as relationship *(CW 16, 489)*, but rather feeling as valuation, analytical psychology now tends to stress the relational aspect. Feeling is generally spoken of as the instrument of connection between persons and between an individual and his outer and inner worlds. To have 'poor feeling' and to be 'unrelated' have become synonymous. Because both anima and feeling are called the function of relationship, they merge with each other.

Now, the two meanings of relationship, that of anima and that of feeling, touch each other only here and there. Yet today in some analytical psychology they have tended to fuse completely, so that anima = relationship = feeling has become the simple formula, nay panacea. Before we swallow any more than tolerable doses of this sweet elixir, or prescribe it to our patients, let us look at its ingredients.

Anima as relationship means that configuration which mediates between personal and collective, between actualities and beyond, between the individual conscious horizon and the primordial realm of the imaginal, its images, ideas, figures, and emotions. Here anima functions as mediatrix and psychopompos (see seven below). The quality of relationship will be determined by this function. So, relationship governed by anima will show unstable paradoxes of longing and trepidation, involvement and skittishness, faith and doubt, and an intense sense of personal significance owing to the importance of the imaginal soul at large. The other main characteristic here, besides the emotional paradoxes and swollen importance, is the uncanny autonomy — the basic unconsciousness — of anima relationship because such relationship reflects her as bridge to everything unknown.

Anima as function of relationship is far indeed from relatedness. It seems odd that anima could ever have been considered as a help in human relationship. In each of her classical shapes she is a non-human or half-human creature and her effects lead us away from the individually human situation. She makes moods, distortions, illusions, which serve human relatedness only where the persons concerned share the same mood or fantasy. If we want "to relate", then anima begone! Nothing disturbs more the accurate feeling between persons than anima. Even when her supposedly higher forms (Diotima, Aphrodite -Urania, Maria, Sophia) enter a relationship, a queenly atmosphere oppresses and her psychopompos role is overshadowed with psychic pomposity.

Feeling as relationship is another kettle of fish. It refers to that function which brings object and subject into an evaluative *relatedness*. I size you up; or an event is discriminated by my scale of values into a particular shape ('feel') so that I recognize its importance relative to other events. "Relationship" here refers to a relatively constant process of assessment and valuation going on between consciousness and its content. By means of this process a relationship is established between consciousness and this content and among the contents themselves. (Thinking, also a rational function, provides relationship as well. It too discriminates, orders, and makes coherent connections between contents and between subject and object. Of course, it thinks these relationships in accordance with principles of thought, rather than feels them as values.)

The relatedness of George and Mary depends upon the specific natures of George and Mary. Their relatedness reflects their living process of feeling, and their relationship is unique to them. If their relationship were anima determined, it would become a reflection less of them and more of an archetypal fantasy playing through them. Then they become collective actors performing an unconscious fantasy, i.e., lovers, quarrelers, cohorts, mother-son, father-daughter, nurse-patient, etc. Even the feeling function is usurped by the dominant fantasy. Then the specific complexity of the relatedness between George and Mary has become upstaged by an archetypal drama directed by the anima. Her purpose? To insist that the human respect her wider, more fateful kind of inhuman relatedness to impersonal factors that are archetypally prior even to human feeling.

The muddling of anima and feeling contributes to that primrose path in analytical psychotherapy which considers the cure of souls to be an anima cultivation of a specific kind, i.e., feeling development. But anima cultivation, or soul-making to use the wider idea, is first of all a complex process of fantasying and understanding of which only part is the sophistication of feeling. Besides, the feeling that is developed through soul-making is perhaps more impersonal, a detailed sensitivity to the specific worth of psychic contents and attitudes, than it is personal. This development does *not* proceed from the impersonal to the personal, related, and human. Rather, the movement goes from the narrower embrace of my empirical human world and its personal concerns towards archetypal events that put my empirical, personal world in a more significant frame. This frame is given not by feeling or relatedness but by the anima whose mythologizing fantasy and reflective function remind of life, fate, and death. She does not lead into human feeling, but out of it. As the function that relates conscious and unconscious, she occludes conscious feeling, making it unconscious and making the human, inhuman. She puts other things in mind than the human world. But should Dante and Petrarch today go into psychotherapy, would they not be told that Beatrice and Laura were immature anima projections, unreal, regressive, revealing inferiority of feeling and unrelatedness to woman and 'the feminine'?

I, for one, have yet to be given convincing demonstration that in dreams a lizard requires development into something warm-blooded and a hyena into something more kindly, or that a little girl calls for development into mature feelings, and an uncanny witch-like woman or one impoverished or primitive is to be upgraded into the human world through feeling and personal relationships.

In these instances, ironically, maybe even tragically, the actual (anima?) images of lizard, little girl, and primitive slattern are not given feelings or evaluated with feeling for themselves as they are. Rather, in the name of feeling/anima development the actual image is depotentiated. All the feeling goes to the development, to the transformational progress of the images into something more human. It is as if the Christian myth of incarnation is continually being applied to the images of the anima, that all images must follow the model of the inhuman becoming human (God incarnating), and that all psychic factors are to enter human relationships. Ridiculous, of course. Yet, putting anima development into the path of feeling development, as feeling is now humanistically understood, means precisely the slaying of the animals, the *daimones,* and the Gods. It means turning the sacred *numinosum* of an archetypal image into something safe, sane, and secular. Analytical psychotherapy, so bent upon humanizing the images and developing archetypal realities into relationships, is not only caught in Darwinism but in the simplest sort of secularism where man is the measure and the Gods aberrations. But did not the Gods always have an aberrant and distorted aspect; were they not always strange forms in animal shapes, grotesque, bizarre, awe-full? Who says they must have warm blood or have human blood at all.

To read the psyche's strange images as signals for feeling development leads right into the "humanistic fallacy", the belief that psyche is a function of the human being and is meant to serve the human life, its images humanized. I still see the connection between man and soul the other way around, as in the main Platonic tradition where man is a function of psyche and his job is to serve it. The therapist of psyche, which in root means "soul-servant", translates human events into the language of the psyche, rather than the psyche into the language of humanism.

At the front of therapy's secular humanism flies the banner of feeling. Where the Church and then psychoanalysis did not quite drive out the devils, 'personal relatedness in a human context' will finally do the job. The anima will become socially presentable, adapted. But if, as Jung says (*CW 13,* 54), "the Gods have become diseases", then curing the soul of its unrelated, inhuman images may also cure it of its Gods. The confusion of anima with feeling and the attempt to humanize by feeling is thus not psychotherapy at all. Rather it is part of contemporary secularism's sickness of soul, or psychopathology. We have yet to discover which archetypal person has captured consciousness through the sentimental appeal of humanism and feeling. At least we know it is not Eros, who prefers the dark and silence to 'relatedness', 'sharing', 'communicating'. Yet some archetypal power does influence therapy by interpreting the psychic movement of our images and their animal-daimonic forms into social relations and personal connections and by raising such guilt over 'unrelatedness'. I suspect Hera, especially in her 'young married' form of Hebe.

4. Anima and The Feminine

We now come to two definitions which put in question anima as image of man's contrasexual genetic structure and experience. Jung calls anima "the archetype of the feminine" *(CW 5,* 266n; cf. *CW 9, i,* 356, 142) and "the archetype of life" *(CW 14,* 646, 313; *CW 9, i,* 66, 56). He further draws analogies between anima and yin *(CW 9, i,* 120; *CW 12,* 192; *CW 13,* 47, 460n) and the Chinese *p'o* soul *(CW 9, i,* 119; *CW 13,* 57f); between anima and the Indian ideas of Maya and Shakti *(CW 13,* 126, 223; *CW 14,* 673; *CW 9, ii,* 20, 24); and he relates anima to the Gnostic Sophia (wisdom) (v. index to *CW 11* and *CW 14,* but especially *CW 11,* 613, and 460, where anima is called "pure Gnosticism".

At this level we can hardly attribute anima to the male sex only. The "feminine" and "life" as well as the Chinese, Indian, and Gnostic analogies to anima are relevant to men and women equally. We are now at an archetypal level of anima, "the feminine archetypal image" *(CW 9, ii,* p21n), and an archetype as such cannot be attributed to or located within the psyche of either sex. We may take this yet one step further, for we cannot be sure that the archetypes are only psychic, belonging only to the realm of psyche, unless we extend psyche first beyond sexual differences, then beyond the human person and psychodynamics (compensation), and beyond psychology too. Jung already made this extension in his notion of the archetype as psychoid, stating that "the archetypes, therefore have a nature that *cannot with certainty be designated as psychic*" *(CW 8,* 439, cf. 964, 419). An adequate notion of anima thus requires that one look beyond men and beyond man, and even beyond psyche. But a metaphysics or metapsychics of the anima is not our direction here. Rather, it is to realize that anima, as archetype, is too wide to be contained by the notion of contrasexuality. Anima, released from this containing definition, bears upon the psyche of women too.

According to the first notion (contrasexuality), there is no anima in women. "The anima, being of feminine gender, is exclusively a figure that compensates the masculine consciousness" *(CW 7,* 328). "The same figure is not to be found in the imagery of a woman's unconscious" *(CW 11,* 48). In accordance with the yoke of opposites women have the animus instead.

But what of "anima women", those women who play the anima for men and are called in analytical psychology "anima types" *(CW 17,* 339; cf. *B, ii,* 231f). Jung says that such women can best play this anima part by being empty themselves *(CW 9, i,* 355, cf. 169). They therefore catch the projections of men, mirroring and mimicking them, so that a man's inner woman is lived out by an anima type.

Here again I believe we have an instance of our psychic premises being determined by an archetypal figure so that we see that which is already given in the premise. We call these women anima types and we connect them with the ancient figure of the hetaera; yet because of theory (no anima in women), we assume that the anima archetype can affect a woman's life only through men and their projections.

Let us look at this more closely. The roles which Jung *(CW 9, i,* 356, 358) assigns to the anima — relation with the mysteries, with the archaic past, enactment of the good fairy, witch, whore, saint, and animal associations with bird, tiger, and serpent (to mention only those he there mentions) — all appear frequently and validly in the psychology of women. Anima phenomenology is not restricted to the male sex. Women have little girls in their dreams, and whores; they too are lured by mysterious and unknown women. The Saint, Sappho, and Sleeping Beauty are part of their inscapes too. And as the images are not restricted to men only, so anima emotion cannot be confined only to the male sex. Women too bear an expectancy, an interiority that is opposed to their outer persona actions. They too lose touch, and may be drawn away to meditate their fate, their death, their immortality. They too sense soul and suffer its mystery and confusion. We say of a woman, "she has soul", and we mean much the same as when we say this of a man.

Women are as salty in their weeping and resentments, as bitchy in their gossip, as abysmal in their dour brooding as men. The intensifications, exaggerations, and mythologizings that belong to the description of anima do appear in women and may not be ascribed to her unconscious feminine personality, the woman within, or attributed to a minority of female genes. Here the anima, archetype of life and archetype of the feminine, influences the psychic process regardless of sex, and we are freed from the masculine-feminine fantasy of anima, from the endless oscillations of compensation, and also from the epistemological deceit of explanations through "projection".

Why do we call the same behaviour in one sex "anima" and in the other "naturally feminine" or "shadow"? What effect does this have on the psychological differences between the sexes, if the same image in a man and a woman is in his case ennobled as a soul-image (anima) while in hers it is part of the realm of shadow. By depriving by definition women of anima — "Woman has no anima, no soul, but she has an *animus*" (CW 17, 338; cf. CW 13, 60; CW 10, 79) — is not analytical psychology willy-nilly continuing a very ancient tradition of denying woman soul and casting the images of this soul into shadow. This is to doubt neither the reality of her shadow nor the pressing spiritual question in woman that is figured by animus.

But I do doubt that woman's psychological development means animus development, for this is an erosion of the categories of psyche and spirit. Animus refers to spirit, to logos, word, idea, intellect, principle, abstraction, meaning, *ratio, nous*. The discrimination of spirit is not at all of the same order as the cultivation of soul. If the first is active mind in its broadest sense, the second is the realm of the imaginal, equally embracing, but very different.

The assumption has been that because women are of the feminine gender they have soul — or rather are soul. As long as femininity and soul are an identity, then of course the soul problem of women is taken care of, again by definition, and by biology. But psyche, the sense of soul, is not given to woman just because she is born female. She is no more blessed with a congenitally saved soul than man who must pass his life in worry over its fate. She is no more exonerated from the tasks of anima cultivation than man; for her to neglect soul for the sake of spirit is no less psychologically reprehensible than it is in man who is ever being told by analytical psychology that he must sacrifice intellect, persona, and extraversion for the sake of soul, feeling, inwardness, i.e., anima.

The immense difficulty which women have with imagination and the torment they go through in regard to a sense of inner emptiness both point to soul as area of their need. No less than men, women need fantasy, mythologizings in which they can read themselves and discover fate. To find a sense of worth, confidence as a person, or "psychological faith" as Grinnell[18] has called it, is as much a need of woman as of man. The hookey substitutes for soul, the anima sentimentalities and anima inflations, are found equally in both sexes; women's attempts at depth, inwardness, sensitivity, and wisdom are as prey to pseudo-soul as those of men. In women perhaps pseudo-soul is even more evident, for in the absence of anima, animus fills the gap, a transvestite travesty.

Animus is given with the civilization, and its psychic representation which we foreshorten into the notion of ego is, as Neumann[19] pointed out, masculine in women too. Ego's archetype is the Hero and so its underside in women too will show the soulful qualities of anima. The neglected area is not animus but anima.

An animus development with which anima does not keep pace will lead a woman away from psychological understanding. This occurs by drying her fantasy, narrowing her range of mood and involvement with life, turning her into at best a spiritual paragon and a psychological dunce, her wisdom, her concern, her counsel all being developed opinion, detached, rather than soul reflection in the midst of her attachments — and this we see even where the preferred field of animus development be psychology itself. The domain of psychology does not guarantee that its inhabitants are particularly psychological. The shingle over the door, "psychologist", unfortunately attests to nothing about the soul of the practitioner. And if the practitioner be a woman, then the epithet "psychologist" even more certainly has nothing to do with soul, since the (animus) developmental process which led to the title has been by definition one of spirit not of soul. To state this implies nothing against the development of logos or against respect for ideas in women, but as spirit is not soul, so animus is not anima, and neither can be neglected nor substituted for the other. The syzygy means both.

The power of our theoretical notions cannot be overestimated. By denying woman anima and giving her animus instead, an entire archetypal pattern has been determined for women's psychology. The *per definitionem* absence of anima in women is a deprivation of a cosmic principle with no less consequence in the practice of analytical psychology than has been the theory of penis deprivation in the practice of psychoanalysis.

While raising this doubt about the animus, I would as well raise a hope that the typically anima constellations in a woman's psyche be treated as such, and no longer as shadow simply because these manifestations are feminine. This in turn would lead to a more precisely refined notion of shadow, perhaps keeping it reserved for the morally repressed. Whenever it comes to a choice between saving the theory and saving the phenomena, the history of thought shows that it profits more to side with the phenomena, even if for a while theory is dislocated and some things we had considered clear fall back into a new obscurity.

Returning now to the emptiness of the anima type woman, we may remember that hitherto her relationship to the anima archetype has had by definition to come through a man. But now we may no longer regard her psychology in this way. The emptiness is no mere void for catching a projection from the opposite sex. Nor may we account for this emptiness through the notions of an unconscious shadow or an undeveloped animus. To derive it from a father-complex again puts the origin onto man, leaving the woman only a daughter, only an object created by projection, an Eve born out of Adam's sleep, without independent soul, fate, and individuality *(CW 9, i, 355)*.

Rather this emptiness would be considered an authentic archetypal manifestation of the anima in one of her classical forms, maiden, nymph, Kore, which Jung so well describes *(CW 9, i, 311)*, and where he also states that "she often appears in woman". Even should we relate this maiden to the daughter, it may remain within the anima constellation. There is no need to search outside for origins in a father.

We all know that fathers create daughters; but daughters create fathers too. The enactment of the maiden-daughter in all her receptive charm, shy availability, and masochistic wiliness draws down a fathering spirit. But its appearance and her victimization is her creation. Even the idea that she is all a result of the father (or the absent or bad father) is part of the father-fantasy of the anima archetype. And so, she must be 'so attached' to father because anima is reflection of an attachment. She creates the figurative father and the belief in its responsibility which serves to confirm the archetypal metaphor of Daughter that owes its source, not to the father, but to the anima inherent in a woman's psyche, too.

"ANIMA"

Moreover, the muse, to whom the nymph has a special connection and towards whom her consciousness is intending, if we follow W. F. Otto,[20] belongs also authentically to the potential of women's psychology in its own right and is not only in reflection to men. It is not *man's* anima, and so it is not a man's inner life that the nymph, hetaera, or muse is reflecting, but anima as archetype, which by other names is psyche or soul. (Cf. *CW 13,* 179ff, 215ff; *CW 14,* 69f on nymphs.)

At this level of distinction Jung himself raises a doubt whether we can truly speak of the anima per se as feminine. He suggests that we may have to confine the archetype's femininity to its projected form *(CW 9, i,* 142). Paradoxically, the very archetype of the feminine may not itself be feminine. One could raise a similar doubt about the "femininity" of life of which anima is the archetype.

The contentless asexual description of the anima archetype as "life", analogous with Maya, Shakti, Sophia, and the *p'o* soul point to a specific kind of life, life which projects out of itself consciousness. In other words, the life which Jung attributes to the anima archetype is *psychic life:* "The anima ... is a 'factor' in the proper sense of the word. Man cannot make it; on the contrary, it is always the *a priori* element in his moods, reactions, impulses, and whatever else is spontaneous in psychic life. It is something that lives of itself, that makes us live; it is a life behind consciousness that cannot be completely integrated with it, but from which, on the contrary, consciousness arises" *(CW 9, i,* 57).

Anima here is not a projection but is the projector. And our consciousness is the result of her prior psychic life. Anima thus becomes the primordial carrier of psyche, or the archetype of psyche itself.

5. Anima and Psyche

We are led to another consideration: the relation of anima to psyche itself. In many places *(CW 9, i,* 55; *CW 14,* 536; *CW 7,* 295; *CW 13,* p 132n; *CW 10,* 243; *CW 17,* 338) Jung uses anima and soul interchangeably. Nevertheless, he applies his main effort to the difficult task of keeping distinct the three terms — anima, soul, psyche. From one side he differentiates anima from soul, saying, "I have suggested instead the term 'anima' as indicating something specific, for which the expression 'soul' is too general and too vague" *(CW 9, ii,* 25). He wants to make sure that his concept, 'anima', is not confused with the traditional ideas of soul in religion and philosophy *(CW 9, i,* 55, 57; *CW 10,* 84; *CW 7,* 302, 371). From another side he also wants to define anima so that it does not refer to psyche, of which it is only one archetype. Neither soul nor anima can be identified with the "totality of the psychic functions" *(CW 6,* 419–21). For this totality the term self is generally reserved. (For more on these differentiations see the editor's and translator's notes, *CW 6,* p467n; *CW 8,* p300; *CW 12,* p8n.)

In another context[21] I attempted to separate some of the threads in the nexus 'anima', 'psyche', 'soul'. I suggested there that the moods and behaviour peculiar to what analytical psychology calls anima is best seen against the archetypal background of Psyche in Apuleius' tale, and that therefore this anima behaviour was precisely where to look for the emergence of psyche. My point there was to show *phenomenologically* that what starts out as mere anima moods and fantasies becomes eventually psychological receptivity, containment, and imagination, so that the way to psychological understanding is through anima. My point here is to show *conceptually* that the process of anima becoming psyche can be deduced from Jung's notion of anima itself. In fact, I think a case can be made for another definition of anima: *archetype of psyche.* Although this definition does not appear in Jung, it can be derived from Jung in the following ways:

a) Jung associates a host of feminine forms with anima; but one in particular he generally keeps outside its confines. This is the mother. "The most striking feature about the anima-type is that the maternal element is lacking" *(CW 10,* 75; cf. *CW 9, i,* 158; *CW 9, ii,* 26; *CW 12,* 92; but *contra CW 9, i,* 356; *CW 17,* 339). The anima makes possible a "purely human relationship" independent of the maternal element of procreation *(CW 10,* 76). Anima thus represents the movement into adulthood and the "growth away from nature" *(idem).*

In alchemy the growth away from nature is spoken of as the *opus contra naturam,* a key concept for the *psychological,* in distinction to the *naturalistic,* understanding of psychic events. The movement from mother to anima represents this shift in perspective from naturalistic to psychological understanding. In alchemy the relationship corresponding with the psychological perspective was exemplified in the adept's relationship with an anima-*soror.* The psychological approach essential to alchemy required anima, so that she becomes the archetypal premise of psychological work.

b) In a series of passages *(CW 9, ii,* p212n; *CW 9, i,* 66; *CW 13,* 262–63; *CW 12,* 505; *CW 14,* 699) Jung demonstrates the identity of anima and Mercurius. Mercurius receives various anima and soul names; and, as Mercurius is called *(CW 13,* 299) "the archetype of the unconscious", so the anima is the archetype who "personifies the collective unconscious" *(CW 10,* 714; *CW 9, ii,* p11n; *CW 11,* 107; *CW 14,* 128).

Mercurius and anima have similar shifty, flighty, iridescent, hard-to-catch, hard-to-fathom natures, a quality imaged by quicksilver in Mercurius and by the anima as elf and Melusine, and by the shimmering wings of *psyché*. Their similarity does not make them one in all respects, but it does help substantiate the idea that the special significance of anima is psychic, since Mercurius is the representation par excellence of psychic nature. (I believe their identity is more pronounced when soul and spirit have not been discriminated; then anima is exaggeratedly mercurial, less the container than seductively elusive — all over the place — and then the spirit is predominately moist, vaporous, and in a soulful flux of uncertainties. It is in this condition when soul and spirit are confounded that the spirit is garbed in white, her colour [the *albedo, anima candida],* and soul appears dressed by his blue or his red. Some of the 'puella' phenomena in young women express this mixture of spirit and soul: an unfixed mercurial spirit that acts as fascinating spark in a soul innocent of what it contains.)

c) But the basic alchemical cluster of ideas associated with anima is that of Luna and Regina and their many other names for the one component of the arcane pair. This component, which, following Jung *(CW 14,* 536, 736), we abbreviate here by Regina, is regarded alchemically in one conjunction to be the counterpart of body, while in another conjunction she becomes the counterpart of spirit. Jung lets Regina stand equally for the feminine, for eros, for soul, the unconscious, the anima, and for the psyche. That is to say, in these alchemical syzygies Regina means psyche itself when psyche is imagined to be different from body or different from spirit.

We should note here that Jung employs the term psyche in two senses. In the narrower and traditional usage, psyche is the soul component of the conjunction. It is in this sense that psyche is phenomenologically and terminologically indistinguishable from anima. In the broader usage, and one rather specific to Jung, psyche means more than a component, and therefore cannot be equated with the anima archetype. Psyche in this sense means all the processes depicted in alchemy, including body, spirit, sun and moon, mercurius, etc. They are each psychological; they are all taking place in the psyche. Anima would only be one of these factors.

This sort of extended notion of soul appears in alchemy, e.g., the soul described by Richard White *(CW 14,* 91–3), which Jung points out, differs extremely from the idea of psyche in "biological and personalistic psychology". This soul is at once the personified anima figured in a female form and the reflective psychological principle. As Jung notes she joins in one the distinction between the wider notion of soul *(anima mundi)* and the narrower one *(anima vagula).* This distinction between soul and *the* soul or *my* soul did not bother the alchemists, and it was a distinction which Neoplatonism refused to make, for Plotinus was able to discuss psychology always on both levels at once: what takes place in psyche of course takes place in man's soul. Archetypal psychology is of course reflected within an individual psyche. Jung sometimes concurs, saying for instance *(CW 16,* 469), "... it often seems advisable to speak less of *my* anima or *my* animus and more of *the* anima and *the* animus. As archetypes these figures are semi-collective and impersonal quantities...". He also regrets *(CW 11,* 759) that: "Man himself has ceased to be the microcosm and eidolon of the cosmos, and his 'anima' is no longer the consubstantial *scintilla,* or spark of the *Anima Mundi,* or World Soul." Because we take the anima personalistically, or she dupes the ego this way, we lose the wider significance of anima. This loss of soul goes on even while we are most engaged in the attempt to gain it: "developing *my* anima" through relatedness, creativity, and individuation.

Unless we understand the "within" in a radically new way — or classically old way — we go on perpetuating the division between my anima and world soul (objective psyche). The more we concentrate her inside and literalize interiority within my person, the more we lose the sense of soul as a psychic reality interiorly within all things. Anima within is not merely within my breast; introjection and internalization do not mean making my head or my skin the vessel inside of which all psychic processes take place. The "within" refers to that attitude given by the anima which perceives psychic life within natural life. Natural life itself becomes the vessel the moment we recognize its having an interior significance, the moment we see that it too bears and carries psyche. Anima makes vessels everywhere, anywhere, by going within.

The means of doing this is fantasy. Phenomena come alive and carry soul through our imaginative fantasies about them. When we have no fantasy about the world, then it is objective, dead; even the fantasy of pollution helps bring the world back to life as having significance for soul. Fantasy is not merely an interior process going on in my head. It is a way of being in the world and giving back soul to the world.

The attempt to take back soul from life outside deprives the outside of its "within", stuffing the person with subjective soulfulness and leaving the world a slagheap from which all projections, personifications, and psyche has been extracted. For this reason, the more we work at our own personalities and subjectivities in the name of the anima, the less we are truly soul-making and the more we are continuing in the illusion that anima is in us rather than we in it. Psyche is the wider notion than man, and man functions by virtue of psyche and is dependent upon it rather than the other way round: "man is in *the* psyche (not in *his* psyche)" *(B, ii,* p188), "The major part of the soul is outside the body", says Jung quoting the alchemist Sendivogius *(B, ii,* p225; *CW 12,* 396). Because the anima notion always implicates the world-soul, or soul of and in the world, a development of anima-consciousness never takes place merely through the development of individual subjectivity.

'*My*' anima expresses the *personalistic fallacy*. Even though anima experiences bring with them a numinosity of person, the feeling of a unique inwardness and sense of importance (exaggerations and mythologizations of mood, insight, or fantasy), to take these experiences literally, as literally personal, puts anima inside '*me*'. The heightened subjectivity of anima events "is anything but personal" because it is archetypal *(CW 16,* 469). The anima is the archetype behind these personalisms and therefore the experiences are archetypally personal, making us feel both archetypal and personal at one and the same instant. But to take the archetypal literally as personal is a personalistic fallacy. So, when under the domination of anima our soulfulness makes us feel most uniquely 'me', special, different, called — this is precisely the moment when, as Jung goes on to say in the same passage, "we are in fact most estranged from ourselves and most like the average type of *Homo sapiens*".

Returning now to the dilemma arising from the two senses of anima — the narrower meaning of one component in the conjunctio and the wider meaning of the place in which the entire process takes place — we may understand it as follows: Anima may be only one ingredient in the alchemy of psychic processes. But because of her conjunctive role *(anima mercurius)* she is that factor through which it all occurs as psychic; she is the means by which (anima as copula and ligament) and in which (anima as vessel) the entire process takes place. Because of her these events become personally experienced as mine, going on in my soul. It is by virtue of the anima ingredient that events which are impersonal and only natural reactions or only spiritual ideas become psychic experiences.

Thus we find the idea in Jung that the more realized the anima (as one archetypal factor in the psyche), the more "psychic existence becomes reality" *(CW 16,* 438). The reality of psyche as an all-too-convincing experience begins in the subjectivized moods and follies of the highly personalized anima. Nowhere do we more stubbornly encounter the reality of soul — in itself such a dim and wispy idea — than in the crosspatch nastiness of bad tempers, the insights that slip away, the sensitive vanities that will not be mollified. Within these commonplace disturbances, as Jung points out *(CW 7,* 318–27), is an anima fantasy; and psychic existence also becomes reality when we recognize the driving power and full import of fantasy itself. Anima refers to a "quintessence of fantasy-images" *(CW 14,* 736) and an "'air-coloured' quintessence" *(idem.,* 749) whose final effect in bringing home the reality of the psyche is a realization "that this fantasy is happening, and it is as real as you — as a psychic entity — are real", "just as if you were one of the fantasy figures" *(idem.,* 753). My conviction that psyche and its fantasies are as real as matter and nature, as real as spirit, depends on how convincing anima has made herself to me. Thus on her depends the psychological calling.

d) The relation of anima and psyche comes out in yet one more way: through Jung's idea of reflection. On the five instinctual drives (hunger, sexuality, activity, reflection, and creation) upon which he elaborates *(CW 8, 237–46)*, his notion of reflection — "bending back" and "turning inwards" away from the world and its object in favour of psychic images and experiences — correlates most closely with his notion of anima. Anima as Luna *(CW 14, 154f)*, passive, cool, breeding, brooding, inward, describes reflection in alchemical language. The archetype corresponding with the instinct of reflection would be the anima.

Primordial images of this bending back and away are presented by the retreating but fecund nymphs and the illusionary voices and ephemera (moonlight, mists, echoes, musings, fantasies) of which we have spoken above, and which I have discussed in more detail in relation with the feminine figures associated with Pan.[22] The turning inwards from the object in favour of internal images correlates again with the endogamous introjection of the anima, or "internalization through sacrifice" *(CW 16, 438; CW 13, 223)*, necessary for psychic consciousness. Another image of reflection associated traditionally with anima is the mirror and the activity of mirroring.

When Jung discourses briefly upon the nature of "unconscious reflection" *(CW 11, 237)*, he says: "Where judgments and flashes of insight are transmitted by unconscious activity, they are often attributed to an archetypal feminine figure, the anima or mother-beloved. It then seems as if the inspiration came from the mother or from the beloved, the 'femme inspiratrice'" *(CW 11, 240)*. At another level he speaks in his Seminars of the same unconscious mental activity as "the natural mind" *(CW 9, i, p88n)*, where we do not think, but are thought, and he holds this natural mind to be exclusively a feminine property.

But the key passages which relate anima to psyche via reflection are these: "The richness of the human psyche and its essential character are probably determined by this reflective instinct" *(CW 8, 242)*. Thus psyche is mainly a result of the instinct of reflection, which in turn is intimately tied with the anima archetype. "Through reflection, 'life' and its 'soul' are abstracted from Nature and endowed with a separate existence" *(CW 11, 235)*. The archetype of both life and soul as distinct from 'only Nature' (procreative, biological Mother Nature) is anima, so that she would be that archetype which both performs the abstraction through reflection and personifies the life and soul in a reflected form. Anima is nature now conscious of itself through reflection. Or, as Jung puts it *(CW 11, p158n)*: "... reflection is a spiritual act that runs counter to the natural process; an act whereby we stop, call something to mind, form a picture, and take up a relation to and come to terms with what we have seen. It should, therefore, be understood as an act of *becoming conscious.*"

*

Far-reaching consequences emerge from these passages. They indicate nothing less than an altogether other vision for the archetypal base of consciousness. If "becoming conscious" has its roots in reflection and if this instinct refers to the anima archetype, then consciousness itself may more appropriately be conceived as based upon anima than upon ego.

We have already heard Jung suggest as much, saying about the anima, "it is life behind consciousness ... from which ... consciousness arises" *(CW 9, i, 57)*. He elaborates upon this notion when discussing the primitive idea that "the name of an individual is his soul" *(CW 8, 665)* which "means nothing less than that ego-consciousness is recognized as being an expression of the soul". He says further *(idem,* 668) that "the sense of the 'I' — ego-consciousness — grows out of unconscious life." And the life he speaks of in these passages is "soul". Again *(CW 14, 129)*, when he says "our consciousness issues from a dark body, the ego", "full of unfathomable obscurities", "a mirror in which the unconscious becomes aware of its own face", we are given a description approaching that of the anima. This kind of ego is reflective; it is a complex of opposites; and like the anima it is defined as "a personification of the unconscious itself". In yet another significant passage Jung contrasts ego and anima as bases of consciousness. When commenting upon a Chinese text, he notes that there "consciousness (that is, personal consciousness) comes from the anima", and says the East "sees consciousness as an effect of the anima" *(CW 13, 62)*. Here the two archetypal bases are contrasted by means of the East-West fantasy.

The ego as base of consciousness has always been an anachronistic part of analytical psychology.[23] It is a historical truth that our Western tradition has identified ego with consciousness, an identification that found formulation especially in nineteenth-century psychology and psychiatry. But this part of Jung's thought does not sit well with either his notion of psychic reality or his therapeutic goals of psychic consciousness. What brings cure is an archetypal consciousness (mediated by the anima as we know from other passages), and this notion of consciousness is definitely not based upon ego:

> It is as though, at the climax of the illness, the destructive powers were converted into healing forces. This is brought about by the archetypes awaking to independent life and taking over the guidance of the psychic personality, thus supplanting the ego with its futile willing and striving ... the psyche has awakened to spontaneous activity ... something that is not his ego and is therefore beyond the reach of his personal will. He has regained access to the sources of psychic life, and this marks the beginning of the cure. *(CW 11, 534).*

The entire movement of Jung's work is away from ego and towards a widening of consciousness that strikes its roots in and reflects other psychic dominants — yet, even in late work, he uses "the word 'consciousness' here as being equivalent to 'ego'" *(CW 14,* p109n, cf. p371n). This equivalence necessitates a series of compensatory operations, e.g., sacrifice of intellect, development of fourth function, development of anima, introversion, shifting consciousness to the second-half of life and its focus on death, all of which is summed up as the "relativization of the ego" *(CW 14,* 504; cf. *CW 9, ii,* 11), for the sake of "psychic consciousness".[24] But precisely this latter is a consciousness structured by the anima archetype.[25]

The "relativization of the ego", that work and that goal of the fantasy of individuation, is made possible however from the beginning if we shift our conception of the base of consciousness from ego to anima archetype, from I to soul. Then one realizes from the very beginning (a priori and by definition) that the ego and all its developmental fantasies were never, even at the start, the fundament of consciousness, because consciousness refers to a process more to do with images than will, with reflection rather than control, with reflective insight into rather than active orientation towards 'objective reality'. We would no longer be equating consciousness with one phase of it, the developmental period of youth and its questing heroic mythology. Then, too, while educating consciousness even in youth, nourishing anima would be no less significant than strengthening ego.

Instead of regarding anima from the viewpoint of ego where she becomes a poisonous mood, an inspiring weakness, or a contrasexual compensation, we might regard ego from soul where ego becomes an instrument for day-to-day coping, nothing more grandiose than a trusty janitor of the planetary houses, a servant of soul-making. This view at least gives ego a therapeutic role rather than forcing ego into the anti-therapeutic position, a stubborn old king to be relativized. Then, too, we might relativize the myth of the Hero, or take it for what it has become today for our psyche — the myth of inflation — and not the secret key to the development of human consciousness. The Hero-myth tells the tale of conquest and destruction, the tale of psychology's "strong ego", its fire and sword, as well as the career of its civilization, but it tells little of the culture of its consciousness. Strange that we could still, in a psychology as subtle as Jung's, believe that this King-Hero and his ego is the equivalent of consciousness. Images of this psychological equivalence are projected from television screens straight and live from the heroic-ego's great contemporary epic in Vietnam. Is this consciousness?

Basing consciousness upon soul accords with the Neoplatonic tradition — which we still find in Blake — where what today is called ego-consciousness would be the consciousness of the Platonic cave, a consciousness buried in the least aware perspectives. These habits and continuities and daily organizations of personality certainly cannot encompass the definition of consciousness, a mystery that still baffles every area of research. To put it together with ego limits consciousness to the perspectives of the cave which today we would call the literalistic, personalistic, practicalistic, naturalistic, and humanistic fallacies. From the traditional psychology (of Neoplatonism) ego-consciousness does not deserve the name of consciousness at all.

Consciousness arising from soul derives from images and could be called imaginal. According to Jung, the *sine qua non* of any consciousness whatsoever is the "psychic image" *(CW 11, 769).* "Every psychic process is an image and an 'imagining', otherwise no consciousness could exist..." *(idem,* 889). On the one hand an image is the inward reflection of an external object. On the other hand, and this is the way Jung prefers to use the word, images are the very stuff of psychic reality. Image is "a concept derived from poetic usage, namely, a figure of fancy or *fantasy-image*" *(CW 6, 743).* They are "inner", "archaic", primordial; their ultimate source is in the archetypes and their expression is presented most characteristically in the formulation of myth. Consciousness arising from anima would therefore look to myth, as it manifests in the mythologems of dreams and fantasies and the pattern of lives; whereas ego-consciousness takes its orientations from the literalisms of its perspectives, i. e., that fantasy it defines as "reality".

Because fantasy-images provide the basis of consciousness, we turn to them for basic understanding. "Becoming conscious" would now mean becoming aware of fantasies and the recognition of them *everywhere* and not merely in a 'fantasy world' separate from 'reality'. Especially, we would want to recognize them as they play through that "mirror in which the unconscious sees its own face", the ego *(CW 14, 129)*, its thought structures and practical notions of reality. Fantasy-images now become the instrumental mode of perceiving and insighting. By means of them we realize better what Jung so often insisted upon: the psyche is the subject of our perceptions, the perceiver through fantasy, rather than the object of our perceptions. Rather than analyzing fantasies, we analyze by means of them; and translating reality into fantasy-images would better define becoming conscious than would the former notion given by ego of translating fantasy into realities. "The psyche creates reality every day. The only expression I can use for this activity is *fantasy*" *(CW 6, 78)*.

In particular, the fantasies arising from and giving insight into attachments would refer to anima consciousness. Because anima appears in our affinities, as the *fascinosum* of our attractions and obsessions, where we feel most personal, here this consciousness best mythologizes. It is a consciousness *bound to life*, both at the level of the vital, vegetative soul as it used to be called (the psychosomatic symptom as it is now called), and at the level of involvements of every kind, from petty passions, gossip, to the dilemmas of philosophy. Although consciousness based on anima is inseparable from life, nature, the feminine, as well as from fate and death, it does not follow that this consciousness is naturalistic, or fatalistic, other-worldly and morose, or particularly feminine. It means merely in these realms it turns; these are the metaphors to which it is attached.

Attachment now becomes a more significant term in anima consciousness than do those more guilt-making, and thus ego-referent, terms like commitment, relatedness, and responsibility. In fact, the relativization of the ego means placing in abeyance such metaphors as:

choice and light, problem-solving and reality testing, strengthening, developing, controlling, progressing. In their place, as more adequate descriptions of consciousness and its activities, we would use metaphors long familiar to the alchemy of analytical practice: fantasy, image, reflection, insight, and also, mirroring, holding, cooking, digesting, echoing, gossiping, deepening.

(To be concluded in *Spring 1974.*)

1   A short list of that literature is given in my *The Myth of Analysis (MA)*, Evanston: Northwestern Univ. Press, 1972, p. 53n. To it I would add: E. Bertine, "The Story of an Anima Projection" in her *Human Relationships*, N. Y.: Longmans Green, 1958; M.-L. von Franz, *The Problem of the Feminine in Fairy Tales*, N. Y./Zürich: Spring Publ., 1972 and her chapter in *Man and his Symbols* (ed. C. G. Jung), London: Aldus, 1964, pp. 177—88. (Even with these additions my list is by no means complete.)
2   C. G. Jung, *Analytical Psychology: its Theory and Practice* (The Tavistock Lectures), London: Routledge and Kegan Paul, 1968; C. G. Jung, *Briefe I* (1906—1945), *II* (1946—1955), (A. Jaffé ed., with G. Adler), Olten und Freiburg im Breisgau: Walter-Verlag, 1972. In these works I refer to page numbers, but in the *Collected Works* of C. G. Jung, Princeton: Princeton University Press — Bollingen Series, I refer to paragraph numbers.
3   For a succinct study of kinds of oppositional pairs and some of the confusions arising when the kinds are not kept distinct, see C. K. Ogden, *Opposition* (1932), Bloomington: University Indiana Press, 1967.
4   *MA*, "Toward an Imaginal Ego", pp. 183—90.
5   I base my analysis of the ancient meanings of *anima* and *psyché* upon R. B. Onians, *The Origins of European thought About the Body, the Mind, the Soul, the World, Time, and Fate*, Cambridge: University Press, 1954[2], Chapters: "The *Psyché*" and "*Anima* and *Animus*"; and from F. E. Peters, *Greek Philosophical Terms*, New York: New York Univ. Press, 1967, sect. "*psyché*".
6   Because of the soul's motility — a prime trait that sometimes even defined soul — some Greek philosophy did associate psyche with fire (Atomists), and Aristotle considered *orexis* (appetite, desire) the ultimate cause of the soul's motion.
7   J. J. Bachofen, *Myth, Religion, and Mother Right: Selected Writings*, Princeton: Princeton University Press — Bollingen Series, 1967, pp. 93ff. W. H. Roscher, *Lexikon d. Griech. u. Röm. Mythologie* Vol. III, i ("Pan", p. 1392f, and "Nymphen", pp. 500ff), Hildesheim: Olms, 1965. E. Jung, "The Anima as an Elemental Being", in her *Animus and Anima*, New York/Zürich: Spring Publ., 1957/72. Cf. T. Wolff's amplification of the hetaera in connection with the anima: "Strukturformen der weiblichen Psyche", in her *Studien zu C. G. Jung's Psychologie*, Zürich: Rhein, 1959, pp. 275—76.   8   *MA*, pp. 61ff.

9   Anima "immediately surrounds herself with a peculiar historical feeling" *(CW 10,* 85). There is a sense of history evoked especially by the anima archetype *(CW 7,* 303, 299; cf. *CW 12,* 112); "She likes to appear in historic dress" *(CW 9, i,* 60), and she "has a peculiar relationship with *time" (CW 9, i,* 356). Her historical associations go down to the archaic, even phylogenetic, past *(CW 9, i,* 518). Although animus may come through the father and be represented by a senex court of fathers and thus show equally strong conservatism, and even in "deepest essence" be "just as historically-minded as the anima" *(CW 10,* 89), nonetheless Jung makes one contrast between anima and animus in terms of a "mystical sense of history". Where anima reaches backward, animus is "more concerned with present and future"*(idem.,* 86). This distinction could be practically extrapolated: Anima draws us into history, so that the struggle with history — of ourselves as cases, and of our ancestors and our culture — is a way of soul-making. The occupation with history, and the historical perspective, reflects anima. Occupation with the present in the political scene, social reform, comment on trends, and all futurology are animus — and this whether in men or women. Anima and animus need each other; for animus can make the past now relevant for the present and future, while anima gives depth and culture to current opinion and predictions. Without each other we are either lost in archeological digs of academic anima refinement or riding the wave of the future, following animus into space-age science-fiction and pollution/population doom. (Cf. C. G. Jung/A. Jaffé, *Memories, Dreams, Reflections,* New York: Pantheon, 1963, p. 286, for Jung's experience and formulation of the historical anima personified in the Galla Placidia incident in Ravenna.)

10 G. Bachelard, *The Poetics of Reverie* (Chap. II on Animus and Anima), Boston: Beacon Press, 1971.

11 For a brief statement by Corbin on soul and imagination, see H. Corbin, *Mundus Imaginalis, Spring 1972,* New York/Zürich: Spring Publ., 1972, pp. 6—7.

12 M. Ficino, *Theologia platonica, XII,* in C. Trinkaus, *In Our Image and Likeness,* Chicago: University Press, 1970, vol. 2, pp. 476—78 and notes.

13 Onians, *Origins,* pp. 168—73 with notes.

14 Porphyry, "Concerning the Cave of Nymphs", in *Thomas Taylor the Platonist: Selected Writings* (ed. G. H. Mills and K. Raine) Princeton: University Press — Bollingen Series, 1969, p. 304. The discourse, too long to quote, is upon nymphs and naiads and the Neoplatonic meaning of the moist element.

15 Bachelard, *Poetics,* p. 66: "... *anima* becomes deeper and reigns in descending toward the cave of being. By descending, ever descending, the ontology of the qualities of the *anima* is discovered."   16   Onians, *Origins,* p. 170n.

17 For a fuller discussion, see my "The Feeling Function", Part Two of *Lectures on Jung's Typology* (with M.-L. von Franz), New York/Zürich: Spring Publ., 1971, especially, "Feeling and the Anima", pp. 121—29.

18 R. Grinnell, "Reflections on the Archetype of Consciousness", *Spring 1970,* pp. 15—39.

19 E. Neumann, *The Origins and History of Consciousness,* New York: Pantheon — Bollingen Series, 1954, p. 42.

20 W. F. Otto, *Die Musen,* Darmstadt, 1945.   21   *MA,* pp. 49—60.

22 J. Hillman, "An Essay on Pan" in *Pan and the Nightmare* (with W. H. Roscher), New York/Zürich: Spring Publ., 1972, pp. xliv-lvi.

23 I have discussed some of the historical background to the ego notion and its anachronistic retention in analytical psychology in *MA,* pp. 148—54, 183ff, 279, 290.

24 J. Layard, "On Psychic Consciousness" *(Eranos Jahrbuch* 1959, Zürich: Rhein), reprinted in his *The Virgin Archetype,* New York/Zürich: Spring Publ., 1972.

25 Here I depart from Onians' *(Origins, p.* 169) analysis of *anima* in Roman contexts and follow Jung and Bachelard. Onians says: "*anima* has nothing to do with consciousness". Much of what we commonly mean by consciousness today

belongs to *animus:* "Consciousness with all the variations of emotion and thought is a matter of *animus.* To contemplate some action is 'to have it in one's animus'; to turn one's attention to something... is 'to turn the *animus* towards it'... to feel faint, to be on the way to losing consciousness, was... 'it goes ill with one's *animus*'". "*Anima* was generic" and thus a far vaguer term, to do with airs of all sorts, located in the head. But following Jung, every archetype by forming a pattern of behaviour and a cluster of imagery, informs consciousness and has a kind of consciousness. If consciousness is defined as it is today, and as Onians regards it, that is, mainly as attention and self-referent experience, it is more an ego-consciousness, and as we suggested above is more associated with animus than anima. Onians' statement in regard to Rome, "*Anima* has nothing to do with consciousness", is applicable to today's term anima, only if we modify his statement to mean: Anima has nothing to do with a certain style of consciousness, e.g., ego-consciousness. Likewise, Bachelard *(Poetics,* p. 64), gives anima the consciousness of images, reverie, and depths (and much more), and assigns to animus "projects and worries", or what we usually call (ego-) 'consciousness'. "Animus is a bourgeois with regular habits" (p. 67) again refers to the continuity of the ego and its adaptation to 'reality'.

THE INCEST WOUND

ROBERT M. STEIN
(Beverly Hills)

The social forms which enable parent, child, and siblings to experience instinctual sexuality without guilt, i. e., fear of violating the incest taboo, have deteriorated. This has resulted in destruction of the intimate kinship connection between mother and son, father and daughter, brother and sister, individual and community. With this gradual deterioration the awareness of the fundamental importance of the incest taboo for psychic development has been lost. Consequently, *the incest taboo instead of being dealt with consciously has fallen into the unconscious and functions autonomously*. This means that the necessity for taking precautions against incest or the danger of violating the incest taboo is no longer a conscious problem. When the sexual instinct threatens to break through the incest barrier, sexuality is experienced as something dangerous and sinful. In this way the moral conflict which rightfully belongs to the mystery of incest becomes focused on instinctual sexuality. Instead of fearing incest, we fear sexuality and our instincts in general.

The elaborate precautions taken by 'primitives' to prevent a violation of the incest taboo suggest that the intensity of the incest desire is too strong to be left to individual responsibility. Much of the structure of primitive societies is in fact related to the incest taboo. In contrast to this, our modern Western civilization lacks viable rituals and social forms for regulating the incest libido. Thus the responsibility

---

This article forms a chapter of *Incest and Human Love — The Betrayal of the Soul in Psychotherapy* to be published by The Third Press, 444 Central Park West, New York City, during the Winter 1973–74. Other papers by Dr. Stein have appeared in *Spring 1970* and *Spring 1971*.

for preventing incest, for dealing with the mystery of incest, has come to rest largely on the individual.

Although there are indications that the incest taboo has become as strong a force in the human psyche as is the incest desire, it takes a high degree of ego consciousness for the *individual* to withstand the fatal touch of incest without being split by the heat of the powerful emotions released. The growing child has, therefore, always been protected from too much exposure to the fascinating temptation of incest. But now little is left of these protective and integrating rituals and the child is thrown into a moral conflict involving the deepest mysteries of life, which he is forced to solve by himself. This results in a repression of sexuality most of the time; but it is not uncommon that open sexual provocation by the adult occurs and that the child then cannot repress the sexuality. In these cases the spiritual feelings of warmth and tenderness are repressed: for example, a woman with a negative father complex could remember no instances where she felt love or closeness to the father. Her only pleasant memories of him were primarily related to sexuality; i. e., actual sexual contact as well as fantasies. In another instance, a man remembered, without the slightest guilt, having had strong sexual desires and fantasies toward his mother; he too could remember no close or warm moments with her. These examples illustrate *that the incest wound causes a split between eros and sexuality*. They also call attention to the fact that it is not the repression of sexuality which is crucial, but the problem of incest.

As we have seen, violation of the incest prohibition is the most horrendous crime for a 'primitive'. Even unsanctioned homicide does not evoke as much horror, nor are the penalties necessarily as severe and final. Since the taboo is so essential for the humanization and cultural development of man, it is understandable that its violation should evoke such guilt and fear. Now a 'primitive' would have to be out of his mind, be totally overwhelmed by an uncontrollable desire, in order to risk the consequences of committing incest. As long as he had a thread of rational control left, he would resist his desire. This is essentially what a child in our culture must do: he must control with repression any spontaneous incestuous sexual impulses he has. Actually the 'primitive' is far better off because he is protected from too much stimulation of his incestuous tendencies by social forms. And by the time he reaches puberty his sexuality has transformed sufficiently so that he need not fear violating the incest taboo if he reacts spontaneously and instinctually. In other words, at least insofar as his incestuous tendencies are concerned, the 'primitive' does not have to fear losing rational control.

For a child in our Western culture quite the opposite is true when he reaches puberty. As long as he was sexually immature he generally had little difficulty controlling and repressing forbidden sexual urges. But with puberty all the repressed sexual urges and fantasies return in full force. This is when he experiences the first real horror about his incestuous desires. He attempts to deal with this guilt and fear exercising constant control over what enters his consciousness. Depending on the severity of his incest wound, he may be forced to repress all sexual imagery in order to be sure none of the guilt-provoking fantasies invade his psyche. Fortunately most children do not have to use such extreme measures, but when they do it results in almost a total cut-off from the sexual instinct. Such children have a tendency to panic at the slightest sign of losing rational control.

The more typical Western pattern is that only a sexuality which is non-incestuous is allowed to enter consciousness. But this means that only those fantasies can enter which are purely sensual and lacking any strong feelings of love and spiritual intimacy. This internal split between love and sex, the spiritual and animal portions of the soul, is a direct consequence of the incest wound. When the tension between the incest desire and prohibition is obliterated, fragmentation results and the essential internal union of the masculine and feminine opposites is not possible.

Most people have great difficulty connecting emotionally to the above phenomenon although they may appreciate its logic. It rings a bell only for those who were unsuccessful or only partially successful in repressing their incestuous sexuality. It is not really essential that one dig up repressed incestuous fantasies and experiences, as long as one becomes aware of how the mind/body and love/sex splits manifest themselves in everyday life.

I believe the severity of the wound can be measured by the degree of fear one has about losing rational control, whether or not it is directly related to sexuality. Those who experience the pain of frequent rejection in relationships are probably also severely afflicted by the incest wound. So too are those who are frequently thrown into states of confusion, loss of identity, and emotional paralysis in their intimate relationships. Of course the most obvious manifestation of the wound occurs when sexuality becomes obstructed except in relationship to fantasies or an actual person toward whom one has neither love nor respect. Why is there such horror of losing rational control, of allowing irrational and spontaneous emotions or desires to express themselves without ego censor? Is it that one fears going amok and committing horrible crimes? Most people have little more to fear than making fools of themselves or, at worst, committing some offensive but forgivable aggressive act. Then why such overwhelming fear of being totally wiped out, should one let go of the reins on the instincts? Surely this has more to to with fantasy, with inner reality, than with the actual dangers confronting one from outer reality. What then is going on inside when one is caught in this ego trap?

I think of a shocking dream I had when I first became aware of the depth of my own incest wound: It was about 11 P.M., and I had to go to my office for something. As I opened the door I suddenly became frightened, sensing some ominous presence in the room. I switched on the light, but saw no one. Suddenly I heard a noise like a whimper coming from behind me. I turned to discover a small, ragged, twelve-year-old boy crouching under my desk. I awakened terrified. Later, using the technique of active imagination which Jung suggests, I re-entered the dream in fantasy. And this is what happened: I pulled the frightened boy out from under my desk and demanded to know what he was doing there. At first he refused to answer, but finally he told me he hides under my desk all the time when I see patients. Then turning to me with a lustful grin he said, "I really dig all those sexy stories your patients tell you". I became furious, calling him a sex maniac, and threatened to turn him over to the police. Then he broke down and my heart went to him. I took him into my arms. Between sobs he told me how I had abandoned him when I was twelve because of my guilt about my own sexuality and that I have forced him to go underground out of fear of my own lust. There was more to the fantasy, but this is the heart of it. Obviously this little boy was that animal-sensual part of myself which I had repressed. In reality, at about the age of twelve I began to have strong sexual desires toward my sisters. I remember feeling terribly guilty and perverse about these feelings and doing everything in my power to block all such thoughts out of my mind. I suspect I must have felt the same terrible dread of incest which a 'primitive' feels. One can imagine how fearful I must have been, at the time of this dream, of losing rational control if all my repressed incestuous sexuality lurked just under the protective front of the physician's desk.

A young woman dreamt of having an hour with her analyst when suddenly the door began to open. She was shocked and furious when she saw who it was, and she quickly rushed to the door and pushed the young teenage girl out of the room. Who was it? Only a girl she had known in high school who was cheap and had the bad reputation of being an easy lay. The dream is obvious: she feared letting her own immoral, lustful, sensual side enter into the analytical relationship. Since the analyst invariably constellates a parental archetype, one may assume the incestuous origins of her fear. In point of fact, until this dream revealed the nature of her fear she had been extremely defensive and resistant to the analytical process.

Such examples of the soul-splitting effects of repressed incestuous sexuality are plentiful and relatively easy to grasp once they have been revealed. However, there are many other expressions of the incest complex which are not so obvious. For example, sexual desire may not become fully aroused except in a triangular situation. And as soon as the triangle is broken, the desire diminishes. This may seem contradictory because one would expect that the incest fear would inhibit sexuality in a triangular situation. We shall have to go deeper into the nature of the wound in order to understand this paradox.

As we have seen, when excessively provoked a child may be unable to repress his sexuality so he is forced to repress his feelings of love and kinship. We must not forget that the purpose of the incest taboo is to prevent a child from having sexual union in those relationships where he feels the greatest spiritual intimacy. Thus incest guilt can be avoided as long as one is unaware of experiencing one of these opposites, love or sex. The repressed opposite will, however, continually threaten to enter consciousness because of the soul's fundamental need for union. In other words the longing for incestuous union, even though repressed, is as powerful as is our horror of violating the taboo. In fact, the more we repress it the more power it gains over us so that we are, for example, continually fascinated and falling into incestuous types of involvements. As long as we remain unconscious of the repressed other half, we do not experience the guilt and painful conflict. Innocently we plunge from one relationship to another, emerging each time fragmented and disillusioned.

I think of a severe, but typical, example of a person who was unable to allow the repressed opposite to enter consciousness. This woman was continually fascinated by men who had authority, position, superior intellect or special talents. She felt always inadequate and incapable of experiencing sexual passion with them. In the few instances in which she did attempt involvement, she felt her soul and body raped and she ended up wounded and furious. This woman had had great love and respect for her father until puberty when he had made several sexual advances toward her. In analysis she at first talked only of her good feelings toward him because she had blocked out the sexual episodes. When they were finally brought back into consciousness, all the fury returned which she had experienced at the age of thirteen. She felt that he was an impotent, dirty old man, who had taken advantage of her trusting youthful innocence. From some of the details which she related of her relationship to her father, it was obvious she was not all that innocent. But she was unable emotionally to accept her own sexual involvement with him. Consequently the pattern continued to repeat itself in relationship to men whom she admired. Her feeling of inadequacy was due to the fact that she was unable to bring her instinctive self into these relationships — how could she if she feared and rejected her sexuality?

But there was another side to this. She also found herself compulsively fascinated by irresponsible, intellectually inferior, psychopathic men. With them her sexual passion was released and to that extent the relationships were much more gratifying. But unable to allow herself to love such a man, she experienced great pain because of the lack of spiritual communion. In addition, she tended to fall into a sexual bondage with them which paralyzed her free will and undermined her self respect. Would she have been able to allow herself to experience consciously her love and kinship feeling toward these men, she would have become free instead of imprisoned and fragmented.

Another very common manifestation of the incest wound is the experience of loving someone sexually and spiritually in fantasy but being cut off or unable to express such feelings in actuality. This is often owing to the fear of consciously embracing the phallic or aggressive aspects of the sexual instinct. The incestuous guilt associated with aggressive sexuality prevents these persons from initiating the flow of eros, although they may be very responsive to the initiating action of others. In this way they can remain unconscious of their own aggressive impulses, and therefore innocent.

Still another important but more complex manifestation of the wound can be illustrated as follows: A woman, caught in a psychological marriage to her father, had repressed her unfulfilled incestuous longings to actually marry him. She hated her father and felt betrayed by him, but she did not know why. Her relationships with men were generally short-lived, ending abruptly and painfully. She was always threatened by spiritual intimacy with a man, but open to sexual intimacy. Typically, as soon as she would become sexually involved she was inundated with all her repressed incestuous longings, except that her current lover took the place of father. In her fantasies, her lover-father would declare his undying love, sweep her off her feet, carry her to the church where they would be married to live happily ever after. These romantic fantasies were so powerful that they became a *fait accompli*. Invariably the actual man had no such feelings, and she was rudely shaken out of her dreams, but always with the conviction that she had been deeply wounded and deceived by the man. It had all been so real for her that she never knew if she had imagined it or if the man had really said such things and led her on. Whenever this happened she was left paralyzed, confused, and humiliated. Essentially the effect of the incest wound on this woman was to make it extremely difficult for her to differentiate inner and outer reality in her relationships. To a lesser or greater extent, this difficulty is an inevitable effect of the wound.

As long as the longing for incestuous union remains unconscious it will be activated in every relationship which offers the possibility of soul connection. This has the effect of obstructing the spontaneous flow of love because the incest archetype always demands eternal commitment in a sacred marriage. Simply put, if everytime love moves me toward union with another I feel compelled to make a permanent commitment, will this not make me cautious and fearful of loving? One must be free to love or not love, to feel and express love in the quick of the moment whether or not it lasts forever. The incest wound interferes with this freedom because of the soul's longing for the sacred eternal union with its mate. This needs to be experienced as an inner reality and not an outer demand whenever one feels love for another.

Apart from love and sex, the incest wound tends to interfere with the experience and spontaneous expression of all the aggressive instincts. In part this is owing to the same fear of losing rational control, but it is also a direct consequence of the guilt-evoking incestuous triangle. A son will fear standing up to his father, revealing his own aggressive potency, because of his guilt about his unconscious incestuous marriage to mother. The same applies for a woman in relationship to mother. The more severe the wound, the more the child experiences the inner parent as rejecting his or her nature. This may ultimately lead to an obsessive need to gain approval and acceptance from others.

The primary function of the incest prohibition is to bring the untamed instincts into the service of love and kinship through a process which stimulates the formation of images of male-female union. This is not the same as the *repression* of instincts, which seems so necessary in our modern civilization. *When the repression of instincts becomes necessary in a culture, it is a sign that something has gone wrong with the societal institutions for the regulation of incest.*

Summary

1) The incest taboo serves to effect a sanctification of Mother and Father and their union. Psychologically, we understand incest, to quote Jung, as *"the supreme union of opposites expressed as a combination of things which are related but of unlike nature"* (CW 14, para 664).

2) An adequate conscious regulation of incest is essential for the formation or crystallization of the archetypal image of the union of opposites best expressed by such symbols as the Royal Marriage or *Hierosgamos* or the Divine Brother-Sister pair. As Jung says, "The psychopathological problem of incest is the aberrant natural form of the union of the opposites, a union which has either never been made *conscious* at all as a psychic task or, if it was conscious, has once more disappeared from view" (ibid., para 108). This, in essence, is what I meant on a cultural level when I said that the incest taboo instead of being dealt with consciously has fallen into the unconscious and functions autonomously. In this way, the moral conflict which rightfully

belongs to the mystery of incest becomes focused on instictual sexuality.
3) The longing for incest and the incest taboo are essential for the development of eros. The taboo enables the child gradually to bring his untamed instinctual urges and energies into the service of kinship and eros.

4) In contrast to the dominant views held from the time of Heraclitus to the present, that man is the "Reasoner" as Descartes felt, or as St. Thomas Aquinas put it, "the behavior of man depends on reason, whereas all animals are governed by instinct", we are asserting that it is eros as psychic relatedness, not reason, that is the crucial differentiating factor between man and animal.

THE PIT AND THE BRILLIANCE

A Study of the 29th and 30th Hexagrams in the *I Ching*

RUDOLF RITSEMA
(Ascona)

Continuing the studies on the *I Ching* published in previous volumes of *Spring*, this article presents two interrelated hexagrams, No. 29, THE PIT, and No. 30, THE BRILLIANCE.* The examples discussed in the previous articles showed the reasons for this new approach to the *I Ching*. So the present study presupposes acquaintance with the procedures outlined in the opening section of last year's article about the 18th hexagram, THE CORRUPTED.

Aiming to retain as much as possible of the rich complexity and imaginal material in the texts of the *I Ching*, this study attempts to evoke the image-concepts of the Chinese terms. Conceptual language alone is inadequate for rendering them because the Chinese terms are at once both so wide and so precise. I have given preference to the primal, often concrete, meaning as the central image to which all the more abstract, secondary, and figurative meanings relate. This primal meaning is rendered systematically by one and the same English word, so that each English word in my translations of the texts represents one particular Chinese character, and this same word is used throughout in a one-to-one systematic equivalence between English and Chinese. This strict method allows the reader to discover exactly where the same Chinese ideogram occurs throughout the *I Ching* texts.

Each of these English primal terms has been filled out in my explanatory notes by a listing of all the meanings associated in the

---

* "Notes for Differentiating some Terms in the *I Ching*" in *Spring 1970*, pp. 111–25, and in *Spring 1971*, pp. 141–52; "The Corrupted, A Study of the 18th Hexagram in the *I Ching*" in *Spring 1972*, pp. 90–109.

Chinese to these primal terms. The English primal terms should therefore be read, not as semantic equivalents, but as signs standing for *a whole of meanings,* a cluster associated around a common central image. Further associations extending beyond what is given are legitimate only where they are related to the central image.

The sometimes awkward constructions in my translations of the texts reflect the multivalent relations within the Imaginal. Very often the Chinese has no syntactic particle, no character specifying the kind of connection between the parts of a sentence. To introduce English pronouns, prepositions, or other connectives would restrict the texts to an arbitrary interpretation imposed by the translator. So I have tried to maintain the unspecific yet precise openness of the original by using a colon (:) to indicate the unspecified relation between the parts of a sentence. The reader may therewith more easily recognize those places where the text allows for a variety of connections.

Hexagram No. 29, K'AN, THE PIT

The name of this hexagram is the same as the name of the two trigrams that compose it. The Chinese character K'AN consists of the graphs for earth and for a pit. K'AN embraces: a pit, a hole in the earth, a cavity, a hollow, the pit as a snare and the pit as a grave; a dangerous place, a precipice or pitfall; to dig a pit, to fall into a snare; and, by extension, a critical time in life leading to the idea of weighing, judging, being tested. The danger resides in the steep sides and the risk of being caught. It is a closed cavity, not a bottomless hole or an abyss.

The image of the trigram K'AN, Stream, streaming water, a flow, applies to the hexagram. Together, pit and stream result in falling, comprising the meanings of falling down, to sink, to drop into, to throw into; and to involve.

The attribute of K'AN both as trigram and hexagram is falling. The image of the stream falling into the pit determines the association of K'AN with HS'IEN, venture, venturing without reserve as the running water that flows of necessity in precipices, abysses, gorges, ravines. (See *Spring 1970,* pp. 112ff.) That in the course of the stream there is a pit, and the inevitable fall into it, provides the image of venture in the *I Ching*. The situation of THE PIT necessarily implies a falling, a wholehearted venturing, till the stream comes up to the brim of the pit and resumes its flow. Thus K'AN is the pit, the stream, and the falling of the streaming water into the pit.

The nuclear trigrams, ☶, KEN, Mountain, above (lines 3,4,5), and ☳, CHEN, Thunder, below (lines 2,3,4), form together the latent hexagram No. 27, YI, THE JAWS, concerned with nourishment. The potential hidden within the situation of falling and venture of THE PIT is the proper control of one's nourishment, both in quality and in quantity.

Contrasted Definitions:

THE BRILLIANCE above, and nevertheless THE PIT below.

The text gives a definition of THE PIT in relation to hexagram No. 30, LI, THE BRILLIANCE. The light of THE BRILLIANCE is above and outside and it apparently prevails; yet it constellates the situation of THE PIT and the falling of the stream into it. The reality of THE PIT is ever present, even though outer brightness may seem to deny it.

The Sequence:

Things do not allow completion of excess.
Hence through this, receiving THE PIT.
THE PIT connotes falling.

The Sequence always connects a hexagram to the immediately preceding one, in this case to the 28th hexagram, TA KUO, THE EXCESS OF THE GREAT. The sentence, "Things do not allow completion of . . .", is a standard formula that occurs very often in the texts of The Sequence. WU, *things,* embraces: matter, substance, essence, the nature of things, anything between heaven and earth, a creature, a being. The meaning of *completion* as the completion of a span or cycle of time (and as such differing from accomplishment as a work done) is discussed in *Spring 1971,* pp. 144 and 147ff. The Sequence tells us that the situation is constellated because the nature of things does not allow one of the main characteristics of the preceding hexagram to be carried through to completion of a time-cycle. Here The Sequence emphasizes the intrinsic impossibility of completing KUO, *excess*, the main feature of the preceding hexagram No. 28, TA KUO, THE EXCESS OF THE GREAT.

Hence through this, receiving (discussed in *Spring 1972*, p. 95) lays stress upon the causal connection: because of the impossibility expressed in the preceding sentence, the oracle presents THE PIT. A situation of excess is thus at the root of receiving THE PIT with its emphasis upon falling. The verb *to connote*, to signify in addition, points out that falling is a meaning or attribute implied in the name of the hexagram THE PIT.*

The Image:
Streams reiterated reach the repeated pit.
The chün-tzu, through the principle of TE, moves.
Repeating: business of teaching.

Stream is the image of the trigram K'AN, the streaming water, the flow. Since this hexagram consists of twice the trigram K'AN, its image, Stream, *reiterates:* the flow of the streaming water arrives more than once. The Chinese word rendered by *reach* means to come to or arrive at the end or summit, as in place, time, or desire. The end at which these reiterated streams arrive is not just one pit, but it is the repeated pit, since that is the name of the trigrams. The Chinese word HSI, *repeat,* contains the image of the repeated movement of (young) birds' wings when practising flight. It includes: to repeat the same act, to practise, and thus, becoming skilled, used to, able to, familiarized with. To repeat occurs six times in this hexagram, i.e., in The Image (twice), The Head, the Commentary on The Head, and in the bottom line *a* and *b*. Although there are eight hexagrams each of which consists of two identical trigrams, only here this combination is called repetition. This notion of repeating as teaching and being taught through practising is very much related to the 29th hexagram, K'AN. The word HSI occurs only at two other places in the *I Ching*. In The Image of hexagram No. 58, TUI, we read in the Wilhelm-Baynes translation: "Thus the superior man joins with his friends for discussion and

---

* In the Sequence of the 18th hexagram *(Spring 1972,* p. 94) I used "means," but "connotes" seems more appropriate to translate the idea of an additional meaning implied in the name of the hexagram.

practice"; and in the second line of hexagram No. 2, KUN, the Wilhelm-Baynes translation renders it by "purpose" (in the *a* and *b* texts and in the Commentary on the Words of the Text at the second line).

The term *chün-tzu* (see below p. 159) denotes a person for whom the oracle makes sense owing to his inner orientation. The repetition of the pit in this hexagram is a matter of teaching. Falling into the pit is the goal reached by the stream. Repeating and practising this falling is a *business* (see *Spring 1972*, p. 95), a matter, of teaching and being taught. The Chinese character HSING, *to move*, shows the graphs for a step with the left foot and for a step with the right foot. It is both transitive and intransitive as the most general and least specific word for motion, movement, to move, comprising the meanings of: to step, to walk; to act, to do. It can be distinguished from the many different and specific notions of movement such as to go, to come (see *Spring 1972*, pp. 101–02), to attain *(ibid.,* p. 105), to reach (see above), etc. TE as the ability to conform one's conduct with TAO has been explained in some detail in *Spring 1972,* p. 96. The word CH'ANG, *principle,* covers the meanings of: a rule, a regular principle, constant, constancy, ordinary, usual, unchanging, to maintain as a law.

The situation is one of flowing water falling into repeated pits. The objective movement of the powerful, and even overpowering streams, and the falling into the pits is a teaching for the chün-tzu who here moves by letting himself be ruled by TE; i.e., he submits to the principle of TE. At many places the *I Ching* uses just the word TE, but here it is the rule or principle of TE, thus emphasizing that here TE rules or presides over every movement of the person concerned.

The Head:

Repeated Pit. Having conformity. Then, heart: Growth.
Movement has honor.

Here again, stress is upon the repeated pit and upon the exercise of falling into it. The interrelated notions of FU, *conformity,* and HSIN, *trustworthiness* (see below, Commentary on The Head), are quite important throughout the *I Ching* and may be distinguished even though the Wilhelm-Baynes translation uses at several places the same English words for both FU and HSIN: trust, faith, dependable, to be believed, etc. Conformity means that outer presentation conforms with inner nature, that form is true to being; appearance can be trusted as conforming with essence. Therefore it embraces the meanings: sincerely, truly, trust, belief, accordant, confidence; all these derive from the concrete sense of to hatch, to brood on eggs. The Chinese character FU, conformity, consists of the graphs for a bird's claws over the graph for a child, thus suggesting the brooding on the eggs from which offspring issue. The child is a true reproduction of its parents' model; it conforms with the standards of its species. Trustworthiness, however, means remaining true to oneself, unaltered by the vicissitudes of life. Its meaning includes: truthfulness, integrity, faith, to confide in, to accord with, to follow. The Chinese character HSIN, trustworthiness, consists of the graphs for a man and for words, suggesting a man of his word.

The verb *having* relates the conformity in a stringent, possessive way with the person concerned. The word *then*, in the sense of 'and so', connects conformity causally with heart and Growth. HENG, *Growth*, is the second of the four cyclical key-terms discussed in *Spring 1972*, pp. 97–99, and stands for the all-pervading extension of the generating principle. *Heart* denotes the physical heart, and the place where the affections of the mind are located. It embraces the meanings of: the center, the middle, the origin or source of the affections, the mind, desire, the moral nature. The juxtaposition of heart and Growth covers the meanings of: Growth in the heart, at the heart, of the heart, by the heart, etc. Here again, as in The Image, *movement* is advocated. We have discussed *honor*, honoring, as deserving the highest rank in *Spring 1972*, p. 108. *Has* stresses that movement and honor are not simply coupled, but that here honor belongs to movement.

The situation presents the objective movement of the stream stopped by its falling repeatedly into a pit. This situation calls for one's moving either oneself or something. Where The Image tells us that TE, ruling as a law, brings about movement, The Head spells out what links the objective situation of the repeated pit and the high importance of one's moving. One's actions conforming strictly with one's inner being is (or will be, or should be) what belongs to one. Thus the primal originating power (YÜAN, Spring) extends and carries through to full Growth the heart (or, in the heart, at the heart, by the heart, or mind).

Commentary on The Head:

Repeated pit. Venture doubled.
Stream flows and nevertheless no overflowing.
To venture movement and nevertheless not losing trustworthiness.
"Then, heart: Growth", thereupon through the solid: center.
"Movement has honor", to go has accomplishment.
Heavens' venture: ascent not possible.
Earth's venture: mountains, rivers, hills, mounds.
King and princes, through instituting venture, guard their states.
The Great even uses the season of venture!

The pit is in a parallel relation with venture. The attribute of the trigram K'AN, The Pit, has two aspects for which the *I Ching* uses two different words: the objective aspect (what is happening to the stream) is falling; the subjective aspect (man's attitude when the stream is halted by falling into the pit) is venturing. The objective aspect cannot be avoided or diverted; it has to be gone through by venturing without reserve. *To double* means: to do over, again, to add. The repeating as a matter of teaching and being taught through practice or exercise implies that one has not only to venture (or is venturing) but must do this over again.

Stream is the image of K'AN, The Pit. Even when falling into the pit, it flows continuously, there is no *overflowing*, no excess. The water does not pass beyond the rim; the stream just resumes flowing when the pit is filled and thereby levelled. (About the connective *and nevertheless* see *Spring 1972*, p. 101.) The two sentences in each of which there is a contrast are parallels. First there is the continuously flowing stream contrasted with the pit that is not overflowing. Then, the following sentence applies these images to one's attitude and action. One ventures movement, (or will or should do so) as we have seen in The Image and The Head. As we mentioned already, HSING, *movement*, is the most general word for to move or motion as opposed to any form of standstill, stopping, resting. *Trustworthiness,* or, as we saw above, remaining true to oneself, corresponds to the image of not overflowing, of filling the pit without going to excess. One ventures movement and at the same time remains unaltered and faithful to oneself. These two sentences provide an explanation of "having conformity" in The Head.

THE PIT AND THE BRILLIANCE

The connection *thereupon* reinforces the causal connotation of "then", indicating that heart and Growth result from venturing movement without losing trustworthiness. *Solid* and *supple* stand for the contrary lines, unbroken and broken, in the hexagrams. Solid refers to the unyielding and strong.* The solid lines are in the center of the two trigrams, i.e., at the second and fifth lines of this hexagram. By means of the solid that results from not losing trustworthiness, centering comes about or is gained. CHUNG, *center*, or centering (discussed in *Spring 1972*, p. 105), means: the middle, the core of, inner, and that which neither bends to one side nor to the other; it points to the center within the person as well as within any situation. This center or the process of centering occurs at many places in the *I Ching* as the point from where man can face the inner and outer vicissitudes of life. So "heart: Growth" is explained as a constellation of the center by means of the solid, of one's unyielding strength.

At this point highest esteem is given to movement, according to The Head, and the Commentary adds *to go* as the specific process that results here from the movement. (WANG, to go or going, has been explained in detail in *Spring 1972*, pp. 101–02). One's action in going, or letting things go, consists in going along deliberately with the continuous flow of objective time and thereby letting things go so that they are passed by and become of the past. The full meaning of KUNG, *accomplishment* as an achievement or a work done, has been outlined in *Spring 1971*, p. 144, where it is defined in contradistinction with toil, maturity, completion, and end. The verb *has* shows that here accomplishment belongs to going.

The last four sentences no longer comment upon the phrasing of The Head. They are wholly concerned with the notion of *venture* since venturing is the main advice for the individual who is in the situation depicted by K'AN. We should recall that venture is: to be confronted with an objective danger which cannot be avoided but has to be gone through by taking risk without reserve. In accordance with this the text enumerates the dangers of the heavens and the earth: heavens' height is beyond any attempts of ascent, earth's surface is scattered with obstacles such as mountains, rivers, hills, and mounds.

---

* In *Spring 1972*, p. 100, in the Commentary on The Head of the 18th Hexagram, I had rendered it by "hard", but solid seems more adequate when paired with the contrasting supple to express the qualities of the unbroken and the broken lines.

It is as if the Commentary wanted to show that venture is inherent in even these most positive fundamentals.

The last two lines show how man avails himself of venture as an instrument in life. The rulers protect their countries by means of instituting venture. Here venture alludes to such a risky thing as armed forces. SHE, *instituting,* denotes: to establish, to arrange, to set up. The Chinese character SHE, to institute, consists of the graphs for words and for to impel, suggesting that an order is given to bring about something. Here we have the deliberate setting up of venture for a social aim.

The last sentence draws a general conclusion from this handling of venture. The *Great* — the faculty to conduct one's own life — will be discussed below, p. 151, and *to use,* to employ something as an instrument, has been explained in *Spring 1972,* p. 107. SHIH, *season,* is the notion of qualitative time. It is the right time, the appropriate moment, timing according to opportunity. Its meaning ranges from the four seasons of the year to any specific moment of time as being in season. The Chinese character SHIH, season, consists of the graphs for sun and for temple thus suggesting sacramental time-determination. The sentence "the Great even uses the season of . . ." occurs at the end of the Commentary on The Head in a number of hexagrams (In the Wilhelm-Baynes translation the phrase reads, "The effects of the time of . . . are truly great"). The word *even* stands for an interjection that draws attention to the statement as in admiration, praise, or surprise. We could here paraphrase this sentence: The Great as the faculty to conduct one's own life even uses for its instrument the season of venture!

The Lines

Six at the bottom line:

a) Repeated pit. Penetrating into the pit: recess. Inauspicious.
b) Repeated pit: penetrating the pit.
Losing TAO: inauspicious.

The Chinese word JU, *penetrating,* denotes entering or going into by one's own activity. The *recess* is a niche or hole at the bottom of the pit. This is a situation of going into the pit by one's own movement instead of falling into it. Man's usurpation of the objective movement (falling) constellates the recess, i.e., a hole beyond the pit. The relation between penetrating into the pit and recess is unspecified and hence multivalent. SHIH, *losing*, embraces the meanings: to omit, to neglect, to fail, without control. The Chinese character SHIH, losing, consists of the graphs for hand and for curved downward, suggesting the image of a hand letting something drop. Numerous renderings have been proposed for the Chinese word TAO, but none seems convincing because the image-concept is so very peculiar to Chinese thought. I shall therefore leave it untranslated. The Chinese character TAO consists of the graphs for walking, moving, and for head, thus suggesting that which presides as a head over all movement, i.e., the principle that is leading ahead. Thus it stands for the leading principle of the motion of the universe as it runs the heavens, the earth, mankind, and the individual. For the image and implications of the *inauspicious*, the ill-omen of the loss of freedom to dispose, the reader may turn to *Spring 1970*, p. 119.

The *b*-text describes the replacement of falling by penetrating as the loss or neglect of TAO. This can be read to mean both that the loss of TAO results in active penetration instead of falling, and that by penetrating one loses TAO.

Nine at the second line:
a) The pit has venture. Seeking attains the Small.
b) Seeking attains the Small. Center not yet issued forth.

The word CH'IU, *seeking*, denotes: to search for, to aim at, to wish for, very desirous of, quest. The reader will find the connotations of *attain*, in *Spring 1972*, p. 105. The *Small* and the *Great* occur in the hexagram-texts with a very specific meaning. The Great stands for the faculty to conduct one's own life and for the capacity to assume leadership within the vicissitudes of one's life. The Small, on the contrary, implies letting oneself be pushed and pulled by outer events and inner impulses (wishes, desires, and aversions). (See also the discussion of the Great's man in contradistinction with the chün-tzu, below, p. 159.) *Center*, as the core, the inner, occurs usually in connection with the second or the fifth line, since they are the central lines of the lower and upper trigrams. It refers to the center of the human person or of a matter under consideration. It is at equal distance from the extremes, right at the middle. The verb CH'U, *to issue forth*, means: coming out of, to proceed from, to spring from, outside. It is the contrary of JU, penetrating (see above, p. 150). The Chinese character CH'U, to issue forth, is traditionally presented as the image of the branches and leaves of plants coming out of the stem.

The particularly close association of venture with the pit constellates here a situation of action, though of a less pronounced kind than in the bottom line. Here we have seeking, but it attains and obtains the Small, the purely reactive to inner and outer influences. It is just the plain statement that seeking cannot at present pretend to anything more. None of the divinatory evaluations is appended to this statement. The *b*-text explains that the center has not yet emerged into the field of the visible and the realm of action. So the quest is at present doomed to obtain nothing but the Small. This is the central line of the lower or inner trigram, so the center has not yet come forth. At the central line of the upper and outer trigram (the fifth line) the *b*-text does speak of the center; by the time of that situation it has appeared.

Six at the third line:

a) The coming of the pit and of falling.
Venture, moreover leaning back.
Penetrating into the pit: recess. Not using.
b) The coming of the pit and of falling.
Completing: no accomplishment.

Here both meanings of K'AN, the pit and falling, *come*, i.e., move with the flow of time into the present. In this situation the objective movement predominates instead of the subjective action that occurs at the bottom and the second line. In accordance with the first statement we find that venture, the attribute of K'AN, is here paired with leaning back. The expression *leaning back* refers to: a pillow, a rest for the back, to recline. This attitude of keeping back from action, beyond the venturing intrinsic to K'AN, is in sharp contrast to penetrating at the bottom line and also to the less pronounced seeking at the second line. The text here is very specific in using the copula *moreover*, introducing leaning back as an addition without any restrictive or negative connotation. *Using* in its literal sense of to employ as an instrument, to make use of something, has been discussed in *Spring 1972*, p. 107. In this situation of equilibrium between venture and leaning back, the inauspicious penetrating into the pit (see bottom line) is not, has not been, and will not be used.

The subtle and very important difference between CHUNG, *completion*, and KUNG, *accomplishment*, has been explained in *Spring 1971*, pp. 144 and 147—51. In short, completion applies to a span of time, or time-cycle, that comes to an end; accomplishment denotes a work done, an achievement. So the *b*-text states that the time of falling into the pit has been or will be completed, but there is no piece of work done. The time of THE PIT is not a time for an achievement.

Six at the fourth line:

a) A wine-cup paired with a dish. Using earthenware.
The window of oneself letting in bonds.
Completing: no fault.
b) A wine-cup paired with a dish. Solid and supple bordering.

The mention of a cup and a plate as a twofold unity suggests a sacrificial situation. The sacrificial vessels for the liquid and the solid were of bronze and had their specific names. But here reference is to ordinary vessels for liquid and solid food. *Using* (see above at the third line) simple earthenware as tools for a sacrifice underlines the informal character of the situation. No formal, official and solemn sacrifice, not even a sacrifice on the level of one's family or clan, but a completely individual, intimate situation. The second sentence underlines this private, individual character of the relation to the extra-human powers or Gods. The *window* stands for the hole in the wall, the window opening. The Chinese word TZU, *oneself*, in addition to the meaning of self, oneself, himself, is also used as a preposition referring to the place where one (or something) comes from, the origin in place or time, the cause. This connotation of origin gives the clue for understanding TZU, i.e., oneself as related to the divine spark that is at the origin of every individual being. The *bonds* embrace the meanings: to bind, to cord up, to bind by contract, to give one's word, to restrain, to moderate, to spare, to economize. These bonds determine the kind of relation to the divine that is established here. It is a contracted obligation and thus it restricts. The verb *letting in* shows that the sacrifice is an opening of oneself to the obligations the divine sends in. Here the sacrifice is not an action of man establishing a relation, but turning to the undefiled original kernel as an opening to the divine.

As at the third line, we have here *completing,* but here it is followed by no fault instead of no accomplishment. At the third line we have a factual statement without any divinatory evaluation. As discussed in *Spring 1972,* p. 103, no fault means not being different from what one ought to be. Here at the fourth line the time of K'AN, the time of falling, is brought to a conclusion. Bringing to an end the time of falling can be related to no fault in a variety of ways; e.g., is no fault, therefore no fault, because there is no fault, will result in having no fault.

Supple and solid, the attributes of the broken and unbroken lines, represent as well the corresponding qualities in life. The word CHI, *bordering,* refers to a line of junction and division. It is the line that partakes in both. The Chinese character CHI, bordering, consists of the graphs for place and for sacrifice. The place of sacrifice is the border between the material world and the world of the spiritual agencies, and also the line they have in common. Within the structure of the hexagram this supple fourth line borders the solid fifth line. The cup and the dish represent the vessels for the liquid (supple) and solid offerings. The situation that partakes in both qualities is one of no fault.

Nine at the fifth line:

a) The pit not overflowing. Merely levelled already. No fault.
b) The pit not overflowing. Center: not yet the Great.

P'ING, *levelled,* comprises the meanings: level, even, equal; and by extension, equitable, uniform, peaceful, tranquil, to restore quiet, to harmonize. Here the situation is at its best within the difficult frame of K'AN. The pit is filled to level, but without any excess of *overflowing* (discussed above). *Merely* indicates that only a filling to the rim is reached, the stream has not yet resumed its course. This is obviously the most to be expected in the situation given by this hexagram. The *b*-text tells us here, in contrast with the second line, that the center has been reached or has come forth, whereas one has not yet reached or obtained the Great, i.e., leadership of one's own life.

Six at the top line:

a) Tied: using cords and ropes.
Dismissed into the jujube hedge.
Three years no attaining. Inauspicious.

b) Top six loses TAO. Three years inauspicious.

The Chinese character HSI, *tied,* consists of the graphs for man and for to connect. It has the literal meaning: to bind, attached to; and by extension, belonging to, devoted to, connections and relatives. The using of cords and ropes shows that the ties are very concrete here. The word translated here as *dismissed* covers the meanings: to let go, to put aside, to place, and also to judge. It has thus a connotation of being dismissed by a sentence. The *jujube hedge* denotes a place that was used as a court of justice, and as a place for literary examinations (that decided about entering upon an official career and about promotions). The name of the thorny jujube bush occurs in several terms applied to judicial courts, probably more those concerned with fact-finding and investigation than with sentencing. Robert H. van Gulik, a specialist in the field of ancient Chinese jurisprudence, writes "one would conclude that in archaic times the CHI (jujube) tree was credited with magic properties that made it especially suitable for marking off a taboo area..."*

Three years may, of course, describe the actual period of being tied and dismissed into the jujube hedge. But, in a more general sense, three applied to some section of time (years, days, etc.) denotes a complete curve: first, ascending; second, culminating; and third, diminishing. Thus, this line describes a full period without *attaining* (see *Spring 1972*, p. 105) or obtaining, during which one is tied and abandoned into a place of examination and trial. These three years of inauspiciousness are explained by the *b*-text as losing TAO, as at the bottom line.

*

The texts of the six lines each give an image of a specific situation that emphasizes one of the aspects belonging to the hexagram K'AN. Though each of these situation-images should be understood in itself and for

---

* *T'ang-yin-pi-shih, Parallel Cases from under the Pear-Tree,* A 13th century Manual of Jurisprudence and Detection, transl. from the original Chinese, with an introduction and notes by R. H. van Gulik. Sinica Leidensia, vol. X, Leiden, E. J. Brill, 1956.

its own merits, we may broaden our understanding by differentiating each of them in relation to the others.

The bottom and the top lines are both inauspicious, the first through one's overdoing, the last through being prevented from doing. The second and the third lines are just plain statements of one's situation: the second rather unsatisfactory, since one attains the Small, the third somewhat more in accordance with the requirements of THE PIT. The fourth and fifth lines have the prudent divinatory qualification of no fault. The center appears in the fifth line as a culmination of the four inner lines (2,3,4,5).

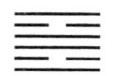

Hexagram No. 30, LI, THE BRILLIANCE

The name of this hexagram is that of the two trigrams which compose it, as is the case with each of the eight hexagrams that are made up of two identical trigrams. According to tradition, the Chinese character LI, consisting of the graphs for bird and for weird, means a yellow bird with brilliant plumage, a fairy, an elf. Brilliance, glaring light, is the main feature of LI. A further meaning of LI is: to cut in two, to part, to divide off, and thus to arrange according to rank or degree. These different meanings should not induce us to think of them as separate notions. They are three angles from which the intellect approaches the image-concept of LI, The Brilliance. The different images and concepts merge on the level of the *mundus imaginalis* into one image-concept that has the bird-like, light-giving, and discriminating powers of consciousness, both cosmic and individual.

At some places the *I Ching* associates the image of HUO, Fire, with the trigram LI, The Brilliance, and in other instances we find the image of MING, brightness. In the texts of this hexagram we find only MING, brightness; it embraces: dawn, daylight, clear, splendor, to shed light on, to illustrate, plain, evident, to distinguish clearly. The Chinese character MING, by joining the graph for moon to the graph for sun, reinforces the idea of light to the exclusion of warmth, for the moon's light is cold. This hexagram, by eliminating the heat aspect of fire, refers to shining light.

The attribute of the trigram LI is *congregating,* and this applies also to the hexagram LI, THE BRILLIANCE. (Although the Chinese word for which congregating stands is also transcribed as LI, it is another word, a completely different ideogram than LI, THE BRILLIANCE). The word LI, congregating, includes these meanings: attached to, to depend on, clinging to, what belongs to a matter, relying, a couple or pair. Traditionally this Chinese character has been taken to represent deer flocking together; LI is that which makes them adhere together as a herd. The English word congregate contains the root *grex,* flock, and *gregare,* flocking together, and thereby refers to the same image of cohesion of similars as does the Chinese.

Summing up we may say that LI, THE BRILLIANCE, refers to both cosmic and human spirit, to consciousness that through brightness brings about clear distinctions; it is the discriminating power of sharp differentiation that, by its congregating quality, constellates the cohesion of what is similar in nature or quality.

The nuclear trigrams are: above (lines 3,4,5) ☱ TUI, Marsh, and below (lines 2,3,4) ☴ SUN, Tree and Wind. The combination of these two nuclear trigrams results in hexagram No. 28, TA KUO, THE EXCESS OF THE GREAT. This is the latent hexagram and shows the potential dynamism within the actual hexagram THE BRILLIANCE. The double brightness of the two trigrams LI tends to an excessive development of the Great. (For the specific meaning of the Great, see above, p. 151.)

The three main relationships of any given hexagram to other hexagrams are to be found in (1) the Contrasted Definitions, (2) The Sequence, and (3) the latent hexagram. These three specific relations of other hexagrams to the hexagram under consideration shed additional light on one's actual situation in terms of the *mundus imaginalis*. In this particular case, (1) the Contrasted Definitions oppose THE BRILLIANCE to hexagram No. 29, THE PIT. They would be above and below, which belong together. (2) The Sequence explains that the situation of THE BRILLIANCE results from THE PIT by connecting the attributes of both hexagrams: falling leads to a place of congregating. (3) The latent hexagram No. 28, THE EXCESS OF THE GREAT reveals, as the inherent potentiality of THE BRILLIANCE, a carrying too far the ability of conducting one's own life. The interrelatedness of the above three hexagrams is further strengthened by a serial connection from No. 30, through (2) The Sequence, back to No. 29, and then again through The Sequence of No. 29 back to No. 28. Thus the two steps of relating back through The Sequence corroborate the importance of (3) the latent hexagram with its idea of excess.

Contrasted Definitions:

THE BRILLIANCE above, and nevertheless THE PIT below.

This text sees THE BRILLIANCE in contrast with hexagram NO. 29, emphasizing that while above and outside THE BRILLIANCE is apparent and dominating, underneath lurks THE PIT and falling. The hidden risks of triumphant brightness are shown both in this text and in the latent hexagram. THE EXCESS OF THE GREAT and THE PIT show where THE BRILLIANCE casts its shadow. The true meaning of THE BRILLIANCE remains obscure unless one sees it together with these relations to hexagrams No. 28 and 29.

The Sequence:

Falling necessarily has a place of congregating.
Hence through this, receiving THE BRILLIANCE.
THE BRILLIANCE connotes congregating.

We have already spoken above of falling and congregating. The word so, *place,* covers the meanings: the place of someone or something, dwelling-place, residence, abode; a building, a house; what the mind is bent on constantly, the object or act the mind is directed to continually. It may be rendered as a relative pronoun: that which, the things which, who, what. As the list of meanings shows, a concept of localization is always strongly implied. Through falling, the water cannot but touch ground again and assemble, i.e., having a place of congregating, and this leads to THE BRILLIANCE of which it is the attribute. In *Spring 1972,* p, 95, we have explained the sentence *hence through this, receiving* as follows: because of the preceding statement, the oracle bestows upon one the present hexagram, THE BRILLIANCE, which corresponds to congregating.

The Image:
Brightness arises twice: THE BRILLIANCE.
The Great's man, through successive brightness,
enlightens into the four cardinal points.

The verb TSO, *to arise,* implies: to generate, to appear, to arouse, to become, to make. The Chinese character TSO, to arise, consists of the graphs for man and for beginning, thus suggesting an activity that brings about something so that it rises and appears. The combination of brightness and to arise shows that this hexagram represents the work of the rising light. Here we find one of the key-terms of the *I Ching,* the *Great's man,* the man who focusses upon that particular quality we described as the Great (see above, p. 151, on Great and Small). The concept of the Great's man becomes clearest if contrasted with its opposite, the Small's man. The Great's man assumes leadership of his life; he has a line of conduct that is in constant interaction with the outer and inner events he meets with. The behaviour of the Small's man is only reactive to the vicissitudes of life and to impulses from within.

There is a distinct difference between the Great's man and the chün-tzu. The Great's man is one who is willing and able to have a line of conduct within the vicissitudes of life. The Great can refer to any kind of guiding line; the term does not imply any specific principles of conduct. It refers to the capacity to conduct, to 'lead life' as one says in English. Whereas the notion of the chün-tzu does imply a specific principle for the guidance of life. The chün-tzu submits to TE, to conforming his life to TAO.

Where the first sentence of The Image has *twice,* the second sentence says *successive* brightness. Whereas twice may be understood to mean a couple or pair, successive points to a sequence, a repetition in time. The *four cardinal points* describe the four quarters of the surface of the earth in their farthest extension. CHAO, *to enlighten,* covers both the concrete and the figurative meanings of bringing light. The Chinese character CHAO, to enlighten, consists of the graph for brightness above the graph for fire, thus confirming that this hexagram is concerned with the shining light of fire and not with the heat of fire. The Image tells us that the one who has inner leadership brings light everywhere through letting it shine repeatedly.

The Head:

THE BRILLIANCE: Harvest, Trial. Growth.
Restraining: female cattle. Propitious.

For a lengthy description of the meaning and implications of the main image-concepts *Growth, Harvest, Trial,* I must refer the reader to *Spring 1972,* pp. 97—99. Here these images are not in the sequence of the time-cycle. The third and the fourth stages — reaping of the crop and testing by ordeal — are directly associated with THE BRILLIANCE. However the nature of the association between THE BRILLIANCE and Harvest and Trial is unspecified. It may be recalled that the colon (:) stands for all the possible kinds of relation between two parts of a sentence, such as: will be, is, should be, results from, results in, therefore, or the prepositional relations: of, by, through, etc. (see *Spring 1972,* p. 94).

Because, as we said above, LI also denotes to cut in two, to part, to divide off, it is very close to the reaping of Harvest and the separating of Trial. Brightness and to cut, suggesting clear-cut as something sharp and distinctive, lead to an additional view of the first sentence: a clear-cut Harvest and Trial, or: a clear-cut through Harvest and Trial.

In the time-cycle of the four key-terms, *Growth* precedes as number two the stages three (Harvest) and four (Trial). Here the situation is different. THE BRILLIANCE is closely related with Harvest and Trial, as we have seen above, and that connection is given here as an explanation for the presence of Growth, of the all-pervading extension of the generating principle. We shall see below that, according to the Commentary on The Head, Growth results from congregating. As the first line of The Head suggests, congregating works through Growth when the multivalent connection of THE BRILLIANCE with Harvest and Trial becomes effective.

Under the title "Accumulation through Restraint" I have dealt at length with the term CH'U, *restraining,* in *Spring 1970,* pp. 123—25. I there exhibited the passages in which CH'U appears and pointed to its association, among others, with animals, their domestication, pasture, and their nourishing. Here restraining is brought into relation with *female cattle* or bovine female which is the height of productive animality in the human domain. Because the text does not specify the relation between restraining and female cattle, I have used a colon (:).

The one statement embraces many possibilities, e.g.: restraining of female cattle, restraining is female cattle, restraining results from, results in, female cattle, etc. LI linked with Harvest and Trial leads to Growth just as restraining connected with female cattle brings about propitiousness.

Commentary on The Head:

THE BRILLIANCE: congregating.
Sun and moon congregate at the heavens.
Hundred cereals, herbs, and trees congregate at the soil.
Doubling brightness through congregating at correctness.
Thereupon transforming and maturing the whole world.
The supple congregates at the center: **correctness.**
Hence Growth.
Through that, restraining: female cattle: propitious.

Congregating as assembling, flocking together and adhering to a place has been discussed above. It is the operational attribute of The Brilliance. The Commentary on The Head describes that congregating operates on the cosmic level, in nature on earth, in human society, and within man's psychic world. *Sun and moon* evoke brightness, the image of LI, since the two Chinese characters form together the character MING, brightness. The one Chinese word JIH, denotes both day and *sun.* Though the connection between sunlight, daylight, day-time is obvious, the English words day and sun are not interchangeable so that I have had to depart here from the rule of one-for-one rendering using either day or sun as the context may require. In The Head of the 18th hexagram *(Spring 1972,* p. 96) days stands for JIH. The numeral *hundred* is used for many, numerous, all. By maintaining the numeral we may keep something of the feeling of concreteness of that round number. The *cereals, herbs, and trees* comprise all kinds of vegetation, the nutrient, the green, and the ligneous plants.

Doubling brightness, by referring to man's action of doing over, is essentially different from the more objective descriptions, "twice" and "successive", that occur in The Image. CHENG, *correctness,* covers these meanings: proper, straight (not inclined to either side), exact, regular, constant, rule, model, to rectify. The Chinese character CHENG, correctness, shows the graphs for to stop and for one, which suggests holding to the one thing (that is right). Correctness is man's attitude and action in order to be exactly according to the rule of what is right and in order to correct by rectifying every deviation. By adhering to correctness and assembling the components of his personality and grouping his fellow-men, a person doubles by repetition the brightness of consciousness. *Thereupon* connects as cause to effect human action in doubling brightness with the subsequent transforming and maturing of the whole world.

HUA, *transforming,* means: to alter, to influence, the gradual and continuous operation of nature; to act upon mind, manners, or nature so as to change them. It is metamorphosis as a process or continuum. The Chinese character HUA, transforming, shows a man upright and a man upside down (a dead man), depicting the whole process of transformations of a man's lifetime. Transforming stands in contrast to PIEN, change, which means: a sudden mutation from one state of being into another, a revolution, and which is used for the change of solid into supple lines and vice versa, when casting the yarrow stalks results in a nine or a six. Different from both transforming and change is CH'ENG, *maturing,* as coming to full growth and the capacity to produce offspring, and which has been discussed at length in *Spring 1971,* pp. 145—47.

The *supple* represents the quality of the broken line, i.e., flexible, pliant, tender, soft. The sentence about the supple congregating at the center refers to the structure of the trigrams LI that have a broken line in the center; the statement about the supple applies to the individual man. The term *center* has been described above, p. 149. The supple assembling and adhering at the core of the person stands to correctness in that peculiar unspecified relation which we have indicated by a colon (:). Thus, the supple results from, results in, is, should be, or will be, correctness. Also this relation may be read as: The supple congregates at the center, therefore correctness, or: The correctness of the supple congregating at the center.

Up to this point the Commentary on The Head explains the first sentence of The Head. The four realms of congregating (heavens, the soil of the earth, the correctness in human society, and the individual's center) show the cause and the reason for the Growth that follows. (For *hence* as causal relation see *Spring 1970,* pp. 121—23). The second line of The Head "Restraining: female cattle. Propitious" comes about through the process of congregating and subsequent Growth. We may read: Through that process, restraining female cattle is propitious, and equally: Through that process, restraining results from (or results in) the propitiousness of female cattle. These readings derive from the phrasing in the Commentary on The Head, however, where propitious is part of the preceding sentence, but in unspecified relationship. In the Head propitious stands all by itself, the preceding sentence ending with a full stop.

The Lines

Nine at the bottom line:
- *a)* When treads confuse. Respecting this. No fault.
- *b)* Respecting confusing treads. Through casting out faults.

The word LÜ, *treads,* is known to the readers of the *I Ching* as the name of the 10th hexagram. It embraces all these meanings: where and on what one puts the foot; footprints, a shoe, a track, a path, a step, to walk on a path; the course of stars and of the seasons; and, by extension, conduct, to act, to practise. The Chinese character LÜ, treads, consists of the graphs for body and for to step again, an image of following the track or trail left by someone. TS'O, *to confuse,* confusing, means: to mistake, to err, in disorder, confused. The Chinese character TS'O, to confuse, shows the graphs for metal and for old, and relates to the original meaning of TS'O, to plate or wash old things with gold. Inducing error by this procedure appears to be the thought that has led to the current meaning, confusing. *When* is used here mainly in the sense of 'at the time of which', with the conditional implication 'in the case of which', 'in the event that'.

For CHING, that feeling of the heart which springs from self-respect and due regard to all positions, we use *respecting,* which includes: reverent, attentive, respectful, to stand in awe, to watch one's self. The Chinese character CHING, respecting, consists of the graph for authority symbolized by the teacher's rod, and the triple graph for to contain, for speech, (to hold the tongue), and for mildness, together suggesting the careful attitude towards authority in learning. Respecting thus denotes the inner attitude towards superiority in knowledge or wisdom and not the exhibition of respect as commanded by official authorities. The verb P'I, *casting out,* has the meanings: to repress, to punish, to expel; the laws or rules that decide what should be excluded; the sovereign who punishes according to the laws. The Chinese character P'I, casting out, consists of three graphs: (1) for the punishment of a crime, (2) for a person in authority, (3) for mouth, i.e., giving order. It shows the authority that throws out the faulty.

In a time when one's own stepping on the way, and/or the trails one is confronted with are confused and thus confuse, the recommendation is to respect those treads. The *b*-text explains that by throwing out whatever is different from what it ought to be (see the description of *fault,* above, p. 154) one respects the confusing treads. One has to admit and to respect that the treads are confusing. This line describes a situation that does not allow light to be shed on the path or to clarify the track ahead. It is a situation of careful and piecemeal throwing out faults.

Six at the second line:

a) Yellow brilliance. Spring propitious.
b) Yellow brilliance: Spring, propitious.
Attaining the center: TAO.

As the color of the soil of central China (the loess) is yellow, so is *yellow* the emblematic color of the country (the Kingdom of the Center or Middle Kingdom); it was the imperial color (dating back to the Yellow Emperor, about 2500 BC). In Chinese charts of the five basic colors yellow holds the center. Here, at the center of the lower trigram appears the brilliance which is qualified by yellow, i.e., imperial, central, earthly. The yellow brilliance as a brilliance related to the earth is appropriate at the center of the lower (inner) trigram. YÜAN, *Spring,* is the first in the time-cycle of the four main image-concepts: Spring, Growth, Harvest, Trial. These image-concepts have been discussed with all their connotations in *Spring 1972,* pp. 97—99. In short, Spring stands for the primal originating power itself, and for the place in space or time where it becomes phenomenal, i.e., the source, the beginning, the head, etc. In the above notes on The Head we showed that in this hexagram the way leads from stages three and four (Harvest and Trial) to stage two, Growth. The first stage occurs only here at the second line as a first culmination of the brilliance at the origin of the generating power. By joining the divinatory term *propitious* the text confirms that the situation presents **favorable conditions,** that it bodes well.

The *b*-text brings yellow brilliance and Spring together in one sentence by means of the peculiar unspecified relation (:) we have discussed above. The same relation is repeated in the explanatory sentence: Attaining the center (results from, is, therefore, through) TAO, which may be understood also as: Attaining the TAO of the center. (For the full implications of *attaining the center*, see *Spring 1972*, p. 105.) We have discussed the word TAO above, p. 151. These sentences that join propitious and TAO to the yellow brilliance show that the intrinsic dangers of the brilliance as depicted in the Contrasted Definitions and the latent hexagram are here in the second line eliminated through the earthly central quality of yellow.

Nine at the third line:

a) Brilliance of the setting sun.
No beating of earthenware drums, and nevertheless singing.
By consequence, the Great: lamenting of old age.
Inauspicious.
b) Brilliance of the setting sun. How possible to last?

The texts of the second line showed the yellow brilliance as a culmination, and the text of the third line confirms this: here the brilliance is that of the setting sun. Musical self-expression shows the mood of this situation. The merry drumbeating has ceased, leaving one with the elegiac *singing*. The elegies without instrumental accompaniment at the time of the setting sun are laments of old-age (lit. the age of seventy or eighty). This *lamenting* of old-age is connected with the *Great*. We have previously discussed the exact meaning of the Great as the faculty to conduct one's own life in accordance with a chosen guiding line (see above, pp. 151, 159). The unspecified relation (:) between the Great and lamenting old-age includes such readings as: the Great's lamenting of old-age and lamenting of the Great's old-age. The emphasis lies on "by consequence, the Great". It is the Great, the determination upon a guiding line in life, that laments at the brilliance of the setting sun. The *b*-text makes the reason for it quite clear by the question "How possible to last?". The Chinese ideogram CHIU, *to last*, longlasting, is traditionally presented as a man with a shackle on one of his legs and who therefore needs a long time when walking. Lasting occurs ten times in hexagram No. 32, HENG, DURATION. The brilliance of the setting sun cannot last, whereas the Great seeks continuity, a lasting line of guidance. Here the intrinsic quest for continuity of the Great leads to inauspiciousness. For the precise meaning of *inauspicious* as ill-omen the reader may refer to *Spring 1970*, p. 119.

Nine at the fourth line:
a) Thus suddenly, thus its coming.
Thus burning, thus dying, thus rejected.
b) Thus suddenly, thus its coming. No place tolerates.

The predominant notion in this line is *suddenly* with the meanings: abruptly, to rush out, precipitate. The important implications of the term *coming* in relation to time have been discussed in *Spring 1972*, p. 101. Five times over the text uses the word JU, *thus*, thereby connecting, and placing in parallel with suddenly coming, the other terms of this process — burning, dying, rejected. *It* refers to the brilliance. At the fourth line one is far from the earth-bound lower center of the yellow brilliance at the second line. Here the tendency to flare up prevails. The text therefore insists that just as sudden as is the coming of the brilliance, so is its burning, dying down, and being thrown away. We have dealt with so, *place*, above at p. 158. JUNG, *tolerate*, embraces the meanings: to contain (as a house its inmates), to endure, to bear with; to receive; the way in which one takes things, countenance. The Chinese character JUNG, to tolerate, consists of the graphs for a streambed or gully and for covering, suggesting a limitation of what can be contained. According to the *b*-text the suddenness of the appearance, flaring up, dying down, and being thrown away, results because the brilliance is nowhere tolerated, cannot be contained anywhere. At the first stage of the upper trigram the brilliance develops its upward flaring without restraint and has no duration at all; this development started already at the third line with the impossibility of lasting.

Six at the fifth line:
a) Issuing forth: either gushing tears or lamenting sadness.
Propitious.
b) Propitiousness of six at the fifth line.
Brilliance: king and princes.

THE PIT AND THE BRILLIANCE

We have discussed above at p. 152 the term CH'U, *to issue forth,* coming out of something so as to be outside. Here at the central line of the upper and outer trigram the brilliance comes fully forth. As the contrast with THE PIT and the latent hexagram THE EXCESS OF THE GREAT each showed an intrinsic shadow within THE BRILLIANCE, so here we find that when the brilliance issues fully forth, there is gushing tears and lamenting sadness. At first sight it may seem startling that this should be considered propitious, i.e., boding well. The *b*-text explains the propitiousness of this line by putting brilliance in the same kind of unspecified relation (:) to the king and princes as does the *a*-text with issuing forth (of the brilliance) and the tears and sadness. The brilliance that proceeds from inside to outside and is associated with the leading task of the king and his princely ministers is not of a gay and lighthearted kind. The actions and decisions of those who bear responsibility for the people are intimately related to tears and sadness. The inclusion of tears and sadness in the situation of the brilliance projected outside is the very essence of its propitiousness. We should recall that the unspecified relationship both in the *a*- and *b*-texts includes: of, by, through; is, will be, results from, results in, etc. The *king and princes* correspond to the first and the third rank of the main dignitaries in government. The princes were the ministers of state to the king (or emperor), his executives. The second rank, the feudal lords, were entrusted with governing functions out in the provinces where they had their fiefdoms (see top line).

Nine at the top line:

a) The king uses issuing forth to chastise. Having excellence. Cutting the heads. Nowise catching those shamed. No fault.
b) The king uses issuing forth to chastise.
Through correctness, fiefdoms.

Above, p. 152, we have discussed *to use,* using. The verb CHENG, *to chastise,* has the meanings: to chastise refractory states, to reduce, to subjugate; to proceed, to start out as on a punishing expedition. The Chinese character CHENG, to chastise, consists of the graphs for to go and for correct thus indicating the undertaking of a rectifying move or expedition. CHIA, *excellence,* means: good, fine, delicious, what is happy, pleased, to rejoice in, to admire. The Chinese character CHIA, excellence, presents the graph for goodness, pleasure, happiness (music) with the graph for to increase or to add, suggesting a high degree of good qualities, of happiness, and of pleasure.

CHE, *cutting*, embraces the meanings: to break off in the middle, to snap in two, to sunder; and, by extension, to decide or discriminate between. The Chinese character CHE, cutting, consists of the graphs for hand and for ax, suggesting the action of cutting into two parts. SHOU connotes much the same as *head* does in English, i.e., the head as part of the human body; a chief or leader; the heads of matter; the beginning, the origin; foremost. The negative FEI, *nowise*, marks an absolute negation: in no manner, in no way, by no means, not at all. The Chinese character FEI, nowise, consists of the graph for to oppose within the graph for chest, the image of a chest filled with opposition, denoting something or someone wholly opposing. Therefore the word FEI occurs also as a noun denoting seditious people, vagabonds, bandits, brigands; all those who deny an authority or order. HUO, *catching*, means: to take in hunting, to catch as a thief, to seize, to get. The word CH'OU, *shamed*, has the meanings: shameful, ashamed, ashamed of, to fill with shame; and, by extension, what causes one to feel shame: the vile, ugly, abominable, disagreeable, or the disgraceful, The Chinese word CH'OU, shamed, presents the graphs for the spirit and for a demon, suggesting the demoniac possession of the spirit that causes shame.

Here, at the top line, issuing forth turns into a tool in the hands of the highest authority who can use it for rectifying and reducing the refractory ones. According to the context of the hexagram, issuing forth applies in the first place to the brilliance, as can be seen from the fifth line where the *b*-text reintroduces the brilliance. The absence of the word brilliance at the top line, though it does not exclude brilliance as an implication, widens the bearing of issuing forth to any kind of coming forth to the outside. This statement is put into parallel with "having excellence", i.e., having a high degree of the good, the pleasant, and the happy. In the definitions of the four cyclic key-terms — Spring, Growth, Harvest, Trial (as we find them in the Wen Yen commentary on the first hexagram) — Growth is expressed in terms of excellence: "Growth (HENG) connotes the gathering of excellence (CHIA)".* So

---

* In the Wilhelm-Baynes translation Book III, hexagram No. 1, Commentary on the Words of the Text (Wen Yen) *a)* 1. "... Succeeding [HENG] is the coming together of all that is beautiful [CHIA] ...".

the occurrence of excellence at the top line refers us to The Head of the actual hexagram where Growth is the main issue. This connection of the top line with the main text of the hexagram as a whole (through the common essence of Growth and excellence) emphasizes the importance of this line as the ultimate culmination of THE BRILLIANCE (a first and inner culmination was reached at the second line).

The second line of the *a*-text shows how the king uses the issuing forth of brilliance for chastising. He breaks the leaders or sunders the deviating principles, but in no way confines those who feel, or can feel, shamed because the demoniac had only been cast upon their spirits by the leaders. This way of chastising implies no fault. The *b*-text shows the positive result of the action outlined in the *a*-text. By means of *correctness* (see above, p. 161) fiefdoms are established, i.e., the realms that were seditious are thus turned into states held and administrated on behalf of the king's central authority.

*

The image of the hexagram receives differing shades of emphasis according to the images in the lines. The image in each of the lines should be read in contrast with the other images so as to sharpen its particular angle of insight. We may summarize the shades of emphasis in these notes on the lines, as follows:

At the bottom line there is not yet any brilliance. The situation allows no light to be shed on the path. Confusion can be lifted only through slow, piecemeal discarding of faults. At the center of the inner (lower) trigram, i.e., at the second line, the brilliance is at the right place insofar as the congregating quality prevents the dangers of flaring up in excess and falling into the pit underneath. At the last line of the inner trigram, i.e., the third line, the decline of the inner brilliance upsets the Great's tendency towards lasting, which now brings about inauspiciousness, since the brilliance follows its natural intrinsic curve. With the fourth line the outer trigram begins, taking the brilliance outside. It is thus without relation to the inner point of congregating at the center of the inner trigram. Having lost its place inside, it remains short-lived. At the center of the outer trigram, i.e., the fifth line, congregating has definitely been replaced by issuing forth. The brilliance that comes to the outside is the brilliance of the highest ruler and his assistants. It is painful and sad and it results from sadness, which is precisely what prevents it from flaring up all of a sudden and dying down as suddenly, as happens at the fourth line. At the top line, the issuing forth of the brilliance broadens to issuing forth in action. Here a special connection with The Head of the hexagram exists through the correspondence between excellence and Growth. The enlightened action takes the place of the sadness of the fifth line. The chastising in the outside corresponds to the casting out faults inside at the bottom line. The confusing (bottom), the sadness (fifth), and the rebellious (top) are turned into vassalage, i.e., autonomous but integrated realms.

THREE EARLY PAPERS

C. G. JUNG

SIGMUND FREUD: ON DREAMS (1901)

Freud begins by giving a short exposition of his work. He first distinguishes the various interpretations which the problem of dreams has undergone in the course of history:

1. The old "mythological" or, rather, mystical hypothesis that dreams are meaningful utterances of a soul freed from the fetters of sense. The soul is conceived as a transcendent entity which either

---

The first of these papers has been translated from a typescript discovered in Jung's posthumous papers. It was apparently a report given (25 January 1901) to his colleagues on the staff of the Burghölzli Mental Hospital, Zürich, where Jung had taken up his post as assistant on 10 December 1900 (see C. G. Jung / A. Jaffé, *Memories, Dreams, Reflections* (New York/London, 1963), end of Ch. III, "Student Years"). The subject was Freud's essay *Über den Traum*, published as part (pp. 307–344) of a serial publication, *Grenzfragen des Nerven- und Seelenlebens*, ed. L. Löwenfeld and H. Kurella (Wiesbaden, 1901); trans., "On Dreams", Standard Edn., V, pp. 631–86. This was a summary of *Die Traumdeutung* (1900); trans., *The Interpretation of Dreams*, Standard Edn., IV–V. Fritz Wittels, *Die sexuelle Not* (Vienna and Leipzig, 1909), was subject of the note by Jung (second paper published here) in the *Jahrbuch für psychoanalytische und psychopathologische Forschungen*, II (1910), pp. 312–15. The third paper was originally entitled "Eine Bemerkung zur Tauskschen Kritik der Nelkenschen Arbeit". It appeared in the *Internationale Zeitschrift für ärztliche Psychoanalyse*, I (1913), pp. 285–88. The writers cited are Victor Tausk, of Vienna, and Jan Nelken, of Zurich. Nelken's paper had appeared in the *Jahrbuch für psychoanalytische und psychopathologische Forschungen*, IV (1912) pp. 504–62. Jung's support of Nelken against Tausk presents arguments of the 'Zurich School' against that of Vienna. For further on the significance of Tausk, see Paul Roazen, *Brother Animal* (New York: Knopf, 1969).

All three papers have been translated by R.F.C. Hull and will appear in *Miscellany*, CW 18, in press for publication in 1974 by Princeton University Press in the United States and by Routledge and Kegan Paul in the United Kingdom. Copyright © 1973 by Princeton University Press. Published here by arrangement with Princeton University Press and the kind permission of the Heirs of C. G. Jung.

produces dreams independently, as [Gotthilf Heinrich von] Schubert still supposed, or else represents the medium of communication between the conscious mind and divine revelation.

2. The more recent hypothesis of [K. A.] Scherner and [J.] Volkelt, according to which dreams owe their existence to the operation of psychic forces that are held in check during the day.

3. The critical modern view that dreams can be traced back to peripheral stimuli which partially affect the cerebral cortex and thereby induce dream activity.

4. The common opinion that dreams have a deeper meaning, and may even foretell the future. Freud, with reservations, inclines to this view. He does not deny the dream a deeper meaning, and admits the rightness of the common method of dream interpretation, in so far as it takes the dream-image as a symbol for a hidden content that has a meaning.

In his opening observations Freud compares dreams with obsessional ideas, which like them, are strange and inexplicable to the conscious mind.

The psychotherapy of obsessional ideas offers the key to unravelling the ideas of dreams. Just as we get a patient who suffers from an obsession to take note of all the ideas that associate themselves with the dominating idea, we can make upon ourselves the experiment of observing everything that becomes associated with the ideas in the dream if, without criticism, we allow all those things to appear which we are in the habit of suppressing as worthless and disturbing. We take note, therefore, of all psychically valueless ideas, the momentary perceptions and thoughts which are not accompanied by any deeper feeling of value, and which are produced every day in unending quantities.

Example, p. 310:[1] On the basis of the results of this method, Freud conjectures that the dream is a kind of substitute, that is, a symbolic representation of trains of thought that have a meaning, and are often bound up with lively affects. The mechanism of this substitution is still not very clear at present, but at any rate we may accord it the status of an extremely important psychological process once we have established its beginning and end by the method just described. Freud calls the content of the dream as it appears in consciousness the *manifest dream-content*. The material of the dream, the psychological premises, that is to say all the trains of thought that are hidden from the dreaming consciousness and can be discovered only by analysis, he calls the *latent dream-content*. The synthetic process, which elaborates the disconnected or only superficially connected ideas into a relatively unified dream image, is called the *dream-work*.

We are now faced with two cardinal questions:

1. What is the psychic process that changes the latent dream-content into the manifest dream-content?

2. What is the motive for this change?

There are dreams whose latent content is not hidden at all, or barely so, and which in themselves are logical and understandable because the latent content is practically identical with the manifest content. Children's dreams are frequently of this kind, because the thought-world of children is chiefly filled with sensuous, concrete imagery. The more complicated and abstract the thoughts of an adult become, the more confused are most of his dreams. We seldom meet with a completely transparent and coherent dream in an adult. Frequently the dreams of adults belong to the class of dreams which, though meaningful and logical in themselves, are unintelligible because their meaning does not in any way fit the thought processes of the waking consciousness. The great majority of dreams, however, are confused, incoherent dreams that surprise us by their absurd or impossible features. These are the dreams, also, that are furthest removed from their premise, the latent dream-material, that bear the least resemblance to it and are therefore difficult to analyse, and have required for their synthesis the greatest expenditure of transformative psychic energy.

Children's dreams, with their clarity and transparent meaning, are the least subject to the transformative activity of the dream-work. Their nature is therefore fairly clear; most of them are wish-dreams.

A child that is hungry dreams of food, a pleasure forbidden the day before is enacted in the dream, etc. Children are concerned with simple sensuous objects and simple wishes, and for this reason their dreams are very simple too. When adults are concerned with similar objects, their dreams as well are very simple. To this class belong the so-called dreams of convenience, most of which take place shortly before waking. For example, it is time to get up, and one dreams that one is up already, washing, dressing, and already at work. Or if any kind of examination is impending, one finds oneself in the middle of it, etc. With adults, however, very simple-looking dreams are often fairly complicated because several wishes come into conflict and influence the formation of the dream-image.

For children's dreams and dreams of convenience in adults the author lays down the following formula: A thought in the optative is replaced by an image in the present.[2]

The second of the questions we asked, concerning the motive for the conversion of the latent content into the concrete dream image, can be answered most easily in these simple cases. Evidently the enacted fulfillment of the wish mitigates its affectivity; in consequence, the wish does not succeed in breaking through the inhibition and waking the sleeping organism. In this case, therefore, the dream performs the function of a guardian of sleep.

Our first question, concerning the process of the dream-work, can best be answered by examining the confused dreams.

In examining a confused dream, the first thing that strikes us is how very much richer the latent dream-material is than the dream-image constructed from it. Every idea in the manifest dream proves, on analysis, to be associated with at least three or four other ideas which all have something in common. The corresponding dream-image frequently combines all the different characteristics of the individual underlying ideas. Freud compares such an image with Galton's family photographs, in which several exposures are superimposed. This combination of different ideas Freud calls *condensation*. To this process is due the indefinite, blurred quality of many dream-images. The dream knows no "either-or" but only the copulative "and".

Often, on a superficial examination of two ideas united in a single image, no common factor can be found. But, on penetrating more deeply, we discover that whenever no *tertium comparationis* is present, the dream creates one, and generally does so by manipulating the linguistic expression of the ideas in question. Sometimes dissimilar ideas are homophonous; sometimes they rhyme, or could be confused with one another if attention is poor. The dream uses these possibilities as a *quid pro quo* and thus combines the dissimilar elements. In other cases it works not only wittily but positively poetically, speaking in tropes and metaphors, creating symbols and allegories, all for the purpose of concealment under deceptive veils. The process of condensation begets monstrous figures that far surpass the fabulous beings in Oriental fairytales. A modern philosopher holds that the reason why we are so prosaic in our daily lives is that we squander too much poetic fantasy in our dreams. The figures in a confused dream are thus, in the main, composite structures. (Example on p. 321.)[3]

In the manifest dream, the latent dream-material is represented by these composite structures, which Freud calls the dream-elements. These elements are not incoherent, but are connected together by a common dream-thought, i.e., they often represent different ways of expressing the same dominating idea.

This rather complicated situation explains a good deal of the confusion and unintelligibility of the dream, but not all of it. So far we have considered only the ideational side of the dream. The feelings and affects, which play a very large part, have still to be discussed.

If we analyse one of our own dreams, we finally arrive by free association at trains of thought which at one time or another were of importance to us, and which are charged with a feeling of value. During the process of condensation and reinterpretation, certain thoughts are pushed on to the stage of the dream, and their peculiar character might easily invite the dreamer to criticize and suppress them, as actually happens in the waking state. The affective side of the dream, however, prevents this, since it imbues the dream elements with feelings that act as a powerful counterbalance to all criticism. Obsessional ideas function in the same way. For example, agoraphobia manifests itself with an overwhelming feeling of fear, and so maintains the position it has usurped in consciousness.

Freud supposes that the affects attached to the components of the latent dream-material are transferred to the elements of the manifest dream, thus helping to complete the dissimilarity between the latent and the manifest content. He calls this process *displacement,* or, in modern terms, a transvaluation of psychic values.

By means of these two principles, the author believes he can offer an adequate explanation of the obscurity and confusion of a dream constructed out of simple, concrete thought-material. These two hypotheses shed a new light on the question of the instigator of a dream, and the connection between the dream and waking life. There are dreams whose connection with waking life is quite evident, and whose instigator is a significant impression received during the day. But far more frequently the dream-instigator is an incident which, although trivial enough in itself, and often positively silly, in spite of its complete valuelessness introduces a long and intensely affective dream. In these cases, analysis leads us back to complexes of ideas which though unimportant in themselves are associated with highly significant impressions of the day by incidental relationships of one kind or another. In the dream the incidental elements occupy a large and imposing place, while the significant ones are completely occluded from the dreaming consciousness. The real instigator of the dream, therefore, is not the trivial, incidental element, but the powerful affect in the background. Why, then, does the affect detach itself from the ideas that are associated with it, and in their place push the nugatory and valueless elements into consciousness? Why does the dreaming intellect trouble to rout out the forgotten, incidental, and unimportant things from every corner of our memory, and to build them up into elaborate and ingenious images?

Before turning to the solution of this question, Freud tries to point out further effects of the dream-work in order to shed a clear light on the purposiveness of the dream-functions.

In adults, besides visual and auditory memory-images, the material underlying the dream includes numerous abstract elements which it is not so easy to represent in sensuous form. In considering the *representability of the dream-content,* a new difficulty arises which influences the dream's performance. At this point the author digresses a bit and describes how the dream represents logical relations in sensuous imagery. His observations in this respect are of no further importance for his theory; they merely serve to increase the stock of the discredited dream in the estimation of the public.

One extremely remarkable effect of the dream-work is what Freud calls the *dream-composition.* This, according to his definition, is a kind of revision which the disordered mass of dream-elements undergo at the moment of their inception — a regular dramatization frequently conforming to all the artistic rules of exposition, development, and solution. In this way the dream acquires, as the author says, a façade, which does not of course cover it up at all points. This façade is in Freud's view the crux of the misunderstanding about dreams, since it systematizes the deceptive play of the dream-elements and brings them into a plausible relationship. Freud thinks that the reason for this final shaping of the dream-content is the regard for intelligibility. He imagines the dream producer as a kind of jocular daimon who wants to make his plans plausible to the sleeper.

Apart from this last effect of the dream-work, what is created by the dream is nothing in any way new or intellectually superior. Anything of value in the dream-image can be shown by analysis to be already present in the latent material. And it may very well be doubted whether the dream composition is anything but a direct effect of reduced consciousness, a fleeting attempt to explain the hallucinations of the dream.

We now come to the final question: Why does the dream do this work? In analysing his own dreams, the author usually came upon quickly forgotten and unexpected thoughts of a distinctly unpleasant nature, which had entered his waking consciousness only to be suppressed again immediately. He designates the state of these thoughts by the name *repression*.

In order to elucidate the concept of repression, the author postulates two thought-producing systems, one of which has free access to consciousness, while the other can reach consciousness only through the medium of the first. To put it more clearly, there is on the borderline between conscious and unconscious a *censorship* which is continually active throughout waking life, regulating the flow of thoughts to consciousness in such a way that it keeps back all incidental thoughts which for some reason are prohibited, and admits to consciousness only those of which it approves. During sleep there is a momentary predominance of what was repressed by day, the censorship must relax and produces a compromise — the dream. The author does not conceal the somewhat too schematic and anthropomorphic features of this conception, but solaces himself with the hope that its objective correlate may one day be found in some organic or functional form.

There are thoughts, often of a pre-eminently egoistic nature, which are able to slip past the censorship imposed by ethical feelings and criticism when this is relaxed in sleep. The censorship, however, is not entirely abrogated, but only reduced in effectiveness, so that it can still exert some influence on the shaping of the dream-thoughts. The dream represents the reaction of the personality to the intrusion of unruly thoughts. Its contents are repressed in distorted or disguised form.

From the example of dreams that are comprehensible and have a meaning, it is evident that their content is generally a fulfilled wish. It is the same with confused dreams that are difficult to understand. They, too, contain the fulfillment of repressed wishes.

Dreams, therefore, can be divided into three classes:

1. Those that represent an *unrepressed wish in undisguised form*. Such dreams are of the infantile type.

2. Those that represent the fulfillment of a *repressed wish in disguised form*. According to Freud, most dreams belong to this class.

3. Those that represent a *repressed wish in undisguised* form. Such dreams are said to be accompanied by fear, the fear taking the place of dream-distortion.

Through the conception of the dream as a compromise we arrive at an explanation of dreams in general. When the waking consciousness sinks into sleep, the energy needed to maintain the inhibition against the sphere of repressed material abates. But just as the sleeper still has some attention at his disposal for sensory stimuli coming from outside, and, by means of this attention, can eliminate sleep-disturbing influences by weaving around them a disguising veil of dreams, so stimuli arising from within, from the unconscious psychic sphere, are neutralized by the periphrasis of a dream. The purpose in both cases is the same, namely, the preservation of sleep, and for this reason Freud calls the dream the "guardian of sleep". Excellent examples of this are waking dreams, which abound in periphrastic inventions designed to make the continuation of the reverie plausible.

Confused dreams are not so clear in this respect, but Freud maintains that with application and good will repressed wishes can be discovered in them too. On this point he adopts a rather onesided attitude, since, instead of a wish, the cause of a dream may easily prove to be just the opposite, a repressed fear, which, manifesting itself in undisguised and often exaggerated form, makes the teleological explanation of dreams appear doubtful.

Freud: Dreams
Contents

Arrangement: Introduction.
1. Example from analysis. Uncritical tracing back of associations.
   a) Manifest dream-content.

b) Latent dream-content.
2. Classification of dreams.
  a) Meaningful and intelligible.
  b) Meaningful and unintelligible.
  c) Confused.
3. Children's dreams.
4. Adults. Dreams of convenience and wish-dreams.
5. Causes of the strangeness of dreams.
  a) Condensation.
    i. by means of the natural common factor.
    ii. by means of a common factor created by the dream itself.
  b) Displacement. Dream-distortion. Distortion of prohibited thoughts.
  c) Concrete representation of inadequate ideas, hence metaphors.
    Sensuous metamorphosis of logical relations.
    Causal: transformation or mere juxtaposition.
    Alternatives = "and".
    Similarity, common factor, congruence.
    Contradiction, mockery, scorn = absurdity of manifest dream.
  d) Dream-composition for the purpose of intelligibility.
  e) Teleological conception: dream as guardian of sleep.

1 Cf. Standard Edn., V, p. 636.
2 Cf. ibid., p. 647.
3 Cf. ibid., p. 651.

MARGINAL NOTE ON F. WITTELS: *DIE SEXUELLE NOT* (1910)

This book is written with as much passion as intelligence. It discusses such questions as abortion, syphilis, the family, the child, women and professions for women. Its motto is: "Human beings must live out their sexuality, otherwise their lives will be warped." Accordingly, Wittels raises his voice for the liberation of sexuality in the widest sense. He speaks a language one seldom hears, the language of unsparing, almost fanatical truthfulness, that falls unpleasantly on the ear because it tears away all shams and unmasks all cultural lies. It is not my business to pass judgment on the author's morals. Science has only to listen to this voice and tacitly admit that it is not a lone voice crying in the wilderness, that it could be a leader for many who are setting out on this path, that we have here a movement rising from invisible sources and swelling into a mightier current every day. Science has to test and weigh the evidence — and understand it.

The book is dedicated to Freud and much of it is based on Freud's psychology, which is in essence the scientific rationalization of this contemporary movement. The two things should not be confused: for the social psychologist the movement is and remains an intellectual problem, while for the social moralist it is a challenge. Wittels meets this challenge in his own way, others do so in theirs. We should listen to them all. Nowhere is the warning more in place that on the one hand we should refrain from enthusiastic applause, and on the other not kick against the pricks in blind rage. We have to realize, quite dispassionately, that what we fight about in the outside world is also a battle in our own hearts. It is high time we realized that mankind is not just an accumulation of individuals utterly different from one another, but that they possess so many psychological factors in common that the individual appears as only a slight variation. How can we judge this question fairly if we do not admit that it also concerns ourselves? Anyone who can admit this will seek the solution first in himself, which is the way all great solutions begin.

Most people, however, seem to have a secret love of voyeurism: they gaze at the contestants as though they were watching a circus, wanting to decide immediately who is finally right or wrong. But anyone who has learnt to examine the background of his own thoughts and actions, and has acquired a lasting and salutary impression of the way our unconscious biological impulses warp our logic, will soon lose his delight in gladiatorial shows and public disputation, and will perform them in himself and with himself. In that way we preserve a perspective that is particularly needful in an age when Nietzsche arose as a significant portent. Wittels will surely not remain alone; he is only the first of many who will come up with "ethical" conclusions from the mine of Freud's truly biological psychology — conclusions that will shake to the marrow what was previously considered "good". As a French wit once remarked, of all inventors moralists have the hardest lot, since their innovations can only be immoralities. This is absurd and at the same time sad, as it shows how out of date our conception of morality has become. It lacks the very best thing that modern thought has accomplished: a biological and historical consciousness. This lack of adaptation must sooner or later bring about its fall, and nothing can stop this fall. And here I am reminded of the wise words of Anatole France:

> Bien que le passé leur montre des droits et des devoirs sans cesse changeants et mouvants, ils se croiraient dupes s'ils prévoyaient que l'humanité future se ferait d'autres droits, d'autres devoirs et d'autres dieus. Enfin, ils ont peur de se déshonorer aux yeux de leurs contemporains en assumant cette horrible immoralité qu'est la morale future. Ce sont là des empêchements à rechercher l'avenir.

The danger of our old-fashioned conception of morality is that it blinkers our eyes to innovations which, however fitting they may be, always carry with them the odium of immorality. But it is just here that our eyes should be clear and far-seeing. The movement I spoke of, the urge to reform sexual morality, is not the invention of a few cranky somnambulists, but has all the impact of a force of nature. No arguments or quibbles about the *raison d'être* of morality are any use here; we have to accept what is most intelligent and make the best of it. This means tough and dirty work. Wittels' book gives a foretaste of what is to come, and it will shock and frighten many people. The long shadow of this fright will naturally fall on Freudian psychology, which will be accused of being a hotbed of iniquity. To anticipate this I would like to say a word in its defence now. Our psychology is a science that can at most be accused of having discovered the dynamite which terrorists work with. What the moralist and general practitioner do with it is not our concern, and we have no wish to interfere. No doubt many unqualified persons will rush in and perpetrate the greatest follies, but that too does not concern us. Our goal is simply and solely scientific knowledge, which does not have to bother with the uproar it has provoked. If religion and morality go to pieces in the process, so much the worse for them for not having more stamina. Knowledge is a force of nature that goes its way irresistibly from inner necessity. There can be no hushing up and no compromises, only unqualified acceptance.

This knowledge does not identify itself with the changing views of the ordinary medical man, for which reason it cannot be judged by moral criteria. This has to be said out loud, because today there are still people claiming to be scientific who extend their moral misgivings even to scientific insights. Like every proper science, psychoanalysis is beyond morality; it rationalizes the unconscious and so fits the previously autonomous and unconscious instinctual forces into the psychic economy. The difference between the position before and afterwards is that the person in question now really *wants* to be what he is and to leave nothing to the blind dispensation of the unconscious. The objection that immediately arises, that the world would then get out of joint, must be answered first and foremost by psychoanalysis; it has the last word, but only in the privacy of the consulting room, because this fear is an individual fear. It is sufficient that the goal of psychoanalysis is a psychic state in which you "ought" and you "must" are replaced by "I will", so that, as Nietzsche says, a man becomes master not only of his vices but also of his virtues. Inasmuch as psychoanalysis is purely rational — and it is so of its very nature — it is neither moral nor antimoral and gives neither prescriptions nor any other "you oughts". Undoubtedly the tremendous need of the masses to be led will force many people to abandon the standpoint of the psychoanalyst and to start "prescribing". One person will prescribe morality, another licentiousness. Both of them cater to the masses and both follow the currents that drive the masses hither and thither. Science stands above all this and lends the strength of its armour to Christian and anti-Christian alike. It has no confessional axe to grind.

I have never yet read a book on the sexual question that demolishes present-day morality so harshly and unmercifully and yet remains in essentials so true. For this reason Wittels' book deserves to be read, but so do many of the others that deal with the same question, for the important thing is not the individual book but the problem common to them all.

THREE EARLY PAPERS

A COMMENT ON TAUSK'S CRITICISM OF NELKEN (1913)

In the first issue of this periodical there was a review by Tausk of Nelken's "Analytische Beobachtungen über Phantasien eines Schizophrenen". In this review I came upon the following passage:

> In the first catatonic attack the patient produced the fantasy that mice and rats were gnawing at his genitals. Nelken derives the symbolic significance of these animals from a suggestion of Jung's, who sees them as symbolizing nocturnal fear. There is no doubt that this interpretation is correct, but it comes from a later elaboration of this symbol and blocks the way to deeper insight. Analysis of dreams and neuroses has taught me beyond question — and I find my view supported by other psychoanalysts — that mice and rats are cloacal animals and that they represent, in symbolic form, the defecation complex (anal complex).

I would like to defend Nelken's view against Tausk's. I do not doubt in the least that Tausk's view is also right. We have known that for a long time, and it has been completely confirmed once more by Freud's rat-man.[1] Further, we know very well that catatonic introversion and regression simply reactivate all the infantile impulses, as is evident from numerous observations in Nelken's analysis. So there is no question of this aspect of the case having escaped us; it merely seemed unimportant to us because by now it is taken for granted. It no longer seems vitally important to know that the anal complex acts as a substitute for normal modes of transference or adaptation, since we know already that the pathological regression of libido reactivates every variety of infantile sexualism, producing fantasies of every infantile kind. Anyone who still thinks that a definite group of fantasies, or a "complex", has been singled out just hasn't seen enough cases. We therefore consider it irrelevant that the castration is performed by cloacal animals. Incidentally, mice are not "cloacal animals" but animals that live in holes, and this is a more comprehensive concept than "cloacal animals".

The only thing we learn from this interpretation is that an infantile complex or infantile interest takes the place of the normal interest. It may be of some value for the specialist to know that in this particular

183

case it was the anal fantasy that contributed a bit of symbolism for the purpose of expressing the introversion and regression of libido. But this interpretation does not supply a generally applicable principle of explanation when we come to the far more important task of discovering the real functional significance of the castration motif. We cannot content ourselves with a simple reduction to infantile mechanisms and leave it at that.

I was once given a very impressive example of this kind of interpretation. In a discussion on the historical fish-symbol, one of those present made the remark that the fish vanishing in the sea was simply the father's penis vanishing in his wife's vagina. This kind of interpretation, which I consider sterile, is what I call sexual concretism. It seems to me that psychoanalysts are confronted with the much greater and more important task of understanding what these analogies are trying to say. What did men of many different races and epochs mean by the symbol of the fish? Why — in the present case too, for that matter — were these infantile channels of interest reactivated? What does this fetching up of infantile material signify? For this obviously is the problem. The statement: "Infantile reminiscences are coming to the surface again" is vapid and self-evident. It also leads us away from the real meaning. In Nelken's case the problem is not the derivation of part of the rat-symbol from the anal complex, but the castration motif to which the fantasy obviously belongs. The rats and mice are the instrument of the castration. But there are many other kinds of castrating instrument which are by no means anally determined. Tausk's reduction of the rats is merely of value to the specialist and has no real significance as regards the problem of sacrifice, which is at issue here.

The Zurich school naturally recognizes that the material is reducible to simpler infantile patterns, but it is not content to let it go at that. It takes these patterns for what they are, that is, as images through which the unconscious mind is expressing itself. Thus, with reference to the fish-symbol, we would reason as follows: We do not deny the Viennese school the possibility that the fish-symbol can ultimately be reduced to parental intercourse. We are ready to assume this provided there are fairly cogent reasons for doing so. But, because we are not satisfied with this relatively unimportant reduction, we ask ourselves what the evocation of parental intercourse or something similar means to the patient. We thus carry the assumption a stage further, because with the reduction to the infantile pattern we have got so far but have not gained an understanding of the real significance of the fact that the reminiscence was regressively reactivated. Were we to remain satisfied with the reduction, we would come back again and again to the long since accepted truth that the infantile lies at the root of the mental world, and that adult mental life is built upon the foundations of the infantile psyche.

Even in the backwaters of the psychoanalytic school one should have got beyond marvelling over the fact that, for instance, the artist makes use of images relating to the incest complex. Naturally every wish has these infantile patterns which it makes use of in every conceivable variation in order to express itself. But if the pattern, the infantile element, were still absolutely operative (i.e., not just regressively reactivated), all mental products would turn out to be unbelievably trivial and deadly monotonous. For it would always be the same old infantile tune that formed the essential core of all mental products. Fortunately the infantile motifs are not in themselves the essential; that is to say, for the most part they are regressively reactivated, and are fittingly employed for the purpose of expressing tendencies existing in the present, most clearly when the things to be expressed are just as far-off and intangible as the most distant childhood — for one should not forget that there is also a future! The reduction to infantile material makes the inessential in art — the limited human expression — the essence of art, which consists precisely in striving for the greatest richness of form and the greatest freedom from the limitations of the conventional and the given.

Herbert Silberer once made the very good observation that there is a mythological stage of cognition which *apprehends symbolically*. This saying holds good for the employment of infantile reminiscences: they aid cognition or apprehension and are expressive symbols. No doubt the infantile reminiscence or tendency is still partly operative and thus has an extraordinarily disturbing and obstructive effect in actual life. That is also the reason why it is so easy to find. But we would be wrong to regard it as a *source of energy* on that account; it is much more a limitation and an obstacle. Because of its undeniable existence, however, it is at the same time a necessary means of expression by analogy, for the furthest reaches of fantasy cannot offer any other material for analogical purposes. Accordingly, even if we do approach the primitive images analytically, we are not content with reduction and with establishing their self-evident existence, but, by comparing them with similar material, we try rather to reconstruct the actual problem that led to the employment of these primitive patterns and seeks expression through them. In this sense we take incest primarily as a symbol, as a means of expression, as Adler too has suggested.

I cannot therefore agree with Tausk when he says that comparison with analogous material "blocks the way to deeper insight". We do not regard the discovery of the anal fantasy as an insight that could be compared in importance with an understanding of the castration motif. I must therefore defend Nelken's attempt to establish general connections in a wider context. We can hardly expect proof of the self-evident existence of infantile fantasies to furnish any insight into the general problem of sacrifice, which makes use of the castration motif among others. That Nelken has this question in mind is clear from his footnote, in which he refers to the snake and scorpion as historical castration animals.

I have taken the liberty of dwelling at some length on Tausk's comment because it seemed to offer a favourable opportunity to sketch out our different approach to these matters. We do not by any means deny the possibility of Tausk's reduction, as should be obvious. But in this and all similar reductions we find nothing that seems to us to offer a satisfactory explanation. We believe, on the contrary, that a satisfactory explanation must make clear the teleological significance of the castration motif. In psychology, as is generally known, you cannot get very far with purely causal explanations, since a very large number of psychic phenomena can be satisfactorily explained only in teleological terms. This does nothing to alter or to detract from the exceedingly valuable discoveries of the Freudian school. We merely add the factor of teleological observation to what already exists. I have devoted a special study to this question, which will shortly appear in the *Jahrbuch*.[2]

Our attempts to develop and broaden the previous insights have given rise to absurd talk of a schism. Anything of that sort can only be the invention of people who take their working hypotheses as articles of faith. This rather childish standpoint is one which I do not share.

My scientific views change with my experiences and insights, as has always been the case in science generally. It would be a matter for suspicion if this were not so.

1 Freud, "Notes upon a Case of Obsessional Neurosis", Standard Edition, vol. 10.
2 "The Theory of Psychoanalysis", *CW* 4; first published in the *Jahrbuch für psychoanalytische und psychopathologische Forschungen,* V (1913), 307—441.

PREFATORY REMARKS TO JUNG'S "REPLY TO BUBER"

EDWARD C. WHITMONT
(New York)

When I was first asked to preface Jung's "Reply to Buber" with a summary of Buber's position I found the task difficult and little to my liking. Now, fifteen years later, when I review what I had written then (cf. *Spring 1957*, pp. 1—3), I find my reaction has not much changed. Perhaps, however, my perspective has. Where, on the one hand, I respect Buber's work now as much as then and find myself quite in sympathy with his intents, I am puzzled with and annoyed by his consistent misunderstandings and consequent misrepresentations of Jung. On the other hand, while endorsing Jung's position and in the face of its very brilliance, I find myself frustrated by what seems an incapacity on Jung's part to bring his position home to his disputant. Although it appears as if the dispute were not subject to resolution through arguments, yet these arguments cannot be lightly dismissed.

Buber's views, which are summarized below, are of interest to us chiefly because they typify an area of confusion between theology and analytical psychology which still today is anything but clear. Buber does not stand alone in his criticism. Similar points have been made not only by orthodox theologians but recently also from within psychology itself. In our day — *mirabile dictu* — humanistic psychology claims to have discovered the realm of the numinous and the religious "peak experience" which Jung is purported to have "dismissed" as "nothing but" psychology.

We may treat all this as absurd and continue to assure ourselves and point out to our critics: that observations such as Buber's are based mostly on misinterpretations and out-of-context quotations — which indeed they are; that views attributed to Jung are quite often diametrically opposite to those he actually held; that the convictions Buber expresses are frequently Jung's no less than his own. Yet, it appears to me that in merely putting Buber's criticism aside, we fail to consider that his projections have found a hook to hang on so that the constant misunderstandings require a reassessment of the positions of both parties.

Jung's reply to Buber, colored as it is by anger and hurt at being misunderstood — and he is misunderstood — sounds convincing to the Jungian. However, it obviously failed to make an impression on his critic, who in his rejoinder again uses Jung's own wording to "show" that Jung indeed denies the reality of the divine, since according to Jung the divine action supposedly arises from one's own inner self, and "God does not exist for Himself, that is, independent of the psyche". (Buber, *Eclipse of God,* pp. 133—34.)

In such an impasse it seems reasonable to assume that some emotionally charged unconscious assumptions must be present which are not being fully confronted by the disputants. With respect to Buber, Jung mentions this fact. But it seems to me that Jung does not confront his own unconscious premises. Indeed, they are being denied by his often repeated demand to be taken as "an empiricist first and last".

In asking to be considered as a pure empiricist, Jung takes the very same position he refused to Freud. Jung claims the capacity for a purely empirical and objective view in his findings about the psyche in general, which capacity he was the first to reject when Freud claimed a similar empiricism in regard to his findings about the person of the patient. Jung could as little be an empiricist as Freud, or as anyone else. Like everyone else, Jung's formulations are bound to be influenced by his personal psychology and philosophy, specifically, in his case, by his introverted emphasis and his suspicions about theology, colored by the problematic relationship to his father, a theologian. To this we may add the need to be accepted by fellow scientists of the late nineteenth century tradition with its Cartesian and positivistic bias. It is thus not difficult to see why conceptualizations might have been used which, if not deliberately anti-theological, at least may sound highly suspect to the theologian.

Perhaps it is the fate of great innovators to be misunderstood. But this does not free those who follow them from the responsibility of utilising their own more removed position for clarifying, and even correcting, some of the ambiguities that have contributed, and continue to contribute, to the confusion. Thus it may, I hope, be not too presumptuous to attempt to point out where perhaps Jung's emotional and philosophical premises led to inadequate definitions that may have given rise to the misunderstandings of Buber. But first let me sum up Buber's critique.

Summary of the Main Points of Buber's Criticism

Jung "transgresses the limitations of psychology in essential respects". In admitting that valid statements can be made only concerning what is within the scope of the knowable — not about the unknowable — Jung admits the limitation of psychology. Yet, he oversteps this limitation when he calls religion "a vital link (lit., living relationship) with psychic processes independent of and beyond consciousness, in the dark hinterland of the psyche" *(CW 9, i^2, § 261).* Buber holds that if religion is a relationship to psychic processes, it cannot be considered a relationship to a primordial Being and Presence *("Urselbständiges Sein und Wesen")* which, much as it may bend itself towards the soul, remains forever transcendent in respect to it. Jung, he says, cannot therefore consider religion the relationship of an "I" to a "Thou".

Jung subsumes metaphysics under psychology. He understands God as "an autonomous psychic content" *(CW 7^2, § 402).* This means not as a Being or Existence to which such a content would correspond but as the content itself, and therefore as something without reality apart from man and his psychology. What the faithful worshipper ascribes to God really originates in his own psyche. The same conclusion follows from the fact that all expressions about the relativity of the Divine are metaphysical statements and Jung claims that "metaphysical assertions, however, are *statements of the psyche,* and are therefore psychological" *(CW 11^2, § 835).* Buber replies that every statement is psychological when considered only with regard to the process by which it is generated and without regard to its meaning and intent. If this sentence is to be taken seriously, psychology would become the only admissible discipline of metaphysics. Any limitation upon psychology is eliminated. Psychology no longer interprets religion but, if the soul experiences itself instead of God, it proclaims a unique new religion of psychic immanence.

Jung disregards moral values. In saying that the mystics have always proclaimed God's immanence, Jung, according to Buber, overlooks the fact that they spoke of this immanence only in souls which had separated themselves from earthly activities and freed themselves from the contradictions inherent in creature existence. In place of this freeing of the whole man, Jung puts the individuation process which is a "separation or withdrawal of consciousness" only. In the place of the union with the Eternal, he puts a psychological Self which, with him, is not a genuinely mystical concept but has a Gnostic twist *(Septem Sermones ad Mortuos,* cf. *Spring 1972,* pp. 206—218). There Jung confesses to a Gnostic God in whom good and evil are united and balanced. Instead of conscience, the inner authority that discriminates between right and wrong, good and evil, Jung proclaims the soul integrated in the Self. Thus, the Self, as the psychological union of opposites eliminates conscience which ought to discriminate between good and evil. The Self, instead of conscience, executes the settlement and balancing of the opposites. And when Jung writes "whoever lives according to his instincts is also able to dissociate himself from them" (I cannot find any such quotation in either of the sources to which Buber refers), this is a statement, according to Buber, "all too well-known to us from certain Gnostic circles".

Jung's view eliminates the need of relating to the Divine. The Self in Jung's conception includes the other or others as well as the I *(CW* 8^2, § 432) and thereby does not exclude, but includes, the world. But these others when so contained in the Self are merely contents of the individual soul and are taken into its possession by the act of enclosing *(Einschluss);* the soul relates to such a content as an "it", or an object only, not as a "Thou". Thus Jung overlooks the necessity of relatedness, of relating to an other, whether man or God, to an otherness of being, impossible to own or possess, and toward which the claim of ownership and possession must be resigned. This necessary attitude for true relatedness Buber holds to be the very opposite of Jung's road to the Self.

Danger of the Self as a "Superman". Since the Self is pure "totality" *(CW* 11^2, §232) which "cannot be distinguished from an archetypal God-image" (ibid, §238), self-realization must be considered the incarnation of God. Buber holds that this God of Jung's who unites good and evil is traceable back to Zurvan, an ancient Iranian deity, never mentioned by Jung. He says that Jung, by treating the Jewish and Christian concepts of God from this basically Gnostic point of view, makes the God of the Old Testament into a semi-satanic demiurge who, because of his "guilt" in respect to the miscarriage of world creation, has been subjected to a ritual killing. And, thereby, Jung unmasks all monotheistic systems as secretly Gnostic. Finally, true to his adherence to the Gnostic God whom he originally confessed, Jung sets the Self, the union of good and evil, upon the throne of the world as the new incarnation. This means, Buber continues, that Jung makes the attempt to put man, or rather the Superman, into the place of God. This implies (here Martin Heidegger is quoted, *Holzwege*, p. 235) "entering a realm, neither divine nor human". "The Superman", Heidegger goes on, "cannot and never will be able to step into the place of God; the realm to which he has access is different; it is differently based upon existence in a different realm of being." These words Buber feels apply ominously to an imminent threat.

Comment

I believe that Buber (as well as other critics) is principally disturbed by what appears to him an inclination to substitute "psyche", "soul", or "contents of the psyche" for the divine or spiritual reality "out there". To him this looks like an attempt to substitute the subjectively human for the objectively transcendent, or at least to treat the latter as if it were a mere epiphenomenon of the former. This was decidedly not Jung's belief or intent; yet ambiguities of terminology, and even attitude, indeed encourage these assumptions.

Foremost among these ambiguities is the tendency in attitude and deed prevalent among many analytical psychologists, particularly of Buber's generation, to give secondary value to personal relationships and to external reality in favor of introversion. Another ambiguity lies in the inadequate definitions and epistemology concerning "soul" and "psyche". The meaning of these terms becomes easily over-extended. A third ambiguity is presented by the concept of projected psychic contents. To anyone — and here I would include Buber — unfamiliar with the secrets of our terminology, the concept of projection may easily seem all too close to denying trans-psychological realities, the very last thing that Jung intended.

PREFATORY NOTE

Already G. R. Heyer, one of Jung's earliest disciples and erstwhile friend and confidant, took issue with what he felt to be Jung's tendency to give insufficient attention to the dynamics and spirit actually inherent in matter itself. Similarly, Heyer believed that Jung in his disquisitions on Tantra yoga rather neglected the body aspects and the psycho-physiological effects that occur through meditation upon the chacras. He felt that Jung emphasized the projections of psychological content which these chacras carry to the exclusion of their intrinsic psycho-physiological dynamics. This kind of criticism has been raised ever and again; for example by Ralph Metzner *(Maps of Consciousness,* MacMillan, N.Y., 1971), who is otherwise very sympathetic to Jung's work. Metzner speaks of a lacuna in respect to the body in Jung's thinking. There has been a well-known reluctance among Jungians to concern themselves with body dynamics and with the social collective "out there", or to include group work in their therapeutic armamentarium.

This introverted bias encourages a tendency to treat external reality as though it were an epiphenomenon or projection of the psyche rather than a facet of a unitary reality encompassing both. The introverted bias also expresses itself in what I believe to be an ambiguous terminology in respect to psyche and projection. It fails to make a clear distinction between the psyche as a vehicle of experience and the non-psychic object "out there" even though that object be endowed with formal qualities, intentionality, and spirit of its own.

The result is a confusion between that which is being observed and the means of observation. The latter is psychical or psychological since the psyche is the inevitable means and datum of all human experiencing, as Jung so often stressed. Whereas the psyche experiences psychological dynamics in a state of introversion, it also observes external objects and dynamics, i.e., objective reality, not only in extraversion, but — a most important point to consider — in introversion as well. Parapsychological research into the *psi* factor has demonstrated conclusively that we do perceive by means of extra-sensory psychic perception both subjective states of others as well as objective, non-psychic events (space-time, distant events and actions). This constitutes an experience by the psyche but *of* non-psychic stuff. Therefore the term psyche or soul has traditionally been reserved for the inner or subjective means and objects of observations, hence to what we Jungians would call the personal psyche, the human psyche. This tradition has failed to recognize as also psychic the impersonal and non-human — what Backster's experiments pointed to (cf. *Spring 1971*, pp. 78—9) when he noted the "emotional reactions" of plants. Likewise the "anima mundi" and the "God" entity may be experienced in this way — impersonal, objective and yet psychic. These phenomena are psychic events without being caused by, or projected by, the personal human psyche.

The term "reality of the psyche", which Jung uses for the "objective" or "transpersonal" psyche, extends the accustomed meaning of psychic reality toward transpersonal events. This usage is unclear to a non-Jungian; it is likely to smell to him of psychologism since what to him is merely personal psyche is claimed to be all-inclusive. The term "objective psyche" sounds self-contradictory because of this generally accepted idea of psyche as personal and subjective. The God image as a content of the non-personal or the objective psyche sounds to the non-Jungian like a reduction to subjectivity.

If the terms psyche and soul are to remain solely in the realm of subjective experience, the transpersonal objects of experience might better be called powers, energies, archetypes, dynamics, or psychoid factors — if we must avoid speaking of Gods and daimons. But, at any rate, they are to be regarded as experiences *sui generis* if we are not to perpetuate the Cartesian mind-object split. Then, it would follow that it is inadmissible to speak of projection of the unconscious psyche when describing the religious experience, the experiments of the alchemist, the perceptions of the astrologer, or the experiences of the yogi. Projection referred originally, and would best remain limited to, a delusional quasi-paranoid tendency to experience in the object an unconscious personal quality of the subject. It is a clinical term that would best remain restricted to clinical distortions of personal material, to qualities capable and in need of assimilation into the conscious personality. We may argue, of course, that all experiencing consists of projection inasmuch as our psychological structuring and sense limitations are our only means of experiencing; but if projection refers to everything, it loses specificity and denotes nothing.

The experience of that which is directly unknowable Jung has defined as *symbolic:* "an image that describes in the best possible way the dimly discerned nature of the spirit, ... that points beyond itself to a meaning that is darkly divined yet still beyond our grasp . . ." *(CW 8², § 644).*

Our anthropomorphizing experiences of the transpersonal and its qualities would therefore more appropriately be called *symbolic perceptions* rather than projections of contents of the psyche. Thereby we would clearly acknowledge their objective reality, yet admit the merely analogical, psychological limitation of our subjective perception. *Symbolic perception* acknowledges objective being as perceived in subjective terms yet differentiates it from the delusion and paranoid distortion inherent in projection. Calling the Divine "the Self" and its image representations "symbolic experiences" of or through the psyche sounds quite different from calling them contents, parts, or projections of the psyche.

Such formulations would offer less offense and misunderstanding to theologians and our humanistic colleagues and would more clearly express for ourselves what we really mean.

RELIGION AND PSYCHOLOGY:
A REPLY TO MARTIN BUBER

C. G. JUNG
(1952)

Some while ago the readers of your magazine were given the opportunity to read a posthumous article by Count Keyserling, in which I was characterized as "unspiritual". Now, in your last issue, I find an article by Martin Buber which is likewise concerned with my classification. I am indebted to his pronouncements at least in so far as they raise me out of the condition of unspirituality, in which Count Keyserling saw fit to present me to the German public, into the sphere of spirituality, even though it be the spirituality of early Christian Gnosticism, which has always been looked at askance by theologians. Funnily enough this opinion of Buber's coincides with another utterance from an authoritative theological source which accuses me of agnosticism — the exact opposite of Gnosticism.

Now when opinions about the same subject differ so widely, there is in my view ground for the suspicion that none of them is correct, and that there has been a misunderstanding. Why is so much attention devoted to the question of whether I am a Gnostic or an agnostic? Why

---

This reply was published in *Merkur* (Stuttgart) in May, 1952, pp 467–73. It was in response to Buber's article in the same journal in February, 1952. Buber's response to Jung's reply appeared in *Merkur* also in May, 1952, pp. 474–76. Buber's arguments are published in English in his *Eclipse of God* (London: Gollancz, 1953). Jung's "Reply" was previously published in mimeographed form in a translation by Robert A. Clark in *Spring 1957*, pp. 1–10. The present translation by R.F.C. Hull (entitled "Answer to Buber") will appear in *Miscellany, CW* 18, in press for publication in 1974 by Princeton University Press in the United States and by Routledge and Kegan Paul in the United Kingdom. Copyright © 1973 by Princeton University Press. Published here by arrangement with Princeton University Press and the permission of the Heirs of C. G. Jung.

is it not simply stated that I am a psychiatrist whose prime concern is to record and interpret his empirical material? I try to investigate facts and make them more generally comprehensible. My critics have no right to slur over this in order to attack individual statements taken out of context.

To support his diagnosis Buber even resorts to a sin of my youth, committed nearly forty years ago, which consists in my once having perpetrated a poem.[1] In this poem I expressed a number of psychological *aperçus* in "Gnostic" style, because I was then studying the Gnostics with enthusiasm. My enthusiasm arose from the discovery that they were apparently the first thinkers to concern themselves (after their fashion) with the contents of the collective unconscious. I had the poem printed under a pseudonym and gave a few copies to friends, little dreaming that it would one day bear witness against me as a heretic.

I would like to point out to my critic that I have in my time been regarded not only as a Gnostic and its opposite, but also as a theist and an atheist, a mystic and a materialist. In this concert of contending opinions I do not wish to lay too much stress on what I consider myself to be, but will quote a judgment from a leading article in the *British Medical Journal* (9 February 1952), a source that would seem to be above suspicion. "Facts first and theories later is the keynote of Jung's work. He is an empiricist first and last." This view meets with my approval.

Anyone who does not know my work will certainly ask himself how it is that so many contrary opinions can be held about one and the same subject. The answer to this is that they are all thought up by "metaphysicians", that is, by people who for one reason or another think they know about unknowable things in the Beyond. I have never ventured to declare that such things do *not* exist; but neither have I ventured to suppose that any statement of mine could in any way touch them or even represent them correctly. I very much doubt whether our conception of a thing is identical with the nature of the thing itself, and this for very obvious scientific reasons.

But since views and opinions about metaphysical or religious subjects play a very great role in empirical psychology,[2] I am obliged for practical reasons to work with concepts corresponding to them. In so doing I am aware that I am dealing with anthropomorphic ideas and not with actual gods and angels, although, thanks to their specific energy, such (archetypal) images behave so autonomously that one could describe them metaphorically as "psychic daimonia". The fact that they are autonomous should be taken very seriously; first, from the theoretical standpoint, because it explains the dissociability of the psyche as well as actual dissociation, and second, from the practical one, because it forms the basis for a dialectical discussion between the ego and the unconscious, which is one of the mainstays of the psychotherapeutic method. Anyone who has any knowledge of the structure of a neurosis will be aware that the pathogenic conflict arises from the counterposition of the unconscious relative to consciousness. The so-called "forces of the unconscious" are not intellectual concepts that can be arbitrarily manipulated, but dangerous antagonists which can, among other things, work frightful devastation in the economy of the personality. They are everything one could wish for or fear in a psychic "Thou". The layman naturally thinks he is the victim of some obscure organic disease; but the theologian, who suspects it is the devil's work, is appreciably nearer to the psychological truth.

I am afraid that Buber, having no psychiatric experience, fails to understand what I mean by the "reality of the psyche" and by the dialectical process of individuation. The fact is that the ego is confronted with psychic powers which from ancient times have borne sacred names, and because of these they have always been identified with metaphysical beings. Analysis of the unconscious has long since demonstrated the existence of these powers in the form of archetypal images which, be it noted, *are not identical with the corresponding intellectual concepts*. One can, of course, believe that the concepts of the conscious mind are, through the inspiration of the Holy Ghost, direct and correct representations of their metaphysical referent. But this conviction is possible only for one who already possesses the gift of faith. Unfortunately I cannot boast of this possession, for which reason I do not imagine that when I say something about an archangel I have thereby confirmed a metaphysical fact. I have merely expressed an opinion about something that can be experienced, that is, about one of the very palpable "powers of the unconscious". These powers are numinous "types" — unconscious contents, processes, and dynamisms — and such types are, if one may so express it, immanent-transcendent. Since my sole means of cognition is experience I may not overstep its boundaries, and cannot therefore pretend to myself that my description coincides with the portrait of a real metaphysical archangel. What I have described is a psychic factor only, but one which exerts a considerable influence on the conscious mind. Thanks to its autonomy, it forms the counterposition to the subjective ego because it is a piece of the *objective psyche*. It can therefore be designated as a "Thou". For me its reality is amply attested by the truly diabolical deeds of our time: the six million murdered Jews, the uncounted victims of the slave labour camps in Russia, as well as the invention of the atom bomb, to name but a few examples of the darker side. But I have also seen the other side which can be expressed by the words beauty, goodness, wisdom, grace. These experiences of the depths and heights of human nature justify the metaphorical use of the term "daimon".

It should not be overlooked that what I am concerned with are psychic phenomena which can be proved empirically to be the bases of metaphysical concepts, and that when, for example, I speak of "God" I am unable to refer to anything beyond these demonstrable psychic models which, we have to admit, have shown themselves to be devastatingly real. To anyone who finds their reality incredible I would recommend a reflective tour through a lunatic asylum.

The "reality of the psyche" is my working hypothesis, and my principal activity consists in collecting factual material to describe and explain it. I have set up neither a system nor a general theory, but have merely formulated auxiliary concepts to serve me as tools, as is customary in every branch of science. If Buber misunderstands my empiricism as Gnosticism, it is up to him to prove that the facts I describe are nothing but inventions. If he should succeed in proving this with empirical material, then indeed I am a Gnostic. But in that case he will find himself in the uncomfortable position of having to dismiss all religious experiences as self-deception. Meanwhile I am of the opinion that Buber's judgment has been led astray. This seems especially evident in his apparent inability to understand how an "autonomous psychic content" like the God-image can burst upon the ego, and that such a confrontation is a living experience. It is certainly not the task of an empirical science to establish how far such a psychic content is dependent on and determined by the existence of a metaphysical deity. That is the concern of theology, revelation, and faith. My critic does not seem to realize that when he himself talks about God, his statements are dependent firstly on his conscious and then on his unconscious assumptions. Of *which* metaphysical deity he is speaking I do not know. If he is an orthodox Jew he is speaking of a God to whom the incarnation in the year 1 has not yet been revealed. If he is a Christian, then his deity knows about the incarnation of which Yahweh still shows no sign. I do not doubt his conviction that he stands in a living relationship to a divine Thou, but now as before I am of the opinion that this relationship is primarily to an autonomous psychic content which is defined in one way by him and in another by the Pope. Consequently I do not permit myself the least judgment as to whether and to what extent it has pleased a metaphysical deity to reveal himself to the devout Jew as he was before the incarnation, to the Church Fathers as the Trinity, to the Protestants as the one and only Saviour without co-redemptrix, and to the present Pope as a Saviour with co-redemptrix. Nor should one doubt that the devotees of other faiths, including Islam, Buddhism, Hinduism, and so on, have the same living relationship to "God", or to Nirvana and Tao, as Buber has to the God-concept peculiar to himself.

It is remarkable that he takes exception to my statement that God cannot exist apart from man and regards it as a transcendental assertion. Yet I say expressly that everything asserted about "God" is a human statement, in other words a psychological one. For surely the image we have or make for ourselves of God is never detached from man? Can Buber show me where, apart from man, God has made an image of himself? How can such a thing be substantiated and by whom? Here, just for once, and as an exception, I shall indulge in transcendental speculation and even in "poetry": God has indeed made an inconceivably sublime and mysteriously contradictory image of himself, without the help of man, and implanted it in man's unconscious as an archetype, an *arche-typon-phos*, archetypal light: not in order that theologians of all times and places should be at one another's throats, but in order that the unpresumptuous man might glimpse an image, in the stillness of his soul, that is akin to him and is wrought of his own psychic substance. This image contains everything which he will ever imagine concerning his gods or concerning the ground of his soul.

This archetype, whose existence is attested not only by ethnology but also by the psychic experience of individuals, satisfies me completely. It is so humanly close and yet so strange and "other"; also, like all archetypes, it possesses the utmost determinative power with which it is absolutely necessary that we come to terms. The dialectical relationship to the autonomous contents of the collective unconscious is therefore, as I have said, an essential part of therapy.

Buber is mistaken in thinking that I start with a "fundamentally Gnostic viewpoint" and then proceed to "elaborate" metaphysical assertions. One should not misconstrue the findings of empiricism as philosophical premises, for they are not obtained by deduction but from clinical and factual material. I would recommend him to read some autobiographies of the mentally ill, such as John Custance's *Wisdom, Madness, and Folly* (1951), or D. P. Schreber's *Memoirs of My Nervous Illness* (first published 1903), which certainly do not proceed from Gnostic hypotheses any more than I do; or he might try an analysis of mythological material, such as the excellent work of Dr. Erich Neumann, his neighbour in Tel-Aviv: *Amor and Psyche* (1952). My contention that the products of the unconscious are analogous and related to certain metaphysical ideas is founded on my professional experience. In this connection I would point out that I know quite a number of influential theologians, Catholics as well as Protestants, who have no difficulty in grasping my empirical standpoint. I therefore see no reason why I should take my method of exposition to be quite so misleading as Buber would have us believe.

There is one misunderstanding which I would like to mention here because it comes up so often. This is the curious assumption that when a projection is withdrawn nothing more of the object remains. When I correct my mistaken opinion of a man I have not negated him and caused him to vanish; on the contrary, I see him more nearly as he is, and this can only benefit the relationship. So if I hold the view that all statements about God have their origin in the psyche and must therefore be distinguished from God as a metaphysical being, this is neither to deny God nor to put man in God's place. I frankly confess that it goes against the grain with me to think that the metaphysical God himself is speaking through everyone who quotes the Bible or ventilates his religious opinions. Faith is certainly a splendid thing if one has it, and knowledge by faith is perhaps more perfect than anything we can produce with our laboured and wheezing empiricism. The edifice of Christian dogma, for instance, undoubtedly stands on a much higher level than the somewhat wild "philosophoumena" of the Gnostics.

Dogmas are spiritual structures of supreme beauty, and they possess a wonderful meaning which I have sought to fathom in my fashion. Compared with them our scientific endeavours to devise models of the objective psyche are unsightly in the extreme. They are bound to earth and reality, full of contradictions, incomplete, logically and aesthetically unsatisfying. The empirical concepts of science and particularly of medical psychology do not proceed from neat and seemly principles of thought, but are the outcome of our daily labours in the sloughs of ordinary human existence and human pain. They are essentially irrational, and the philosopher who criticizes them as though they were philosophical concepts tilts against windmills and gets into the greatest difficulties, as Buber does with the concept of the self. Empirical concepts are names for existing complexes of facts. Considering the fearful paradoxicality of human existence, it is quite understandable that the unconscious contains an equally paradoxical God-image which will not square at all with the beauty, sublimity, and purity of the dogmatic concept of God. The God of Job and of the 89th Psalm is clearly a bit closer to reality, and his behaviour does not fit in badly with the God-image in the unconscious. Of course this image, with its Anthropos symbolism, lends support to the idea of the incarnation. I do not feel responsible for the fact that the history of dogma has made some progress since the days of the Old Testament. This is not to preach a new religion, for to do that I would have to follow the old-established custom of appealing to a divine revelation. I am essentially a physician, whose business is with the sickness of man and his times, and with remedies that are as real as the suffering. Not only Buber, but every theologian who baulks at my odious psychology is at liberty to heal my patients with the word of God. I would welcome this experiment with open arms. But since the ecclesiastical cure of souls does not always produce the desired results, we doctors must do what we can, and at present we have no better standby than that modest "gnosis" which the empirical method gives us. Or have any of my critics better advice to offer?

As a doctor one finds oneself in an awkward position, because unfortunately one can accomplish nothing with that little word "ought". We cannot demand of our patients a faith which they reject because they do not understand it, or which does not suit them even though we may hold it ourselves. We have to rely on the curative powers inherent in the patient's own nature, regardless of whether the ideas that emerge agree with any known creed or philosophy. My empirical material seems to include a bit of everything — it is an assortment of primitive, Western, and Oriental ideas. There is scarcely any myth whose echoes are not heard, nor any heresy that has not contributed an occasional oddity. The deeper, collective layers of the human psyche must surely be of a like nature. Intellectuals and rationalists, happy in their established beliefs, will no doubt be horrified by this and will accuse me of reckless eclecticism, as though I had somehow invented the facts of man's nature and mental history and had compounded out of them a repulsive theosophical brew. Those who possess faith or prefer to talk like philosophers do not, of course, need to wrestle with the facts, but a doctor is not at liberty to dodge the grim realities of human nature.

It is inevitable that the adherents of traditional religious systems should find my formulations hard to understand. A Gnostic would not be at all pleased with me, but would reproach me for having no cosmogony and for the cluelessness of my gnosis in regard to the happenings in the Pleroma. A Buddhist would complain that I was deluded by Maya, and a Taoist that I was too complicated. As for an orthodox Christian, he can hardly do otherwise than deplore the nonchalance and lack of respect with which I navigate through the empyrean of dogmatic ideas. I must, however, once more beg my unmerciful critics to remember that I start from *facts* for which I seek an interpretation.

1   *VII Sermones ad Mortuos*, by Basilides of Alexandria (n.d 1916), privately printed. English translation by H. G. Baynes, privately printed 1925; included in the 2nd edition of *Memories, Dreams, Reflections*, appendix. (Jung's "sin of my youth" was "perpetrated" when he was 41 years old; for an article relating it significantly to his later work see James W. Heisig, "The *VII* Sermones: Play and Theory", *Spring 1972.*)
2   Cf. G. Schmaltz, *Östliche Weisheit und westliche Psychotherapie*, 1951.

JUNG AND THEOLOGY: A BIBLIOGRAPHICAL ESSAY

JAMES W. HEISIG
(Cambridge)

It would, I think, be fair to characterize the present state of scholarly relations between Jungian psychology and theology as chaotic. If one takes the trouble to study the shelves of books and reams of articles that have appeared on the subject, one is consistently left with the impression of an adventuresome, potentially fruitful and perhaps even revolutionary inter-disciplinary project that has somehow failed to make a presentable case for itself. The initial skirmishes between uninformed critics and uncritical devotees have gone on unabated and the few flashes of brilliance have done little to enlighten matters. Darkness continues to hover over the waters. Perhaps every human process of creativity requires such a period of chaos; but until we can acknowledge this state for the *rudis indigestaque moles* that it is, we can have no hope of moving through it.

This, then, is the principal motive behind the present essay, which will attempt to set forth in a systematic fashion the literature available on the topic "Jung and theology", and to sketch the broad outlines of its achievements. I proceed within certain limitations which it is best to clarify at the outset. To begin with, we shall adhere strictly to our subject matter, dealing only with those works which attempt to describe, compare or evaluate the religious dimensions of Jung's thought. Related questions (such as the archetypes, the collective unconscious, the theory of symbolism and the like) will only be considered if they are presented in such a context. Likewise, historical treatments of the psychology of religion, later developments of the Jungian school and the adaptation of Jungian principles in theological investigation are mentioned only when they form part of an explicit and extensive confrontation with Jung's own thought. Very brief commentaries, short reviews and *obiter dicta* have been excluded for the most part.

Within those limits, I have made every effort to gather together as comprehensive a bibliography as I was able, omitting nothing that fit the theme, however outdated, insignificant or useless it appeared. To that end, the standard European, North and South American and Australian indices of periodical literature (up to August 1972) have been consulted, as well as scores of more specialized bibliographies. Entries which I was unable to locate and read, but whose titles suggest that they ought to find a place in such a study, have been marked with an asterisk (*) in the actual bibliography, although reference to them has been omitted in the text of the essay.

The adoption of a scheme for organizing the material at hand is more a matter of convenience than of rigid logical classification. Jung's writings on the psychology of religion form an organic whole and do not take easily to neat categories. It is to be expected that commentaries on his work will tend to reflect this, and that the apparent tidiness of the outline which follows will have to be taken occasionally *cum grano salis*.

It only remains to mention in passing that to my knowledge nothing of this scope has yet been undertaken. A much more modest attempt at a bibliographical study on Jung and religion was compiled in 1956 by STRUNK (345), but contained no more than a dozen entries of secondary material, most of which were lifted out of *Psychological Abstracts*. Other efforts to review the relevant literature on the subject have been equally restricted (v. HAENDLER 146, 149; HOSTIE 182, pp. 109—10; MANN 245; STEFFEN 338). Indeed, as we shall see, this is only symptomatic of a more general state of affairs in which needless repetition has helped to maintain constructive criticism at a sub-standard level.

1. General Studies - I

We begin with the more thoroughgoing confrontations with Jung's psychology of religion, among which can be found the most solid description and criticism that has appeared on the subject. Even here however, certain fundamental lacunae have gone unattended. For one thing, no one has yet bothered to do a proper job of investigating and reporting on the primary source material. The more than fifty volumes of unpublished seminar notes, accessible for the past twenty-five years, have all but gone totally ignored. Also, Jung's personal correspondence, which is now beginning to appear and which, when fully published, will be seen to shed considerable light on almost every facet of his views on religion, has not yet found its rightful place. Those two areas aside, one still looks in vain for a definitive study embracing the whole of Jung's published corpus.[1] The situation with secondary sources is hardly more satisfying. Large areas of critical work seem somehow to escape the notice of even the best commentators, and, in more than a few cases, there are wide gaps between the promising listings of a concluding bibliography and the internal textual evidence of what has actually been examined with care.

With these reservations, we can turn first to the work of VICTOR WHITE, whose sympathetic understanding of Jung's thought and deep appreciation of the Christian tradition served him admirably in the years he devoted to the dialogue between psychology and theology. A Dominican priest and lecturer on scholastic thought, FR. WHITE'S growing interest in psychology led him to Zurich, where he studied at the newly-founded Jung Institute and came to form a lasting, if finally somewhat turbulent, friendship with Jung himself. From the very start he was convinced of the rich possibilities that archetypal psychology,[2] in marked contrast to the Freudian approach, held for the theologian (396, 397, 398). In time this led him to *God and the Unconscious*, a book organized about a number of earlier lectures and essays (401). Its reception, undoubtedly aided by Jung's superb foreword, was overwhelmingly favorable, the chief reservations centering on his shaky interpretation of non-Jungian psychology (STERN 339, ALLERS 10, SCHWARTZ 327; cf. FORDHAM 108, LEAVY 232, MESEGUER 261). Others were skeptical of his use of St. Thomas (STEVENS 340, BARTEMEIER 23) and one reviewer accused him of being unversed in theology (LEONARD 235). From the Catholic side, however, his most vigorous opponent was the Italian Franciscan AGOSTINO GEMELLI, who concluded a short and unsympathetic book on Jung with an attack on WHITE'S orthodoxy (127; cf. 128). At a conference in 1957 which both men attended, WHITE (404) took the opportunity to conclude a paper on the therapeutic value of dogma with a reply to these attacks, to no apparent avail. For in 1959, while lying in a semi-conscious state after cracking his skull in a motor-scooter accident, WHITE received a letter from his Master General, informing him that the Holy See had ordered the suspension of the sale of his book. A humble consent from FR. WHITE and not so humble complaints from his superior helped to lift the ban and the book went into several reprints and foreign translations. At that time, he had also been preparing a second book of lectures for publication, which carried the themes of the earlier volume to greater depth and concluded with a number of appendices on specific questions relating to Catholic theology (408; cf. LAYARD 231). Shortly after its appearance, he died. Appropriately enough, the book ends with a brief appendix on the problem of evil, which had been a matter of considerable tension between him and Jung during those final years, as their correspondence amply demonstrates.

The only attempt to trace the development of Jung's religious thought through his writings was undertaken by a Belgian Jesuit and professor of theology at the Louvain, RAYMOND HOSTIE (182; cf. 183). His chronological outline of Jung's career into three periods of increasing openness to religion quickly, if rather unquestioningly, became a classic reference among those within and without the Jungian school. In spite of the artificiality of the scheme, the dubious selection of material and the frequent errors in footnoting, this book has long been the only developmental study available, and for that reason alone deserves careful attention. His actual confrontation with Jung, on the other hand, has been less well received, arguing as he does from a dogmatically Catholic standpoint and thereby often failing to appreciate Jung's arguments (LAMBERT 224; A. JUNG 203; HOBSON 176; WHITE 402, 405). On the more favorable side, CROWLEY (78), THIRY (352), and RÜSCHE (304) seem to have accepted HOSTIE'S arguments *tout court*.

No less comprehensive than the works of WHITE and HOSTIE, HANS SCHÄR'S (317) study on Jung's psychology of religion leaves much to be desired from a critical point of view. He accepted Jung's wide-ranging researches and conclusions without question, and greatly overestimated his scholarly achievements. The merit of the book lies in the early recognition (1946) by a Protestant pastor of the need for both theoretical and practical theology to take Jung seriously. But, as FRISCHKNECHT (122) has pointed out, SCHÄR presumes that a mere summary of Jung's ideas solves the problem of integrating them into patterns of Christian thought. LEONARD (236) has also questioned SCHÄR'S theological competence and is suspicious of his tacit assumptions.

Somewhat in this same vein is a more recent book by CHARLES HANNA (152) which is a popularization of Jung's religious ideas, aimed at pastors and seminary students. Even more facilely than SCHÄR he weds Jungian theory to traditional Christian dogmatics with surprisingly little sense for the complexities involved. JOLANDE JACOBI'S (194) treatise on the individuation process, which represents her only attempt to deal at length with Jung's religious psychology, is a tribute to her customary flair for making more order out of Jung than he was able to make of himself.

An avid disciple of Jung's and a German Jewish convert to Russian Orthodoxy, GERHARD ZACHARIAS (423) has climbed out rather far and rather alone on a limb in an imaginative attempt to use Jung's ideas to reformulate a contemporary Christian theology. His approach centers around viewing the Self as an image of Christ, which he supports by weaving together theological and psychological insights on the notion of transcendence. As WHITE (402) has noted, ZACHARIAS' allusions to the Christian biblical and doctrinal tradition are far too amateurish and his use of Jung far too uncritical to provide the kind of support his case needs (cf. HOCH 178).

In a light, popular and preachy book, J. M. HONDIUS (181) undertakes the same project of reconciling the doctrine of Self to that of Christ, approaching the matter from the opposite end of the spectrum by seeing psychology as an *ancilla* to theology, the perennial *regina scientiarum*.

More dependable from a theological point of view is the work of JOSEF GOLDBRUNNER, a Catholic priest and noted authority in catechetics. Already in 1940 (131) he showed enthusiasm for the possible uses of depth psychology in problems of pastoral care. At the same time, however, he accused Jung of "psychologizing" religious dogmas away and disagreed with his understanding of the sacraments — to which judgments MESEGUER (259) gave his support. In a later and more mature book, GOLDBRUNNER (134) made use of Jung's later writings and as a result was slightly more charitable in his estimation, even though he persisted in adhering to the supremacy of Catholic dogma and to his inadequately argued criticism of Jung's "positivistic agnosticism". JACOBI (192) was quick to refute these charges, which, however, had once again earned MESEGUER'S (261) unqualified approval.

Even stronger than the judgments of GOLDBRUNNER are those of MAX FRISCHKNECHT (121), who concluded in a little booklet on Jung that he could find nothing other in his psychology than a subtle variety of atheism. What he saw in Jung was an ambivalent attitude towards religion, which actually masked a divinization of the Self in place of Freud's supreme Sexuality. Curiously enough, nearly 20 years later FRISCHKNECHT (123) published his highly laudatory reflections on Jung's autobiography, citing his own book as an example of the kind of unfortunate misunderstanding that had arisen between Jung and the theologians.

VIKTOR VON GEBSATTEL, a Catholic psychotherapist and one of the inspiring lights of existential psychology, took over many of the arguments of FRISCHKNECHT'S book in his own critical *auseinandersetzung* with Jung (383). His main complaint was, and remained (384), that Jung had misconstrued religion by ignoring the whole realm of the "personal", seeing God instead in the inadequate categories dictated by his model of the psyche. WALDER (387, pp. 152—58) criticized VON GEBSATTEL at some length for misrepresenting Jung's actual methods, only to show that he himself had quite missed the fundamental sense of the objections. Some years later WINGENFELD (414) made the same accusations in a more systematic and thorough fashion. Nevertheless, as FREI (118) has noted, the book is riddled with misinterpretations of Jung's ideas.

Arguing from many of the same premises, RUDOLF AFFEMANN (4) has presented us with a more systematic piece of work, confronting Jung's religious psychology on six major points with the teaching of the Bible, and concluding with a chapter on the division of labor between theology and psychology. In the process, Jung emerges as a pantheist of gnostic stamp. An intelligent and consistent book, it suffers, however, from a virtually total isolation from secondary material, which leads in this case to a simplistic and overbearing tone in his biblical theology and a lack of appreciation for the finer points of archetypal psychology. (My own suspicion is that AFFEMANN intended the book as a response to ZACHARIAS [423], from whom he would have picked up his interpretation of Jung.)

WALTER BERNET (38), now professor of practical theology in the University of Zurich, attempted to find a place for Jung within the theological circle by pasting together a montage of insights from liberal theology, existentialism and his own special reading of the theory of archetypes. While Jung was not personally pleased with the results, there is much to commend the work as a piece of philosophical theology, and indeed BERNET'S central idea concerning the Self as man's hint to a God-beyond-experience deserves far more attention than it has hitherto received (cf. HOCH 178).

In a massive and impressive study on religion in Marx, Freud and Jung, H. M. M. FORTMANN (114) has given us what may well be the most organized presentation of Jung's religious thought, along with some of the most perceptive evaluation. Descriptively, only his conception of Jung's notion of "faith" is questionable. Critically, his strong point is his rejection of the adequacy of Jung's articulated methodology and of his understanding of the historical aspects of Christianity. Moreover, as he stated in an article prefiguring the main ideas of the book (113), he considers Jung to have given us the best psychology of religion to date: full of brilliant questions and untenable answers!

Of all the longer studies mentioned in this section, by far the least convincing seems to be that of ANTONIO MORENO (269). His book is so full of misinterpretations, faulty judgments and technical and grammatical errors that it would hardly merit mention, were it not for the fact that his attempt to compare Jung with Eliade, however unsatisfactory the results, stands alone. Elsewhere I have criticized the book in detail (165).

The most ambitious work in Italian has been done by LUIGI PINTACUDA (277), who unfortunately did not understand Jung at any depth. His book shows a decisive lack of linguistic rigor and an overall unevenness of style. Furthermore, the reader is annoyed to find so many unidentified quotations, typographical errors and faults of information in a study that is obviously aimed at an educated audience, not to mention the more serious complaint of an almost Inquisitional Catholic orthodoxy which is used to steamroll Jung's achievements into "mere dilettantism".

Finally I would refer to various unpublished dissertations. RIU-KAS (287) has done a lengthy and moderately competent job of summarizing Jung's notion of the God-archetype according to its genesis, structure and function. When he goes on to find in Jung's ideas on religion in general a viable answer to the challenge of the "death-of-God" movement in theology, his judgments of that radical theology are too hasty and his appreciation of the critical literature surrounding Jungian psychology too meagre (despite a considerable, but deceptive bibliography) to uphold his cause. An earlier thesis by DAWSON (85; cf. 84) is somewhat less impressive in its understanding of Jung's writings, bringing the author to the point where he cannot finally decide for himself what rôle Jung is to play within the Christian theological tradition. BEVERIDGE (45), on the other hand, does take a firm stand on the rapport between theology and archetypal psychology, stressing the value of Jung's thought for making the Gospel relevant to modern man. Although he is suspicious of the consequences of Jung's quaternity theory, most of what he writes is too vague and undisciplined to be of much use.

2. General Studies - II

In addition to the longer pieces cited above, there are numerous shorter attempts to deal with Jung's religious psychology in an equally general, but for the most part less impressive manner.

A first class of entries comprises non-critical descriptions and popularized accounts. Among these, a paper by ELEANOR BERTINE (42) recommends itself for clarity of approach; after a brief personal introduction (cf. EVANS 101), she summarizes Jung in five points of increasing specificity, clarifying these with examples from her own psychotherapeutic practice. In a later, more loosely organized essay (43) she adds to her résumé something of the methodological polemics in which Jung got involved. E. B. HOWES (184) has written the closest thing to a "primer" on the subject, presuming almost no knowledge of psychology at all. FRIEDA FORDHAM's (105, pp. 69—83) chapter on religion in her excellent little introduction to Jung, if read in context, is as fine a short summary as there is. The Portugese equivalent to it was done by E. CALLUF (62, pp. 19—23, 277—98), who has only slightly weakened his effort by incorporating HOSTIE's (182) theories on Jung's development; and in Dutch there is E. CAMERLING's (63, pp. 41—45) far more simplified account.

Without intending to write an account of Jung's religious psychology, ANIELA JAFFE (199) has done an admirable job of summarizing his major thoughts on religion against the broader context of his life-myth. In contrast, ELLENBERGER (99, pp. 723—26), who has done a mammoth job of research into the origins of depth psychology, somehow falls flat in his treatment of Jung's writings on religion, denying them the importance they deserve. CHARLES BAUDOUIN (28, ch. 15) — founder of the school of "psychopedagogy" in Geneva in which he embodied his lifelong concern of combining the theories and therapeutic methods of Freud and Jung — included a chapter on Jung's views on religion in his last and posthumously published book (cf. BAUDOUIN 27, pp. 101—07, 112—28). A less reliable attempt to contrast Freud and Jung on religion was undertaken by ZUNINI (430), unfortunately without reference to the work of BAUDOUIN. HAENDLER (148), KIRSCH (218), ROCHEDIEU (288), WILWOLL (413, pp. 38—45, 54—55), and RÖSSLER (290) write of Jung's religious psychology in contrast to Freud's atheism, as does GOTTSCHALK (137, pp. 56—66), who, like WEHR (391, pp. 59—72), adds a section on the subject in the course of his rather loose and journalistic portrait of Jung (cf. also PRUYSER 281).

TONI WOLFF (420), in a brief but typically precise lecture, has approached the topic from the aspect of the "religious function". JACOBY (196) deals with the same topic from a more clinical point of view. JACOBI (191) also chose the religious function as a starting point for her rigidly orthodox reconstruction of Jung's notion of the *homo religiosus*. FROBOESE (124) assumed a similar stance in a paper contributed to a special edition of *Der Psychologe,* although her own ideas are indiscriminately mixed up with those of Jung. M. E. HARDING (153, 154) took religious symbolism as her *point de départ* in two papers condensing Jung's ideas on religion. Similar comments in a later article (155) sparked a discussion with DOUGLAS (92 and HARDING 156).

A second class of entries under the same heading comprises the endeavors to relate Jung's ideas on religion to his personal experiences. M.-L. VON FRANZ (382) has recently published an interesting and readable essay on Jung's life and thought which begins with a chapter relating Jung's boyhood experiences to the dominant concern of his life: the *imago Dei*. ALM (13), THURNEYSEN (356) and FRISCH-

KNECHT (123) had all previously noticed this aspect of the autobiography and commented on it at some length. LOOSER (240) has given us a short, simple commentary on the childhood prayer Jung refers to early in his memoirs, drawing the somewhat improbable conclusion that it enables one to see in the four-year old Jung the direction of his later work. FORDHAM (112) argues more convincingly for the influence of childhood experiences on adult religious attitudes, drawing on Jung's autobiographical account as an example. We can also mention here THORNTON (354), who adopted Jung's thought patterns to interpret his own mystical experiences; finding in Jung "a mystic of the first order", he gives a number of interesting personal impressions of Jung's religious nature. Similarly SERRANO (331), in his flowery and naive study of Jung and Hermann Hesse.

In the third place, we include those works which go beyond mere description to take up the debate between Christian tradition and archetypal psychology. As we might well expect, SCHÄR (319) and ZACHARIAS (422) are unconditionally optimistic in finding a place for Jung among the theologians, stubbornly oblivious of any difficulties other than the possible narrowmindedness of the theologians themselves. MERLIN (258), BENZ (37), DE HAAS (86), and CARLSSON (64) concur with a similar lack of theoretical rigor. Only slightly more reserved in their judgments are RYCHNER (306), SAURAT (309), and KÖBERLE (219, pp. 185—200), to whom HAENDLER (146, 149) lent support in his brief surveys of the relevant literature. To these names we should also add that of J.-W. HEIDLAND (161), an Evangelical Bishop who has given Jung high praise for his services to the Church.

JOSEF RUDIN (301), whose essays on the dialogue between theology and Jungian thought are among the most intelligent available, is more circumspect, more conscious of the complexities, but no less excited by the possibilities. Similarly, WHITE (400), in a BBC radio broadcast, pleaded the cause of Jung's psychology to Christian theologians and believers, always within the limits of doctrinal tradition. A serious-minded attempt to subordinate Jung's religious psychology to Christianity by means of a comparison of the notions of Eros and Agape was undertaken by LANTERO (227); finally, however, the relations turn out to be more linguistic than conceptual and his conclusions, consequently, remain unconvincing. H. KIENER (210) presents an enthusiastic defense of Jung's psychology of religion and elsewhere (212) goes to lengths to refute some casually made theological criticisms levelled against Jung, mustering to her aid a flurry of quotations from Jung's writings.[3] CARLO PETRO (274), a noted Italian psychotherapist and professed Jungian, returns frequently in his book on Jung to insist that he finds Catholicism wholly compatible with Jung's views. Essays by E. METMAN (262) and P. METMAN (263) on Jung suffer from a certain vagueness in logic, as do KIENER and PETRO, confusing description with argument.

We can now turn to a number of less favorable general studies, and here the spectrum runs wide and varied. On the one hand, we have as intelligent and informed a thinker as SBOROWITZ (312, 314) seeking to find in Christianity an answer to certain inadequacies in Jung's opinions on religion. Whatever one may think of such an approach, it is surely easier to come to grips with SBOROWITZ than with the bias of someone like GLOVER (130, pp. 54—64), who throws together in a kaleidoscopic fashion various unidentified bits of Jungiana and then concludes, with no premises other than his own occasional parenthetical jibes, that it is all basically irreligious nonsense. DRY (94, pp. 192—227) disagrees with Jung's views for more solid reasons, questioning in her account his understanding of Christian doctrine and Christian mysticism. BISHOP'S (47) criticisms represent a one-sided attack from a viewpoint which sees theology as unassailable by psychology but quite able to show up its shortcomings. SMITH (333), KIJM (216), and RUMPF (305) are slightly more positive, but basically operate from the same position, as does MAIRET (244), who is skeptical of those who would find in Jung's psychology a surrogate religion. GRANJEL (138) demonstrates the same preference for orthodoxy in his criticisms of Jung, but he is far from convincing, if only for the many tell-tale hints in his essay of insufficient acquaintance with the material. MACINTOSH (242, pp. 68—73) finds a subjectivistic psychologism in Jung's writings on religion, but fails to note any development beyond the earlier, Freudian-influenced writings. It is easier to exonerate REIK (284), writing in 1921, for holding like views. To a generally favorable account, HINDEL (175) appends his objections to Jung's attack on the *sacrificium intellectus* and the metaphysical reality of God. Similarly partial to Jung, VETTER (378) and WURM (421) have only to complain about the use of an immanentistic, mechanical model of the psyche to describe the rapport between man and God in religion. NORDBERG (271), in a death notice on Jung which appeared in a prominent American Catholic weekly, accused him of preaching a "hazy pantheism" which had been grossly over-rated as to its usefulness for Christian theology.

In conclusion, I mention briefly three studies which approach the problem of Jung's psychology of religion from the question of the "soul". ROTH (296) defends Jung against his critics without a trace of personal objection; PYE (282) goes even further to uphold Jung's very vagueness of language as an indication of the therapeutic need for ambiguous words in which the religious emotions can find repose. In contrast, STOCKER (343, pp. 323—25; cf. 342, pp. 104—25) attacks Jung for his emphasis on collectivism which, he holds, does grave injustice to the traditional doctrine of the dignity of the individual soul.

3. Methodology

Almost every entry of the bibliography upon which this essay is based makes some mention of Jung's methodology. Still, it seems worthwhile to bring together under that heading a number of the more specific and extensive treatments. It should be noted parenthetically that from here on almost no reference will be made to the general studies contained in the previous sections, which by definition treat to one degree or another most of the particular subjects that follow.

Among those who have undertaken to extract and evaluate Jung's methods, few seem to have had as keen an appreciation of the problems as did FREI (117), who yet persisted in championing Jung's right to treat theological matters from a psychological viewpoint. SIERKSMA (332, pp. 113—95), ADLER (2), and ALM (12, pp. 98—107) present comparable arguments, but tend to weaken their case by adhering rigorously to Jung's often unjust criticisms of Freud. FORDHAM (111) is one of the few who is fair to Freud, and as a result dispels many of the commonly-held prejudices stemming from Jung. ABENHEIMER (1), BARZ (26), and BINSWANGER (46) all stress the coherence of Jung's own statements regarding his strictly empirical and non-metaphysical methods (cf. JOHNSON 201). KELSEY (208) asserts that Jung has bridged the gap between philosophy and theology by providing a "consistent pragmatic realism within a phenomenological base which can deal with religious experience"; but from a purely philosophical point of view, his defense of Jung's methodology is far too simple and uninformed to justify his conclusions. SANFORD (308) reflects the same point of view, although he is careful to point out a certain inconsistency between Jung's articulated epistemology and his actual analytical methods, which depend on both scientific and quasi-religious models of knowledge-acquisition. One of the most competent attempts to assess Jung's methodology has been done by BURRELL (59). In the course of a lengthy reconstruction of Jung's "language of the soul" he argues that Jung's implicit metaphysic and his theological finesse suggest that psychology may yet prove a reliable handmaid for theology. CAHEN (61) (Jung's French translator) has contrasted the languages of psychology and what he calls "traditional religion" in order to support his conclusions on the value of Jung's psychology for faith in search of understanding. Similarly, KELLER (205) has seen in the methodological limits Jung set himself a means to distinguish nature from grace and to appreciate their interactions. ALLENBY (6) also faces the question from a standpoint within archetypal psychology, outlining four ways in which its methods have a bearing on our current religious situation; one of her points, the balance between inner and outer experience, is taken up as the leitmotif of a similarly-orientated essay by SUMNER and ELKISH (349; cf. VON LOWENICH 385, pp. 197—218). VON MORAWITZ-CADIO (268) concludes from a brief summary of Jung's career that he has offered us *the* Christian psychology (cf. also Anon. 433). The frequent criticisms of "relativism" and "psychologism" are met by VON FRANZ (381) in the course of an article where she insists that Jung's personal, non-scientific convictions were in favor of an objective God, transcendent to the psyche. Accepting Jung's opposition between creed and experience in a far more dogmatic fashion, FRENKLE (119) has applied it to case material under the illusion that he is thereby lending support to Jung's fundamental approach to religion. And HAYES (158) muddles her defense by indiscriminate quotations from philosophers and poets, with no apparent sense for speaking with precision.

Criticisms of Jung's methodological positions towards religious phenomena range from caution to condemnation. A. BRUNNER (55) finds the Jungian approach a wholly unsuitable tool for appreciating religion, to judge by the results which it yields. STROJNOWSKI (344) likewise finds Jung incompatible with Christianity, and strikes a warning against the possible penetration of his brand of 20th century gnosticism into Polish-speaking lands. MACQUARRIE (243, pp. 96—97, 109—11) sees Jung as unduly subjective, non-metaphysical and "naturalistic" in his conceptualization of religion. In a short treatise embracing the whole of Jung's religious psychology, STAUB (337) comes to conclude that Jung has not understood what religion is all about; with far more detail and evidence at hand, he arrives at the same basic complaints as MACQUARRIE. Both LIRAN (238) and DE LA CROIX (87), in contributions to a 1958 symposium on Jung and religion, attacked his methodological distinction between faith and experience as inadequate, and DE LA CROIX added some important criticisms of Jung's avowed empiricism. Many of the same ideas appear in ULANOV (367, pp. 5—12, 111—27), who is otherwise not particularly conscious of adverse criticism to Jung. JÄGER (197) disagrees with Jung's claims to empiricism, insisting that "mystical" elements not answerable to scientific canons form an essential part of his psychology. SCHARFENBURG (323) raised a number of complaints against Jung's invasion into theology, to which BARTNING (24) wrote a rather unimpressive and defensive reply. PIMENTA DE SOUZA (276) found the professed agnosticism towards matters metaphysical in Jung's writings an inconsistent and unsatisfactorily grounded posture. Along the same lines, BEACH (29) has argued that Jung had set up an unsuitable line of demarcation between metaphysics and science, which might have been more profitably drawn according to a model like Paul Tillich's.

WHITE'S attitude to these matters is mixed. On the one hand he argues for the identification of the concepts of soul and psyche in both psycholgy and theology (408; cf. BURNS 58), and yet on the other hand he objects to Jung's tendency to a subjectivism that leaves out the reality of a transcendent Other (407). GOLDBRUNNER'S (132, 133) evaluation is similarly ambivalent, except that it is more harsh in its judgment of Jung's psychologizing of God. In fact, this latter is the most common of all methodological complaints against Jung. CARUSO (65; 66, pp. 373—97), a student of VON GEBSATTEL and founder of his own depth psychology circle in Vienna, returns to this charge again and again. And DAIM (80, 82), who seems to be waging in one form or another a continual battle with Jung, raises the same issues, accusing Jung of a sort of psychological idolatry which is kept alive by the "esoteric-gnostic community" of loyal Jungians.

Given such objections, it is not surprising to find a number of thinkers, like BEIRNAERT (32, 34), who consider Jung's theories more dangerous to Christian thought than Freud's explicit atheism (cf. Anon. 432). BODAMER (50, pp. 218—23, 227—28), MCPHERSON (255, pp. 170—75) and RÜÖSLI (289) find a faith-destroying undercurrent to Jung's therapeutic pragmatism; and POHIER (279) sees the same fundamental psychic reductionism in Jung albeit in a more covert and subtle form, which Jung had attacked in Freud's attitudes to religion. BERNET (39), who seems to have grown more distant from Jung over the years, finds a similar deceptiveness in Jung, adding elsewhere (40), however, that he considers the almost total lack of attention paid by theologians to Jung a regrettable oversight.

4. God, Christ and Self

Jung never tired of pressing the distinction between God as he is in himself and the God-image as it appears in the psyche, this latter being at times indistinguishable from the central archetype of the Self. The way was thus open for Christian thinkers such as SCHÄR (322), COX (74, 76), and HEYER (169) to argue that a transcendent God was wholly compatible with Jung's theories. In his later works, however, Jung was to identify Christ with the Self, while the God-image was identified with the collective unconscious, an idea frequently overlooked (e. g., GUT 142, pp. 161—69), although it had already been developed to some length in *Aion* (summarized in BENNET 35, pp. 113—25 and BACH 19). But for those more or less committed to reconciling the Jungian position with traditional theology, this did not cause any grave problems, as COX (75) and BOCKUS (49) have shown. H. WOLFF (418) and HOWES (186) get into exegetical waters well over their heads in similarly trying to validate Jung's Christological notions. On the other hand, EDINGER (97) obviously preferred the earlier version, to which he returned by maintaining the Father as an image of the Self and aligning Christ to the individuating ego.

MANN (247, 249) has approached the question of the suitability of Jungian psychology to theology from another angle, insisting that Jung was in fact unable to uphold his distinction between *Deus* and the *imago Dei*, but was forced to enter into theological speculation every bit as much as today's responsible theologian is forced to enter into the world of psychology. In his own massive but undisciplined study of the development of the God-image, MANN (248) operates wholly under the inspiration of Jung's researches, except for the fact that he is more conscious of its hybrid character. LANG (226), by way of contrast, feels that contemporary anthropology — and here he seems to mean the direction initiated by Fr. Wilhelm Schmidt — renders Jung's approach valid for examining the origins of polytheism, but not of monotheism. HILLMAN (171) could hardly agree with the assumptions of such an approach, but has argued that a certain theological bias lay behind Jung's tendency to elevate the Self and its imagery to the rank of a quasi-eschatological norm. In so doing, he claims, the possibilities of a "polytheistic psychology" have been unjustly ignored.

Several critics, such as RORARIUS (292, 293), UHSADEL (366), and GOLDBRUNNER (135), have objected to a psychologistic immanentism in Jung that leaves no room for a transcendent God except as an occasionally hygienic illusion. HAENDLER (147) ran into objections from the more orthodox Jungians in making similar complaints (cf. ZACHARIAS 424). SCHWERMER (328) attempts to exonerate Jung from the charges by affirming that he was too passionately preoccupied with his own psychological investigations to do more than simply refuse to affirm or deny the reality of the God of the theologians. MARTINS (253) and DAVIES (83, pp. 18—25) take the opposite view, insisting that Jung should have admitted to the objective reality of a non-psychic God.

5. Trinity and Quaternity

Nothing has caused so much consternation among Christian theologians as Jung's suggestion to complete the Trinity with the addition of a fourth figure, alternatively woman or devil — a notion that few indeed seem able to describe without critical comment in the way FABRICIUS (103, pp. 96—105) does. LEIBBRAND (234), for example, has some very intelligent comments to make in his attack on Jung's idea. For him, Jung errs in treating the Trinity, after the manner of the modernists, as if it were an *object d'art,* capable of being interpreted according to one's personal aesthetic inclinations, instead of the *dogma purum* which it is. BLEUEL (48) resists Jung's attempts to compare the Christian trinity with "pagan" parallels and claims that he is trying to preach a sort of "Gospel of Nature" that supplants faith with reason. WILSON (412, pp. 176—97, 704—17) dismisses Jung's "Quaternity" as wholly unbiblical, somehow supposing that such a judgment suffices to dismiss what Jung was in fact trying to do. Within the Jungian school, MANN (246) defended Jung's right to handle such questions psychologically and saw in the Quaternity theory a goad for theologians to come to grips with the scientific and comparative approaches to religious phenomena. EDINGER (96) attempted to take some of the sting out of the concept by suggesting that the Quaternity be reserved for symbolizing the eternal and static qualities of God (or the Self), while Trinity be related only to the dynamic and developmental aspects. GORDON (136) backed up this idea, while ADLER (3) took fundamental issue with it. ANRICH (18, pp. 534—83), on the other hand, rejected the Quaternity because of his own prejudice for models of three, around which his lengthy, woolly treatise on the philosophic roots of body and soul gravitates.

Predictably enough, when Jung tried to feminize the image of the Deity by interpreting the Assumption of Mary as a transformation of the Trinity, theologians of every persuasion complained. SCHULZE (326) called it a kind of "allegorical exegesis" that was entirely unbiblical and gnostic. DOYLE (93, pp. 867—70) dismissed it as contradictory to the official *magisteria* of the Roman Church, to which CREHAN (77) added that it was an infiltration of pagan idolatry into accepted Christian tradition. No less partial to official dogmatics, O'MEARA (272) nevertheless appears to accept in some vague fashion the validity of Jung's insights for mythology, if not also for theology (cf. HÜBSCHER 189). The most favorable and extensive commentary on this question has been done by ULANOV (367), who approached the problem from the broader context of the reintroduction of the feminine into theology via Jungian psychology.

The idea that evil might find a place within the Godhead has hardly met with universal approval either. After a sketchy summary of Jung's views, MICHAELIS (266) jumps to the conclusion that they are an indication of what VON GEBSATTEL (383, p. 52) had already called "the mystical power of paganism". DAIM (81) sees Jung's distortion of trinitarian dogmatics as rooted in his basic error: the relativizing of good and evil by substituting for absolute transcendence the mechanical interaction of conscious and unconscious mind. WHITE (399) had also been a constant opponent of Jung's general notion of evil, eager to defend the scholastic notion of the *privatio boni* against alleged misinterpretations. HAENDLER (150) felt that the more acceptable conception of the "wrath of God" would cover the data to which Jung refers, without having to assume Satan into heaven. RUDIN (299, 303) has done his best to defend Jung here and to translate him into theologically acceptable terms, although he has not succeeded in giving more than a selective paraphrase. BERTINE (44) takes Jung with far less difficulty, as does SEIFERT (329) whose facility with philosophical jargon masks a certain unclarity of thought. But the most sustained attempt to confront Jung on evil has also been the most disastrous. I am referring to PHILP'S (275) book, which is built around a correspondence between him and Jung, and is so full of annoying misunderstandings that it is impossible to follow any consistent line of argument. LAMBERT (224, 225) attacked PHILP for misconstruing Jung, and WHITE (408, pp. 258—59) rightly accused both sides of obstinacy and incoherence.

6. *Protestantism and Catholicism*

Attempts to describe and evaluate Jung's desultory comments on the relative merits of Protestantism and Catholicism have been few. In an article that was praised by Jung for its "objectivity", KIESOW (213) sketched a plan of what was later to become his doctoral thesis (214), in which he presented a synoptical view of Jung's attitudes to the two traditions, concluding that Jung remained a Protestant in his convictions, but was compelled by his empiricism to acknowledge the psychological value of many things in Catholicism (cf. HILTNER 172, 174). By contrast, DILLISTONE (91) has argued that Freud corresponded better to Protestantism and Jung to Catholicism, which is supposedly clear from his attitude to the sacraments. Far more naive is a little book by WITCUTT (417) whose hagiographical loyalty to Jung and utter unfairness to Freud render his arguments for Jung's relevance to Catholicism wholly unconvincing, as WHITE (395) has observed. MCLEISH (254) is hardly an improvement, despite the fact that he writes nearly twenty years later. CHOISY (68, pp. 135—59), whose leanings are basically Freudian, counsels the Catholic to caution in the face of Jung's immanentistic "paganism". Similarly, at least one editorial in a Catholic journal warned its readers against the destructive pantheism that lies hidden underneath Jung's religious psychology. Finally, we note in passing an irresponsible and often flippant piece of work (RITCHY 286) in which the author presumes to argue from Jung's writings to the total rejection of what is loosely called "the Church".

7. Prophecy or Gnosticism?

We have heard Jung called everything from atheist to mystic. For some, the placing of Jung at the fringes of Christianity via some appropriate label is a matter of prime critical importance. Jung's pastor in Küsnacht, W. MEYER (264) characterized Jung in his funeral eulogy as a prophet whose voice deserves to be heard by Christians everywhere. For RIEFF (285) and HOCH (179), this same title is used ironically, to dismiss him as possessed of messianic illusions of grandeur.

But by far the most frequently encountered title applied to Jung is that of "gnostic", which — in spite of its exceedingly complex historical connotations — offers a convenient dust-bin for complaints against his psychology of religion. MANUEL (250), VERGOTE (377), and FRIEDMAN (120) use it to accuse Jung of radically psychologizing all forms of transcendence, while KÜNZLI (222) and BEIRNAERT (33) take it to represent Jung's indomitable rationalism and opposition to religious belief. Others, like HERWIG (167, pp. 86—90) and KIESOW (215), mean thereby to attribute a pantheistic-dualistic metaphysic to Jung's psychology. ALTIZER (15) (whose theological views, *malgré lui*, show considerable influence of Jungian thought [cf. NOEL 270, pp. 154—61 and ALTIZER 16]) refers to the ego-destructive metaphysics which Jung appears to share with gnostic thinkers.

The most celebrated attack of Jung's gnosis is that of MARTIN BUBER (56, 57), who accused Jung both of denying the validity of faith and of distorting the Judaeo-Christian notion of God. As he himself stated, it was the "VII Sermones ad Mortuos" which revealed to him the personal confession of a gnostic deity. QUISPEL (283) takes the critique as a compliment and goes on to draw some ambiguous connections between Jung's *opusculum* and what he reconstructs as the doctrine of Basilides. FODOR (104) has described the rather odd events surrounding the composition of the sermons. JAFFE (200) gives a fuller account of Jung's activity during this period and quotes for the first time from Jung's "Red Book" of visionary poetics. As for the psychological interpretation of the sermons, I remain partial to my own views (163), which, however, disagree on every significant point with those of HUBBACK (188).

8. Psychotherapy and the Cure of Souls

Perhaps no one in the Evangelical tradition has been so consistently and unambiguously positive in his assessment of the service Jungian psychotherapy can perform for the pastoral care of souls than SCHÄR (315, 316, 320, 321), who somehow manages to summarize, defend and expand on Jung's views without a hint of criticism. STICKELBERGER (341) and VON DER HEYDT (380) give similar approval, while MEIER (256) departs from Jung only in admitting to the metaphysical aspects of including religious problems in therapy. HAENDLER (145) early adopted Jungian psychology as a ground for a theology of preaching without, in contrast to his later writings, questioning the ontological *epoché* of a transcendent God. WHITE (396), in one of his first published essays on Jung, suggested that archetypal psychology could offer us solutions to many of the ethical dilemmas of psychotherapy. In a book on dreams, SANFORD (307) totally subordinates the cure of souls to a loyal and unquestioning obedience of Jung's views. HEUN (168) and THURNEYSEN (357) are more conscious of the differences and consequently admit to a *mutual* enrichment of theology and psychology. WHITMONT (409) intimates the same notions in his analysis of the Jungian position. KELSEY (206) has done what is surely the most comprehensive American study on the topic, leaving no doubt throughout how influential Jung has been in shaping his own personal convictions. Elsewhere KELSEY (209) argues from his own experience in favor of the benefits of Jungian psychology for the priest in the modern world. ALEX'S (5) advice to an ex-priest at sea with his God is far less satisfactory: a random selection of Jung's thoughts bound together only by the author's rather odd conception of theology. MACAVOY (241, pp.

1154—56, 1161—64) finds Jung's psychology useful for the spiritual direction of Catholics precisely because it cultivates values long familiar to the Roman Church. Minus the creedal attachments, MORAWITZ-CADIO (267) agrees in seeing the lasting advantages of an encounter between Christian spirituality and archetypal psychology. On like grounds, ALLENBY (8) describes Jung's brand of psychotherapy as a form of monasticism in modern dress.

On the negative side, DESSAUER (89) claims no honorable minister would ever send anyone under his care to a disciple of Jung, whom he considers a pseudo-mystic. UHSADEL (365, pp. 54—84) is far less rash in his judgments, but insists all the same on the need to maintain proper frontiers between psychotherapy and spiritual guidance. The same arguments, though not the same competence, appear in VOGEL'S (379) references to Jung. VAN DE WIENCKEL (369) finds Jung of inestimable relevance to Catholic asceticism, provided one rejects his notions of evil, the Quaternity and Christology. MESEGUER (260) approaches Jung with optimism and tries to suggest his usefulness for Christian believers, but in the end he yields to the pressures of his Catholicism in rejecting Jung's basic world-view.

In terms of more specific contributions, SPENGLER (334) has tackled with admirable success the difficult problem of extrapolating from Jung's writings a theory of conscience, contrasting it with that of Freud. RUDIN'S (298, 300, 302) concern with the therapeutic interpretation of what Jung called the "imago Dei" merits careful attention. In attempting to distinguish unhealthy distortions from genuine experiences of revelation, he has gone a long way in posing the questions in an intelligent and workable fashion. JACOBI'S (193) confident interpretation of God-symbolism found in certain of her patients' paintings has the curious, but ironic, advantage of exemplifying the sort of issues RUDIN is raising. From a more general and methodological perspective, an essay of mine (164) restates these problems in a somewhat different fashion. DU PEREZ' (95, pp. 108—27, 177—82) application of Jung to religious education and the case-study arguments of FROBOESE-THIELE (125) and ALLENBY (7) appear to me too incomplete to perform even that function. Finally, I would include a reference to ZIEGLER (429) who has suggested that, along Jungian lines, physical illnesses might often be viewed with profit as a kind of psychosomatic "incarnation of religious interests".

9. Archetypal Hermeneutics

Jung's idea that the rites, symbols and dogmas of religion might be read as the language of unconscious psychic processes has caused no little stir. No less a theologian than TILLICH (358, 359) has admitted to the revolutionary potential of such an approach. FRAYN (115) had suggested the same thing nearly twenty years earlier, under Jung's influence. Nevertheless, while men like WALLACE (389), UNDERWOOD (368), KELSEY (207), and J. G. WILLIAMS (411) continue to plead Jung's cause, little significant impact has been made on formal theology itself. Endeavors to evaluate critically Jung's own adoption of this approach have been motley. In a ponderous and sloppy doctoral dissertation, SPINKS (336, pp. 1213—46) has suggested certain amendments to the archetypal theory to render it more suitable to theology. LONDERO (239) arrived at much the same position in a more sustained study without, however, facing the more fundamental philosophical issues. WISSE (416), who devotes a good deal of attention to Jung in his book on the religious symbol, gets trapped in questioning the psychic mechanics of the system and the apparent immanentism involved HEPBURN (166, pp. 104—18), on the other hand, has presented what seems to me the most important and informed criticism in this area yet to appear. His whole essay should serve as an angel's warning to those who would rush into theology armed only with Jungian archetypal theory. And many there are who have rushed in, as a brief survey by STEFFEN (338) shows; perhaps the most cavalier and light-hearted of these is ROLFE'S (291) attempted reinterpretation of Christianity. Standing over against HEPBURN, FORDHAM (110) and MAUD BODKIN (51, pp. 167—80) have argued in favor of the Jungian approach and its scientific merits.

The most tempting road for archetypal psychology into Christian tradition is, of course, the richly symbolic world of the Bible. As early as 1933 TUINSTRA (364, pp. 192—200) had ventured in with a theory of symbols that drew considerably from Jung. Not much later, WESTMAN (393, 394) undertook an even more explicitly Jungian interpretation of two stories from the Pentateuch, for which THUM (355) singled him out in his criticisms of Jungian exegesis. But from the theologian's point of view, boldness had surely reached the borders of folly in two studies by HOWES (185, 187) who went at the Gospels with a regrettable lack of scriptural finesse, only to come up with a suspiciously one-sided confirmation of Jung's views. COPE (70) did little better, linking psychology at its weakest point (biblical hermeneutics) with theology at its weakest (depth psychology) to argue that Jung had cleverly and subtly demonstrated the truth of Christianity! SUARES (346, 347, 348), although convinced that Jung's rationalism and his theoretical explanations of the psyche were an anachronistic residue from the last century, nonetheless appears to accept the purely descriptive qualities of the archetype theory, which he uses in studying the myths of Genesis.

ALM (11) has argued in an intelligent manner that Jungian psychology may help provide us with a more suitable model for appreciating mysticism. Where he may have gone too far is to conclude from his work that the collective psyche is equivalent to what Jung's theological critics refer to as the "Thou", the God who transcends the psyche. DILLISTONE (90) and EVANS (102) are less impressive in their interpretations of Christian symbolism à la Jung. WHITE (408, pp. 248—57) treads very carefully in integrating Jung's understanding of the Mass (cf. CURTISS 79) with the theological notion of sacrifice. GAFFNEY (126) is more direct, bringing a rare sort of hard-nosed logic and historical competence to bear on Jung's over-simplifications and inaccuracies concerning the Mass. BARZ (25) has tried to give an archetypal interpretation of the Christian baptismal rite in the form of an extended dialogue between a theologically well-read layman and an analytical psychologist, where the author's bias stacks all the cards on the side of the latter. BEIRNAERT (32), on the other hand, has clearly opted for subordinating the archetypes involved in Christian sacramentalism to the Divine Power which he claims theology finds at work there.

10. Comparative Studies

Given the enormous breadth of his researches and his highly suggestive and imaginative style, Jung lends himself readily to comparison with a wide range of thinkers. For instance, VASAVADA (372, 373) has tried to bring Western and Eastern philosophies together by adopting Jung's concepts as both a bridge and a protective filter. At the same time, he insists that archetypal psychology can learn from the spiritual superiority of the East the need to abandon its strictly scientific prejudices and don the robes of the guru (371, 374, 375). To judge from his comments on Western philosophy, one might be righteously suspicious of what VASAVADA says about the "East" as well. Indeed, the highly unfavorable treatment which JACOBS (195) has Jung's theories of religion suffer at the hands of Indian metaphysics gives us cause to wonder. Generally speaking, however, there is wide recognition of Jung's genius in enlightening for the West the spiritual traditions of the Orient (WEHR 391, pp 83—99): everything from Zen (JOHNSTON 202) to the Vedanta (THORNTON 353) to Vipassana meditation (BYLES 60). R. C. ZAEHNER (427, 428) even went so far as to refer to Jung as a "new Buddha", prepared for the role in a special way by the mystical experiences of his childhood. Elsewhere (425) he makes considerable use of Jung's notion of the collective unconscious, which he feels finds its proper place in religion. In his Gifford Lectures, ZAEHNER (426) qualified his admiration by admitting that he finds Jung more illuminating for Oriental religions than for Western Christianity. LINSSEN (237) has given a synoptic summary of Jung and Krishnamurti, commenting on the notion of the Self in particular as their main point of contrast. LAUTERBORN (229) has produced a similarly-orientated study on Jung and Swami Omkaranda.

Because of Jung's attachment to the East, as well as to alchemy, astrology and mystical traditions of every kind, it has never failed to surprise and annoy the savants of anthroposophy how Jung could so deliberately and totally ignore the work of Rudolf Steiner. As one commentator observed not without irony, had Steiner written in Latin, Jung would have gone at his books wholeheartedly (HEYMANN 170)! HUPFER'S (190) comparison of the concept of spirit in the two thinkers offers little more than a summary of two positions, without critical appraisal. LAUER (228) attempts to get at their roots in a common *Zeitgeist*, before suggesting how Steiner could complement the work of Jung. A new book by WEHR (392) is by far the best thing on the subject, fair in its judgments and always conscious of fundamental differences.

There has been no lack of attempts to compare certain aspects of Jung's religious psychology to the thought of the spiritual and intellectual giants of Christian tradition. DAVID COX (73) has gone to great lengths to compare St. Paul's soteriology to Jung's psychology of individuation. His proposed technique of using "common language" as a methodological tool actually comes to mean reducing each to its lowest common denominators, at which point it is relatively easy to draw connections. (GUN [141] and LAMBERT [224] present contrasting evaluations of the book.) ALLENBY (9) has drawn attention to certain similarities between Jung and Joachim of Fiore. BECK (31) sees in the theology of St. Francis de Sales a means to correct the positivistic humanism of Jung's psychology. MEISSNER (257) found what he considered a remarkable correspondence between Origen's allegorical exegesis of the Song of Songs and certain of Jung's psychological categories. SUMNER (351) had attempted the same feat with John Climacus' meditations. Earlier (350) he had dealt with St. John of the Cross, disagreeing somewhat with the result of FORDHAM'S (107; cf. 106) interpretation. Yet a third attempt to understand the great Spanish mystic on Jungian principles was made by BAUDOUIN (27, pp. 234—67).

Closer to modern times, KOPLIK (221) uses Jung's psychology to get at the meaning of the plays of O'Neill, convinced that both men shared a common concern for the religious plight of contemporary man. Likewise, MARTIN (252), writing under the spell of archetypal psychology, compares Jung with Toynbee and T. S. Eliot. Apart from the serious questions that such efforts raise in terms of literary criticism, the level of psychology strikes one as amateur and full of abstractness.

BARNES (20) put forward the thesis that the metaphysics of Plotinus can be compared to Jung's conception of the psyche, gnostic literature serving as the common ground. SCHÄR (318) is on more solid footing in indicating Jung's ties to Burkhardt. GILEN (129) only slightly develops the theme of Jung's ideational attachments to the modernist movement — a fascinating and suggestive area for future research. BARONI (21) compares Jung and Nietzsche, effectively skirting the question of actual dependence and remaining at the surface of Nietzsche's thought. MORENO (269, pp. 216—50) is more ambitious, but hardly more successful, in taking up the same task (cf. HEISIG 165). WINKLER'S (415) comparison of Jung to the theological currents at the end of the last century is weak and not always accurate. Worthy of special notice, however, is J. M. CLARK'S (69) exposé of the scholarly blunders and erroneous arguments inherent in the picture Jung gives of Meister Eckhart in *Psychological Types*.

In the area of contemporary religious thought, DE ROUGEMONT (88) sets Karl Barth and Jung in contrast to one another: "possibly the greatest theologian and the greatest psychologist of our century". KIENER (211) rather carelessly finds a place for Jung in the ranks of Bonhoeffer, Tillich, Bultmann and John Robinson; and NOEL (270, pp. 158—61) attributes to Jung much of the inspiration behind the theology of Thomas Altizer, the man who sired death-of-God theology. Predictably, there have been various attempts, none of them particularly solid, to bring together Jung and Teilhard de Chardin. TOWERS (360) is the clearest of the lot, while BRAYBROOKE (53) does little more than piece together unidentified quotations from the two men, leaving the reader on his own to draw the conclusions. LECOURT (233) basically does the same thing by means of paraphrase. An essay by BENOIT (36), which compares both Jung and Teilhard to Whitman, is a fairly superficial and imprecise bit of work. ULANOV (367, pp. 96—110) has seen similarities in the theories of symbolism found in Jung and Tillich, while COWLES (72) parallels their ideas in terms of Christian ethical concerns. JAEGER (198) argues that Jung advanced beyond the theories of Rank by breaking free of the I-Thou dichotomy, precisely the opposite view from those who side with Buber against Jung. TRÜB (361, 362, 363), who made the confrontation between Jung and Buber his life work (cf. SBOROWITZ 311), owes much to each of his masters, although in the end he sides with Buber in matters of faith. WALDER (388) takes him to task for this and for his "extraordinarily subjective" interpretation of Jung. SBOROWITZ (310) repeats many of TRÜB'S views in a slightly different approach to the two men. PROGOFF (280) brings in Tillich as well, comparing the inner myths of all three (or their "dynatypes" as he calls them), and ends up with a misty and colorless generality. Last of all, we cannot fail at least to mention the work of Erich Neumann (reviewed by SBOROWITZ 313), who in developing his own approach to myth carried out many of the ethical and religious consequences of Jung's thought.

11. Reviews

We conclude our guided tour through this bibliographical wonderland by referring to the more substantial and important book notices that deal specifically with Jung and religion.

Jung's Terry Lectures on psychology and religion (1938) were generally well received in America, as reviews by LAWS (230) and ROSENFELD (294) attest. BARRETT (22) and BOISEN (52), however, did take issue with the way in which Jung appeared to reduce religion to a function of the collective mind (cf. also ELLARD 98). FREI'S (116) remarks on the occasion of the appearance of the German edition, written from a Catholic point of view, represent the same cautious enthusiasm that was to characterize all his later writings on archetypal psychology. A later review by SCHARPFF (324) summarized Jung's arguments without critical comment. By the time the eleventh volume of Jung's *Collected Works* appeared, some twenty years later, attitudes were becoming more sophisticated — and more hardened (cf. WHITE 406, PLAUT 278, SPIEGELBERG 335).

But if there is one single touchstone which can serve to test the metal of both Jung's disciples and his critics, it is surely that passionate, ironic and divisive little book, *Answer to Job*. FORDHAM (109) and LAMBERT (223) were able to assimilate the book with apparent ease by subordinating its various arguments to the general genre of a kind of active imagination by proxy. GUETSCHER (143) took a similar stance as a theologian, insisting that Jung was avoiding all speculation about the transcendent. HILTNER (173) maintained his loyalty to Jung by simply sidestepping the difficult points, for which he was later taken to task (CHAMBERLIN 67). EVANS (100) accepted the book with only minor reservations, as did O. WOLFF (419), who set out to defend Jung's right to a psychological approach to the Incarnation. CORBIN (71) had no apparent problems in reconstructing the book around one of its sub-themes, the doctrine of Sophia, the eternal feminine, leaving nothing to complain about for an historian of alchemy. JAFFE (199, pp. 101—11) embraced Jung's ideas more fittingly by locating them in the broader context of his life-concerns.

The overwhelming majority of commentators, however, were less easy to please, as ROTH (295) has shown in his brief survey of the book's acceptance. MANN (245) raised his typical complaint about the inadequacy of Jung's espoused scientific empiricism, finding in *Job* a clear instance of what he called "psychotheology". VELASQUEZ (376) referred to it as a brand of non-scientific esotericism, and WATKIN (390) and MICHAELIS (265) saw it as a presumptuous and wholly grotesque venture into religion. SCHMIDT (325) claimed that it was Jung's over-rationalistic approach which was responsible for his frequent distortions of scripture and Christian tradition.

Jung has fared no better at the hands of the exegetes. An unsigned article in a Jewish monthly (431) listed a number of scriptural errors (one of which, an incorrect reference in the book's motto, was corrected in later editions). BERNHARDT (41), SEMMELROTH (330) and GRILL (140) were of the opinion that Jung had distorted and would even have destroyed faith in the Bible as the Word of God. VON WEIZSÄCKER (386) concurred in a somewhat distasteful *ad hominem* attack on Jung. KEHOE (204) specifically goes at Jung's notion of the figure of Satan. In an impressive and thorough essay on the book, VAN DEN BERGH (370) accuses Jung of, among other things, abusing the book of Job for the sake of his own psychological fantasies, which might have found a less blasphemous romping-ground. Likewise WILDBERGER (410) thoroughly rejects Jung's interpretation of the Book of Job and of the New Testament image of God as wild and frivolous speculation, concluding that it has far more affinity with Indian thought than with anything recognizably Christian.

And finally WHITE (403; 408, pp. 233—40), who has nowhere attacked Jung with such unexpected vehemence, criticized him for reading the Bible with "deliberately distorted glasses". As FORDHAM wrote to WHITE concerning the harsh reviews he had given, "Jung is on Job's side and you are on the side of God."[4]

For others, the main complaint is Jung's seemingly apparent refusal to take theology seriously. Thus RUDIN (297) accuses him of blending shabby biblical scholarship with a cavalier dismissal of the transcendent God of Christian theology. Similarly, HOCH (177) and BERNET (38, pp. 189—96) claim that Jung has overstepped the frontiers of psychology in a radical immanentizing of God within the human psyche. For the same reasons, HOFFMAN (180) and HABERLANDT (144) find in *Job* an insensitivity to the meaning of revelation, and MARTI (251) asserts that Jung' is divinizing man via an "enlightened rationalism with a gnostic costume". HEDINGER (160) and KOEP-

GEN (220) both contrast Buber's faith with Jung's psychologistic relativism. PANNWITZ (273), in the course of a more general commentary, refers to Jung's handling of the Job-myth as a twisted approach to Christian doctrine. HEAVENOR (159) criticizes Jung for totally missing the point of Protestantism. From a "freethinking" standpoint, HARTWIG (157) objects, in opposition to Jung's other critics, that Jung had lacked the courage to carry his insights to their logical and inevitable conclusion: atheistic humanism.

*

If I have argued anything in the preceding pages, it is that scholarship on the borderlands between theology and archetypal psychology has grown tired. What it needs to avoid declining into an eremitic glass-bead-game is not so much the flair of revolutionizing ideas, as the painstaking re-examination of fundamental assumptions. Given such discipline, and not a little perseverance, the night may yet pass into dawn.

1   As might be expected, there is a personal project hiding in the shadows of this polemic: I am now in the final stages of completing a study of Jung's notion of the *imago Dei*, a preliminary sketch of whose main arguments appeared in 1971 (162).
2   I deliberately use the word "archetypal", in place of "analytical", "complex" or "Jungian" to characterize Jung's psychology, because it seems to me the most precise and unambiguous. In so doing, I express agreement with Hillman's reasons for suggesting the term. (Cf. J. Hillman, "Why 'Archetypal' Psychology?", *Spring 1970*, N.Y., Spring Publications, pp. 212—19.)
3   The work referred to is: Pierre Barthel, *Interprétation du langage mythique et théologie biblique*. Leiden, Brill, 1967. Unless the original thesis differs considerably from its published version, Barthel's criticisms are all made *en passant* and not argued at any length.
4   Quoted with the permission of the author.

Bibliography

1 ABENHEIMER, Karl M. "Notes on the Spirit as Conceived by Dynamic Psychology." *Journal of Analytical Psychology* 1 (1956) pp 113–31.
2 ADLER, Gerhard. "A Psychological Approach to Religion." In his: *Studies in Analytical Psychology.* London, Hodder and Stoughton, 1966, pp 176–216.
3 —. A discussion on EDINGER [96]. ibid. pp 28–9.
4 AFFEMANN, Rudolf. *Psychologie und Bibel: eine Auseinandersetzung mit C. G. Jung.* Stuttgart, Ernst Klett, 1957.
5 ALEX, William. "When Old Gods Die." In: Hilde Kirsch, ed. *The Well-Tended Tree: Essays into the Spirit of our Times.* New York, G.P. Putnam's Sons, 1971, pp 33–47.
6 ALLENBY, Amy Ingeborg. *Jung's Contribution to the Religious Problem of Our Time.* Guild of Pastoral Psychology, Lecture No 91. London, 1956.
7 —. "The Church and the Analyst." *Journal of Analytical Psychology* 6 (1961) pp 137–55.
8 —. "The Life of the Spirit and the Life of Today." *Harvest* 13 (1967) pp 18–29.
9 —. "Religionspsychologie mit besonderer Berücksichtigung von C. G. Jung." In: Wilhelm Bitter, *Psychotherapie und religiöse Erfahrung.* Stuttgart, Ernst Klett, 1968, pp 212–25.
10 ALLERS, Rudolf. "Mental Trouble and Moral Life." *Books on Trial* (June 1953) pp 342–43.
11 ALM, Ivar. "Die analytische Psychologie als Weg zum Verständnis der Mystik." In: *Die Kulturelle Bedeutung der Komplexen Psychologie. Festschrift zum 60. Geburtstag von C. G. Jung.* Berlin, Julius Springer, 1935, pp 298–313.
12 —. *Den Religiösa Funktionen I Människosjälen. Studien Till Fragan om Religionens Innebörd och Människans väsen I Modern Psychologi Särskilt Hos Freud och Jung.* (Doctoral dissertation). Stockholm, Svenska Kyrkans Diakonistyrelses Bokförlag, 1936.
13 —. "C. G. Jungs Erfahrungen in theologischer Sicht." *Theologische Zeitschrift* 19 (1963) pp 352–59.
14* ALTIZER, Thomas J. J. *A Critical Analysis of C. G. Jung's Understanding of Religion.* (Doctoral dissertation). University of Chicago, 1955.
15 —. "Science and Gnosis in Jung's Psychology." *The Centennial Review* 3 (1959) pp 304–20.
16 —. "Response I." In: John B. Cobb Jr., *The Theology of Altizer: Critique and Response.* Philadelphia, Westminster, 1970, pp 194–98.

17* ANGHINETTI, P. W. *Alienation and Myth: A Study of the Works of Nietzsche, Jung, Yeats, Camus and Joyce.* (Doctoral dissertation). Florida State University, 1969.
18 ANRICH, Ernst. *Moderne Physik und Tiefenpsychologie. Zur Einheit der Wirklichkeit und damit der Wissenschaft.* Stuttgart, Klett, 1963.
19 BACH, Hans Israel. *C. G. Jung's "Aion". A Synopsis.* Guild of Pastoral Psychology, Lecture No 74. London, 1952.
20 BARNES, Hazel E. "Neo-Platonism and Analytical Psychology." *Philosophical Review* 54 (1945) pp 558—77.
21 BARONI, Christophe. "Dieu est-il mort? De Nietzsche à Jung." *Synthèses* 19 (1965) pp 328—43. [A shorter version of this essay appeared in his: *Introduction à la psychologie des profondeurs.* Lausanne, L'Homme sans Masque, 1966, pp 76—80.]
22 BARRETT, Clifford. "Jung on Religion." *New York Times Book Review* (20 March 1938) p 14.
23 BARTEMEIER, Leo H. "Psychoanalysis and Religion." *Bulletin of the Menninger Clinic* 29 (1965) pp 237—44.
24 BARTNING, Gerhard. "Hebräische wider griechische Psychologie? Zum Gespräch mit C. G. Jung." *Quatember* 26 (1962) pp 117—20.
25 BARZ, Helmut. *Die altkirchliche Taufe: Versuch einer psychologischen Interpretation.* (Diploma thesis). Zurich, 1967.
26 —. "Fragen der Tiefenpsychologie an die Kirche." In: Hans Jürgen Schultz, ed. *Was weiss man von der Seele?* Stuttgart, Krenz, pp 186—94.
27 BAUDOUIN, Charles. *Psychoanalyse du symbole religieux.* Paris, Fayard, 1957.
28 —. *L'Oeuvre de Jung et la psychologie complexe.* Paris, Payot, 1963.
29 BEACH, B. Y. "Jung on metaphysics." (Paper delivered to the New York Association of Analytical Psychology, 4 December 1968.)
30* —. *Jung and Tillich: A Critical Appraisal.* (M.A. Thesis). Drew University, 1967.
31 BECK, Irene. "Franz von Sales und C. G. Jung. Aktuelle psychologische Aspekte der salesianischen Theologie." *Jahrbuch für salasianische Studien* (1969) pp 5—16.
32 BEIRNAERT, Louis. "The Mythic Dimensions in Christian Sacramentalism." *Cross Currents* 1 (1950) pp 68—86.
33 —. "Jung et Freud au regard de la foi chrétienne." *Dieu Vivant* 26 (1954) pp 95—100.
34 —. Contribution to: "Débat sur psychologie et religion." In: *L'Armée et La Nation.* No 30 of: *Recherches et Débats.* Paris, Fayard, 1960, pp 200—06.
35 BENNET, E. A. *C. G. Jung.* London, Barrie and Rockliff, 1961.
36 BENOIT, Ray. "Whitman, Teilhard and Jung." In: Harry J. Cargas, ed. *The Continuous Flame: Teilhard in the Great Traditions.* St. Louis, B. Herder, n.d. [ca. 1969] pp 79—89.

37 BENZ, Ernst. "Psychologie et religion chez C. G. Jung." *Schweizerische Zeitschrift für Psychologie und ihre Anwendungen* 25 (1966) pp 230–35.
38 BERNET, Walter. *Inhalt und Grenze der religiösen Erfahrung. Eine Untersuchung der Probleme der religiösen Erfahrung in Auseinandersetzung mit der Psychologie C. G. Jungs.* Bern, Paul Haupt, 1955.
39 —. "Fragen der Theologie an der Tiefenpsychologie." In: Schultz [26 supra]. pp 195–202.
40 —. "C. G. Jung." In: Hans Jürgen Schultz, ed. *Tendenzen der Theologie im 20. Jahrhundert. Eine Geschichte in Porträts.* Stuttgart, Krenz, 1966, pp 150–55.
41 BERNHARDT, W. H. Review of *Answer to Job*. *Journal of Religious Thought* 12 (1955) pp 127–28.
42 BERTINE, Eleanor. "The Jungian Approach to Religion: An Introductory Paper." *Spring* (1958) pp 33–48.
43 —. "Jung's Psychology and Religion." *Religion in Life* 28 (1959) pp 365–75.
44 —. "The Perennial Problem of Good and Evil." *Spring* (1960) pp 21–33.
45 BEVERIDGE, W. E. *The Jungian Psychology and the Origin of Religion.* (B. Litt. dissertation). Trinity College, Dublin, 1952.
46 BINSWANGER, Kurt. "Der Heilweg der analytischen Psychologie C. G. Jungs." In: L. Szondi, ed. *Heilwege der Tiefenpsychologie.* Bern, Hans Huber, 1956, pp 35–48.
47 BISHOP, John Graham. *Jung and Christianity.* London, S.P.C.K., 1966.
48 BLEUEL, Josef. "Der trinitarische Urglaube." *Natur und Kultur* 48 (1956) pp 37–42.
49 BOCKUS, Frank M. "The Archetypal Self: Theological Values in Jung's Psychology." In: Peter Homans, ed. *The Dialogue between Theology and Psychology.* University of Chicago Press, 1968, pp 221–47.
50 BODAMER, Joachim. *Gesundheit und technische Welt.* Stuttgart, Ernst Klett, 1955.
51 BODKIN, Maud. *Studies of Type-Images in Poetry, Religion and Philosophy.* London, Geoffrey Cumberlege, 1951.
52 BOISEN, A. T. Review of *Psychology and Religion*. *American Journal of Sociology* 44 (1939) pp 612–13.
53 BRAYBROOKE, Neville. "C. G. Jung and Teilhard de Chardin: A Dialogue." In: Cargas [34 supra] pp 90–100. [Reprinted from *Month* 225 (1968) pp 96–104; it also appeared later in the *Journal of General Education* 20 (1969) pp 272–80.]
54* BROOKS, Henry Curtis. *The Concept of God in the Analytical Psychology of Carl Gustav Jung.* (Doctoral dissertation). Boston University. [Cf. *Dissertation Abstracts* 25 (1964) p 3134.]

55 BRUNNER, A. "Tiefenpsychologische Deutung der Religionsgeschichte." *Stimmen der Zeit* 154 (1955) pp 390–92.
56 BUBER, Martin. "Religion and Modern Thinking." In his: *The Eclipse of God. Studies in the Relation between Religion and Philosophy.* London, Victor Gollancz, 1953, pp 87–122, 179–84. [Originally in *Merkur* 6 (1952) pp 102–20.]
57 —. "Reply to C. G. Jung." ibid. pp 171–76. [And *Merkur* 6 (1952) 474–76.]
58 BURNS, Charles. "The Catholic Psychotherapist and the Future." *The Wiseman Review* 498 (1963–4) pp 383–94.
59 BURRELL, David. "Jung: A Language for the Soul." Ch. 5 of a forthcoming book to be entitled *Exercises in Theological Understanding.* [privately circulated, 61pp.]
60 BYLES, Marie B. "Vipassana Meditation and Psychologist Jung." *Maha-Bodi* 68 (1960) pp 362–66.
61 CAHEN, Roland. Contribution to "Débat sur psychologie et religion." [v. 34 supra] pp 150–87.
62 CALLUF, Emir. *Sonhos, complexos e personalidade. A psicologia analítica de C. G. Jung.* Sao Paolo, Mestre Jou, 1969.
63 CAMERLING, Elizabeth. *Inleiding tot het denken van Jung.* Assen, Born, 1955.
64 CARLSSON, Allan. "Jung on Meaning and Symbols in Religion." *Journal of General Education* 22 (1970) pp 29–40.
65 CARUSO, Igor. *Existential Psychology: From Analysis to Synthesis.* London, Darton, Longman and Todd, 1964. [Originally published as *Psychoanalyse und Synthese der Existenz.* Wien, 1952.]
66 —. *Bios, Psyche, Person.* Freiburg, Karl Alber, 1957.
67 CHAMBERLIN, J. Maxwell and HILTNER, Seward. "Jung and Christianity." *Pastoral Psychology* 7 (1956) pp 53–6.
68 CHOISY, Maryse. *Psychoanalyse et catholicisme.* Paris, L'Arche, 1950.
69 CLARK, James M. "C. G. Jung and Meister Eckhart." *Modern Language Review* 54 (1959) pp 239–44.
70 COPE, Gilbert F. *Symbolism in the Bible and the Church.* London, SCM Press, 1959.
71 CORBIN, Henry. "La Sophie éternelle." *Revue de culture européenne* 3 (1953) pp 11–44.
72 COWLES, Ben Thomson. *The Ethical Implications of a Christian Estimate of Man, with Special Reference to the Anthropologies of Carl Jung and Paul Tillich.* (Doctoral dissertation). University of Southern California, 1960.
73 COX, David. *Jung and St Paul: A Study of the Doctrine of Justification by Faith and its Relation to the Concept of Individuation.* London, Longmans, Green and Co., 1959.

74 —. *God and the Self*. Guild of Pastoral Psychology, Lecture No 112. London, 1960.
75 —. "The Self and God." *Harvest* 7 (1961) pp 3–13.
76 —. *History and Myth*. London, Darton, Longman and Todd, 1961.
77 CREHAN, J. H. "Maria Paredros." *Theological Studies* 16 (1955) pp 414–23.
78 CROWLEY, T. "Jung and Religion." *Irish Theological Quarterly* 23 (1956) pp 73–9.
79 CURTIS, Monica Mary. *Jung's Essay on the Transformation Symbol in the Mass*. Guild of Pastoral Psychology, Lecture No 69. London, 1951.
80 DAIM, Wilfred. *Umwertung der Psychoanalyse*. Vienna, Herold, 1951.
81 —. "Der Grundfehler C. G. Jungs. Zu einer gnostischen Entgleisung." *Wissenschaft und Weltbild* 6 (1953) pp 58–67.
82 —. *Tiefenpsychologie und Erlösung*. Vienna, Herold, 1954.
83 DAVIES, D. V. *An Investigation of the Attitude of Abnormal Personalities towards the Idea of God*. (Doctoral dissertation). King's College, London, 1956.
84 DAWSON, Eugene E. "The Religious Implications of Jung's Psychology." *Transactions of the Kansas Academy of Science* 52 (1942) pp 88–91.
85 —. *The Religious Implications of Jung's Psychology*. (Doctoral dissertation). University of Wisconsin, 1959.
86 DE HAAS, Clement H. "Psychology and Religion." *Cross Currents* 4 (1954) pp 70–5.
87 DE LA CROIX, Michele-Marie. Contribution to "Débat sur psychologie et religion. [v. 34 supra]. pp 206–14.
88 DE ROUGEMONT, Denis. "Le Suisse moyen et quelques autres." *Revue de Paris* 72 (1965) pp 52–64.
89 DESSAUER, Philip. "Bemerkungen zum Verhältnis von Psychotherapie und Seelsorge." *Anima* 7 (1952) pp 112–20.
90 DILLISTONE, F. W. *Christianity and Symbolism*. Collins, London, 1955.
91 —. "The Christian Doctrine of Man and Modern Psychological Theories." *Hibbert Journal* 54 (1959) pp 154–60.
92 DOUGLAS, W. "Influences of Jung's Work: A Critical Comment." *Journal of Religion and Health* 1 (1962) pp 260–72. [v. 156].
93 DOYLE, Eric. "God and the Feminine." *The Clergy Review* n.s. 56 (1971) pp 866–77.
94 DRY, Avis Mary. *The Psychology of Jung: A Critical Interpretation*. London, Meuthen, 1961.
95 DU PREEZ, Jan Petrus van Albertus. *Opvoeding en die ombewuste – 'n bydrae van die analitiese sielkundeskool van C. G. Jung tot die*

opvoedkunde. (M. Ed. dissertation). University of South Africa, Pretoria, 1961.

96 EDINGER, Edward F. "Trinity and Quaternity." *Journal of Analytical Psychology* 9 (1964) pp 103–14. [Reprinted from: Adolf Guggenbühl-Craig, ed. *Der Archetyp.* Basel, Karger, 1964, pp 16–28.]

97 —. "Christ as Paradigm of the Individuating Ego." *Spring* (1966) pp 5–23.

98 ELLARD, A. G. Review of Jung's *Psychology and Religion. Thought* 14 (1939) pp 335–36.

99 ELLENBERGER, Henri F. *The Discovery of the Unconscious. The History and Evolution of Dynamic Psychiatry.* London, Allen Lane The Penguin Press, 1970.

100 EVANS, Erastus. *An Assessment of Jung's "Answer to Job".* Guild of Pastoral Psychology, Lecture No 78. London, 1954.

101 —. *A Pilgrim's Way between Psychotherapy and Religion.* Guild of Pastoral Psychology, Lecture No 79. London, 1954.

102 —. "The Phases of Psychic Life." In: Philip Mairet, ed. *Christian Essays in Psychiatry.* London, SCM Press, 1956, pp 109–26. [Reprinted in Pastoral Psychology 8 (1957) pp 33–46.]

103 FABRICIUS, Johannes. *Drommens virkelighed. Freud og Jung.* Copenhagen, Arnold Busck, 1967.

104 FODOR, Nándor. "Jung's Sermons to the Dead." *Psychoanalytic Review* 51 (1964) pp 74–8.

105 FORDHAM, Frieda. *An Introduction to Jung's Psychology.* Harmondsworth, Penguin, 1953/1968.

106 FORDHAM, Michael. "The Dark Night of the Soul." In his: *The Objective Psyche.* London, Routledge and Kegan Paul, 1958, pp 130–48. [Revised from an earlier version: "The Analytical Approach to Mysticism." *Revue suisse de psychologie et de psychologie appliquée* 4 (1945) Nos 3–4.]

107 —. "Analytical Psychology and Religious Experience." ibid. pp 113–29. [Revised from his: Guild of Pastoral Psychology, Lecture No 46. London, 1947.]

108 —. Critical notice. *British Journal of Medical Psychology* 26 (1953) pp 319–22.

109 —. "An Appreciation of *Answer to Job.*" *British Journal of Medical Psychology* 28 (1955) pp 271–73.

110 —. "The Relevance of Analytical Theory to Alchemy, Mysticism and Theology." *Journal of Analytical Psychology* 5 (1960) pp 113–28.

111 —. "Is God Supernatural? Freud, Jung and the Theologian." *Theology* 69 (1966) pp 386–96.

112 —. "Religious Experience in Childhood." [v. 5 supra]. pp 79–89.

113 FORTMANN, H. M. M. "De godsdienstpsychologie van Jung." *Gawin* 10 (1962) pp 265–74.

114 —. *Als ziende de Onsienlijke. Een cultuurpsychologische studie over de religieuze waarneming en de zogenaamde religieuze projectie.* Hilversum, Paul Brand, 1968, 3 Vols.
115 FRAYN, R. Scott. *Revelation and the Unconscious.* London, Epworth Press, 1940.
116 FREI, Gebhard. "C. G. Jung: Psychologie und Religion." *Schweizerische Rundschau* 40 (1940) pp 329—31.
117 —. "C. G. Jung zum 70. Geburtstag." *Schweizerische Rundschau* 45 (1945) pp 312—19.
118 —. "Zur Darstellung Wingenfelds über C. G. Jung." *Arzt und Seelsorger* 7 (1956) pp 5—7.
119 FRENKLE, Norbert J. *Konfessionalismus und Religion aus der Sicht einiger analytischer Prozesse.* (Diploma thesis). Zurich, 1972.
120 FRIEDMAN, Maurice. "Jung's Image of Psychological Man." *Psychoanalytic Review* 53 (1966) pp 595—608. [This essay appeared later in his: *To Deny our Nothingness: Contemporary Images of Man.* London, Victor Gollancz, 1967, pp 146—67.]
121 FRISCHKNECHT, Max. *Die Religion in der Psychologie C. G. Jungs.* Bern, Paul Haupt, 1945.
122 —. Review of SCHÄR [317]. *Theologische Zeitschrift* 2 (1946) pp 388—93.
123 —. "Neue Begegnung mit C. G. Jung." *Reformatio* 12 (1963) pp 307—15.
124 FROBOESE-THIELE, Felicia. "Die religiöse Funktion des Unbewussten." *Der Psychologe* 2 (1950) pp 343—51.
125 —. *Träume: Eine Quelle religiöser Erfahrung?* Göttingen, Vandenhoeck u. Ruprecht, 1957. [pp 27—41 of this book were reprinted in: Jutta von Graevenitz, ed. *Bedeutung und Deutung des Traums in der Psychotherapie.* Darmstadt, Wissenschaftliche Buchgesellschaft, 1968, pp 298—320.]
126 GAFFNEY, James. "Symbolism of the Mass in Jung's Psychology." *Revue de l'Université d'Ottawa* 33 (1963) pp 214*—31*.
127 GEMELLI, Agostino. *Psicologia e religione nella concezione analitica di C. G. Jung.* Milano, Vita e Pensiero, 1955.
128 —. *Psychoanalysis Today.* New York, P. J. Kenedy and Sons, 1955.
129 GILEN, Leonhard. "Das Unbewusste und die Religion nach C. G. Jung. Zugleich ein Beitrag zur Religionspsychologie des Modernismus." *Theologie und Philosophie* 42 (1967) pp 481—506.
130 GLOVER, Edward. *Freud or Jung?* London, Allen and Unwin, 1950.
131 GOLDBRUNNER, Josef. *Die Tiefenpsychologie von Carl Gustav Jung und Christliche Lebensgestaltung.* (Doctoral dissertation). Freiburg im Breisgau, 1940.
132 —. *Holiness is Wholeness.* London, Burns and Oates, 1955. [Originally published as *Heiligkeit und Gesundheit.* Freiburg, 1949.]

133 —. "The Structure of the Psyche and the Personalist View of Man: A Critical Study of the Depth-Psychology of C. G. Jung." *Journal of Psychological Researches* 5 (1961) pp 97—102.
134 —. *Individuation.* University of Notre Dame, 1964. [A German edition of the same title appeared in 1966, published by Erich Wewel Verlag, Freiburg.]
135 —. "Die Bedeutung der Tiefenpsychologie für das christliche Leben." In his: *Sprechzimmer und Beichtstuhl. Über Religion und Psychologie.* Basel, Herder, 1965, pp 47—56.
136 GORDON, Rosemary. "Symbols: Content and Process." In: Joseph Wheelwright, ed. *The Reality of the Psyche.* New York, C. G. Jung Foundation for Analytical Psychology, 1968, pp 293—304.
137 GOTTSCHALK, Herbert. *C. G. Jung.* Berlin, Colloquium, 1960.
138 GRANJEL, Luís S. "La psicología de C. G. Jung en la historia de las relaciones entre medicina y religión." *Archivos ibero-americanos de historia de la medicina* 1 (1949) pp 189—297.
139* GRIFFIN, Graeme Maxwell. *The Self and Jesus Christ. A Critical Consideration of the Nature of the Self and its Place in Christian Theology and Life, with Particular Reference to the Thought of Dietrich Bonhoeffer and Carl Jung.* (Doctoral dissertation). Princeton, 1965. [cf. *Dissertation Abstracts* 26 (1965) pp 3508—09.]
140 GRILL, S. "Psychoanalytiker als Exegeten." *Der Seelsorger* 25 (1955) pp 322—26.
141 GUN, George S. Review of COX [73]. *Scottish Journal of Theology* 13 (1960) pp 192—94.
142 GUT, Gottlieb. *Schicksal in Freiheit.* Freiburg, Karl Alber, 1965.
143 GUTSCHER, Klaus. "Brücke zu Jung." *Kirchenblatt für die reformierte Schweiz* 108 (1952) pp 226—28.
144 HABERLANDT, H. "Diskussion um Hiob." *Wissenschaft und Weltbild* 6 (1953) pp 52—8.
145 HAENDLER, Otto. *Die Predigt. Tiefenpsychologische Grundlagen und Grundfragen.* Berlin, Alfred Töpelmann, 1941/1949.
146 —. "Komplexe Psychologie und theologische Realismus." *Theologische Literaturzeitung* 78 (1953) pp 199—215.
147 —. "Unbewusste Projektionen auf das christliche Gottvaterbild und ihre seelsorgerliche Behandlung." In: Wilhelm Bitter, ed. *Vorträge über das Vaterproblem in Psychotherapie, Religion und Gesellschaft.* Stuttgart, Hippokrates, 1954, pp 187—212. [Summary in *Arzt und Seelsorger* 5/2 (1954) pp 6—8.]
148 —. "Tiefenpsychologie." In: Kurt Galling, ed. *Religion in Geschichte und Gegenwart.* Tübingen, J.C.B. Mohr, 1956—, Vol 6 pp 886—95.
149 —. "C. G. Jung." *Theologische Literaturzeitung* 84 (1959) pp 561—88.
150 —. "Theologische Einleitung." In: von Graevenitz [125 supra]. pp 5—18.

151* HANG, Thadée. *La struttura dell'anima nella psicologia di C. G. Jung.* (Doctoral dissertation). Milan, Università Cattolica del Sacro Cuore, n.d.
152 HANNA, Charles Bartruff. *The Face of the Deep: The Religious Ideas of C. G. Jung.* Philadelphia, Westminster, 1967.
153 HARDING, Mary Esther. "The Psyche and the Symbols of Religion." In: Werner Wolff, *Psychiatry and Religion.* New York, M.D. Publications, 1956, pp 3—7.
154 —. "Jung's Contribution to Religious Symbolism." *Spring* (1959) pp 1—16.
155 —. "Jung's Influence on Contemporary Thought." *Journal of Religion and Health* 1 (1959) pp 247—59.
156 —. Reply to DOUGLAS [92] with rejoinder. *Journal of Religion and Health* 1 (1959) pp 269—72.
157 HARTWIG, Theodor. "Antwort auf Hiob." *Befreiung* 3 (1955) pp 103—11.
158 HAYES, Dorsha. "Religion: An Individual Search." *Harvest* 14 (1968) pp 35—50.
159 HEAVENOR, E. S. P. "Answer to Job." *Scottish Journal of Theology* 20 (1967) pp 120—21.
160 HEDINGER, Ulrich. "Reflexionen über C. G. Jungs Hiobinterpretation." *Theologische Zeitschrift* 23 (1967) pp 340—52.
161 HEIDLAND, Hans-Wolfgang. "Die Bedeutung der analytischen Psychologie für die Verkündigung der Kirche." In: Wolfgang Böhme, ed., *C. G. Jung und die Theologen: Selbsterfahrung und Gotteserfahrung bei C. G. Jung.* Stuttgart, Radius, 1971, pp 46—59.
162 HEISIG, James W. "La nozione di Dio secondo Carl Gustav Jung." *Humanitas* 26 (1971) pp 777—802.
163 —. "The *VII Sermones:* Play and Theory." *Spring 1972,* pp 206—18.
164 —. "Depth-Psychology and the *Homo Religiosus.*" Shortly to be published in the *Irish Theological Quarterly.*
165 —. "A Note on A. Moreno's *Jung, Gods and Modern Man.*" Awaiting publication with the *Journal of Analytical Psychology.*
166 HEPBURN, Ronald W. "Poetry and Religious Belief." In: Hepburn et al. *Metaphysical Beliefs.* London, SCM Press, 1957, pp 85—166.
167 HERWIG, Hedda J. *Therapie der Menschheit. Studien zur Psychoanalyse Freuds und Jungs.* Munich, Paul List, 1969.
168 HEUN, Eugen. "Psychotherapie und Seelsorge." *Zeitschrift für Psychotherapie und medizinische Psychologie* 3 (1953) pp 76—81.
169 HEYER, Gustav R. "Komplexe Psychologie (C. G. Jung)." In: Viktor Frankl et al., eds., *Handbuch der Neurosenlehre und Psychotherapie.* Munich, Urban u. Schwarzenberg, 1959—60, Vol 3, pp 321—25.
170 HEYMANN, Karl. "Ein Weg zur Psychologie: Die Autobiographie von C. G. Jung." *Abhandlungen zur Philosophie und Psychologie* 8 (1965) pp 14—20.

171 HILLMAN, James. "Psychology: Monotheistic or Polytheistic?" *Spring 1971,* pp 193—208.
172 HILTNER, Seward. "Man of the Month: Carl Gustav Jung." *Pastoral Psychology* 6 (1956) pp 79—81.
173 —. "Answer to Job by Carl Gustav Jung." *Pastoral Psychology* 6 (1956) pp 82—3. [v. 67].
174 —. "Carl Gustav Jung." *Pastoral Psychology* 12 (1961) pp 7—9.
175 HINDEL, Robert. "Der archetypische Gott C. G. Jungs und die Religion." *Wort und Wahrheit* 7 (1951) pp 565—71.
176 HOBSON, Robert. Critical Notice of HOSTIE [182]. *Journal of Analytical Psychology* 3 (1958) pp 64—9.
177 HOCH, Dorothee. "Antwort auf Hiob." *Kirchenblatt für die reformierte Schweiz* 108 (1952) pp 165—68.
178 —. "Von der 'prophetische Sendung' C. G. Jungs für Kirche und Theologie." *Kirchenblatt für die reformierte Schweiz* 111 (1955) pp 197—201.
179 —. "Zum 'Credo' von C. G. Jung." *Kirchenblatt für die reformierte Schweiz* 119 (1963) pp 66—8.
180 HOFMANN, Hans. "Real God and Real Man." *Christian Century* 72 (1955) pp 452—53.
181 HONDIUS, J. M. *Religie en werkelijkheid in het licht der psychologie van C. G. Jung.* Deventer, 1948.
182 HOSTIE, Raymond. *Religion and the Psychology of Jung.* London, Sheed and Ward, 1957.
183 —. "Carl Gustav Jung." *Lexikon für Theologie und Kirche.* Ed. by J. Höfer and Karl Rahner. Freiburg, Herder, 1960, Vol 5, p 1207.
184 HOWES, Elizabeth Boyden. *The Contribution of Dr. C. G. Jung to Our Religious Situation and the Contemporary Scene.* Guild for Psychological Studies, No 1. n.d., n.p.
185 —. *Analytical Psychology and the Synoptic Gospels.* Guild of Pastoral Psychology, Lecture No 88. London, 1956.
186 —. *Son of Man — Image of the Self.* Guild of Pastoral Psychology, Lecture No 109. London, 1960.
187 —. *Die Evangelien im Aspekt der Tiefenpsychologie.* Zurich, Origo, 1968.
188 HUBBACK, "VII Sermones ad Mortuos." *Journal of Analytical Psychology* 11 (1966) pp 95—111.
189 HÜBSCHER, Arthur. "C. G. Jung über das Mariendogma." *Glaube und Erkenntnis* 3 (1953) p 13.
190 HUPFER, Joseph. "Der Begriff des Geistes bei C. G. Jung und bei R. Steiner." *Abhandlungen zur Philosophie und Psychologie* 1 (1951) pp 57—79.
191 JACOBI, Jolande. "Aspects psychologiques de l'homme religieux." *Etudes Carmélitaines* (1949) pp 115—35.

192 —. "On the Frontiers of Religion and Psychology." London *Times* (23 May 1958).
193 —. "Das Religiöse in den Malereien von seelischen Leidenden." In: Josef Rudin [v. 302]. pp 123–66.
194 —. *The Way of Individuation*. London, Hodder and Stoughton, 1967.
195 JACOBS, Hans. *Western Psychotherapy and Hindu Sâdhanâ. A Contribution to Comparative Studies in Psychology and Metaphysics*. London, Allen and Unwin, 1961.
196 JACOBY, Mario. "Religious Problems Encountered by the Analyst." Lecture delivered to the Analytical Psychology Club of London, 19 October 1972.
197 JAEGER, M. "Reflections on the Work of Jung and Rank." *Journal of Psychotherapy as a Religious Process* 2 (1955) pp 47–57.
198 JÄGER, Otto. "Ein Gespräch über C. G. Jung." *Deutsches Pfarrerblatt* 61 (1961) pp 83–5.
199 JAFFE, Aniela. *The Myth of Meaning in the Work of C. G. Jung*. London, Hodder and Stoughton, 1970. [First published as *Der Mythus vom Sinn*. Zurich, Rascher, 1967.]
200 —. "The Creative Phases in Jung's Life." *Spring 1972*, pp 162–90.
201 JOHNSON, Paul E. *Psychology of Religion*. New York, Abingdon, 1959.
202 JOHNSTON, William. "Zen and Christian Mysticism: A Comparison in Psychological Structure." *International Philosophical Quarterly* 7 (1967) pp 441–69.
203 JUNG, A. "Buchsprechung von R. Hostie, *Jung und die Religion*." *Anima* 4 (1957) pp 374–75.
204 KEHOE, Richard. Review of *Answer to Job*. *Dominican Studies* 5 (1952) pp 228–31.
205 KELLER, Adolf. "Analytische Psychologie und Religionsforschung." [v. 11 supra]. pp 271–97.
206 KELSEY, Morton T. *Dreams: The Dark Speech of the Spirit. A Christian Interpretation*. Garden City, Doubleday, 1968.
207 —. "God, Education and the Unconscious." *Religious Education* 65 (1970) pp 227–34.
208 —. "Jung as Philosopher and Theologian." [v. 5 supra]. pp 184–96.
209 —. "Rediscovering the Priesthood through the Unconscious." *Journal of Pastoral Counseling* 7 (1972) pp 26–36.
210 KIENER, Hélène. "Le problème religieux dans l'œuvre de C.-G. Jung." In her book of the same title: Fontainebleau, Ferrière, 1968, pp 1–17.
211 —. "L'apport de C.-G. Jung au débat théologique actuel." ibid. pp 19–38.
212 —. "Réponse à quelques critiques sur la portée religieuse de l'œuvre de C.-G. Jung." ibid. pp 39–58.
213 KIESOW, Ernst-Rüdiger. "Der Protestantismus in der Sicht C. G.

Jungs." *Monatsschrift für Pastoraltheologie* 47 (1958) pp 445—50.
214 —. *Katholizismus und Protestantismus bei Carl Gustav Jung.* (Doctoral dissertation). Humboldt, University of Berlin, 1962.
215 —. "Bemerkungen zu C. G. Jungs Selbstdarstellung." *Wege zum Menschen* 17 (1965) pp 146—50.
216 KIJM, J. M. "De katolieke godsdienst en de complexe psycholgie van C. G. Jung." *Gawin* 1 (1952—3) pp 39—49.
217* KIRSCH, James. Four lectures on religion and Jungian psychotherapy, broadcast on KPFK Radio, Los Angeles, April 1960. Never published, but in private transcript form.
218 KIRSCH, Thomas B. "Psychiatry and Religion." *Journal of Religion and Health* 6 (1967) pp 74—9.
219 KÖBERLE, Adolf. *Christliches Denken: von der Erkenntnis zur Verwirklichung.* Hamburg, Furche, 1962.
220 KOEPGEN, Georg. "Hiob, das grosse Lehrgedicht des Alten Testaments. Zu den Deutungen C. G. Jungs und Martin Bubers." *Gloria Dei* 7 (1952) pp 228—37.
221 KOPLIK, Irwin Jay. *Jung's Psychology in the Plays of O'Neill.* (Doctoral dissertation). New York University, 1966.
222 KÜNZLI, Arnold. "Carl Gustav Jung." *Deutsche Rundschau* 81 (1955) pp 942—44.
223 LAMBERT, Kenneth. Critical notice on Jung's *Answer to Job. Journal of Analytical Psychology* 1 (1955) pp 100—08.
224 —. "Can Theologians and Analytical Psychologist Collaborate?" *Journal of Analytical Psychology* 5 (1960) pp 129—46.
225 —. Critical notice on PHILP [275]. *Journal of Analytical Psychology* 5 (1960) pp 170—76.
226 LANG, R. "Die Frage der Urreligion in der Tiefenpsychologie." *Wissenschaft und Weltbild* 5 (1952) pp 46—53.
227 LANTERO, E. H. "Agape and Jung's Eros." *Journal of Religious Thought* 5 (1948) pp 186—95; 6 (1949) pp 49—66.
228 LAUER, Hans Erhard. *Die Rätsel der Seele. Tiefenpsychologie und Anthroposophie.* Freiburg, die Kommenden, 1960/1964.
229 LAUTERBORN, Eleonore. *Swami Omkaranda und C. G. Jung. Der psychologische Schatten und das überpsychologische Selbst.* Zürich, A.B.C., 1970.
230 LAWS, Frederick. "The Mystic in the Laboratory." *New Statesman and Nation* 15 (1938) pp 660, 662.
231 LAYARD, Doris. Review of WHITE [408]. *Harvest* 6 (1960) pp 76—7.
232 LEAVY, Stanley. Review of WHITE [401]. *Bibliography for the Guild of Scholars* 14 (1953) No 5, pp 1—3.
233 LECOURT, Jacques. *Carl Gustav Jung et Pierre Teilhard de Chardin: leur combat pour la santé de l'âme.* Dammartin-en-Goele, Institut Coué, 1967.
234 LEIBBRAND, Werner. "C. G. Jungs Versuch einer psychologischen

Deutung des Trinitätsdogmas." *Zeitschrift für Religions- und Geistesgeschichte* 3 (1951) pp 122—34.

235 LEONARD, A. "La psychologie religieuse de Jung." *Supplément de la Vie spirituelle* 5 (1951) pp 325—34.

236 —. "Incertitudes et perspective en psychologie religieuse." *Supplément de la Vie spirituelle* 7 (1953) pp 215—42.

237 LINSSEN, Râm. *Etudes psychologiques de C. G. Jung à J. Krishnamurti.* Bruxelles, "Etre Libre", n.d. [ca. 1950].

238 LIRAN, Bernhard. Contribution to "Débat sur psychologie et religion." [v. 34 supra]. pp 187—97.

239 LONDERO, Carissimo. *Il simbolismo religioso nel pensiero di C. G. Jung.* (Doctoral Dissertation). Pontificio Ateneo Antoniano, Rome, 1959.

240 LOOSER, Günther. "Jung's Childhood Prayer." *Spring* (1966) pp 76—80.

241 MACAVOY, Joseph. "Direction spirituelle et psychologie." In: Charles Baumgartner et al., eds. *Dictionnaire de Spiritualité.* Paris, Beauchesne, 1957, Vol 3, pp 1143—73.

242 MACINTOSH, Douglas Clyde. *The Problem of Religious Knowledge.* London, Harper and Brothers, 1940.

243 MACQUARRIE, John. *Twentieth-Century Religious Thought. The Frontiers of Philosophy and Theology, 1900—1960.* London, SCM Press, 1963.

244 MAIRET, Philip. "Presuppositions of Psychological Analysis." [v. 102 supra]. pp 61—72.

245 MANN, Ulrich. "Tiefenpsychologie und Theologie." *Lutheranische Monatshefte* 4 (1965) pp 188—92.

246 —. "Quaternität bei C. G. Jung." *Theologische Literatur-Zeitung* 92 (1967) pp 331—36.

247 —. "Symbole und tiefenpsychologische Gestaltungsfaktoren der Religion." In: Charlotte Hörgl und Fritz Rauh, eds. *Grenzfragen des Glaubens. Theologische Grundfragen als Grenzprobleme.* Zürich, Benzinger, 1967, pp 153—75.

248 —. *Theogonische Tage. Die Entwicklungsphasen des Gottesbewusstseins in der altorientalischen und biblischen Religion.* Stuttgart, Ernst Klett, 1970.

249 —. "Die Gotteserfahrung des Menschen bei C. G. Jung." [v. 161 supra]. pp 7—24.

250 MANUEL, André. "C. G. Jung, gnostique et agnostique?" *La Nation* (3 August 1961).

251 MARTI, Kurt. Review of *Answer to Job. Kirchenblatt für die reformierte Schweiz* 108 (1952) pp 168—69.

252 MARTIN, Percival William. *Experiment in Depth: A Study of the Work of Jung, Eliot and Toynbee.* London, Routledge and Kegan Paul, 1955.

253 MARTINS, Diamantino. "Posiçâo analítico-existencial do problema de Deus." *Revista portuguesa de filosofia* 32 (1970) pp110–20.
254 MCLEISH, John. "Carl Jung, Psychology and Catholicism." *Wiseman Review* No 489 (1961) pp 264–76; No 490 (1961-2) pp 313–18.
255 MCPHERSON, Thomas. *The Philosophy of Religion.* New York, Van Nostrand. 1965.
256 MEIER, C. A. "Einige Konsequenzen der neueren Psychologie." *Studia Philosophica* 19 (1959) pp 157–72.
257 MEISSNER, W. W. "Origen and the Analytic Psychology of Symbolism." *Downside Review* 79 (1961) pp 201–16.
258 MERLIN, E. A. "Faith and Psyche: A Role for Jung in Theology." *Catholic World* 209 (July 1969) pp 172–75.
259 MESEGUER, Pedro. Review of GOLDBRUNNER [131]. *Razón y fe* (May 1943) pp 465–68.
260 —. "La aceptación de la 'sombra', según C. G. Jung, y su paralelo cristiano." *Razón y fe* 145 (1952) pp 166–78; 393–402.
261 —. "Psicología compleja (Jung)." *Razón y fe* 149 (1954) pp 87–90.
262 METMAN, Eva. *C. G. Jung's Essay on "The Psychology of the Spirit".* Guild of Pastoral Psychology, Lecture No 49. London, 1947.
263 METMAN, Philip. *C. G. Jung's Psychology and the Problem of Values.* Burning Glass Paper No 21. Kent, n.d. [ca. 1954].
264 MEYER, Werner. "In memoriam Carl Gustav Jung." *Reformatio* 10 (1961) pp 331–36. [Reprinted, with omissions, from: *Zur Erinnerung an Carl Gustav Jung.* (Gedenkfeier anlässlich der Bestattung). Küsnacht, 1961. pp 7–18.]
265 MICHAELIS, Edgar. "Le livre de Job interprété par C.-G. Jung." *Revue de théologie et de philosophie* 3 (1953) pp 183–95.
266 —. "Satan – die vierte Person der Gottheit? Zu C. G. Jungs Deutung des Buches Hiob." *Zeitwende* 25 (1954) pp 368–77.
267 MORAWITZ-CADIO, Alice von. *Spirituelle Psychologie. Zur Psychologie Jungs als Notwendigkeit der Gegenwart.* Wien, Amandus, 1958.
268 —. "Dem Andenken C. G. Jungs." *Natur und Kultur* 53 (1961) pp 211–13.
269 MORENO, Antonio. *Jung, Gods and Modern Man.* London, University of Notre Dame Press, 1970.
270 NOEL, Daniel C. "Thomas Altizer and the Dialectic of Regression." [v. 16 supra]. pp 147–63.
271 NORDBERG, Robert B. "Jung: Passing of a Mystic." *America* 105 (1961) p 699.
272 O'MEARA, Thomas Aquinas. "Marian Theology and the Contemporary Problem of Myth." *Marian Studies* 15 (1964) pp 127–56.
273 PANNWITZ, Rudolf, "C. G. Jung's Wissenschaft von der Seele." *Merkur* 7 (1953) pp 418–38. [Later included in his: *Beiträge zu*

einer europäischen Kultur. Nürnberg, Hans Carl, 1954, pp 104–31.]

274 PETRO, Carlo. *Le psicologie del profondo ed in particolare la psicologia analitica di C. G. Jung e l'igiene mentale*. Cremona, Mangiarotti, 1963.

275 PHILP, Howard L. *Jung and the Problem of Evil*. London, Salisbury Square, 1958.

276 PIMENTA DE SOUZA MONTEIRO, José Alfredo. "A psicologia analítica de Jung." *Revista portuguesa de filosofia* 16 (1950) pp 48–72.

277 PINTACUDA, Luigi. *La psicologia analitica di Karl Jung*. Rome, Paoline, 1965.

278 PLAUT, A. Critical notice on vol 11 of Jung's Collected Works. *Journal of Analytical Psychology* 4 (1959) pp 68–73.

279 POHIER, J. M. "Psychologie et religion de Carl G. Jung." *Revue des sciences philosophiques et théologiques* 44 (1960) pp 639–45.

280 PROGOFF, Ira. "The Man Who Transforms Consciousness: The Inner Myths of Martin Buber, Paul Tillich and C. G. Jung." *Eranos-Jahrbuch* (1966). Zurich, Rhein, 1967, pp 99–144.

281 PRUYSER, Paul W. "Some Trends in Psychology of Religion." *Journal of Religion* 40 (1960) pp 113–29.

282 PYE, Faye. *The Soul as a Function of Relationship in Psychology and Religion*. Guild of Pastoral Psychology, Lecture No 121. London, 1963.

283 QUISPEL, Gilles. "C. G. Jung und die Gnosis: Die 'Septem Sermones ad Mortuos' und Basilides." *Eranos-Jahrbuch* (1968). Zurich, Rhein, 1970, pp 277–98.

284 REIK, T. "The Science of Religion." *International Journal of Psychoanalysis* 2 (1921) pp 80–93.

285 RIEFF, Philip. "C. G. Jung's Confession: Psychology as a Language of Faith." *Encounter* 22 (May 1964) pp 45–50.

286 RITCHEY, Melvin S. *Light from the Darkness: Modern Man in Search of a Meaningful Church*. (Diploma thesis). Zurich, 1969.

287 RIUKAS, Stanley. *God: Myth, Symbol and Reality. A Study of Jung's Psychology*. (Doctoral dissertation). New York University, 1967.

288 ROCHEDIEU, Edmond. "C. G. Jung a redonné à la psychologie ses dimensions spirituelles." *La Vie protestante* (16 June 1961).

289 RÖÖSLI, Josef. "Der Gottes- und Religionsbegriff bei C. G. Jung." *Schweizerische Kirchenzeitung* 26 (1944) pp 302–04.

290 RÖSSLER, Dietrich. "Tiefenpsychologie als theologisches Problem." *Evangelische Theologie* 21 (1961) pp 162–73.

291 ROLFE, E. *The Intelligent Agnostic's Introduction to Christianity*. London, Arrow Books, 1963.

292 RORARIUS, Winfried. "Der archetypische Gott. Über das Verhältnis

von Glauben und Psychotherapie bei Freud und Jung." *Zeitwende* 37 (1966) pp 368—81.

293 —. "C. G. Jungs Einsicht in die Seele und die Anrede des Evangeliums." *Zeitwende* 34 (1963) pp 225—39.

294 ROSENFELD, Paul. "Psychoanalysis and God." *Nation* 146 (1938) pp 510—11.

295 ROTH, G. "Die Lehre C. G. Jungs in der Kritik ihrer Hilfswissenschaften." *Wissenschaft und Weltbild* 9 (1956) pp 39—44.

296 ROTH, Paul. *Anima und Animus in der Psychologie C. G. Jungs*. Winterthur, P. G. Keller, 1954.

297 RUDIN, Josef. "Antwort auf Hiob." *Orientierung* 17 (1953) pp 41—4. [Reprinted in his: *Psychotherapie und Religion*. Olten, Walter, 1964. English version: *Psychotherapy and Religion*. London, University of Notre Dame Press, 1968, pp 135—54.]

298 —. "Das kranke Gottesbild." *Orientierung* 22 (1958) [Reprinted ibid. pp 155—72.]

299 —. "Gott und das Böse bei C. G. Jung." *Arzt und Seelsorger* 12 (1961) pp 4—8. [Also in the *Neue Zürcher Zeitung* (30 July 1961.)]

300 —. "Misstrauen gegen das religiöse Erleben." In his: *Religion und Erlebnis. Ein Weg zur Überwindung der religiösen Krise*. Olten, Walter, 1963, pp 15—29.

301 —. "C. G. Jung und die Religion." *Orientierung* 28 (1964) pp 238—42. [Reprinted v. 9 supra. pp 73—86.]

302 —. "Psychotherapie und religiöser Glaube." In his *Neurose und Religion. Krankheitsbilder und ihre Problematik*. Olten, Walter, 1964, pp 65—94.

303 —. "Das Schuldproblem in der tiefenpsychologie von C. G. Jung." In: Rudin et al., *Schuld und religiöse Erfahrung*. Freiburg, Herder, 1968, pp 61—71.

304 RÜSCHE, Franz. "Über ein bedeutsames Buch zum Thema 'C. G. Jung und die Religion'." *Theologie und Glaube* 54 (1964) pp 81—90.

305 RUMPF, Louis. "C. G. Jung, Déchiffreur de l'âme en souffrance." *Revue de théologie et de philosophie* (1962) pp 250—69.

306 RYCHNER, Max. "C. G. Jung zu seinem 80. Geburtstag." In his: *Arachne: Aufsätze zur Literatur*. Zurich, Manesse, 1957, pp 206—17.

307 SANFORD, John A. *Dreams: God's Forgotten Language*. Philadelphia, J. B. Lippincott, 1968.

308 —. "Analytical Psychology: Science or Religion? An Exploration of the Epistemology of Analytical Psychology" [v. 5, supra]. pp 90—105.

309 SAURAT, Denis. "Le rôle historique et l'avenir des idées de Jung." *Le Disque vert* (1955) pp 220—30.

310 SBOROWITZ, Arië. "Beziehung und Bestimmung. Die Lehren von

Martin Buber und C. G. Jung in ihrem Verhältnis zueinander." *Psyche* 2 (1948) pp 9—56.
311 —. "Nachwort" to TRÜB [363]. pp 117—24.
312 —. "Das religiöse Moment in der Tiefenpsychologie." *Psyche* 5 (1951) pp 278—89.
313 —. "Eine religiöse Konzeption in der Nachfolge C. G. Jungs." *Psyche* 8 (1955) pp 22—31.
314 —. "Freud, Jung und die Möglichkeit einer christlichen Psychotherapie." In his: *Der leidende Mensch: Personale Psychotherapie in anthropologischer Sicht*. Darmstadt, Wissenschaftliche Buchgesellschaft, 1965, pp 62—105.
315 SCHÄR, Hans. "Die Bedeutung der Religionspsychologie." *Schweizerische Zeitschrift für Psychologie* 2 (1943) pp 175—85; 255—65.
316 —. "Voraussetzungen der Seelsorge beim Pfarrer und beim Arzt." *Schweizerische Zeitschrift für Psychologie* 4 (1945) pp 238—62.
317 —. *Religion und Seele in der Psychologie C. G. Jungs*. Zurich, Rascher, 1946. [English edition: *Religion and the Cure of Souls in Jung's Psychology*. London, Routledge and Kegan Paul, 1951.]
318 —. "C. G. Jung und die Deutung der Geschichte." *Schweizerische Theologische Umschau* 22 (1952) pp 91—6.
319 —. "Die Religion in der Psychologie C. G. Jungs." *Psychologia-Jahrbuch* (1955) pp 96—110.
320 —. "Vie spirituelle saine et maladive dans la religion." *Le Disque vert* (1955) pp 236—52.
321 —. *Seelsorge und Psychotherapie*. Zurich, Rascher, 1961.
322 —. "Gotteserfahrung, Gotteserkenntnis und Seele." *Schweizerische Theologische Umschau* 35 (1965) pp 16—28.
323 SCHARFENBERG, Joachim. "Zum theologischen Gespräch mit C. G. Jung." *Quatember* 26 (1962) pp 21—7. [Also printed in: *Wege zum Menschen* 14 (1962) pp 3—8].
324 SCHARPFF, Wilhelm. "Der Tiefenpsychologe C. G. Jung und die Religion." *Wort und Tat* 9 (1955) pp 76—9.
325 SCHMIDT, Ernst Walter. "Hiob, Jung und Bultmann." *Neue Deutsche Hefte* 1 (1954) pp 699—705.
326 SCHULZE, W. A. "Die Himmelfahrt Mariens bei C. G. Jung." *Theologische Zeitschrift* 25 (1969) pp 215—18.
327 SCHWARTZ, Charlene. "Jung and Freud." *Integrity* 7 (July 1953) pp 20—4.
328 SCHWERMER, Josef. "Religiöse Termini bei C. G. Jung." *Theologie und Glaube* 49 (1959) pp 386—74.
329 SEIFERT, Friedrich. "Gut und Böse als Antinomie und als Polarität." [v. 96 supra] pp 63—79.
330 SEMMELROTH, Otto. Review of *Answer to Job*. *Scholastik* 28 (1953) p 139.

331 SERRANO, Miguel. *C. G. Jung and Hermann Hesse. A Record of Two Friendships.* New York, Schocken, 1970.
332 SIERKSMA, Fokke. *Phaenomenologie der religie en complexe psychologie: een methodologische bijdrage.* Assen, Van Gorcum, 1950.
333 SMITH, J. W. D. "A Study of Sin and Salvation in Terms of C. G. Jung's Psychology. *Scottish Journal of Theology* 3 (1950) pp 397–408.
334 SPENGLER, Ernst. *Das Gewissen bei Freud und Jung, mit einer philosophisch-anthropologischen Grundlegung.* Zurich, Juris, 1964.
335 SPIEGELBERG, Friedrich. Critical notice on Vol 11 of Jung's Collected Works. *Journal of Analytical Psychology* 4 (1959) pp 79–83.
336 SPINKS, Alfred G. S. *Archetypes and Apocalypse.* (Doctoral dissertation). University of London, 1945.
337 STAUB, Josef. "Die Auffassung von Gott und Religion bei C. G. Jung." *Annalen der Philosophischen Gesellschaften Innerschweiz und Ostschweiz* 4 (1948) pp 1–37.
338 STEFFEN, Uwe. "Tiefenpsychologie und Theologie. Zum 80. Geburtstag von C. G. Jung am 26. August 1955." *Monatsschrift für Pastoraltheologie* 44 (1955) pp 416–30.
339 STERN, Karl. "Jung and the Christians." *Commonweal* 58 (1953) pp 229–31.
340 STEVENS, George. Review of WHITE [401]. *Theological Studies* 14 (1953) pp 409–505.
341 STICKELBERGER, Rudolf. "Seelsorger als Arznei. Nach dem Tode Jungs." *Reformatio* 10 (1961) pp 295–99.
342 STOCKER, Arnold. *Psychologie du sens moral.* Geneva, Suzerenne, 1949.
343 —. "L'anima nelle dottrine psicologichie contemporanee." In: Michele Federico Sciacca, ed., *L'Anima.* Brescia, Morcelliana, 1954. pp 293–329.
344 STROJNOWSKI, Jerzy. "Psychologia religii K. G. Jung." *Zeszyty Naukowe Katolickiego Uniwersytetu Lubelskiego* 6 (1963) pp 35–45.
345 STRUNK, Orlo. "Psychology, Religion and C. G. Jung: A Review of Periodical Literature." *Journal of Bible and Religion* 24 (1956) pp 106–13.
346 SUARES, Carlo. *Le Mythe Judéo-chrétien d'après la Genèse et les Evangiles selon Matthieu et Jean.* Paris, Cercle du Livre, 1950.
347 —. "Jung et l'experience religieuse." *Le Disque vert* (1955) pp 339–45.
348 —. "C. G. Jung. Le vieil homme de la terre." In his *De quelques apprentis-sorciers.* Paris, Etre Libre, 1961, pp 113–34.
349 SUMNER, Oswald and ELKISH, F. B. "Modern Psychology and Introspection." *Downside Review* 65 (1947) pp 33–44.
350 SUMNER, Oswald. *St. John of the Cross and Modern Psychology.* Guild of Pastoral Psychology, Lecture No 57. London, 1948.

351 —. *St. John Climacus: The Psychology of the Desert Fathers.* Guild of Pastoral Psychology, Lecture No 63. London, 1950.
352 THIRY, A. "Jung et la religion." *Nouvelle revue théologique* 79 (1957) pp 248–76.
353 THORNTON, Edward. "Jungian Psychology and the Vedanta." In: James Aylward et al., *Spectrum Psychologiae.* Zurich, Rascher, 1965, pp 131–42.
354 —. *The Diary of a Mystic.* London, Allen and Unwin, 1967.
355 THUM, Beda. "Theologie und Psychologie." *Gloria Dei* 5 (1950-1) pp 81–91.
356 THURNEYSEN, Eduard. "C. G. Jungs 'Erinnerungen, Träume, Gedanken'." *Kirchenblatt für die reformierte Schweiz* 119 (1963) pp 162–65; 178–81.
357 —. *Seelsorge und Psychotherapie.* Munich, Kaiser, 1950.
358 TILLICH, Paul. "The Impact of Psychotherapy on Theological Thought." New York, Academy of Religion and Mental Health, 1960. [Published with revisions in *Pastoral Psychology* 11 (1960).]
359 —. Contribution to: *Carl Gustav Jung 1875–1961: A Memorial Meeting.* New York, 1962, pp 28–32.
360 TOWERS, Bernard. "Jung and Teilhard." [v. 36 supra] pp 79–87.
361 TRÜB, Hans. "Individuation, Schuld und Entscheidung. Über die Grenzen der Psychologie." [v. 11 supra] pp 529–55.
362 —. *Vom Selbst zur Welt. Der zweifache Auftrag des Psychotherapeuten.* Zurich, Speer, 1947.
363 —. *Heilung aus der Begegnung. Eine Auseinandersetzung mit der Psychologie C. G. Jungs.* Stuttgart, Ernst Klett, 1951.
364 TUINSTRA, Coenrad Liebrecht. *Het symbool in de psychanalyse. Beschrijving en theologische Critiek.* (Doctoral dissertation). Amsterdam, 1933.
365 UHSADEL, Walter. *Der Mensch und die Mächte des Unbewussten. Begegnung von Psychotherapie und Seelsorge.* Kassel, Johannes Stauda, 1952.
366 —. "Zum Problem der Transzendenz in der Psychologie C. G. Jungs." In: Theodor Bovet et al. *Forschung und Erfahrung im Dienst der Seelsorge.* Göttingen, Vandenhoeck u. Ruprecht, 1961. pp 66–70.
367 ULANOV, Ann Belford. *The Feminine in Jungian Psychology and in Christian Theology.* Evanston, Northwestern University Press, 1971.
368 UNDERWOOD, Richard Arnold. *The Possibility of the Word in the "Time of the World-Picture" — Prolegomena to a Study of the Depth Psychology of C. G. Jung in Relation to Contemporary Theological Interpretation.* (Doctoral Dissertation). Drew University, 1962.
369 VAN DE WIENCKEL, Erna. *De l'inconscient à Dieu. Ascèse chrétienne et psychologie de C. G. Jung.* Paris, Montaignes, 1959.

370 VAN DEN BERGH VAN EYSINGA, Gustav Adolf. "Jung en Job et cetera." In his: *Godsdienstwetenschappelijke Studiën XIV*. Haarlem, H. D. Tjeenk Willink en Zoon N. V., 1953, pp 34—44.
371 VASAVADA, Arvind. *Dr. C. G. Jung ka nislesanatmaki manovijñan. Ek samksipth Paricay*. Varanasi, Chowkhamba Vidyabhawan, 1963.
372 —. "The Place of Psychology in Philosophy." Presidential address to the 38th session of the Indian Philosophical Congress of Madras, 1964.
373 —. *Tripurá-rahasya*. Varanasi, Chowkhamba Sanskrit Offices, 1965.
374 —. "Philosophical Roots of the Psychotherapies of the West." [v. 353 supra] pp 143—54.
375 —. "Jung's analytische Psychologie und indische Weisheit." In: *Abendländische Therapie und östliche Weisheit*, ed. by Wilhelm Bitter. Stuttgart, Ernst Klett, 1968, pp 236—44. [English translation: *Journal of Analytical Psychology* 13 (1968) pp 131—45.]
376 VELAZQUEZ, José M. "Jung: psicólogo de la religión." *Universidad de la Habana* 25 (1961) pp 140—44.
377 VERGOTE, Antoine, "Interpretazioni psicologiche dei fenomeni religiosi nell'ateismo contemporaneo." In: *L'Ateismo contemporaneo*. Ed. by the Faculty of Philosophy of the Pontificia Università Salesiana, Rome. Turin, Società Editrice Internazionale, 1967, Vol 1 pp 327—80.
378 VETTER, August. "Die Bedeutung der unbewussten Seele bei C. G. Jung." *Zeitwende* 12 (1936) pp 213—24.
379 VOGEL, Gustav. *Tiefenpsychologie und Nächstenliebe*. Mainz, Matthias Grünewald, 1957.
380 VON DER HEYDT, Vera. *Psychology and the Cure of Souls: Standards and Values*. Guild of Pastoral Psychology, Lecture No 81. London, 1954.
381 VON FRANZ, Marie-Louise. "Die Selbsterfahrung bei C. G. Jung." [v. 161 supra] pp 25—45.
382 —. *C. G. Jung. Sein Mythos in unserer Zeit*. Stuttgart, Huber, 1972.
383 VON GEBSATTEL, Viktor Emil. *Christentum und Humanismus. Wege des menschlichen Selbstverständnis*. Stuttgart, Ernst Klett, 1947.
384 —. *Imago Hominis: Beiträge zu einer personalen Anthropologie*. Schweinfurt, Neues Forum, 1964.
385 VON LOEWENICH, Walther. *Luther und der Neuprotestantismus*. Witten, Luther, 1963.
386 VON WEIZSÄCKER, Viktor. Review of Jung's *Answer to Job. Psyche* 2 (1952) p 30. [Partially reprinted as "Nochmals C. G. Jungs *Antwort auf Hiob*." *Kirchenblatt für die reformierte Schweiz* 109 (1953) p 319.]
387 WALDER, Peter. *Mensch und Welt bei C. G. Jung*. Zurich, Origo, 1951.

388 ——. "Zu einer Auseinandersetzung mit der Psychologie C. G. Jungs." *Psyche* 7 (1953) Referat pp 26—33.
389 WALLACE, Anthony F. C. *Religion: An Anthropological View.* New York, Random House, 1966.
390 WATKIN, E. "Religion?" *Dublin Review* 229 (1955) pp 337—40.
391 WEHR, Gerhard. *C. G. Jung in Selbstzeugnissen und Bilddokumenten.* Reinbek bei Hamburg, Rowohlt, 1969.
392 ——. *C. G. Jung und Rudolf Steiner. Konfrontation und Synopse.* Stuttgart, Ernst Klett, 1972.
393 WESTMANN, H. *The Old Testament and Analytical Psychology.* Guild of Pastoral Psychology, Lecture No 3. London, 1939.
394 ——. *The Golden Calf.* Guild of Pastoral Psychology, Lecture No 10. London, 1941.
395 WHITE, Victor. "St. Thomas and Jung's Psychology." *Blackfriars* 25 (1944) pp 209—19.
396 ——. "Psychotherapy and Ethics." *Blackfriars* 26 (1945) pp 287—300.
397 ——. "Psychotherapy and Ethics: A Postscript." *Blackfriars* 26 (1945) pp 381—87.
398 ——. Review of Jung's *Die Psychologie der Übertragung* and *Aufsätze zur Zeitgeschichte. Blackfriars* 28 (1947) pp 138—40.
399 ——. Review of Vol 9/2 of Jung's Collected Works. *Dominican Studies* 5 (1952) pp 240—43.
400 ——. "Four Challenges to Religion: II. Jung." *Blackfriars* 33 (1952) pp 203—07. [Reprinted in *Commonweal* 55 (1952) pp 561—62.]
401 ——. *God and the Unconscious.* London, Collins 1952/1967.
402 ——. "Two Theologians on Jung's Psychology." *Blackfriars* 36 (1955) pp 382—88. [Reprinted in abridged form in *Cross Currents* 7 (1957) pp 283—87.]
403 ——. "Jung et son livre sur Job." *Supplément de la Vie spirituelle* (1956) pp 199—209.
404 ——. "Dogma and Mental Health." In: *Conducta religiosa y salud mental: VII Congreso católico internacional de psicoterapia y psicología clínica.* Madrid, 1957, pp 97—101.
405 ——. Critical notice on HOSTIE [182]. *Journal of Analytical Psychology* 3 (1958) pp 59—64.
406 ——. Critical Notice on Vol 11 of Jung's Collected Works. *Journal of Analytical Psychology* 4 (1959) pp 73—8.
407 ——. "Theological Reflections." *Journal of Analytical Psychology* 5 (1960) pp 147—54.
408 ——. *Soul and Psyche. An Enquiry into the Relationship of Psychotherapy and Religion.* London, Collins, 1960.
409 WHITMONT, Edward. "Religious Aspects of Life Problems in Analysis." *Spring* (1958) pp 49—64.
410 WILDBERGER, H. "Das Hiobproblem und seine neueste Deutung." *Reformatio* 3 (1954) pp 355—63; 439—48.

411 WILLIAMS, Jay G. "Other-Worldly Christianity: Some Positive Considerations." *Theology Today* 28 (1971) pp 328–36.
412 WILSON, John Richardson. *Psychodynamic Structure and Trinitarian Foundations.* (Doctoral dissertation). University of Edinburgh, 1968.
413 WILWOLL, Alexander. "Vom Unbewussten im Aufbau religiösen Erlebens." *Annalen der philosophischen Gesellschaft Innerschweiz* 2 (1945) pp 25–55.
414 WINGENFELD, Berard. *Die Archetypen der Selbstwerdung bei Carl Gustav Jung.* Pfullendorf/Baden, Schmidt und Sohn, 1955.
415 WINKLER, Klaus. *Dogmatische Aussagen in der neueren Theologie im Verhältnis zu den Grundbegriffen der Komplexen Psychologie C. G. Jungs.* (Doctoral dissertation). Berlin, 1960.
416 WISSE, Stephen. *Das religiöse Symbol. Versuch einer Wesendeutung.* Essen, Ludgerus, 1963.
417 WITCUTT, W. F. *Catholic Thought and Modern Psychology.* London, Burns, Oates and Washbourne, 1943.
418 WOLFF, Hanna. *Anima Jesu.* (Diploma thesis). Zurich, 1969.
419 WOLFF, Otto. "C. G. Jungs Antwort auf Hiob." In: Gerhard Zacharias, *Dialog über den Menschen.* Stuttgart, Ernst Klett, 1968, pp 153–68.
420 WOLFF, Toni. *Christianity Within.* Guild of Pastoral Psychology, Lecture No 42. London, 1946.
421 WURM, Alois. "Zu dem Thema: C. G. Jungs Stellung zum Christentum." *Die Seele* 30 (1954) pp 148–50.
422 ZACHARIAS, Gerhard Paulus." Die Bedeutung der Psychologie C. G. Jungs für die christliche Theologie." *Zeitschrift für Religions- und Geistesgeschichte* 5 (1953) pp 257–69. [Reprinted in French: *Synthèses* 10 (1955) pp 381–90.]
423 —. *Psyche und Mysterium. Die Bedeutung der Psychologie C. G. Jungs für die christliche Theologie und Liturgie.* Zurich, Rascher, 1954.
424 —. et al. "Aussprache über den Vortrag von Professor Haendler." [v. 147 supra] pp 213–23.
425 ZAEHNER, Robert Charles. "The Religious Instinct." In: Alan Pryce-Jones, ed. *The New Outline of Modern Knowledge.* London, Victor Gollancz, 1956, pp 64–85.
426 —. *Mysticism: Sacred and Profane. An Inquiry into Some Varieties of Preternatural Experience.* Oxford, Clarendon, 1957.
427 —. "A New Buddha and a New Tao." In his: *Concise Encyclopaedia of Living Faiths.* London, Hutchinson, 1959.
428 —. *Concordant Discord: The Interdependence of Faith.* Oxford, Clarendon, 1970.
429 ZIEGLER, A. "Der Beitrag der analytischen Psychologie C. G. Jungs zur Psychosomatik." *Therapeutische Umschau und Medizinische Bibliographie* 23 (1966) pp 251–55.

430 ZUNINI, Giorgio. *Homo Religiosus*. Milan, Il Saggiatore, 1966. [English translation: *Man and His Religion: Aspects of Religious Psychology*. London, Geoffrey Chapman, 1969.]
431 [Anon.] "Antwort auf Jungs *Antwort auf Hiob*." *Für ein jüdisches Lehrhaus Zürich* 2 (September 1952) pp 22–24.
432 [Anon.] "A Little Jung is a Dangerous Thing." *America* 92 (1955) p 612.
433 [Anon.] "Carl Gustav Jung gestorben." *Arzt und Seelsorger* 12/3 (1961) pp 1–4.

The following material arrived only after the above had gone to press. It has therefore not been included in the essay, but a reference to the relevant sections has been included in square brackets.

434 BARTH, Hans. Critical review of Jung's "Die Beziehungen der Psychotherapie zur Seelsorge." *Neue Zürcher Zeitung*, 3 August 1932. [Sec. 8]
435 BURI, Fritz. "C. G. Jungs *Antwort auf Hiob*." *National-Zeitung* (Basel), 27 April 1952. [Sec. 11]
436 HOMANS, Peter. "Psychology and Hermeneutics: Jung's Contribution." *Zygon* 4 (1969) pp 333–55. [Sec. 9]
437 KELSEY, Morton. *Encounter with God: A Theology of Christian Experience*. Minneapolis, Bethany Fellowship, 1972, pp 102–121 *et passim*. [Sec. 2]
438 OATES, Wayne. *Christ and Selfhood*. New York, Association Press, 1961, pp 230–33. [Sec. 5]
439 POSTLE, Beatrice. "Religion in the Psychologies of Jung and Freud." *The Ohio State Medical Journal* 43 (1947) pp 947–50. [Sec. 2]
440 SCHÄR, Hans. "Zum Gedächtnis von Carl Gustav Jung, 26. Juli 1875–6. Juni 1961." *Freies Christentum* 13 (1961) pp 111–13. [Sec. 8]
441 WERBLOWSKY, R.J.Z. "Psychology and Religion." *The Listener* 49 (1953) pp 677–9. [Sec. 2]
442 —. "God and the Unconscious." *The Listener* 49 (1953) pp 758–9. [Sec. 1]

AGAINST IMAGINATION:
THE *VIA NEGATIVA* OF SIMONE WEIL

ROGER WOOLGER
(Oxford/Zürich)

"La fin de la vie humaine est de construire
une architecture dans l'âme."
Simone Weil, *La Connaissance surnaturelle*, p. 16.

Blake wrote: "The world of Imagination is the world of eternity',[1] epitomising an assumption that is axiomatic to Jungian psychology. If Freud opened the royal road to the unconscious with the study of dreams only to find the potentially subversive vestiges of infantile sexuality and aggression, it was Jung who showed that deeper and closer contact with this primal psychic sludge revealed transforming symbols that could make of this road a *Heilsweg* of potential religious significance. Indeed, so impressive is the extent of Jung's demonstration of the redemptive and regenerative power of the imagination that we are apt to forget another approach to wholeness that is emphatic in rejecting the imagination *tout court*. This other approach is the mystical doctrine loosely termed the *via negativa* or sometimes "apophatic theology". It stems, in the Christian tradition, from the works of the obscure fifth century Church Father, Dionysius the Areopagite, who was probably influenced by the Neoplatonism of Plotinus.[2] In this essay I shall sketch some of the ways in which this doctrine not only contrasts with but explicitly repudiates that cultivation of the imagination so much a cornerstone of Jungian practice. In doing so my presentation of both schools of thought will necessarily be simplified, and I have chosen to examine a somewhat extreme example of the *via negativa* in order to sharpen the issues raised.

The via negativa

The doctrine of the *via negativa* and its corresponding practice in contemplative or mystical prayer is to be found, in one form or another, in all religions where mysticism has flourished: in Hinduism we meet the characterisation of Brahman as *neti, neti,* (not this, not this); in Buddhism there is the doctrine of not-Self and *sunja* (void); the Sufis of Islam called it *Al Haqq,* the Real or abyss of Godhead underlying Allah; in Judaism we meet the teaching of *tsimtsum* or the *Deus absconditus* (the absent God); in Taoism it emerges partly in the elusive and utterly indefinable quality of the *Tao* itself.

The mystic who pursues the *via negativa* as praxis follows an ascetic path of abandonment *(l'abandon* in De Caussade, *die Gelassenheit* in Silesius), suffering, darkness, void (Eckhart, Sankaracharya, St. John of the Cross), dryness, emptiness, *accidie,* purgation, and the stripping away of self. The emphasis upon this ignorance and nothingness is expressed in the titles of the two classic Christian treatises, *The Cloud of Unknowing* and *The Dark Night of the Soul.* The following two quotations are excellent examples of the doctrine: the first, Christian, illustrates its practical or ascetic aspect; the second, Buddhist, shows its metaphysical side:

> In order to arrive at having pleasure in everything,
> Desire to have pleasure in nothing.
> In order to arrive at possessing everything,
> Desire to possess nothing.
> In order to arrive at being everything,
> Desire to be nothing.
> In order to arrive at knowing everything,
> Desire to know nothing. (St. John of the Cross, *Ascent of Mount Carmel,* I, 14)

> There is ... a state of being where there is neither earth nor water, fire nor air ... neither this world nor the next nor both together, neither sun nor moon. There, I say, there is neither coming nor going nor standing still, neither falling nor arising: it is not based on anything, does not develop, and does not depend on anything. That is the end of suffering.

> There is an unborn, unbecome, unmade, uncompounded; and were there not an unborn, unbecome, unmade, uncompounded, then no escape could be discerned from what is born, becomes, is made, and is compounded. *(Udana,* VIII, 1, Pali Canon)

The resemblance of the mystic's states of dryness, void, *accidie,* etc., to depression was examined long ago with great sympathetic insight by William James in his chapter on the "Sick Soul" in *The Varieties of*

Religious Experience; more recently, Dr Frank Lake[3] has discussed the Psalms of David both as a document of the depressive temperament and as a potential source of therapy. What emerges is a typical state of the total withdrawal of energy in both the ordinary sufferer and the mystic. In this state the mystical aspirant (for so he is) can no longer pray nor take solace in worship; in comparison the depressive is often without dreams or fantasy, in a state of acute psychic dryness.

If one were to take the clinical typology which sees manic-depressive psychosis as a polar opposite to schizophrenia[4] one might be tempted to say that the dryness of the depressive and that of the mystic in his "dark night" together stand at the other end of the continuum from both the schizophrenic overwhelmed by voices, visions and presences, and the religious visionary like Blake or Bunyan rapt in his divine revelation. In the way that many mystics eschew visions and the practice of the imagination there is certainly a marked exclusiveness about the two states. St. John of the Cross writes of the approach to mystical contemplation as follows:

> The spiritual person who would enter upon the spiritual road (which is that of contemplation) must leave the way of imagination and of meditation through sense, when he takes no more pleasure therein and is no more able to reason. *(Ascent of Mount Carmel,* II, 14)

One contemporary commentator upon St. John, Dom Chapman, does indeed seem to regard this as a matter of temperament. He recommends that, in the life of prayer, some people should employ imagery if it suits them (what he calls, following St. John, meditation) while others should abandon images in favour of imageless contemplation.[5] Whether or not visionary and mystic are opposite types as are, apparently, schizophrenics and manic-depressives (even allowing the adequacy of such classification) is a problem we shall return to. Clearly, if they are, therapists and spiritual directors should have much to learn from a study of each other's methods and recommendations.

Simone Weil on Affliction and the Void

Simone Weil (1909-1943) was a contemporary practitioner of the *via negativa* in an extreme form. She is of particular interest in that she never belonged to any religious denomination or sect and is thus free from doctrinal influence or constraint other than of her own choosing;

her adoption of the *via negativa* was therefore entirely spontaneous. She opposed without compromise the use of imagination in the spiritual life, coming to spiritual illumination through a way of unattenuated suffering, darkness, and void. Trained as a philosopher she was able to articulate her experiences and insights with razor sharp, Pascalian precision. Although she never achieved any final systematic synthesis, her posthumously published notebooks and letters reveal an extraordinary thousand-page spiritual odyssey which contains no less than a complete mystical doctrine of the void.[6]

Many religious personalities have been tormented by mental anguish: for Pascal it was *la misère de l'homme;* for Kierkegaard the *Angst* of the isolated and alienated individual. Simone Weil saw the reflection of her own suffering in the social conditions of the European workers of the Thirties and in the lives of all those oppressed by political tyranny and poverty. Like many of her generation she first sought solutions in Marxism and activism, going so far as to relinquish her teaching position as an *agrégé* of the Sorbonne in philosophy to become actively engaged in *syndicalisme* (trade union movements) and left-wing politics. She worked for a year, at intense cost to both body and soul, in three factories in Paris and later among farm labourers; she travelled in Germany at the beginning of Hitler's ascendancy, was briefly at the front in the Spanish Civil War and later, in exile from her native France, identified herself passionately with the French resistance movement from 1940 until her death. She died, virtually unknown, in England, of tuberculosis aggravated by a refusal to eat more than French p.o.w. rations. She was 34. Although a Jewess she was never involved with either Orthodoxy or the struggles of Zionism but with the oppressed, *deraciné* masses she worked with. It was among these people that, she wrote, she "received for ever the mark of a slave, like the branding of a red-hot iron which the Romans put on the foreheads of their most despised slaves". Here too she became convinced that "Christianity is pre-eminently the religion of slaves".

In attempting to express her vision of physical and mental suffering she gave to the French word *malheur* (roughly translated: affliction) a new and terrible meaning:

> In the realm of suffering, affliction *(le malheur)* is something apart, specific, and irreducible ... Affliction is inseparable from physical

suffering and yet quite distinct from it ... There is not real affliction unless the event which has seized and uprooted a life attacks it, directly and indirectly, in all its parts, social, psychological and physical. *(Waiting on God,* pp. 77—8)

Simone Weil did not analyse such conditions, for the purpose of affliction is to learn that it has no purpose, that it is "the supreme contradiction". On the intellectual level affliction is "the problem of evil", the insolubility of which she came to regard as a means of undermining the fixity of the ego. Evil, and indeed all the classic problems of philosophy, can have this function for they are all ultimately contradictions, intellectual surds, comparable to the *koans* of the Zen masters or to the riddles posed in fairy tales:

> The riddles contained in these tales are no doubt *koans.*
> Riddles of the princess who kills all her suitors (found in innumerable tales). Riddles of Solomon and the Queen of Sheba. Riddle of the Sphinx at Thebes. Death of those who do not manage to solve them. To solve them is to understand that there is nothing to be solved, that existence possesses no significance for the discursive faculties ... Having solved the riddle you marry the princess, you inherit the kingdom. *(The Notebooks,* p. 446)

Ultimately, philosophy is not an intellectual but a contemplative discipline:

> The real method in philosophy consists in clearly conceiving insoluble problems in their insolubility, then simply contemplating them fixedly, tirelessly, waiting attentively for years without any hope. *(La Connaissance surnaturelle,* p. 365, my translation)

Religion too must be subjected to this *negatio*. She sees the essence of the religious attitude, initially at least, as one of doubt, not faith; atheism, according to her, must be a purification, a making bare of all the inherited ego structures. St. John of the Cross too speaks of a "dark night of the intellect" when all faith is lost, seemingly forever.

This state of doubt, of waiting, of insoluble contradiction and meaningless pain produces a state of extreme tension; in her writing she expresses it in the form of metaphysical paradox in which the anguish of a powerful intellect divided against itself is very apparent:

> To explain suffering is to console it, therefore it must not be explained. Whence the eminent value of the suffering of the innocent.
> It resembles the acceptance of evil in creation by God, who is innocent. To be innocent is to bear the weight of the entire universe. It is to throw away the counterweight. *(The Notebooks,* p. 229)

The image of weight here is significant. By concentrating so much libido in maintaining these conflicts in consciousness, an opposite is predictably constellated. Psychologically we would call it depression, Simone Weil uses the term void:

> Suffering is defined by efforts in the void. If one has a headache, one continually makes an effort to get rid of it, without any result. The acceptance of suffering is thus the acceptance of the void. *(The Notebooks,* p. 227)

The void can be produced by:

> Sudden death, betrayal, absence of one we love, sudden loss, something to which our thoughts for the future were attached. *(The Notebooks,* p. 198)

It is a state "when there is nothing external to correspond to an internal tension" which "produces an anguish, a desperate revolt, followed, as a result of exhaustion, by resignation" *(The Notebooks,* pp. 147, 137). This tension and anguish is caused by a refusal to fill the void by the gratification of desires or by the acceptance of any false consolation for the suffering. Gratifications and consolations create what Simone Weil calls a "balance" which is the *natural* or human response to suffering or deprivation. Denial of such a balance perpetuates the void but allows the possibility of *supernatural* consolation instead:

> Need of reward, for the sake of a balance; need to receive the equivalent of what one has given . . .; but if, doing violence to this need, powerful as gravity we leave a void, there takes place as it were an inrush of air, and a supernatural reward supervenes. It does not come if we receive any other wages; it is this void which causes it to come. *(The Notebooks,* p. 135)

Because the void is a condition of such extreme suffering men will flee from it at all costs, ignorant of its spiritual function, and seek a balance. One of the chief ways by which this is achieved is the imagination:

> The imagination (when uncontrolled) is a producer of a balanced state, a restorer of balances and filler up of voids.
> Men exercise their imaginations in order to stop up the holes through which grace might pass, and for this purpose, and at the cost of a lie, they make for themselves idols, that is to say, relative forms of good conceived as being totally unrelated forms of good.
> In no matter what circumstances, if one arrests the imagination which fills voids, there is a void (Poor in spirit).
> In no matter what circumstances (but sometimes at the price of what degradation!), the imagination can fill the void. That is why average human beings can become prisoners, slaves, prostitutes, and pass through no matter what suffering without being purified. *(The Notebooks,* pp. 139, 145)

Simone Weil clearly did not suppose, then, that the endurance of affliction constitutes an automatic process of "soul-making", precisely because she recognised the ever-present capacity of the ego to rationalise and of the imagination to create illusory distractions and false hopes; suffering may lead us to the brink of the void, but it cannot lead us to experience it in its fulness while these alternatives remain. Both psychologically and spiritually, suffering and its attendant void hurl us into the depths of hell; only when the flames of hell are accepted do they become a refining fire.

Simone Weil shunned the way of imagination, it seems, because she considered that it could all too easily create a *paradis artificiel* that turns men from contemplating the stark reality of their condition and from learning that patience and humility alone are the true conditions of the spiritual life. In striking contrast to the Blakean attitude which sees the imagination as divine, she sees it rather as a form of sin:

> Christ experienced all human misery except sin. But he experienced everything that renders man capable of sin. It is the void which renders man capable of sin. All sins are attempts to fill voids. *(The Notebooks,* p. 149)

Where Blake in his *Vision of the Last Judgement* calls Jesus "the Human Imagination", Simone Weil notes: "What comes to us from Satan is the imagination." *(The Notebooks,* p. 218)

Where the Jungian attitude would be to acknowledge, in the words of Zimmer (and Blake), that "all the gods are within us", Simone Weil would have us reject them:

> To empty oneself of one's false divinity, to submit oneself unconditionally to the condition of human misery. Submission, acceptance and irreducible bitterness. *(The Notebooks, p. 285)*

For her, the imagination is opposed to the spiritual life because imagination prevents the valuation of both the object and the person — and ultimately God — *in themselves,* freed, we might say psychologically, from all projections:

> *To try to love without imagining.* To love appearance in its nakedness, devoid of interpretation. What one then loves is truly God.
> The imagination is always linked with desire, that is to say, with value. It is only desire without an object that is empty of imagination. Beauty is naked, unshrouded by imagination. God's real presence is in everything that is unshrouded by imagination. *(The Notebooks, pp. 273, 553)*

Here is the attitude of the contemplative *par excellence*. It is an attitude we find strongly expressed in St. Teresa and St. John of the Cross when they castigate those who would go in search of, or are dazzled by, visions. It is the attitude that prevents one of Blake's most eminent critics, Northop Frye, from calling Blake a mystic, but rather a visionary.[7] Indeed, it would seem to be an attitude that is opposed to what has been called "the symbolic life" and hence to the very practice of analytical psychology.

Spirit and Psyche

Are the way of imagination and the mystical way of negation and emptiness irreconcilably opposed then? Does there exist a middle path? One answer would be to say that the realms of psychology and of religion are not to be confused by the drawing of spurious and fanciful analogies between depressions and mystical "dark nights", between active imagination and meditation; to object, in other words, that it is a *question mal poseé*. But I feel that such a reply is only to return to the kind of restrictive definition of psychology that Jung helped us break free from when he advanced his key concepts of the archetypes and the collective unconscious. Moreover, Jung himself never attempted to hide either the religious implications and applications of his psychology or the religious connotations of such terms as "individuation" or "Self"; most recent psychologies of religion acknowledge a sizeable debt to his works. Jung re-introduced the soul into psychology and in doing so extended its borders into territory that has traditionally been the province of religion.

If then, we admit the conflict to be a real one, we must return to examine it more closely. The first thing that deserves mention is the way in which the opposition of the two ways has been expressed so far. From the remarks cited it could be argued that Simone Weil does not take *imagination* to mean the deeper levels of the psyche. She does not appear to be concerned with those archetypal levels from which artistic and creative imagination issue nor with visionary experience at all, but rather with the distractions, false goals, and *paradis artificiels* that conscious fantasy is apt to dwell upon as an escape from the harsh realities of life and our darker nature. Actually the evidence of her later notebooks is that she became increasingly interested in myths and fairy tales, though for her they were not so much expressions of the psyche at large but rather *allegories* of spiritual development. Such allegories are strictly the language of the spirit speaking through the imagination and giving it an inner coherence and moral dynamic; they are not to be confused with the spontaneous symbols and fantasies of the imagination that can "run away" with us. She would therefore probably have accepted Paracelsus' distinction cited by Henry Corbin between *Imaginatio vera* and fantasy and particularly Corbin's comment on this:

> Whenever the imagination strays and is wasted recklessly, when it ceases to fulfil its function of perceiving and producing the symbols that lead to inner intelligence, the *mundus imaginalis* ... may be considered to have disappeared.[8]

Yet even if, as these remarks show, Simone Weil is opposed rather to fantasy than to the imaginal or visionary path, it nevertheless is the case that the path she does describe is still not the path of the visionary. It is obscuring the issue to say, as Michael Fordham does in his otherwise valuable essay on St. John of the Cross,[9] that the Night Sea Journey (which is the mythological paradigm of a classical Jungian analysis) is a direct parallel of the Dark Night of the Soul. For the fact remains that analysis requires a living encounter with the images of our unconscious and their active cultivation through artistic practices or active imagination, whereas the mystical journey of St. John only begins, as we saw earlier, when the capacity to produce or meditate upon images appears to have irrevocably dried up. Indeed, to attempt to characterize the Dark Night of the Soul as an archetypal process is to give to the archetypes wider explanatory power than they warrant. The Dark Night of the Soul is not a *process,* it is a state, a state which may include visionary experience but which is not to be exclusively identified with it. In the darkness there are no bearings.

In Fordham's attempted parallel we meet a tendency that is not uncommon in Jungian writing on religion: to see spiritual processes only from the viewpoint of the psyche. Such is, of course, a legitimate, if not *the* legitimate viewpoint for psychology. But religion, and particularly its mystical element, asserts another realm over against the psyche, namely that of the spirit. Kathleen Raine made this point with regard to Blake in *Spring 1971* and I wish to repeat and emphasise it here. "Possibly", she writes, "the Jungian system is somewhat confused through an insufficient distinction between the psychological and the spiritual levels".[10] From the spiritual viewpoint, the viewpoint that asserts spirit as a *separate reality,* (cf. Plato's dualism of *being* and *becoming* and Kant's *noumenal* and *phenomenal),* spirit or the spirit is no more an archetype *sui generis* than God is, though both may of course appear in archetypal form. To call it "psychoid", moreover, is only to beg a very slippery metaphysical question.

The contrast of spirit and psyche is expressed in the mystical tradition as a difference of *levels,* that is, hierarchically. The most common image is that of a *scala* or ladder leading up from earth to heaven, and we are also familiar with the mountain to be ascended, the hierarchy of the spheres, the notion of various psychic planes, the ascending *cakras* in the bodily microcosm of Kundalini yoga, and so on.[11] Blake in his "fourfold vision" saw levels of Generation, the Soul, the Spirit and the Transcendent, according to Kathleen Raine.[10] In Avicenna and most Muslim writers on psychology it is common, according to R.C. Zaehner and Henry Corbin, to distinguish two parts in the human soul itself, "the higher or rational soul which naturally strives upward and whose goal is the acquisition of knowledge of God, and the lower soul usually called the *nafs* or 'self', which is tripartite, being composed of the imagination, anger, and lust".[12] This is paralleled, though not exactly, by the various Hindu doctrines of higher and lower self, such as *saksin* and *jiva* in Advaita Vedanta or *purusha* and *prakrti* in the Sankhya.

In all such doctrines where the *via negativa* plays a part, the "dark night" is seen to belong specifically to the level of the spirit, of higher self, where it is, in some sense, *beyond, outside, other than,* or *transcending* psyche. Furthermore, there is often play with the images of ascent and descent, of height and depth: the dove descends from on high, the mystic ascends Mount Carmel, the cloud of unknowing lies above us, all emphasising the "higher" nature of spirit as contrasted with the "lower" nature of the body, of the descent into Hell, the depths of the unconscious, imagination, and so on.

But such metaphors are often misleading and paradoxical, particularly with regard to how they affect spiritual progress. Simone Weil herself often echoes the Heraclitan "the way up and the way down are one and the same" with her philosophy of gravity:

> To humble oneself is to ascend from the point of view of moral gravity. Moral gravity makes us fall towards the heights. *(The Notebooks,* p. 221)

What is more profitable here, however, is to consider that area of transition from psyche to pure spirit where spirit seemingly interacts with and interpenetrates psyche, the realm often designated as that of *intermediaries*.[13] To illustrate this general idea we could take a simplified schema of two overlapping circles (for which there exist several Gnostic and theosophical antecedents'[14]

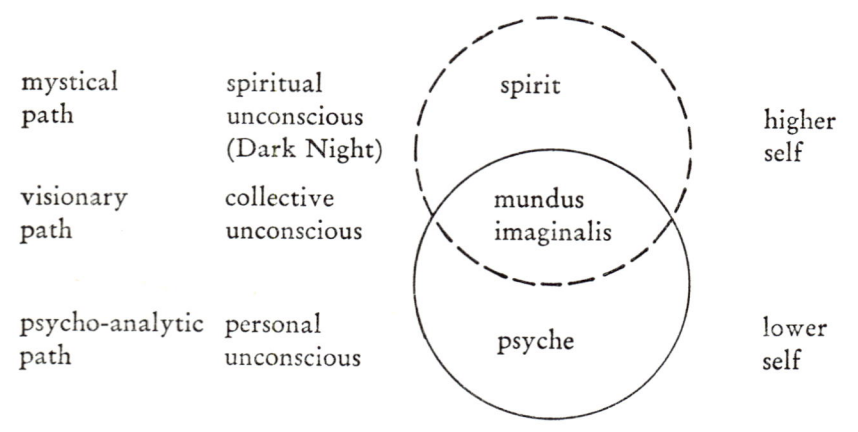

mystical path	spiritual unconscious (Dark Night)	spirit	higher self
visionary path	collective unconscious	mundus imaginalis	
psycho-analytic path	personal unconscious	psyche	lower self

The overlapping area represents that region of the soul where psychic contents become contaminated and transformed by the spirit to take on the primordial and numinous character of the archetypes. This area would correspond to Jung's collective unconscious. Henry Corbin, similarly, writing of visionary experience, calls it the "the world of Idea-Images" or the *mundus imaginalis,* which is "the intermediary between the world of pure spiritual realities, the world of Mystery, and the visible, sensible world".[15] Commenting on Blake, Northrop Frye describes the visionary (as opposed to the mystic) as one who "creates, or dwells in, a higher spiritual world, in which the objects of perception in this one have become transfigured and charged with a new intensity of symbolism". *(Fearful Symmetry,* p. 8.) To live in this world is to live the visionary life and to perceive with what Blake calls "spiritual sensation" and Corbin calls "spiritual imagination".

It is not my purpose in this essay to enumerate and discuss the many spiritual topographies that exist — the exploratory and theoretical work of contributors to this annual like Corbin and Gilbert Durand[16] already does this outstandingly — but rather to plead for an awareness of the complexity and variety of visionary and mystical phenomenology. If we cast our net widely enough to include *mundi imaginales* as diverse as, say, St. Teresa's *Interior Castle,* Bunyan's *Pilgrim's Progress,* the *Fioretti* of St. Francis, Plato's *Republic, The Lord of the Rings,* or the tales of Juan Luis Borges, then distinctions between visionary, contemplative, creative imagination, intellectual intuition, fancy, allegory, *paradis artificiels* become, it seems to me, imperative.

Of all the metaphysical, psychological, and moral problems that would arise from a closer study of the distinctions, one seems of central importance. In the contrast between spirit and psyche is the *mundus imaginalis* to be regarded as an ultimate resting place or as a terrain to be traversed? As we have seen, the visionary is one who is impelled to live in this intermediary world, while the contemplative passes through and beyond it. What is curious is that often mystical traditions, particularly within Christianity and Buddhism, would by-pass this imaginal world altogether, moving directly to the spiritual unconscious of the "dark night". Such attempts to ignore or to suppress psyche rather than transform it not infrequently have dire psychological consequences. There results a kind of spiritual narcissism, a spirituality all "in the head", which is ultimately schizoid, for the *askesis* has omitted the "lower" rungs of the *scala* leaving them psychically unconscious and unregenerate. Not for nothing is the traditional antidote for spiritual pride, humility — the practice of being grounded in one's *humus*.

Where the contemplative wishes to dwell in the higher reality of spirit, waiting on God, the visionary mystic, being closer to psyche, is more intimately bound up with the archetype of incarnation. Thus for Blake, Jesus was the Imagination, and for Jung, an image of the numinous Self.

Herein, also, are two very different attitudes to the body. Blake exults in "the human form divine", Tantric yoga deifies sexuality, Christian marriage is a sacrament, yet the ascetic path of the contemplative subjects the body to the greatest of austerities — "Brother Ass" was what St. Frances called his hard used frame. The mystic does not seek to transform the body, to transfigure the imagination through the agency of spiritual sensation, but to quieten the body so that it may receive the spirit in the prepared vessel of the soul, sometimes to unite with it,[17] sometimes to be consumed by it in ecstasy (cf. Quarles: "For I was flax and he was flames of fire"). The body, senses and imagination are left far behind, and very often (though by no means always) the ego is dissolved in a sea of unutterable bliss.

Norman O. Brown has criticised the ascetic strain of Christian mysticism for its rejection of the incarnational aspect of Christianity. He sees their practices as repressive in a Freudian sense, negating "instinctual reality".[18] But he is wrong in thinking that mysticism necessarily works against instinct, however much against nature it may appear to the outsider. As the nineteenth-century mystic Coventry Patmore wrote: "The power of the soul for good is in proportion to the strength of its passions. Sanctity is not the negation of passion but its order ... Hence the greatest saints have often been the greatest sinners."[19] "Ordina questo amore, o tu che m'ami", cries Jacopone da Todi. But this is not to say that such an ordering of our instincts is by any means an easy process, as both Simone Weil and Freud too realized:

> To go down to the source of our desires in order to tear away the energy from its object. It is there that desires are true, in so far as they are energy. It is the object that is false. But there is an indescribable wrenching apart of the soul at the separation of a desire from its object. This wrenching apart is the condition of truth. *(The Notebooks,* p. 203)

A conversion of psychical instinctual force into various forms of activity can no more be achieved without loss than a conversion of physical forces. *(Leonardo)*[20]

Simone Weil believed quite simply that it is the action of the spirit that brings about the transmutation of instinctual into higher energies and that this is only possible when instinctual desires have become *detached* from their real or fantasy objects:

> The acceptance of the void in oneself is a supernatural thing. Whence find the energy for an act without counterpart? The energy has to come from elsewhere.
> Detachment. Indifference (in the elevated sense) ... Silence all the incentives in yourself, and you will nevertheless act, impelled by a source of energy which is other than the motives and incentives. *(The Notebooks,* pp. 135, 247)

Detachment, non-attachment or "holy indifference" are prescriptions in writings as diverse as Meister Eckhart, François de Sales and the *Bhagavad Gita* and offer, in some respects, the key to the transition from psyche to spirit in the mystical life. For by separating psychic energy from an object, or image of an object, there occurs a split level of consciousness, what we may call a higher and lower level. Thus, for example, a common recommendation for dealing with the problem of distracting thoughts in contemplation is to *observe* the flow of images rather than participate in them; in this way the centre of consciousness stands outside them (cf. Aldous Huxley, *The Perennial Philosophy,* Ch. 23 on "Spiritual Exercises"). Dom John Chapman says that the imagination "must have something to do" while the will is fixed upon God. He calls this split in consciousness a "ligature" which he desribes thus:

> There is a curious feeling that *these imaginations are not you* — they are mechanical, like those in a dream. You leave them as uncontrolled as possible in order to have the will fixed on nothing in particular — which is God, of course. *(Spiritual Letters,* p. 58)

Elsewhere he describes this state in contemplative prayer as one where "the images and emotions cease to be *me:* they are peripheral" (p. 76).

It may seem peculiar to regard the imagination as peripheral but it is a good illustration of the kind of difference I have been trying to bring out between the way of imagination and the *via negativa*. When all is said and done, as remarked earlier, it depends what our perspective is, whether we view from the psyche or the spirit or somewhere between. From his essay on "The Phenomenology of the Spirit in Fairy Tales" *(CW 9, i)* it is clear that Jung as a psychologist took his perspective from the psyche. In his concern with the archetypal world of the collective unconscious he shares the attitude of the visionary. The contemplative mystic, on the other hand, views from the lofty and detached perspective of the spirit, which is of itself imageless, devoid of all psychic accretions, "unborn, unbecome, unmade, uncompounded", *ein lauter Nichts* in the phrase of Silesius. Unless the spirit enters into the psyche to transform mundane imagination into vision or numinous dreams, spirit remains unknowable or unconscious in a more absolute sense than our unconsciousness of personal memories, and even of archetypal images; hence I have borrowed from Assagioli the term *higher* or spiritual unconscious.[21] The ego, detached from psyche, may enter into the spirit but only at the loss of all that is rich in the psyche.

Whichever path we choose — or are chosen by — depends of course on our individual destinies, but it may also depend on whichever philosophies we adopt consciously or unconsciously from our cultural heritage. All psychologies, systems, and teachings embody certain archetypal motifs which act as pointers to unfamiliar areas of *gnosis* and experience; they may also contain what Peter L. Berger calls, in contradistinction to the archetypes, "signals of transcendence", which point out of and beyond all experience.[22]

I have briefly sketched here a philosophy of spirit which is a *via negativa,* a philosophy which contains many explicit, if paradoxical, signals of transcendence, but which regards the *via imaginalis* as circumscribed and incomplete. There is opposition between the two ways certainly, but it may simply be an instance of the Gestalt figure and ground principle: when spirit is seen in fixed perspective as the conceptual figure, psyche necessarily recedes to the background and *viceversa*. But although it is well-nigh impossible to entertain the perspective of psyche and spirit simultaneously they do, nevertheless, complement each other as a paradoxical union of opposites. For without psyche, spirit would have no rootedness or receiving vessel, and without spirit, psyche could not evolve and grow. The mystery of their

AGAINST IMAGINATION

interaction is a *coniunctio* as Jung saw. The spirit is made flesh in the darkest and most lowly dwelling place of human existence. In the surpassing words of the English fourteenth-century mystic Dame Julian of Norwich: "In the self-same point that our soul is made sensual, in the self-same point is the City of God ordained to him from without beginning."[22]

1. William Blake, *Poetry and Prose,* ed. Keynes, 1961, "Vision of the Last Judgement", text to p. 69.
2. cf. V. Lossky, *The Mystical Theology of the Eastern Church,* London, 1957, Chs. 1 and 2. Other major sources on mysticism from which I have drawn are: Evelyn Underhill, *Mysticism,* 12th ed., London, 1930; R.C. Zaehner, *Mysticism, Sacred and Profane,* London, 1957; Aldous Huxley, *The Perennial Philosophy,* London, 1944; St. John of the Cross, *Works,* 3 vols., trans. Peers, London, 1934—5.
3. F. Lake, *Clinical Theology,* London, 1966.
4. e.g., Kretschmer's as schematized in H.J. Eysenck, *The Structure of Human Personality,* London, 1953, 1970, pp. 25ff.
5. Dom John Chapman, *Spiritual Letters,* London 1935. Throughout this essay I follow Chapman's distinction and use *meditation* to refer to spiritual practices involving imagery and *contemplation* to mean imageless practices. This matter is confused by the fact that Eastern "meditation" frequently means both practices and St. Ignatius Loyola called his practice of visualizing the Gospels "contemplation".
6. The standard biography of Simone Weil is: Jacques Cabaud, *Simone Weil, Fellowship of Love,* London, 1964. Her major religious writings are to be found in *Waiting on God,* London, 1951; *The Notebooks of Simone Weil,* London, 1956; *The First and Last Notebooks,* London, 1971; *Science, Necessity and the Love of God,* London, 1968. Provocative but very unrepresentative selections from her notebooks are given in *Gravity and Grace,* ed. Thibaud, London, 1952. Cf. also the present author's *Simone Weil's Philosophy of the Spiritual Life,* unpublished M. Phil. Dissertation, University of London, 1970.
7. Northrop Frye, *Fearful Symmetry,* Princeton, 1947. Cf. also R.C. Zaehner who regards Blake as a seer not a mystic: *op. cit.,* p. 35; Underhill appears to regard him as both, however.
8. Henry Corbin, "*Mundus Imaginalis,* or the Imaginary and the Imaginal", *Spring 1972,* p. 14.
9. Michael Fordham, *The Objective Psyche,* London, 1958, p. 140. Cf. also the very helpful paper of Dom Oswald Sumner, "St. John of the Cross and Modern Psychology", Guild of Pastoral Psychology, Lecture 57, London, 1948.
10. Kathleen Raine, "Response" to James Hillman, "Psychology: Polytheistic or Monotheistic?", *Spring 1971,* p. 218. Hillman has, however, clearly acknowledged a spiritual dimension in other writings: e.g., "On Psychological Creativity", *Eranos Jahrbuch, 35,* Zurich, 1966, pp. 357ff.
11. cf. A. Lovejoy, *The Great Chain of Being,* New York (1936), 1960.
12. Zaehner, *op. cit.,* p. 106, referring to Henry Corbin, *Avicenna and the Visionary Recital,* New York, 1960.
13. Simone Weil also evolved a semi-historical theory of intermediaries (though not of an intermediary universe) which she termed *metaxu.* It derives, like all such theories of intermediaries, from a key passage in Plato's *Symposium* (202): "Love (eros) is an intermediary (Greek: *metaxu*) between that which is mortal

and that which is immortal ... it is a great *daimon* ... God does not mingle with men, it is uniquely by means of love, or the *daimon* that there is intercourse and dialogue between the gods and men." (trans. Simone Weil in *Intimations of Christianity*, London, 1957, p. 125.) Simone Weil saw Christ as the most perfect form of *metaxu* in his cosmic as well as human incarnation as *logos*.

14 cf. The Gnostic diagram of the Ophite System cited in A. Nygren, *Agape and Eros*, London, 1953, p. 304. This consists of three circles: God's realm (pneuma), the Middle Realm (spirit and soul), the centre of which is darkness, and Cosmos (spirit, soul and body). Cf. also the vision from Boehme's *Theosophische Werke* reproduced in J. Jacobi, *The Psychology of C.G. Jung*, 6th, ed., London, 1962, which has a circle of creation and a circle of paradise above it, with dove and cross as intermediaries.

15 Henry Corbin, *Creative Imagination in the Sufism of 'Ibn Arabi*, Princeton and London, 1969, p. 217.

16 cf. Gilbert Durand, "Exploring the Imaginal", *Spring 1971*.

17 It is important to realize that the union of the soul with the spiritual principle — in Christian and Sufi mysticism, God, — is quite distinct from the *hieros gamos*, which is what takes place *in the soul, prior to* mystical development. When Jung writes in *The Psychology of the Transference* (CW 16, para 532), "this inner unity, or experience of unity is expressed most forcibly by the mystics in the idea of the *unio mystica*", etc., we are forced to admit that all the evidence is to the contrary. This is a consequence of Jung's reluctance to admit that God can exist *independently* of our experience of Him in the soul, a metaphysic that has often been criticised. Cf. the discussion on this crucial point in Zaehner, *op. cit.*, Ch. 6 and *passim* and in Martin Buber, *Eclipse of God*, New York, 1952, Ch. 5.

18 Norman O. Brown, *Life Against Death*, Wesleyan University, 1959.

19 Coventry Patmore, *The Rod, the Root and the Flower*, London, 1907: "Aurea Dicta", 132.

20 Freud, *Leonardo*, trans. Strachey, Penguin Books, London, 1963, p. 168.

21 Roberto Assagioli, *Psychosynthesis*, New York, 1965, Chs. 1 and 2. Assagioli's remarks on spiritual awakening (Ch. 2) are particularly valuable.

22 Peter L. Berger, *A Rumour of Angels*, London, Penguin Books, 1970. "I would suggest that theological thought seek out what might be called *signals of transcendence* within the empirically given human situation. And I would further suggest that there are *prototypical human gestures* that may constitute such signals ... By signals of transcendence I mean phenomena that are to be found within the domain of our 'natural' reality but that appear to point beyond that reality ... By prototypical gestures I mean certain reiterated acts and experiences that appear to express essential aspects of man's being, of the human animal as such. I do *not* mean what Jung called 'archetypes' ... The phenomena I am discussing are not 'unconscious' and do not have to be excavated from the 'depths' of the mind; they belong to ordinary everyday awareness." (p. 70.)

23 Julian of Norwich, *Revelations of Divine Love*, Ch. 55.

from Princeton

✣ C. G. Jung: Letters

Volume 1: 1906—1950
Selected and Edited by GERHARD ADLER, in collaboration with ANIELA JAFFE
Bollingen Series XV

$17.50
$30.00
the set (Vol. 2, fall 1973)

✣ The Collected Works of C. G. Jung

Volume 2: Experimental Researches
Translated by LEOPOLD STEIN, in collaboration with DIANA RIVIERE
Bollingen Series XX:2

$17.50

new paperbacks...

✣ Answer to Job

C. G. JUNG, Translated by R.F.C. HULL
Bollingen Series   #283 $2.95

✣ C. G. Jung: Psychological Reflections

A New Anthology of His Writings, 1905—1961
Edited by JOLANDE JACOBI and R.F.C. HULL
Bollingen Series   #284 $2.95

✣ Synchronicity

An Acausal Connecting Principle
C. G. JUNG, Translated by R.F.C. HULL
Bollingen Series   #297 $1.45

✣ Dreams

C. G. JUNG, Translated by R.F.C. HULL
Bollingen Series   #298 $3.95

PRINCETON UNIVERSITY PRESS   PRINCETON, NEW JERSEY 08540

OBSERVATIONS IN TRANSIT BETWEEN ZURICH AND MILAN

LUIGI ZOJA
(Milano)

Archetypes and Codified Labels

I often ask myself whether the passing of years might bring to Jung's formulations a progressive loss of actuality, as in a way happened to Freud with the general revaluation of sexuality. On its own, Jung's great theme of the collective unconscious forms more of an experiential whole than a doctrinaire system. The archetype is born with the human psyche, not with a particular society; it never dies, but merely changes its clothing. This implies an ever-renewed reality, provided we ever-renew our own experiental verifications.

Jung unfortunately is dead and only we Jungians are left. Often because of insecurity and laziness we dare not venture into the unconscious and rather label it with presupposed conscious ideas. The archetype then tends to acquire fixed clothing and to become standardized. And, as opportunity makes the thief, the ready-to-wear archetype lessens the possibility of a personal archetypal experience. The psychologist, buoyed by the collective projections on him, continuously tends to join the cult of archetypal theorists rather than to risk personal archetypal experience. He does this, moreover, with the advantage of being officially recognized as a pious person. We have all, for example, had experiences of clever professional debates in which everyone rigorously says what everyone has known in advance. Granted, this is not necessarily negative; the psychologists too need their initiation rituals and knowledge of who is pious and who impious. But, even though reassurance is often a necessary phase, we ought to remember that the impious Publican still possesses the archetype, while the pious Pharisee has already substituted it with a stereotype — not for temporary reassurance, but *in a definitive way*, thereby fixing his libido at an "anal" level.

The risk of mummifying the archetype seems to me proportionally greater the further analytical psychology travels from its original birthplace, transported as the luggage of memories rather than as an inner experience. Secondly, this deadening seems to me to increase with the passing of years as we get further from Jung's own generation. Thirdly, we now witness a certain sociological phenomenon: as social insurance more and more recognizes psychotherapy, a larger and larger slice of the population, once excluded, is allowed to benefit from and participate in psychotherapy, thus greatly modifying its field of application.

The Thief as an Archetypal Role and as a Moralistic Label

Let us consider a figure often appearing in dreams: the thief. How frequently our reaction to him is a simplistic, prejudiced interpretation: "that's a shadow". What are we going to do with the fact that in some societies raid and theft are more shameful for the robbed than for the robber? Or that in others, the bride has to be, symbolically at least, stolen? Do we consider the divine thieves of classical antiquity shadows or psychopomps? To moralize about theft is probably a quite recent bourgeois attitude, still hardly accepted in traditional Mediterranean cultures nor in general in cultures not influenced by Protestant moralizing. One needn't cite Apache clans to find a society in which theft has a positive value. It is enough to consider the world of our Sardinian pastors who for centuries have administered their own law, themselves convinced that the true thieves are not sheep thieves, but the land owners and the politicians on the 'continent'.

An Italian coming to Switzerland for analytical training may resent the fact that the Swiss, including his analyst, have different ideas and experiences of law and property. This can be the beginning of mutual negative projections, leading the analysand to perceive both the analyst and analytical psychology as part of a foreign culture. Then depth psychology, a means to eliminate projections, becomes itself *an object* for projections.

Although the archetype of the shadow is universal, it depends on individual and collective consciousness for its concrete expression — both of which hold certain elements unacceptable. Thus in Zurich, in a typical bourgeois sitting-room conversation, one might be ashamed to admit that he had made a false declaration on his income tax form.

Just three hundred kilometers to the south, in a corresponding situation, one might be ashamed to admit he had made an honest one. Some young people I know from Zurich admit to stealing little objects in the supermarkets, but they confess to returning them shortly after. They say they wanted to see how a thief might feel! (Evidently an "introverted" interest). They were, so to speak, trying to cast some light on a heavy collective shadow that for centuries their ancestors have managed to keep far from consciousness.

The juvenile impulse to nonconformity takes many forms, but I have never met in Italy anyone similar to the Zurich "returning thief". Italians on the whole are probably too extraverted to be interested in the inner experience of stealing and more concerned with the newly "acquired" object. It is of course possible that such a thief might exist in Italy, but it is also probable that he would be more ashamed to confess the restitution than the theft.

The respect for authority (or the superego experience) in Latin countries is not only quantitatively different from that in the countries where depth psychology was born, but it also has a different quality. What is "acceptable" or "right" often tends to be officially ambivalent, to contain openly the polarities, the acceptable thing and its shadow at the same time. This accounts for the lesser urgency for depth psychology, or at least for its contributions to the superego and the shadow. The discovery of the compensatory function of the unconscious is in a way less dramatic south of the Alps, since consciousness tends somehow to be already "compensating" in its attempt to hold the polarities. Of course this situation is not without neurotic suffering, but the dissociation responsible for this suffering tends more to be contained *within the persona* than battled out between ego and shadow. For centuries it has been understood in Mediterranean civilizations that it is not only one's right, but one's duty, to assume a certain duplicity. In the Prometheus myth what is relevant is Prometheus' cleverness; from this alone the positive aspects of the theft far outweigh its negative aspects. The Roman god Mercury (and his correspondents, the Greek Hermes and the Etruscan Turms) is the official consecration of cleverness. Psychologically, this cleverness may be understood as bringing something out of the unconscious in an intuitive, unpredictable, almost magical way, and transforming it into available psychic energy.

Puer and the Related Mother Complex

The collective shadow of the Swiss, more than having a content different from that of the Mediterranean, seems to stand in a different relationship to its own collective consciousness: namely, the shadow seems more in contrast with the conscious attitude. This is emphasized by the sociological fact that the Swiss, for all their regional and local differentiation, have a marked lack of subculture (the main exceptions being the recent group of foreign immigrants and the more Pan-European tradition of Geneva). Wilhelm Tell, rebel in front of Austrian law, becomes, the moment he is accepted collectively, a prototype of Swiss lawfulness; he does not remain an ambivalent hero. In more psychological terms he soon loses a certain puer flavor.

In Italy the large sub-cultural slices of the population are not always aware of official heroes. They might, for instance, through their oral traditions praise people such as "Passatore" (1824-1851) or Salvatore Giuliano (1922-1950) — not by chance both dead in their twenties. They endow these men with a certain ideological and political value, and yet laud them *as bandits*. Their popular tales are filled with the details of the deeds of these "good brigands". Historical evidence shows official acceptance and integration of several marked "shadow figures". So too with the sexual shadow. It was in Italy, official houser of the Catholic Church, that the legend of Giacomo Casanova was born and praised, and in most Catholic Spain, where Don Juan entered the European psyche.

Seen in the light of history, today's rebellious movements are in Italy more a continuation of national traditional splits in the collective consciousness than they might be in Germanic countries. Today, however, such splits tend to assume political guises.

The Italian collective consciousness, it seems, dissociates into its opposing components, each projecting its shadow on the other. Probably it is this domestic recipe, experienced so long ago in Marius and Silla, among Guelphs and Ghibellines (representatives of the same culture and yet so mortally opposed), more than any chimerical Italian sweetness, that restrains fanatical racism or nationalism, and keeps the shadow closer to consciousness. (How superficially applied were, for instance, racial laws during the last World War, if we compare them with those of Germany!) The Italian collective is traditionally characterized by strong irreconcilables; personal rivalries are so underlined that it is hardly necessary to make another nation, race, or minority the scapegoat. Psychologically, this situation can be interpreted as a collective equivalent of the previously mentioned individual tendency to live more markedly the pairs of opposites within the conscious situation. The Italian collective persona shows marked splits, as does the individual.

Strong oppositions characterize the puer archetype when oedipally linked with the mother archetype. In Germanic countries, where the Italian *madreterra* becomes *vaterland,* the puer archetype is traditionally less accepted and tends to be rejected, thus becoming a most important component of the Germanic collective shadow. From another perspective, as that of M. Moreno,[1] for example, the student rebellions may be viewed and revalued as expressions of a constellated puer aeternus archetype. But a problem still waiting, and with which every Italian interested in analytical psychology is faced, is the revaluation of the puer in terms of a revaluation of the Mediterranean cultural background. As far as I know, everything else, except for Moreno, written on the puer comes from north of the Alps, and is therefore conditioned by that which is for the north traditionally repressed. This frequently diffident attitude is perhaps due, together with older factors, to a direct influence of Protestantism with its repression of powerful feminine archetypal figures, a theme often expanded upon by Jung. The puer, whether or not disentangled from the mother complex, is not necessarily a *pathological* complex, since is has been probably one of the most creative archetypal components of the Mediterranean civilization.

Returning briefly to the typically Mediterranean God Hermes, we should remember that he is a Child God as well as Divine Thief and Trickster. Italian fairy tales show these two latter personages consecrated also in the Christian age in the figure of St. Peter, though tempered by a certain moralizing.[2] All in all, the "morality" of the Classical Mediterranean culture has probably been changed less than it might appear by the subsequent coming of Christianity and of the present technological age.

It is still a rigorous task to define Mediterranean morality by means of intellectual categories. Persona and shadow, law and anti-law, have an emotional, not an intellectual, delimitation. It is not the problem of law in the classical sense — as has been seen in examples of the many out-of-the-law situations acceptable in the social dimension. Law interpreted as the necessity of staying within the boundaries of a formal dictate belongs to societies stressing the Father archetype. Those stressing the Mother archetype, on the other hand, while easily stretching the law, tend to oblige the individual to stay within the subtle boundaries of some emotional security emanating from this feminine figure. In a sense, respect for the traditional positive law (archetypally Father's or God's law) is often an intolerable condition: how can one reach the Mother through it?[3]

Mediterraneity as a Polarity

In speaking here of "Mediterraneity" I must emphasize that I refer to an abstract polarity. The concrete situation in Mediterranean populations is evidently coalescing this polarity with other more general Western features. Particularly today one notices that the traditional attitude does not correspond to the demands of a technologically advanced society. The old attitudes, therefore, are becoming more and more officially repressed. Nevertheless, this does not change much of the substantial (depth psychological) reality. We could even say that this very gap between official attitudes and psycho-sociological reality is one of the most visible features of Mediterranean life. Modernization has not altered significantly the Mediterranean soul.

Historically, "official" Italy has always displayed a rationality and efficiency mistrusted and unknown by the "other", more true, Italy. Official Italy has given the world Rome, "mother of the law", and invented the *res publica* along with its Empire. Nevertheless, history shows that the law has rapidly emigrated or become a refined discussion in restricted circles, and has had to bow to terminological contradictions such as the "crime for reasons of honor". And the Empire quickly accepted an alliance with a power — the Church — which was substantially foreign to the still pagan, or even pre-pagan Italic populations; it underwent through Charlemagne a transformation, becoming the *Sacro Romano Impero Germanico*, which was often to re-enter Italy, but as a foreign influence. But the ancient Italic populations, true representatives of Mediterranean polarity, were never affected by those monumental events. They never had a state, nor divinities in a formal sense, nor codes of law. Since the colonizations of Aeneas and the Greeks, those cunning Italian peasants refused to absorb the spirit, nay the entire culture, of the conquerors. Their life has always been to work the earth for their families. This earth was never fertile ground for the divinization of politics and for sky Gods which might lead to such expressions as *"Gott mit Uns"* or "My country right or wrong", but rather nourished such old popular sayings like *"Venga la Francia, venga la Spagna, purchè se magna"* (France or Spain might come, provided that we eat) — which is much less of a joke than it might at first seem.

Among the best descriptions of the traditional Italian soul, I find Carlo Levi's *Cristo si è fermato a Eboli* (Christ Stopped at Eboli).[4] His southern peasants have their own beliefs, and their own national wars, which they never hesitated to fight heroically. Those wars, however, were not bound up either with the megalomanias of Caesar or those of Charles V or with the Austrian-Italian frontiers or the East African Empire, though so many in fact died in those wars. They first fought Aeneas and his military theocracy and then, though totally defeated, never accepted it. They held their position for centuries without identifying with the dominating culture, always linked to the chthonic divinities and to their black madonnas, refusing sky Gods and the Eastern state Gods. Their other national wars were, as Carlo Levi explains, the Italic wars against Rome, then the wars against the Angiò, and finally, the brigand wars. As it is historically evident, all were absurd wars, lost from the beginning, "negative" wars fought for the non-law and for the non-state, though without anarchical ideology — in fact without any ideology. Thus when we look beyond appearance and beyond political manipulation at incoherent protests, such as the present Reggio Calabria guerrillas, we will ascertain that even in the present technological Italy, the antique rebellious soul of the non-state remains strong.

Prospect

Each human being is undeniably in a unique relationship with his origins, his country, his duties and destiny. Such a relationship appears, even upon hasty examination, to be of a fundamentally archetypal character. We should attempt to distinguish according to the circumstances whether we are observing the same archetypes in different clothing or different archetypes constellating in the collective premises.

Analytical psychology is not an encyclopedia that we might pack up and mail through time and space, but something living and for whose life we are responsible. It is better not to forget that it was born approximately in 1912 — i.e., some generations ago, and in a *vaterland* not a *madreterra*, traditionally Protestant and not Catholic, and that Jung frequently alludes to Nietzsche and Goethe, both quite foreign to the Italian, and that he has dealt with Grimm's Fairy Tales and not with Italian tales, the body of which is just beginning to surface from its rich history, and that his studies on alchemy usually refer to German material and not to the alchemists of the Italian Renaissance.

"Renaissance" brings me to my last point in these remarks. In Jung we find a frequent return to the ancient Orient as a source for psychology. But the movement eastwards too is connected with a traditional Germanic interest, which, when reproduced in our Mediterranean culture, tastes slightly artificial. Instead, we have our Renaissance. It seems evident that a still unrealized Italian task could be to understand this Renaissance, not just as an artistic movement, but as the first real step toward depth psychology formulated by a Western psyche.

1 M. Moreno, *Psicodinamica della contestazione,* Torino: Eri, 1969.
2 See I. Calvino, *Fiabe Italiane,* Torino: Einaudi, 1956.
3 One might recall the poem *La Madre* by the modern Italian poet Ungaretti. Here the author, speaking to his mother with the emotional tension of a lover, seems to show that he will try to reconcile himself with God only in order to be back with his mother...
E solo quando mi avrà perdonato
Ti verrà desiderio di guardarmi.
Ricorderai di avermi atteso tanto
E avrai negli occhi un rapido sospiro.
(And only when He will forgive me
You shall long to look at me.
You will remember how long you waited
And have in your eyes a swift sigh.)
4 Carlo Levi, *Cristo si è fermato a Eboli,* Torino: Einaudi, 1946

ART INTERNATIONAL

(incorporating THE LUGANO REVIEW)

announces the forthcoming publication of two of James Hillman's Yale Terry Lectures of 1972:

Pathologizing, or Falling Apart (June)
and
Psychologizing, or Seeing Through (September)

Other contributors to current and forthcoming issues include: W.A.C. Adie, Daniel Bell, Max Beloff, Maurice Cranston, Brian Crozier, George Feaver, Michael Foot, Clement Greenberg, John Holloway, Sidney Hook, G.F. Hudson, Brian Inglis, Morton Kaplan, Elie Kedourie, Bernard Lewis, Seymour M. Lipset, John Lukàcs, Robert Moss, John Passmore, David Rees, Harold Rosenberg, Eugene V. Rostow, Sir Kenneth Strong, Edward Teller, Sir Robert Thompson, Justus M. van der Kroef, John Wain, Alec Waugh, Bertram D. Wolfe, and many others.

Readers of SPRING may obtain a one-year trial subscription at a discount of one third, provided they send their subscriptions directly to the publisher. Simply send your name and address, together with your check for $ 16.00 (or 60 Swiss francs) to:

ART INTERNATIONAL, Via Maraini 17-A, Lugano, Switzerland: Editor, James Fitzsimmons.

ARAS

Archive for Research in Archetypal Symbolism
A Department of the C. G. Jung Foundation for Analytical Psychology, Inc.

Collection of photographs showing archetypal imagery of Paleolithic, Neolithic, ancient Anatolian, Egyptian, Near Eastern, Minoan, Mycenaean, Greek, Etrusco-Italic, Roman, Judaic, Mithraic, and Christian cultures. More than 7,000 examples prepared for study; thousands in progress, including those from other cultures.
A unique collection of source material of value to students of analytical psychology and related fields. Of particular interest to those intent on discovering, for themselves, evidence of archetypal stages in the movement of consciousness in individual spheres of culture, relevant to the individual today.

Open: Tuesday through Thursday 10 AM—6 PM   Closed: July and August
130 East 39th Street   Suite 516   New York City

THOREAU GOES WEST:
Footnote to a Footnote

PHILIPP WOLFF-WINDEGG
(Basel)

In a note on "Jung and Transcendentalism" *(Spring 1971,* pp. 136-40) William McGuire mentions a rumour that C. G. Jung had written an essay on Thoreau but says that there is no reference to Thoreau in Jung's published or unpublished works, nor does he appear to have possessed a copy of *Walden.*

Jung did know Emerson, and has quoted him, but apparently Jung missed Emerson's close friend and fellow-citizen of Concord, Mass., Henry David Thoreau. This, in a way, seems a pity, for he would certainly have agreed to Thoreau's definition of myth: "In the mythus a superhuman intelligence uses the unconscious thoughts and dreams of men as hieroglyphics to address men unborn."[1] There is not much point in haggling over the question of what relation Thoreau's "superhuman intelligence" might bear to Jung's "collective unconscious". What is more important is the style of thinking common to both: first of all, to take myth seriously (a sufficiently audacious act in Thoreau's era of pragmatic Yankeeism); secondly, the stress on the unconscious and on dreams; thirdly, the insistence on the necessity of interpretation immanent in all myths ("hieroglyphics"); and finally, the trans-temporal significance of myth ("to address men unborn").

What myth meant to Thoreau personally is obvious from *Walden,* the book that has made him famous. It has become particularly popular in our time, since Thoreau seems to offer a way of opting out of civilisation. One generally overlooks the fact that he only spent two years in the tame wilderness near Walden pond, quite close to civilisation, and that he then broke off his experiment. A romantic secondary myth has grown up round *Walden* which is, however, refuted by the book itself.

283

It was Thoreau's fate to enter into world literature as a *homo unius libri*. And for the very reason that this book is so popular, I prefer to deal here with a passage from his voluminous works which is not so well known and in which Thoreau's thinking shows itself to be fundamentally mythical. The passage is from the essay "Walking":[2]

> When I go out of the house for a walk, uncertain as yet whither I will bend my steps, and submit myself to my instinct to decide for me, I find, strange and whimsical as it may seem, that I finally and inevitably settle southwest, toward some particular wood or meadow or deserted pasture or hill in that direction. My needle is slow to settle, varies a few degrees, and does not always point due southwest, it is true, and it has good authority for this variation, but it always settles between west and south-southwest. The future lies that way to me, and the earth seems more unexhausted and richer on that side. The outline which would bound my walks would be, not a circle, but a parabola, or rather like one of those cometary orbits which have been thought to be non-returning curves, in this case opening westward, in which my house occupies the place of the sun. I turn round and round irresolute sometimes for a quarter of an hour, until I decide, for a thousandth time, that I will walk into the southwest or west. Eastward I go only by force; but westward I go free. Thither no business leads me. It is hard for me to believe that I shall find fair landscapes or sufficient wildness and freedom behind the eastern horizon. I am not excited by a walk thither; but I believe that the forest which I see in the western horizon stretches uninterruptedly toward the setting sun, and there are no towns or cities in it of enough consequence to disturb me. Let me live where I will, on this side is the city, on that the wilderness, and ever I am leaving the city more and more, and withdrawing into the wilderness. I should not lay so much stress on this fact, if I did not believe that something like this is the prevailing tendency of my countrymen. I must walk toward Oregon, and not toward Europe. And that way the nation is moving, and I may say that mankind progresses from east to west. Within a few years we have witnessed the phenomenon of a southeastward migration, in the settlement of Australia; but this affects us as a retrograde movement, and, judging from the moral and physical character of the first generation of Australians, has not yet proved a successful experiment. The eastern Tartars think that there is nothing west beyond Tibet. "The world ends there", they say; "beyond there is nothing but a shoreless sea". It is unmitigated East where they live.
>
> We go eastward to realize history and study the works of art and literature; we go westward as into the future, with a spirit of enterprise and adventure. The Atlantic is the Lethean stream, in our passage over

which we have had an opportunity to forget the Old World and its institutions. If we do not succeed this time, there is perhaps one more chance for the race left before it arrives on the banks of the Styx, and that is the Lethe of the Pacific, which is three times as wide.

I know not how significant it is, or how far it is an evidence of singularity, that an individual should thus consent in his pettiest walk with the general movement of the race ...

Every sunset which I witness inspires me with the desire to go to a West as distant and as fair as that into which the sun goes down. He appears to migrate westward daily, and tempts us to follow him. He is the Great Western Pioneer whom the nations follow. We dream all night of those mountain-ridges in the horizon, though they may be of vapor only, which were last guilded by his rays. The island of Atlantis, and the islands and gardens of the Hesperides, a sort of terrestrial paradise, appear to have been the Great West of the ancients, enveloped in mystery and poetry. Who has not seen in imagination, when looking into the sunset sky, the gardens of the Hesperides, and the foundation of all those fables?

Columbus felt the westward tendency more strongly than any before. He obeyed it, and found a New World for Castile and Leon. The herd of men in those days scented fresh pastures from afar ...

To use an obsolete Latin word, I might say, *Ex Oriente lux; ex Occidente frux.* From the East light, from the West fruit ...

If the moon looks larger here than in Europe, probably the sun looks larger also. If the heavens of America appear infinitely higher, and the stars brighter, I trust that these facts are symbolical of the height to which the philosophy and poetry and religion of her inhabitants may one day soar. At length, perchance, the immaterial heaven will appear as much higher to the American mind, and the intimations that star it as much brighter. For I believe that climate does thus react on man, — as there is something in the mountain air that feeds the spirit and inspires. Will not man grow to greater perfection intellectually as well as physically under these influences? I trust that we shall be more imaginative, that our thoughts will be clearer, fresher and more ethereal, as our sky, — our understanding more comprehensive and broader, like our plains, — our intellect generally on a grander scale, like our thunder and lightning, — and our hearts shall even correspond in breadth and depth and grandeur to our inland seas.

In the first place, Thoreau observes a "west spin" which he instinctively follows and, having observed it, is happy to follow. He has enough intuition (and is sufficiently well read) to see this orientation or, more properly speaking, this "occidentation", not simply as a casual whim, but rather as the repetition of the movement which European and American history has taken — the path of occidental culture from Greece to Western Europe, the leap across the Atlantic, the penetration of North America by the settlers following the setting sun — that movement which in our time, and probably for the last time, continues in Brazil with the gigantic project of exploring and developing the Amazonas Basin.

It is a remarkable fact that Europe and America do not think of themselves as "centre", as for instance China does, but that expressions such as "Western World" and, in German, *Abendland*" have prevailed. This shows a conscious and sharply felt contrast to the "East", the origin of threatening hordes of invaders from the Persians in Greek times to the Turks at the beginning of the modern age, and at the same time the origin of a refined style of life and an entirely different style of thinking and believing, which might conceivably be superior to ours. The "West", by sticking to this name, stresses its essentially eccentric position. It does not repose in itself, but is always on the verge of the uncertain, the undiscovered, the yet-to-be-explored.

Thinking in mythical terms, Thoreau experiences as a replica of the space of world history the area in which he moves physically. He expressly rejects for this area the centre-orientated symbol of the circle, preferring that of the comet's path which he thinks of as open on one side. The more the two branches diverge, the larger the scope for expansion and for freedom. When Thoreau ambles through the Massachusetts woods, his muscles and his organs of perception and orientation obey the orders of a supra-personal topography. The astonishing thing, however, is that he himself is capable of experiencing his individual, personal movement as an expression of the transpersonal, collective and archetypal, although he formulates it somewhat guardedly: "I know not how significant it is, or how far it is an evidence of singularity..."

The movement to the West, however, is at the same time a vertical one. America will produce philosophers, poets, and founders of religion such as the world has never seen before. It is true that the initial impulse has come from the East, but the West will reap the harvest: *lux* in the East, *frux* in the West. At this point, Thoreau's mythical consciousness merges with the American ideology, better known as the American dream, the feeling of superiority of him who believes that he can begin from scratch without having to repeat his predecessor's mistakes. We remember that the Atlantic was, in Thoreau's eyes, the Lethe in which everything that is old, used-up, and rotten is washed away. America is the country of the New Man who will come one day, and Thoreau, in other respects rather sceptical of the idea of progress, has never allowed his doubts seriously to question the validity of the "American dream".

The land of promise which he sees in the sunset, the gardens of the Hesperides and the Isle of Atlantis, is a target symbol of perfection and of the life without illness and age, a garden of Paradise; at the same time, it must be seen as the primeval forest, though an open and friendly one, in which every plant develops to the full in accordance with its own innate law, and even the rank growth is subject to the general divine harmony. The paradise is garden as well as virgin forest, and in exactly the same way, Thoreau's gardens of the Hesperides are "the Wild", as he likes to call it, out of which everything that is new will arise, on the one hand, the West being the goal of the most strenuous efforts and the most wearisome voyages to the region of at least potential perfection, and at the same time virgin land, i.e., not only a terminal point, but also a new beginning. And all civilisation takes its strength from the roots it has in "the Wild": "The story of Romulus and Remus being suckled by a wolf is not a meaningless fable. The founders of every state which has risen to eminence have drawn their nourishment and vigor from a similar wild source. It was because the children of the Empire were not suckled by the wolf that they were conquered and displaced by the children of the northern forest who were."[3]

The dialectics between the Wild and civilisation have been the theme of Thoreau's life and work. In the present "Footnote to a Footnote" this cannot be elaborated upon. The above remarks are not meant as a commentary but merely as an indication from which a more thorough commentary could start. Only one hint more: there is yet another symbolic aspect in Thoreau's walks through the woods which unconsciously pattern themselves on the movements of world history, an aspect which he himself, being essentially an optimist, does not mention. But it is that aspect which we in our time, who no longer believe in myths and who doubt to an ever-increasing degree the potentialities of man, may prefer, particulary when thinking of America. The West is also the region of death and destruction. In American slang, "to go West" means "to die".

1 "A Week on the Concord and Merrimack Rivers" in *The Concord Edition of Henry D. Thoreau,* Boston and New York: Houghton and Mifflin, 1929, vol. 1, p. 61.
2 Op. cit., "Walking", vol. 5, p. 217 ff.
3 Ibid., p. 224.

THE BELL-BRANCH RINGS
Poems by Dorsha Hayes

"— technically enviable." — *Louis Untermeyer*
"— they ring true." — *Edward F. Edinger, M.D.*
"— a rare beauty." — *Ross L. Hainline, M.D.*
"— compassion. poetic skill." — *T. O'Conor Sloane, III*

Publisher:
WILLIAM L. BAUHAN
Dublin, N.H. 03444 $ 3.95, hard cover.

JAMES HILLMAN
THE MYTH OF ANALYSIS:
THREE ESSAYS IN ARCHETYPAL PSYCHOLOGY
(Studies in Jungian Thought) $ 9.00

WILLIAM WILLEFORD
THE FOOL AND HIS SCEPTER:
A STUDY IN CLOWNS AND JESTERS AND THEIR AUDIENCE
$ 8.50

ANN BELFORD ULANOV
THE FEMININE IN JUNGIAN PSYCHOLOGY AND IN CHRISTIAN THEOLOGY
$ 10.50

NORTHWESTERN UNIVERSITY PRESS
1735 BENSON AVENUE   EVANSTON, ILLINOIS 60201 USA

INDIANA UNIVERSITY PRESS

PSYCHE AND SYMBOL IN SHAKESPEARE
By Alex Aronson

This first systematic study of Shakespeare in terms of Jungian psychology develops a consistent and comprehensive terminology and shows that Jung's concept of the archetype and his affirmative attitude toward art make his theory particularly fruitful for the interpretation of poetic drama.

352 pages $ 10.00

BLOOMINGTON, INDIANA 47401

From the C. G. Jung Foundation

The Feminine Psychology Women have been waiting for...

Knowing Woman

by Irene Claremont de Castillejo

A wise woman wrote this book — a warm woman — a woman who speaks in simple words, uncluttered with psychological jargon. Mrs. Castillejo saw the necessity for women to assert their independent individualities — to work for equality of opportunity and reward — long before Women's Lib. She saw, too, "Man's collective fear of woman's rivalry and his passionate desire to 'keep her in her place'."

A major contribution is the author's recognition of how a woman's mind operates at a level of *diffuse awareness* very different from the *focused consciousness* into which she is educated by our society. At this diffuse level a woman has understanding and power beyond the usual range of a man; here she is in closest harmony with her deep feminine self, with nature, and with those who surround her.

Every woman will want to read this book ... discerning men, too!

190 pages, with index $ 7.50

Neumann's Last Book

The Child

... Structure and Dynamics of the Nascent Personality

Erich Neumann was the one among C. G. Jung's pupils who was most creative in building on Jung's work and carrying it forward.

The Child is an examination of the structure and dynamics of the earliest developments of ego and individualities — the first of his proposed explorations into the detailed psychology of the various stages of life – and unfortunately the last, for he died shortly before its full completion.

In this work we progress from the primal relationship of child and mother through to the emergence of the ego-Self constellation, via the child's relationship to: its own body, its Self, the thou, and being-in-the-world. *The Child* is an incisive, richly rewarding book which reveals deep insights into the processes whereby man achieves consciousness.

222 pages, with index $ 7.50

Published by G. P. Putnam's Sons for the C. G. Jung Foundation
At better bookstores, or order direct from
THE C. G. JUNG FOUNDATION, Dept. PP 14
815 Second Avenue, New York, N.Y. 10017

A LETTER

RE: "IS ANALYTICAL PSYCHOLOGY A RELIGION" — NOTES ON A TALK GIVEN BY C. G. JUNG (1937)

May 20, 1972

This is a very important document. I was distressed to discover that it varied significantly from my copy (given me by Esther Harding). Evidently the editor in smoothing out the grammar has inadvertently changed the meaning in several places. For example:

1. The first paragraph in my copy is missing in the version published by *Spring [1972*, pp. 144–48].

2. In the *Spring* [p. 147] version we read: "If we are philosophers in the old sense of the word, we are lovers of wisdom."

In my copy: "We are philosophers in the old sense of the word, lovers of wisdom."

3. In the Spring version we read: "When we recognize the Spirit alive in the unconscious of every individual, then we become brothers of Christ."

In my copy: "Then we may recognize the Spirit alive in the unconscious of every individual. Then we become brothers of Christ."

In view of the importance of these remarks by Jung I think that future scholars should be alerted to the fact that there is another version of Jung's remarks than the one printed.

Edward F. Edinger, M.D.
New York City

REPLY

The first paragraph of these notes, which Dr. Edinger points out as missing in *Spring 1972*, is as follows: "I hardly know what to say to you tonight. I have talked so much, twice already this evening. I do not know what more there is. I can only hope that something will come to me that I can give you."

The editing of the notes (as explained in *Spring 1972*, p. 144) was done by Mrs. Jane Abbott Pratt, who was one of the original contributors to the compilation of 1937.

J. H.

The earth is a living Mandala

MANDALA by José & Miriam Argüelles
with a Foreword by Chögyam Trungpa

This book is the first to deal with the Mandala in a comprehensive manner, and in this respect alone it is a unique achievement. The authors demonstrate that Mandala is a universal principle, a vision, a way of growth, a ritual technique, and essential life process. Deceptively simple yet capable of the most sophisticated refinements, "the principle of the center" is a basic aesthetic form and philosophical device employed by almost all pre-technological world cultures to express the powerful experience of unity and inter-relatedness.

As the authors indicate, the world situation today has once more called forth from the depths of consciousness the eternally renewing principle of the Mandala, the magic circle, the ground of the harmony of the opposites. Not only do the authors discuss with learning and imagination the concepts and history of the Mandala in its widespread and diverse uses through the various world-cultures and symbolic systems, but they have provided a great number of original illustrations which give a vivid authenticity to their ideas. In addition, they also present fundamental techniques for the creation of Mandalas that the reader may follow or adopt according to his own inclinations. Timeless, yet immediately of the moment, the Mandala speaks to our present situation as a vision and means to wholeness. By the very manner in which the authors have presented and illustrated this book, the healing power of the Mandala is evoked as a practical aid to regaining the ability to walk once again the Beauty Way.

In the words of Chögyam Trungpa, this book itself is "Mandala in action." Profusely illustrated in full color and monochrome. Cloth $ 12.50, Paper $ 5.95.

At your bookstore or postpaid from the publishers:
SHAMBALA PUBLICATIONS, INC., 1409 Fifth Street, Berkeley, CA 94710

To be published Summer 1973 by E. J. Brill, Leiden, Netherlands

The Eranos Yearbooks in a new style. Every volume, clothbound, with several major papers in English, and English summaries of the French and German papers.

ERANOS 1970   MAN AND SPEECH

In **English:** Toshihiko Izutsu, Sense and Nonsense in Zen Buddhism — Gilles Quispel, From Mythos to Logos.

In French and German with **English** Summaries: Ernst Benz, Henry Corbin, Gilbert Durand, H. Jacobsohn, Adolf Portmann, S. Sambursky, Gershom Scholem, Th. von Uexküll.

*

ERANOS 1971   THE STAGES OF LIFE IN CREATIVE PROCESS

In **English:** James Hillman, Abandoning the Child — Graham Hough, W.B. Yeats, a Study in Poetic Integration — Geoffrey S. Kirk, Old Age and Maturity in Ancient Greece — Gilles Quispel, The Birth of the Child, Some Gnostic and Jewish Aspects.

In French and German with **English** Summaries: Ernst Benz, Henry Corbin, René Huyghe, Aniela Jaffé, Adolf Portmann, S. Sambursky, Jean Servier.

*

ERANOS 1972   THE REALMS OF COLOUR

In **English:** Peter Dronke, Tradition and Innovation in Medieval Western Colour Imagery — Toshihiko Izutsu, The Elimination of Colour in Far Eastern Art and Philosophy — Christopher Rowe, Conceptions of Colour and Colour Symbolism in the Ancient World — Dominique Zahan, White, Red and Black, Colour Symbolism in Black Africa.

In French and German with **English** Summaries: Ernst Benz, Henry Corbin, René Huyghe, Adolf Portmann, P.A. Riedl, S. Sambursky, Gershom Scholem.

*

Still available:

ERANOS 1969   THE IMAGE OF MAN: ITS MEANING AND CHANGES

In **English:** James Hillman, First Adam, then Eve, Fantasies of Female Inferiority in Changing Consciousness — Toshihiko Izutsu, The Structure of Selfhood in Zen Buddhism — G. Quispel, Gnosis and the New Sayings of Jesus — Gershom Scholem, Three Types of Jewish Piety.

In French and German with **English** Summaries: Ernst Benz, Henry Corbin, Gilbert Durand, H. Jacobsohn, Adolf Portmann, S. Sambursky.

Price per volume: $ 22.00 or Sfr. 70.—
If ordered from Eranos Foundation, 6612-Ascona, Switzerland, 20% off the list price — $ 18.00 or Sfr. 56.—

PSYCHOTHERAPY
THEORY, RESEARCH AND PRACTICE

The Quarterly Journal of the Psychotherapy Division of the American Psychological Association

EUGENE T. GENDLIN, Editor
BEGINNING OUR TENTH YEAR
Publishing quarterly articles relevant to psychotherapy

PSYCHOTHERAPY
is not limited to research only, but also specializes in direct descriptions of cases, with emphasis on the therapist's description of his problems and choices.

PSYCHOTHERAPY
is open to differing viewpoints and strong arguments going on in the field.

Subscription Rates $ 10.00 per year
Single Copies $ 2.50
Student Rate $ 5.00
Foreign Rate $ 11.00
Back issues are available
Volumes 1—7 at $ 10.00 per volume, $ 2.50 single issue, $ 2.75 foreign

Please enter a one year subscription beginning with the current issue ....
Also send back issues, Vol. I ....; Vol. II ....; Vol. III ....; Vol. IV
..........; Vol. V ....; Vol. VI ....; Vol. VII ....; Vol. VII ....
Name .... Address ....
City .... State .... Zip ....
Check enclosed ....

Send to: E. T. Gendlin, Editor, Dept. of Psychology, University of Chicago, 5848 S. University, Chicago, Illinois 60637, USA

Inward Light . . .

a semi-annual "little magazine", now in its 36th year. It is sponsored by the Friends Conference on Religion and Psychology and aims "to be an organ of expression and intercommunication among those concerned with cultivating the inner life and relating it to the problems of our time".
Inward Light publishes many articles by Jungians and the editor is a Jungian analyst, Elined Kotschnig. The two current issues contain a two-part article by Dr. Edith Wallace of New York on "Chaos and the Creative".
Subscription: $2.— a year

3518 Bradley Lane, Washington D.C. 20015

The Monist

An International Quarterly Journal of General Philosophical Inquiry
Founded 1888 by **Edward C. Hegeler** — Editor, Eugene FREEMAN

Editorial Board: William P. Alston, Monroe C. Beardsley, Lewis White Beck, William A. Earle, Dagfinn Follesdal, William Frankena, Maurice Mandelbaum, R. Barcan Marcus, Richard Martin, Mary Mothersill, Joseph Owens, Richard Rorty, J. B. Schneewind, Wilfrid Sellars, John E. Smith, Richard Wasserstrom.

Managing Editor: Ann FREEMAN

EACH ISSUE IS LIMITED TO ARTICLES ON A SINGLE GENERAL TOPIC. Submitted papers should be received by the editor nine months prior to the scheduled publication date of the issue.

GENERAL TOPICS for recent and forthcoming issues:

SCHEDULED PUBLICATIONS DATES:

Vol.	No.	Date	Year	Topic
57	2	Apr.	1973	Pragmatism Reconsidered
57	3	July	1973	Philosophic Analysis and Deep Structure
57	4	Oct.	1973	Philosophy of War
58	1	Jan.	1974	The Philosophy of Thomas Aquinas
58	2	Apr.	1974	Language of Art
58	3	July	1974	"Sidgwick" and Moral Philosophy
58	4	Oct.	1974	The Philosophy of Moral Education
59	1	Jan.	1975	The Philosophy of Husserl
59	2	Apr.	1975	Philosophical Problems of Death
59	3	July	1975	Language, Thought, and Reality
59	4	Oct.	1975	The Phenomenology of Mysticism

Editorial Office: Department of Philosophy, California State University San Jose, California 95114
Business Office: Box 599, La Salle, Illinois 61301

SUBSCRIPTION RATES: United States: Annual (4 issues): Institutions, $8.00; individuals, $6.00. Single copies: Institutions, $2.00; individuals, $1.75. Foreign postage: Add 15 cents to single copy rate or 60 cents to subscription rate.

PSYCHOLOGICAL PERSPECTIVES

A semi-annual review
Published by: **C. G. Jung Institute of Los Angeles, Inc.**
WILLIAM WALCOTT, EDITOR

The current psychological outlook on contemporary and historical people – events and issues – political, religious, social, scientific, artistic – Essays, reviews, fiction and poems by psychologists and non-psychologists – readable, exciting, provocative – significant, thoughtful, illuminating – A whole new dimension of intelligent and creative human commentary – **Psychological Perspectives** upon the world of people and events.

Annual Subscription:
$ 5.00 USA
$ 6.00 Foreign

Write: **Psychological Perspectives**
595 E. Colorado Blvd., Suite 503
Pasadena, Calif. 91101